THE
PADEREWSKI MEMOIRS

To Miss Mary Lawton
with heartfelt thanks of
I J Paderewski

J J Paderewski

The PADEREWSKI MEMOIRS

by

Ignace Jan Paderewski

and

Mary Lawton

NEW YORK

CHARLES SCRIBNER'S SONS

1939

New York City
April 19, 1933

I herewith wish to state that
my Autobiography, which I am now preparing
in collaboration with Miss Mary Lawton and
which Charles Scribner's Sons is to publish,
is the authentic record of my life, and the
only one that has my authorization and
approval.

J. J. Paderewski

Contents

Illustrations

THE
PADEREWSKI MEMOIRS

I

Boyhood

The beginning of my life was quite ordinary. I was born a very long time ago in a little country village in Podolia, a former Province of the old Polish Republic, which does not belong any more to Poland. The name of the village was Kurylowka.

It was one of the most beautiful places in existence. I cannot tell you enough about the country, the softness and freshness of the air, the picturesque, undulating landscape, the soil and the richness of that. And the beautiful fruit! The finest orchards I have ever seen were in the place where I was born. Hundreds of acres of fruit trees—all kinds of fruit; they were marvellous. It was a joy to me, a small boy. I have recollections still concerning that delicious fruit—and how, when it was all gathered together in store, the fragrance that filled the air was still sometimes stronger than the fragrance of the most beautiful flowers.

Our home was very far from civilization; we were hundreds of miles from the primitive railway station, so that all travelling (and there was very little travelling then) was done by horse, of course.

When I was three years old, I already showed some disposition for music. I was attracted by the piano. I began to play with one finger, with one small finger I tried to find the melodies—and when I was four, I began then to use all my fingers. So after I had attained my fourth year, I possessed that much musicianship.

My father was interested in all this and wanted to give me some education in this direction. From the beginning he was convinced that I had a great talent, and as he was a man with a strong sense of duty and also of really exceptional justice, he considered it his duty not to waste a talent which God had given.

At this time my father was administrator of very large estates. His name was John Paderewski—Jan, we call it in Polish. My middle name, too, is Jan; I was named for my father. He was very artistic in his tastes and had a feeling for all art. He was a painter and a sculptor too, in a modest way. For instance, he used to make certain little religious statues for the churches. He was, you see, a very pious man, extremely pious, and from time to time, when he had some leisure, he would make these little statues and quite charming they were too. He did it out of his religious feeling, which was very deep. He was always busy—always cheerful—always fond of work. I can never remember my father as idle.

My father was a very handsome man too, a strong man. So far as I can remember, he was not very exuberant, but he had a deep sense of humor and was very conscientious and extremely kind to man and beast.

I think I neglected to tell you he played the violin. He played very little, just simple tunes, principally dance music for the servants and children to dance to. I did not dance—I have never been fond of dancing, nor has my sister either, but when other children came to our house, and there was a little fête there, he was very fond of contributing to it by playing his dance music to add to the gaiety. Otherwise his musical ability was far below his gift for sculpture and painting.

My father was everything to us, father and mother both; he was all we had as my mother died soon after my birth. I was born November 6, 1860, and a few months later the mother, whom I was never to know, died. I grew up without a mother. My mother's name was quite unusual—Polixena, and her family name was Nowicki.

There was no woman in our house when we were small except my aunt, who came only from time to time to visit us, before my father was sent to prison.

My mother, from what I know, was a very artistic woman.

Boyhood

She had a fine education. She was the daughter of a professor of the university of Wilno, who was an exile himself, because he was sent into the interior of Russia by the Russian government after the last war for independence against the Russians in '30 and '31, and my mother was born in exile.

An uncle of my mother was a member of the Cabinet of Poland, and he was murdered, during the last war. Of her family there is now no one left. According to those who knew her she was very musical. Perhaps it was from her that music came to me. She was very distinguished in appearance I have always heard, and very gentle. There is a little picture of her that I shall give you later, which reveals a certain charming quality, as you will see.

I started piano by my own intuition. There were no lessons, no effort to teach me. With one finger I was always seeking, always trying to find the melodies, and then when I was three my first teacher (a violinist alas, and not a pianist) came to give me lessons. That was the beginning, and it was during the time he was giving me these lessons that my father was taken from us and sent to prison. That was the first tremendous happening in my life—I was only three years old.

For many years, as you know, the political condition of Poland had been revolutionary and the principal point in the revolution (many years before I was born), in 1817, 1847, and 1854 was the emancipation of the serfs. At that time they were attached to the places where they lived; they had no right to move and were practically slaves. The Polish nobility, which owned the great estates on which these peasants lived, applied to the Russian government repeatedly asking them to free them, but the government always refused. It was a revolutionary move on their part and they insisted on keeping the poor peasants in serfdom, and their dependents. They wanted to create strife and discontent between the nobility and the peasants. That was their sole object. The government wanted to free them at their own time and not then, and it was not until 1861 that they were, by order of the Emperor, made free everywhere.

[3]

The Paderewski Memoirs

My country was always torn with revolution. My first childish knowledge of it was revolution, and it was in the revolution of 1863 that my father was taken to prison. It was very sad and very terrifying to us, and we cried bitterly together, my sister Antonina and I. We could not understand it when our father, who was so good, was taken away from us and we were left alone.

This revolution of 1863 brought disaster to my father and all his house. Like every one belonging to the same class of small nobility, my father took part—not actively—but he was always encouraging his friends to participate, and naturally he was arrested and put into prison. He remained there for more than a year.

It was this revolution of '63 and '64 which ruined many thousands of people in Poland. Many were executed or sent to Siberia; their properties were confiscated and given away to Russian functionaries, to those, for instance, who had discovered that they had been guilty of some intrigue or some participation in the propaganda against the Russian government. My father supported all that. Whatever he could do he did, except that he could not take an active part in the fighting, for that was against his nature.

I still remember very well what happened the day they came to take him away. Suddenly the house was surrounded by Cossacks, and nobody was permitted to leave before a thorough search was accomplished. There was a large company of the Cossacks, perhaps 150 on horseback. They seemed very big and terrifying to a small boy. They completely encircled our house, and proceeded with the search. I was frightened of course, and could not realize then what was going on, and I wanted to know, to understand; so I approached a Cossack very timidly and asked him about my father, because he was the most important thing in our lives. I was rather badly received, with the knout!

That incident was of great importance in my young life—my first contact with the Russian authorities. They were searching our house to find forbidden things—papers and propaganda and so on. Of course I had no idea who they were—I was only inter-

Paderewski's father, sister, and mother

The children with their father (*right*) and the music teacher

ested in the fate of my father. He was very dear to us—there was a tremendous bond.

When the Cossacks first surrounded the house I felt that something terrible was going to happen, but when they entered the house, then I knew that it was for my father they had come. I realized the danger. So I ran again to the tallest of the Cossacks, frightened as I was, and cried, "What is happening to my father?" But he never answered or even looked at me. But I insisted and I kept on asking, as a child will, what had happened—why they were taking my father away, and if he would soon be back again. And then, the tall Cossack laughed, threw back his head and again gave me several very heavy strokes with the knout.

This first contact with the Russian authorities affected me very deeply—it will always affect me. First of all it was very painful, it cut my flesh, but I also considered it a supreme insult—in the pride of boyhood, not quite four years old! It wounded my spirit.

During the imprisonment of my father, of course we could not stay alone—so our good aunt, who was living at a distance of a hundred miles or more, came to take us away and we stayed with her while our father was in prison. Even after his release, we remained with our aunt because he had to look for new work, some other occupation. So during the time of his being in prison and out of work, we stayed on in that little village under the tuition of our aunt. She was my father's sister and I remember gratefully how very kind she was to us. And she was always sickly, I remember that too, but in spite of it she watched over us carefully and became our mother for the time being.

I think I told you that my first teacher was a violinist. My father had engaged him before he was sent to prison, as there was no music teacher within reasonable distance. The only one available was a violin player and that violinist gave me my first rudiments of piano playing. Being a violinist, naturally he knew nothing about the piano. But he was a nice and very conscientious old man, and said that although he could not really give me any instruction in piano music (and evidently I was talented for the piano) I could play quite well enough, he thought, for duets. So duets with my sister were the main object of his lessons. Poor man! He worked very hard with us, beating time faithfully at the side of the piano with his thin old hands.

Now, young as I was, I soon realized that he could do nothing for me, he could not teach me how to play. So I used to play by myself, improvising. That suited me quite well for I wanted to play—I was always playing, but I did not want to study. Like every child, my love for music was not so strong then as to make me want to work. So the old violin teacher pleased me very well at that time.

My father, of course, thought all was well, poor man! He had done his duty by supplying a teacher and that brought him happiness in his exile.

During our stay with my aunt, I learnt reading and writing but I really do not know how. It must have come quite naturally, I think, for I do not remember ever learning to read or write. We started with a French governess, and while she was there I learnt to read by myself in Polish, and then, I think by some miracle, I learnt Russian too. I could write by the time I was four, because in 1864 I began writing letters to my father in prison, but they were not very interesting letters, I'm afraid—just a child's letters —and brought little comfort to him. I remember the first one I wrote him—it was a great effort. It was all about my cousin Florian and his beautiful green boots. It is a tradition among the Polish people to wear with their Polish costumes very gay boots of different colors, yellow, green, red, etc. Florian, who was a year older than I, got a pair of these splendid boots which he displayed on every possible occasion, to the envy of all his playmates. They seemed magnificent to me and I was so impressed that my first letter to my father was full of news of the green boots—I could write of nothing else. Now, your natural conclusion is that I was envious —that I wanted a pair myself, and that my father perhaps after reading my letter would send me the money. But, as a matter of fact, that was not the case. I remember very distinctly and for the very good reason that I have never envied any one. No, I have never known envy in my life, believe me. But this is not a virtue; it is perhaps some lack in my own make-up. It is very curious, but it was always so from the beginning. When, later in my student days, for instance, certain boys reached very good results in their studies which made them a little bit prominent, I, too, was delighted and rejoiced with them. Then I would say to myself, "I am glad, yes, very glad, but how is it that I do not envy them their success?" And so I would think about it a little, and realize that perhaps I, too, could accomplish certain fine results in the future —even more brilliant than theirs. I felt convinced of this and these convictions acted as a spur to my ambitions even as a child—and helped later in building my career.

After a year or more of imprisonment, my father was set free, and this is of interest because it came about in a most remarkable way. The peasants from the surrounding villages went in great numbers to the prison and asked the authorities to release him.

You know the peasantry of that country were called Ruthenians. The upper class—the owners of the estates, the administrators, physicians, and teachers—all were Polish. There was a very harmonious life between the two classes, until the Russian government tried to wipe out every vestige of former rule in that province and to create hostility between the two. But in spite of this constant trouble-making, the peasants were extremely devoted to my father and *they* obtained his release by their loyalty and insistence.

My father, as I think I have already said, had a deep sense of humor, but he had something much more valuable too—he was a very equitable, just man. His position was a responsible one because he had practically to rule an enormous tract of land, and he had under him thousands of people. So he must have been an extremely just and good administrator of all that multitude of servants, because after he was thrown into prison, those poor peasants went in an immense crowd to the headquarters of the district, and demanded his release. I like to remember that he inspired such loyalty. And he continued practising that equity throughout his whole life. His justice never failed even in the smallest incident, as you will see when I tell you the following story.

Although I was always attracted to the piano as a child, I was even more attracted by nature. I loved to climb trees. A regular boy. I liked to climb trees for the fruits. Fruit was always a passion with me. I remember once when I hung myself on a tree, because I ruined my only good clothes—and new clothes came rarely in our family. We could not afford them. The day of my tragedy I had on the beautiful new clothes which my father had just bought me, at great sacrifice, including a particularly beautiful little vest, and after putting them on the first thing I did, boylike, was to climb a tall pear tree filled with unexpected spikes, in pursuit of a most magnificent pear with rosy, luscious cheeks, hanging at the very top of that perilous tree. I forgot everything until I slipped —slipped and completely tore my new shirt and beautiful vest, and hung there by the collar caught by one of the sharp spikes of the tree. There I hung crying for help. The spike saved me, but it destroyed my clothes. The new coat was in rags. The beautiful vest was ruined.

But I was not punished by my father, not at all; and now comes the point of this story, and something to note. He sent for me at once, and I was led in weeping and terribly frightened—I felt that a great punishment was in store for me. But to my surprise he said very quietly, "Well, Ignace, this is a very unfortunate accident you have had—very, and you have been very careless and very selfish. You have ruined your beautiful new clothes—the clothes that have cost so much to buy, and that I have taken so much trouble to get for you." By this time I was crying more than ever and expecting the punishment at once. I stood waiting my doom. "But I am not going to punish you," my father continued. "No. But you will have to wait a long time before you get another suit. *That* will be your punishment—that will be punishment enough. I shall not add to it." And then he turned and went out of the room. Ah, this made a deep impression on me then. I was overwhelmed with emotions I was too young to analyze. But I did realize then what the serfs realized about my father—that his sense of justice never failed.

The petition of the serfs eventually had the desired effect upon the authorities and my father was released from prison. But we did not see him for some months after that. Everything was upset then throughout the Province. The property he had managed was in receivership. The owners had left, and my father had to look for another position. What a discouragement that must have been for him. But he finally got a new post in Sudylkow. It was a little township of only about 2000 population, of which 1800 were Jews.

It was a sad place to live in, very sad—but one gets accustomed to everything. Our house stood on a small hill, overlooking a little pond and a large Jewish cemetery. It was frightful —just a few steps from the cemetery. Our house overlooked that at a distance of only a hundred yards. When we moved there I was only seven years old and very impressionable, and at least twice a week I had to see from our little garden the funerals of those poor Jews and hear the laments. It was terrible.

It was the custom among the Jewish people to go to the cemetery and pray by the graves of the departed ones. In Jewish funerals the women never take part, only the men. These funerals were always accompanied by laments. After the funeral begin the long hours of crying. The sound of it was like a great wail rising up into the air. I remember the agonizing picture it made on my childish mind.

There was no bier, no coffin. The body was simply wrapped in a large black cloth and one saw it carried thus on the shoulders of the bearers to the grave. The sight was awful; it was very sinister and terrible. Then they buried the body and went home, and a few hours later the women came and began their laments over the grave. They prayed and prayed and from time to time cried out, even shouted, with such an expression of pain, of agony! It was really distressing and it went on for hours. Their wails still linger in my ears.

Yes, all the year round we had to see those Jewish funerals. It was an ugly place to live in. But at that time conditions were such that new houses could not be built. It was almost a state of war still in Poland. My father was always trying to get another house, but it was not possible. Whenever he applied for a house, some reason was given to prevent him from having it. And so we had to stay on there and spent several years in that depressing place. Every detail of it is stamped on my memory forever.

When I was a very little boy I was very boisterous and full of temperament and vigor, always ready for any mischief. This lasted for a few years only, because when I was seven, I became rather sickly. I was melancholy and always thinking about death, and was afraid of being buried alive. I do not know what happened, but I think the Jewish cemetery and constant funerals really affected me deeply. All my boyhood was under the influence of that ugly neighborhood.

Every Friday in the summer, the whole masculine population of the Jews came to bathe in the pond opposite our house—hundreds of them. They just took off their clothes and went into the water. What a sight—those bathing Jews! It was impossible to have a guest in our house on Friday during the summer.

You ask me about the Jewish priests with their long black robes dragging on the ground, the strange little round hats they wear and the curls hanging down on either side of their faces. Well, first let me tell you that costume and the curls do not apply to the priests alone, all the Jews in Poland dress like that. They have long beards, long clothes, and long curls. They have been exactly the same for eight hundred years in Poland, because the first Jews who came into Poland, you must know, came during the first Crusades, and they obtained privileges, and even advantages over the native population in Poland. They still preserve their customs and their costumes too. They always remain the same. And this reminds me of a rather amusing incident which developed into an unexpected situation for my father.

Every Jewish community, wherever it may be, considers the Rabbi as their leader, not only in religious matters, but in politics too. They settle all their misunderstandings through the

Boyhood

Rabbi, but their Rabbi must be a very highly respected and perfectly reliable man. Now, the Rabbi in the town where we lived was not, shall we say, up to the mark! Though he was a very nice man, the Jewish people had no confidence in him, so whenever there was a dispute, a quarrel, a little conflict, as there always was among the Jews, they came to my father en masse and he had to be the judge. So he became practically the Jewish judge of that neighborhood and they all loved him; he was most popular among the Jewish people.

His sense of justice and his absolute integrity were such that in many cases the Jews came to him with their little quarrels instead of going to the Rabbi. In such cases there were always plenty of witnesses, sometimes 200 or 300 Jews surrounding our house, and 30 or 40 more waiting for my father's verdict, inside the house. He always gave his opinion in a satisfactory way for all. He was not only extremely just, but also had plenty of tact. Tact is the foundation of diplomacy, and my father became practically the Rabbi of that neighborhood, and it was really an amusing situation when you come to think of it. Whatever he did was absolutely right in the eyes of the Jews. I remember one particular instance of this. There were in this place a tailor and a shoemaker, both of whom were devoted to my father. The tailor was a good man—punctual and reliable, but the shoemaker (who was really a genius as a shoemaker) was a frightful drunkard. That happens very rarely with the Jews, because usually they are sober men.

My sister and I were always running about the fields and in the great forests, so we were always out of shoes, and it was necessary every few months to have new ones. The good shoemaker was called upon to provide us with strong, new shoes very frequently. One morning when we were practically barefoot, our father sent for him in great haste and asked him to make us some new shoes very quickly. The shoemaker promised and took the measurements, but the days passed and the shoes were not delivered, as the good shoemaker was on a grand spree and drunk all the time.

After many weeks of delay and excuses he finally brought them, but, alas, they were useless—so badly made that they fell to pieces immediately and my sister and I found ourselves at the beginning of winter still without shoes.

My father was so upset and deeply indignant that after one look at the shoes, he himself went without a moment's delay, and called upon the shoemaker, and gave him then and there, without any explanations or conversation, a few corrections (not verbal but with a whip)—a good, sound thrashing, just like a good father. He thrashed the shoemaker well. The poor man wept and wailed, but my father paid no heed to that.

The neighbors, at the sound of the crying, had gathered round the shoemaker's house, but my father enjoyed such tremendous popularity and authority that they did not pay the slightest attention to the lamentations of the shoemaker. They only laughed and shouted at him in a chorus, "It serves you right, because you are a drunkard, and a disgrace to the community." And then they came in a body to our house and shook hands with my father and thanked him heartily for what he had done.

The one real enjoyment in that dreary place was in the summer when I could climb the trees, especially the fruit trees. It was such a pleasure, especially to pick the fruits which were ripe enough, and then sometimes to climb so high to the top of a tree as to fall crashing down with a broken branch! That was a thrill—for a small boy. An experience—an adventure, and I had so few.

I was a very lonely boy. My surroundings were so sad and impressed me to such an extent that I became a very melancholy child. I was the only boy in the family—I had no playmates and my sister was my only companion. We amused ourselves as best we could, but there were not very many resources for amusement under such circumstances. We were very lonely children.

And now I want to tell you a little about my sister. She was two years older than I. She was also of sad disposition, and I think she was just as affected as I was by that dreary neighborhood—the Jewish funerals and the laments. She was musical and played rather well, but she was not very ambitious. Ambition develops with age, of course, and later on she became more serious, but I had the ambition of the family then. We played together, duets, but we played only when the teacher was there, otherwise we had no desire to sit down and play by ourselves. My sister Antonina was very fond of crying, I recall, a privilege of her sex! She was devoted to me and watched over me in her way like a little mother.

When I was a small boy I was a great friend of horses, and I had a favorite horse when I was about seven years old. He was my only real companion. I used to ride that horse without a saddle. We were very good friends, and I felt toward him as though he were my brother. I loved him very much. And whenever I got any sweets, some particular delicacy, I never failed to go at once to my horse to partake of that little feast with him. On one occasion he was in the meadow (it was a feast day in the family) and I had received quite an extra number of delicious little cakes, and hurried to share them with my dear horse. I saved a generous share for him. He ran quickly toward me and ate greedily, profusely, from my hand, and then suddenly, without warning, wheeled about quickly and kicked me in the stomach with his hind legs, so terribly that I fell down as dead and remained unconscious for hours. And there they found me, the family, after a long search—lying in the meadow still unconscious.

And why did my horse do that? Yes, why? I have asked myself that question many times because that horse loved me, and was my friend. I cannot feel that he did it purposely. But I have watched many horses since then and have come regretfully to the conclusion that the horse is a very stupid—an unreasoning—animal. The old saying that a dog bites the hand that feeds it—one can argue it this way and that, there is no satisfactory answer.

At any rate, I lost faith in my horse then; I never went to him again with little cakes in my hand and affection in my heart. I lost a comrade—that is a hard thing for a small boy.

I do not like talking about myself, but you have made it easy for me—too easy. You do not conform to that I see. So be it, but if I decide to talk on about the happenings of my youth, of my existence altogether, it is with the view of its being perhaps of interest and even of use to some one else.

Now there are a great many people in this world who are struggling constantly, students especially, aspiring to some ideal, striving to satisfy their ambition, and who are handicapped in their striving, and constantly defeated in their efforts. I know well what such discouragements mean, for I have had great difficulties in my life, beginning from my earliest childhood. As early as my fourth year, when we were thrown from one place to another, no home, no security, no father or mother even. As a child I sensed that life was hard, and I know, as well as most, the despair that can beset the human heart.

It is my feeling that perhaps these difficulties which I have had to overcome in my work, this little story of my own poverty and strife, may stimulate and even help some one in that vast, always increasing army of young strugglers. And so we shall go on.

But first let us turn back for a moment, for I want to speak about something that happened while my father was in prison, which was of great importance to me, for it brought about the advent then of a new teacher.

II

My first instructor, the violinist, had accomplished nothing, and my aunt, who was a kind and just woman, felt that something should be done about a proper teacher, for me especially, while we were at her house.

Now, coming to that important event, there was, at a distance of some fifty miles, an old gentleman who was reputed to be a bonafide musician. He was the brother of a very well-known musician, Albert Sowinski, who lived in Paris and had quite a reputation there. The name of my new teacher was Peter Sowinski. They came of a musical family. He was also the uncle of a Polish poet of some distinction. And so his entrance into my musical life certainly seemed a step forward. My aunt asked him to come and give

Boyhood

lessons to my sister and myself and for two years he came every week and always stayed a day or two. But these lessons proved not very important after all, because he was not a *real* piano teacher, but was just a poor musician who was giving lessons to the children of the nobility. Just to let us play four-handed—my sister and myself—all the arrangements of opera, etc., was all he expected while he sat by the piano listening. So, after all, he proved to be no better than the violinist. It was my fate!

Well, naturally, I did not profit much from his instruction, but those lessons continued nevertheless for several years, even after father came out of prison, but now only once a month when our teacher came and remained five or six days. He still continued to teach us to play arrangements for four hands, always duets. That is as far as we ever went. It was then the fashion to play duets, because music at that time was considered by the majority of people as a recreation, not as an art.

We had a wretched piano. An old piano made in Vienna by Graff. It was an old small piano with a very weak tone and hoarse in sound and scratchy. However, that was the best we could have then.

I preferred always to improvise rather than practise. I did not know *how* to practise. My first teacher, the violin player Runowski, knew nothing about the technique of the piano. Sowinski, who succeeded him, was not very well acquainted either with piano technique, so he could not teach me anything. One was as bad as the other. So, unfortunately, all that time was absolutely lost.

We knew operas by Donizetti and Rossini. We played "Il Barbiere," "Norma," and "Lucia di Lammermoor," but always four-handed, my sister and I, and I always played the bass. I did not object to this minor rôle at all and rather enjoyed that basic education, which was perhaps my budding sense of courtesy—to give first place to a lady. At any rate, let us hope so. My sister Antonina was then about eight years old. She always played the treble, and I, as you know, the bass, and sometimes our performances were very exciting, especially when we fought each other with our elbows, which we generally did very vigorously, accompanied by sudden little kicks as well. In fact our duet playing was very often more acrobatic than musical!

I've already said my sister was very talented for music, but she lacked ambition, whereas I think I may say that I had a real ambition to become an artist. I, perhaps, did not realize it then, but there was already working in me some inner force. I was *sure* that I would attain something, and it must be said now that my true object—my great object—already, at the age of seven, was to be useful to my own country, which was then, as you know, partitioned, having no existence of her own and very oppressed. My great hope was to become *somebody,* and so to help Poland. That was over and above all my artistic aspirations. I was always ready and planning to fight for Poland, and my sister and I were always playing soldier when we were not playing duets! I was born a patriot. Even from my sixth year my head was filled with dreams and hopes for Poland. I longed to go forth and liberate my country. As children, Antonina and I played "soldier" nearly every day. My part was, I must say, the most interesting one, for I, of course, was the warrior and rode the horse—the charger on which I set forth to victory. The steed was represented by a long stick on which my sister arranged a bag stuffed with all kinds of things to represent the horse's head, even the ears. My costume too, the Polish uniform, was made by my sister of white and red paper with a red square cap. The crowning glory, the sword, was a piece of wood cut with my jack-knife. On this splendid charger I rode all over the house pretending to fight a battle. And my patriotism was always encouraged by my father and my teachers. There were no protests to our playing soldier in the house. Patriotism and music marched hand in hand. My life began like that.

But in spite of our deficient teacher, I was always at the piano and so my poor father did not realize that I was really learning nothing. How could he? He trusted the teacher. He thought that his duty was performed when he found a teacher, and he had faith in him. In the meantime, my only real musical enjoyment was just to sit down to the piano and improvise, which I did constantly.

The boy and his sister

Always at the piano

Boyhood

It was while I was studying with Sowinski that my father made a large book full of music paper, and then before I had written one single note, there was already a title beautifully written by him: "Compositions of Ignace Paderewski"—all done with the most beautiful flowing lines and scrolls, in the fashion of the day.

Well, the book was filled after a certain time with my musical compositions—my first little pieces, and my father was so proud. But what interested me most when I started composing was that the caligraphic part of the composition should be beautiful, that it should *look* beautiful. Sound, I did not attach much importance to, then.

I did not write music instinctively. I did it by *comparison* when looking at the piano music which I played myself. I followed the way it was printed, if you understand what I mean.

Somehow, through the long years, that book has disappeared —it would be interesting to see it now, I think.

My father realized keenly then the great necessity of our being educated, and first of all we had a governess who taught us French. Her knowledge of other subjects was not very extensive; she only gave us quite a good accent in French. That was her one duty. Finally, we had a real tutor, and in the person of a former Polish refugee. He fled to France after the disastrous war of 1830–31. After a long stay in Paris he was pardoned and came back to Poland, and it was then he started as a tutor to children. My father asked him to undertake the education of my sister and myself, which he did for several years. He was a very highly educated man. His name was Michael Babianski.

Mr. Michael Babianski came in 1868. He had been recommended to my father as a very successful and experienced teacher. With him I had regular lessons in grammar, both in Polish and French, in mathematics, geography, history and so on, just according to my needs and age. He devoted all his time and all his heart to our early education, especially to mine, and I learnt a very great deal from him. He concentrated on me. His French was perfect and his knowledge of various subjects was very considerable. He remained with us until his death. He was very attached to me, and a great believer in my ability as a musician. I also got from him a great knowledge of Polish history and he confirmed in me my ardent patriotism—he fed it continually. He was in entire sympathy with me and he understood my childish ideas about things, my patriotism and longing to help my country. In that way, he always encouraged me. It is a fact that I owe to him a great deal of my patriotic feelings, my aspirations. He fostered them continually. He was a very old man when he died, and he died under my father's roof.

There is, in this connection, a fact which I think I should now mention. When I was ten years old, I read the description of the battle of Grünwald, which was fought in 1410 against the Knights of the Cross (the Germans) and which was a tremendous victory for the Poles. I conceived then the idea that as the year 1910 would be the 500th anniversary of that victory how wonderful it would be if I, at that time, could erect a monument for that great anniversary. I thought of that during the whole of my life. Years later I realized this dream. In 1910 I gave that monument to the City of Cracow. But that story comes later.

No, I never talked about it with any one. I kept that dream all to myself until 1908, when I found the sculptor to execute the monument. It came as a surprise even to those who were nearest to me, for I can rarely talk about things before they happen. Early in life, as a small child, I learnt to keep everything to myself. Even now I cannot talk about things close to my heart—I cannot. It is a feeling I have—a superstition, never to speak about anything that I intend doing.

But I am far ahead of my story. Although Babianski did so much for my education, my *piano* progress was absolutely nil. I did not get even the first rudiments of piano technique. It was a tragedy. And I was just beginning to realize it myself. I was then about ten years old. I tried to play, but I did not know *how*. I had absolutely no knowledge of fingering—the correct position of the hands. But, fortunately, I had that so-called *inborn tech-*

nique. I could play anything—not perfectly, of course, but I could overcome certain technical difficulties with comparative ease, because, as I have already said, it was *inborn* and natural.

As a boy I was very much interested in poetry too, and I learnt some of our great poems without any effort. It was nothing to me to learn by heart three or four pages of poetry, but I had no musical memory then. I had absolutely no musical memory until I was fifteen or sixteen. It was not strange, because I did not like to concentrate on music. I did not receive any kind of serious musical education as a child, and what was given me in the form of pretended education bored me terribly. I had no interest for this playing of chords, basses, etc., in operatic arrangements. The eternal duets!

The only enjoyment I could find was in improvising, and that does not mean an effort of memory. In connection with that lack of musical memory, it is very curious that I had, for instance, a great memory for figures. When I was a small boy I could multiply four figures by four figures in my mind with great ease. My want of memory as a musician then was a great drawback to me. My first memory for music was absolutely *aural*. I could remember those things that I had heard. My memory for poetry and figures was *visual*. I could remember easily the things that I saw. I had only those two kinds of memory then, but the third memory, which is for a musician the principal one, the surest of all, his *automatic* memory, that was lacking then. That third memory I did not have until much later. It developed with time, and when I learned *how* to play.

When a boy I could not concentrate except on things which I liked, which interested me. At that time my father was fond of chess, and I had to play it with him. In a village, very far from cultured people, there was often nobody else. It was not every day that we could have guests. It was a long journey of many hours to reach our house, and the roads were often impassable for horses. Sometimes we were so stuck in mud, especially in the spring, that we had to ask for oxen to pull the carriage out.

So I often played chess with my father; and I acquired such

technique that I could easily play two or three games at once from memory, without the chess board. Now I would not remember one single figure. I could play chess when a boy of ten and play the game from another room without even seeing the pieces, dictating my moves. I could play two games of chess simultaneously, but at that time I could not memorize music at all. I do not know how to account for this, except that I had *emotion* for music then, but no memory.

One of the remarkable things at that period, as I have already mentioned, was that I learnt Russian. Nobody taught me, but I learnt Russian well enough to read the newspapers. At that time no Polish newspaper was permitted. The only postal station was about 25 kilometers away and the roads were almost impassable in winter, and so it was only once a week that we received our mail.

It was then I began to read the newspaper—and I became the official reader for the family. About this time my life began to have new interests. A great change came in our surroundings and this event happened when I was about eight years old. My father married again in 1867, and I acquired a stepmother. He had married into a large family, it seems. There were many brothers and sisters, and life suddenly became quite different, because then many people came to our house—we were constantly surrounded by people, after being entirely alone for so many years. This change affected me deeply in various ways. I was then in the midst of a large family, my stepmother's family, and I had to adjust myself to it. You see my father hired a small house near ours for my stepmother's family and they would often come in the evening for news and social intercourse, and generally stayed for meals, and these new relatives became a part of our daily life. They were poor and my father supported them all, and our household took on new ways—it changed completely.

My stepmother was very kind, a good woman, and especially with me, she was very sweet, but she did not make herself so popular with my sister. She was not at all artistic or musical, but

Boyhood

she liked me because I was rather a nice boy, I suppose, and then too I was a *boy*. She was very good to me, and many extra sugar plums came my way, and very good little cakes. When I was a child I was very fond of cakes. I still am! But there was always friction between my stepmother and my sister, and it was the unhappy part of my childhood with my sister that while I was on the best of terms with my stepmother, it was just the opposite with her. There were constant quarrels and of course plenty of cause for tears, while with me it was quite different, which added to my unhappiness. Sometimes I had very earnest discussions with my stepmother about my sister, because she was not always right, in fact neither of them was, and even as a small boy I was always trying to bring about harmony between them, and sometimes I almost succeeded—then peace for a day or two —and then, all the little quarrels began over again. I could not reconcile them no matter how hard I tried. This conflict lasted until the very last moment of my sister's stay at home. They were always opposed to each other, temperamentally I think, and there was no help for it.

Aside from my father and stepmother the majority of the guests of the family were very old people. I was always, as a child, with older people. Besides my father, my stepmother and my sister, there were also my tutor, Mr. Babianski, my stepmother's father, my grandfather, and there was too, my music teacher, Mr. Sowinski. Those four gentlemen represented about 300 years! The youngest of them was 78 years old. My companions!

My father at this time was suffering greatly with his eyes—he was menaced with blindness. He could not read at all. It was then that he would ask me to read or play for him. He would lie on the sofa and listen to the music and I would play in the dark, the old cracked piano—sometimes for several hours. But I enjoyed myself then, for I loved to improvise. My sister never took part in these improvisations. She was reading or amusing herself in other ways, or sometimes quarrelling violently with the stepmother, which she also enjoyed. And so I served my father and that community of old men. During the long winter evenings I sat there in the dim candlelight, reading aloud to them. This went on for hours every night. But it was really very interesting, very touching. These old men drinking in the news as I read it to them. It was always very exciting when the weekly newspapers came to the house. Then they all crowded eagerly around me. They could not read a word of Russian, and had to depend upon me. They could hardly wait for me to begin.

So I was the reader and I read whatever I liked! At that time Polish newspapers were extremely rare, and in our district they were absolutely forbidden because the government wanted to completely Russianize the whole country, to wipe out the traces of the ancient Polish culture altogether. So we had to receive the news through the *Russian* newspapers. Well, I read them the news, and according to the content of the news I sometimes changed it a little just to please them, to make them happy. Then I used to read the new books just published, novels of rather good writers, but mostly historical. There was always great enthusiasm for these historical novels, particularly and especially tales from the war, because most of the old men had seen the Napoleonic war of 1812 and still talked about it. Their talk contributed enormously to my patriotism and intense desire to be of some use to my country.

There were two generations of revolutionaries in our house—that old tutor, Babianski, and my own father. Then from the neighborhood came a number of people who had been pardoned through some influence or other, and who had returned from Siberia or from exile. All this exercised an enormous influence upon my childish mind. No wonder there was for years, and still is, in me, that preference for patriotic activity rather than for anything else. That is always above everything. And I was as eager for the war news as they were—those Russian newspapers were a great excitement to me too.

But there came a moment when the readings brought a little drama—a very serious one—into the family. It was during the Franco-Prussian war. I had among my listeners people who even remembered seeing Napoleon. All of them were born in the eighteenth century. My grandfather remembered perfectly well the Napoleonic wars. My tutor also remembered them. He was still imbued with the Napoleonic spirit, having spent thirty years in France. The rest of the company was absolutely pro-French. France had not done any harm to Poland, whilst the Germans, the Russians, and the Austrians had all mutilated our country, and so naturally all our sympathy was always on the side of the *French* during that war.

My little tragedy happened shortly after the declaration of the Franco-Prussian war in 1870. My father, as I've said, became very ill with his eyes, and the doctor absolutely forbade him to read. He tried very hard to remain quiet, but the excitement over the war was intense. He wanted news of what was happening; every one wanted news. Newspapers were the one thing that mattered, and my father sent the long distance to the neighboring village to fetch them once, sometimes twice a week, and I was the reader. There were many listeners and all were very anxious for news of the French. There was one important person who always came—a Jewish barber by the name of Schmul, he was assistant doctor too. He made hot compresses for my father's eyes and fulfilled the duties of nurse. A good, kind man. And so he too always attended the readings, and with the others waited for good news of the Franco-Prussian war.

Well, I would glance at the papers quickly first—and I saw only the most frightful news, the disastrous events of the battle-field. There was no good news to be found anywhere for these poor old men. What was I to do? I had not the courage to read them what was really happening. I felt that it would break their hearts, they were keyed up to such a pitch of excitement and anxiety about the war. There was only one thing to do, I decided. I would read just the *opposite* of what was really in the newspapers. I made up my mind quickly, and I must confess I did not have the slightest hesitation. I turned all the bad news into good! No, I could not do it now. I probably could not have done it then if I had been a little older. But then, I just improvised, I made a little plan, a little story, and instead of reading what really happened—I sent all the French victorious to the Rhine! And then there was such enthusiasm! Such happiness! They shouted with delight at the news. Why, on one occasion when I located the French already at Cologne (which was just the opposite from the truth) my father sent to the cellar for a bottle of the finest old wine, and together they drank the health of the victors. These old people were actually crying with emotion and, well, I was delighted—delighted with what I had done.

I continued the readings for several weeks. I did not know how it would end, but I hoped for the best. I had some slight hesitation when I started, I confess, but I soon got accustomed to my improvisations, and it was a great pleasure to me. And there was another incentive, and excitement, too, the overcoming of a difficulty—a technical difficulty, because it was, after all, no easy matter to transpose a Russian newspaper into Polish at sight. Russian was not my language and I had to translate very quickly as I read, without showing the slightest hesitation. So it became a kind of sport—a stunt. Of course, I saw the tragedy too, coming nearer and nearer. I was safe for a time, for we had no neighbors and the nearest place was many miles away. The real war news was not brought in, but I knew the truth would appear sooner or later, and it did!

My father suddenly became much better and went to the town to see the doctor. There was nothing more terrible for me at that time than that visit of my poor father to his physician. I knew he would then hear everything. I was caught. I said to myself, "Something serious is going to happen." So I took all the papers from which I had read such brilliant news of the great French victories, and put them into my own little room ready to burn in the oven, and then I waited. My father returned from his visit to the doctor looking very serious. He sent for me at once. I had never seen him so agitated. He found it difficult even to speak. At last he said, "Well, Ignace, where are the newspapers from which you have read such wonderful news to us? I should like to see them for myself. Bring them to me." I hurried from the room only too glad to go. I gathered them up quickly, and put them into the oven and burned them. Then I returned to my father. It was a strange scene. My tutor, the old grandfather, and the little Jewish barber were gathered around my father. He was very angry. I had never seen him like that before. "He has lied to us, that boy," he said, pointing to me. "Lied! He has read us things that were not so. I have just come from the doctor and he has told me the truth. When I said, 'Thank God, I can now read again of the wonderful French victories, the doctor laughed at me." The old men stared at my father, who became more excited. "Yes, he laughed at me and said, 'What is the matter with you? Are you mad? What French victories are you talking about?' And then I told him how every evening my boy had read to us the glorious news in the newspapers. 'Glorious news; why that is something fantastic. There is no glorious news! It is just the opposite that's happened! The French are *beaten everywhere*—everywhere!' When I told him he was mistaken, that the French were already at Cologne, the doctor said, 'You are crazy, my friend, crazy! You are making of yourself a laughing-stock.' " The poor old men were stunned at all this. They simply stared at my father, speechless, and then they turned and looked at me. My heart seemed to fall right down through my body. "What have you to say for yourself?" my father shouted. "What about all these lies you have told us?" "I did not lie," I cried, "I did not lie. I only read what I hoped—what you wanted." Then my father said, "No more arguing. You deserve a good punishment." And then and there he gave me a few hard whacks. It was really very painful. I was overwhelmed.

At that moment the good little Jewish barber intervened. "No, no," he cried, "do not punish that boy. It is true he has made a laughing-stock of you, of us all, but he meant no harm. He tried to please us, the poor child, and I shall suffer with the rest," he went on, "because I have been all over the district telling the great news and now everywhere I shall be considered a liar! I shall suffer more than anybody in this house. But that boy of yours—he is a good boy. He is such a clever boy. I beg of you to pardon him. If I had a boy like that I should put him on a pedestal. He has a brain, that son of yours." It was a crucial moment! He was a good friend of mine, the little Jewish barber, and he saved the day. My father forgave me, and so did they all in the end.

My motive was to make them happy. That has always been a very important motive in my life—to make other people happy, sometimes at a dreadful cost. It began very early, for I cannot stand a sad expression on some one's face—I cannot. I wish to see every one happy, smiling, and enjoying himself.

So the incident was closed. There was no more reading aloud for a time.

It was my father's great pleasure in the evening after his work when he could call upon me and say, "Well, now improvise something, my child." It seemed he never had enough of my playing. He realized, I believe, even then that I was something apart. He felt that. It was an intuition with him; although he had no musical education himself, he understood it. He felt that I was going to be an artist. He realized that I had a future, a line in life, to follow. It comes to me now how often these thoughts and hopes must have filled his mind, and how he worked and dreamed in his own way, to help me and accomplish this. A talent God had given could not be wasted. Such was his simple faith in destiny.

I used to improvise for hours for my father—it soothed him and brought him a kind of peace, and sometimes when he was very tired and in great pain, he would fall asleep, or so I thought, but the moment I stopped playing, he would start up and cry, "Why do you stop, why do you stop? Go on." "But," I would say, "you are already asleep and I·am playing for more than an hour." "Oh, well, just a few minutes more. Go on, my child, go on."

It was about this period, my sister and I took part in a concert in the neighborhood—a little place where there were perhaps only a hundred people, but we considered it a very great event. Yes, a little charity concert, and our very first.

Boyhood

I was twelve then—it was in '72. Just we two children performed. We were known then in the neighborhood as being rather musical children, and some one who wanted to organize a charity concert asked my father to let us play.

No, I was not nervous at that age when playing, I was never frightened. The fright came later through the sense of responsibility. At our first little concert, we were well received by the audience—they applauded loudly and we were given some sweets as a reward. Then later on (before leaving for Warsaw that same year) I played two or three concerts more, quite by myself. My sister sat in the audience. There were no more duets this time! I was the soloist. One extraordinary feature of these concerts was that after I had finished my so-called program, some one in the audience, as a great test, came and held a towel over the keyboard, completely hiding the keys, and without seeing them I played again. That was a great effect! And for that extra concert I actually received some pay!

There was also a concert at Zaslaw, the city of the Administration, and a second concert in another district, Ostrog. This one in a tiny hall that held only some fifty people. But in both these concerts the towel test was repeated. The news had spread, you see, and I had become quite famous through it.

My father could not go with me, but as it was a little distance from home, my tutor, Mr. Babianski, and my stepmother's father accompanied me. These two old men were greatly moved and excited by my first public appearances. My programs were quite modest, as you can imagine, and not very long. I seem to remember that, for lack of pieces, I improvised a good deal, for I did not have access to any musical compositions at that time. I knew only a few things myself. I played some little arrangements from operas that I knew. We were so far away from cities and artistic centers that we did not even have a musical library. I played pieces by Kalkbrenner and Tedesco, a musician who was enjoying some reputation then, and last of all—the Carnival of Venice. What was the effect on the people, you ask. Well, they liked it very much. Of course, they could not expect great things from a boy of twelve, and then you know *their* musical ideas were not very high. I think I was quite serious about it all and glad to play, but I was not so very much excited. I had absolutely no sense of responsibility then. Playing was second nature to me.

I was already attracting the attention of certain people, important people, too, in our district. There was one very wealthy family, the family of Count Chodkiewicz, friends of my father's, who insisted on taking me at this time to Kieff for a few weeks' visit. I was looked upon then as a very talented boy—a promising musician. So they decided to take me to Kieff where I could hear some music. You must realize that I had never heard any concerts at that age, nor any music really. I had never heard an orchestra, a pianist, violinist, or even a singer. So this was a great adventure—my first. At Kieff I heard my first concert. They took me to the opera, too, and I even saw some very great artists performing dramas and first among them all was Adelaide Ristori, an Italian. She was a very famous actress and I had a tremendous impression of her. She thrilled me. Her voice was another kind of music to my ears.

An interesting thing comes to my mind now in my memory of Madame Ristori. Twenty-five years later when I was playing at a great concert in Rome, at the Royal Palace, I again saw this amazing artist, then a very old woman. It was after the concert at a soirée that I saw Ristori sitting in a great chair just as I first saw her—years before, as a small boy. She was still magnificent. An air of grandeur still enveloped her like a mantle and her noble voice was still music to my ears.

During the visit in Kieff another friend of my father's, Baron Horoch, came across my path. He was administrator of a large forest belonging to the family of Count Chodkiewicz. Baron Horoch was also interested in me and anxious to help. To them I was then a kind of musical prodigy. You must remember that in those days people lived very far away from each other—our neighbors were very much dispersed and we saw them rarely. But, from time to time, they came to our house and on such occasions my father always made me play for them. So it was that they

Boyhood

became interested in my musical future, and it was one of these good friends, this same Baron Horoch, whom my father had asked to bring me home from Kieff.

The journey back was a very eventful one. We went by sleigh, of course, and on the journey there happened a serious incident which might have been fatal. On our way home we were attacked by a great pack of wolves and we had to defend ourselves quickly. It was at night, very late at night, in deep, deep snow and bitterly cold. I was asleep in the bottom of the sleigh, wrapped in a great fur robe. There was still a distance of 120 miles to go from where we were then, to my father's house. Baron Horoch had two sleighs, which was the custom, a small one for the luggage and a big sleigh for the travellers. We had started late and I fell asleep at once. Suddenly I was frightened and awakened by the shrill crying of wolves. There was, so far as I can remember, not a very great distance between them and us—that hungry, shrieking pack. The horses, I recall, were terribly frightened—they were trembling all over. They scented the wolves first. They realized the danger before we did.

The first thing I noticed when I awakened was several small lights, sharp, glowing little lights shining in the night—the eyes of the wolves in the darkness. I did not know how far away they were for I was just awake—and bewildered. The night was bitter cold and very frosty—all about us the deep, white snow, and nothing to be seen but the glowing eyes of the wolves.

Baron Horoch had a gun with him, of course, but what was one gun against a pack of wolves? The coachman of the first sleigh acted quickly. "We must have a fire. That will frighten the wolves. We must make a fire. There is nothing else to do," he shouted. "We must burn the other sleigh." So all the luggage was quickly transported into the big sleigh and the other was set on fire at once. The fire took very quickly because the sleigh was filled with straw. It blazed up like a great torch and quieted the frightened horses for a few moments, but, as we all realized, it was only for a few moments. Luckily, at a distance of perhaps a hundred yards there were enormous heaps of straw still in the

fields, left from the harvest. It was extremely fortunate for us—
that straw saved our lives. The fire kept the wolves at bay. It
frightened them as fire always does. But we thought of only one
thing. The burning sleigh would last only a few minutes, a quarter of an hour perhaps—after that? So we left the burning sleigh
and ran for the straw—all of us. There were six or seven of these
tremendous heaps and when the coachman saw them he shouted,
"God be thanked! Thank God, we are saved!" Then Baron
Horoch ordered them to be burned, one after the other. The
great fires were started. It took a long, long time—hours, to burn
them all. But it saved us. The moment we set fire to that straw
there was perfect quiet. We no longer heard the crying of the
wolves or saw the shining little lights of their eyes in the darkness. The horses were quiet again. They, too, knew that we
were safe.

Of course, in the morning many sleighs appeared and we went
on with the journey home. We arrived late in the afternoon and
the first thing I saw were candles alight in the big room. This did
not surprise me because I already knew that something was
going to happen in my father's house. I felt this the day before
I left Kieff. I was very restless. I said to myself, "Something happens now in our home. There will be a great change when we
return." I could not sleep that night. I have always had a certain
sensitiveness or intuition which made me foresee and expect
things, especially death. So when I saw the candles burning, I
knew that what I felt had happened. For there in the big room lay
the body of my grandfather. He had died the day before.

I have had several such experiences. I often had them as a
child. Now I use more logic. Perhaps I am not as wise as I used
to be, because now I apply logic to my intuition, and logic and
intuition do not go hand in hand.

II

Student Days In Warsaw

I

About this time my father began to speak of sending me to Warsaw to the Conservatory. He wanted me to have a real musical education. He realized at last the need of it. The interest of Count Chodkiewicz had made an impression, and my father had very serious thoughts about it, and there was a great deal of discussion because it was an important thing in our little household to launch me forth in the Conservatory. I do not remember my stepmother's feelings at that time; I think she was glad for me because she really loved me very much, but she had no voice in the matter. She was not musical—she was a good hausfrau, as the Germans say. She was absorbed in her children—they filled her life. It is hard to remember after all these years my feelings then, but I do remember that I was a little afraid. Of course I was only a small boy and the great unknown had not very much attraction for me then. I was going away, to leave my family and everything I was accustomed to and all the life that I had known, and I was frightened—a little.

Fortunately for our plan, a railway was being built that connected our village with Warsaw, and that gave my father the idea that he could really take me there at last. And so we went on the first train that was organized. There were no cars for the people, there were only cars for merchandise. And on that little train we went to Warsaw and my father put me in the Conservatory there—the real beginning of my musical life. I was twelve years old.

At the Conservatory, I was immediately and kindly received. The Director was a remarkable man. His name was Kontski. He was a fine violinist and the founder of that Conservatory in Warsaw. A very strong, striking personality.

When he spoke to me, he looked straight into my eyes; he had such piercing eyes. But I understood his look at once and was not surprised when he said, "We'll take this boy immediately, without any examination." You see, I had withstood that look —I faced him. We understood each other from the beginning.

And so I was received at the Conservatory and my father was so happy. He decided to look for a piano for me. He looked in several places, but the pianos were all too expensive. Then somebody mentioned the name of Kerntopf, the famous piano-maker, and we went there at once.

The factory, shop, and living quarters occupied a tremendous floor of some twenty or more rooms in a very ancient house. The owner, old Mr. Kerntopf, was a very sympathetic and lovable man. He received us so kindly and said, "Yes, I have several pianos here, but I don't know whether they will meet your approval, they are rather expensive." He felt, of course, that we were not rich people, and he made a very low price, to which my father finally agreed. He wanted to buy that piano at once but while we were talking, suddenly the eldest son, Edward Kerntopf, came in. He looked at me keenly and listened to my playing. My playing was, as could have been expected, very incorrect, but still there must have been something in it, some expression that pleased him, for he said immediately to my father, "What do you want to do with your boy?"

My father replied quickly and so proudly, "Oh, he has just been accepted for the Conservatory without even an examination!" He was very proud, you see, of the fact that I was not examined, that the reception was so cordial. He was very pleased about it, for I had justified his own opinion. So he said to Kerntopf, "This piano is for my boy here."

"Nonsense," said young Kerntopf, "you don't want to buy a piano; it would be worthless after a year. I will give him a piano to practise on and for nothing." Ah! That was love at first sight, real friendship.

And from that moment began Edward Kerntopf's interest in me. In that instant he befriended me as a small boy and until the day of his death he never failed in his devotion. At that moment, so many years ago, when I was left alone he came to the rescue. He was my good Fate.

My father was greatly touched by this kindness. He talked freely to them and said, "I do not know quite where to put my boy. I would like to find a family to leave him with—he is so young. You could perhaps give me some advice." I stood by my father listening to all this and very anxious—I was still a little frightened, you see. Again Edward Kerntopf came to the rescue.

"Oh, let him live here with our family," he said. "We are already ten children in the family. One more will make no difference, or you can pay a trifle to my mother just for the food if you wish, because we are not rich." Well, that was charming. "Leave your boy here and then he will have a piano too. He can practise on any piano—there are plenty here. It will cost us nothing, and it will not cost you anything either."

My father was overjoyed, of course, and very grateful for that good arrangement. It took a great weight from his heart.

So I was left there. I returned with my father to the hotel that day, but the next morning he took me to the Kerntopfs' and then he left me. Oh, that was pathetic, that final moment when my father left me and said good-by! I cried aloud. And when she saw that, old Mrs. Kerntopf came to me. She was terribly fat, but she had a heart even larger than her body, for she immediately took me to that heart and tried to console me. She said I would not feel so much my father's departure after a little time, because they would be very kind to me and loved me already, and so it proved. I stayed with them until I finished my studies at the Conservatory.

It was a good fate. Life suddenly became very different for me. I was in the midst of a huge family and everything was completely changed. I no longer had a little room to myself at the

Kerntopfs', but I was put into a perfectly enormous room where there were four of the Kerntopf boys sleeping. It was a sort of dormitory—an immense room. I had never seen anything like it before. Although there were five of us in that great place, every one had a little space for himself for his books (if he had any) and his little belongings, and there was a table, a kind of desk for writing, I remember.

No, there was no carpet on the floor; it was very plain and humble, but it was very comfortable. I no longer dressed by candle light, for there were already in Warsaw lamps, petrol lamps. There was no piano in that big room that we lived in. I used to have to go into other rooms in the warehouse to practise, and according to the circumstances I played on different pianos —whatever piano happened not to be in use. Whenever a client came, of course, I had to run away from that piano and go to the other end of the warehouse and look for one that I could practise on.

You know it was such an immense house—I cannot seem to give you any idea of its size as we talk. It was a whole floor of a tremendous building—some twenty or more rooms—and always in some part of the place there were piano workmen laboring. In fact, we were all mixed up together, piano workmen and the good Kerntopf family.

They became my family too. Our relations were very happy with one exception—one of the boys. That was not quite so harmonious at first. He was four years older than I, and from the beginning always tried to show his superiority. He corrected me, for instance, on my Polish. He very often used slang—and I had been fed on poetry and the best literature, and I knew my language much better than he. But I came from the Provinces, and he lived in the capital, Warsaw. So he simply had to show the country boy the superiority of the city young gentleman. So we quarrelled very often and sometimes violently. But finally everything adjusted itself because—he fell in love and alas! could not express himself. So he begged me to write for him his first love letter! There must be no slang in that—only poetry! Then our quarrels ceased immediately and all was well. But the rest of the family were always like brothers and sisters to me from the beginning.

I may perhaps mention now that for the first time I then had the company of some real boys, when I entered the Conservatory. Up to then I had spent my life only with my sister. I had no playmates really. I was practically alone, and it is a very tedious life for a boy always to be with a girl, and only one girl—and that girl, a sister!

But we digress. Let us return to the Conservatory. There I found boys of my own age. Some of them were very lively and it had a great effect upon me and I changed in a short time into quite a different creature; a new energy came to me. I became extremely mischievous, quick in my movements, and sometimes even did things which were not at all pleasant particularly to the older students, the young men of twenty-two or more, who did not relish my pranks! As I was so very quick in my movements and my hair so very red at that time, all my colleagues called me "squirrel." (We had only red squirrels in Poland. We knew nothing about these gray squirrels in America.) So "squirrel" was an appropriate name for me at that time in the mischievous days.

Then at the same time I was rather afflicted with two little shortcomings. I could not pronounce "s" very well, there was a kind of whistling in my mouth, and when I was playing the piano I used to make the most dreadful grimaces at very difficult passages. The first thing, the bad articulation, I practically got rid of. I studied that, not exactly like Demosthenes, by keeping small pebbles in my mouth, but I practised with other means. I have always tried to overcome things from my early youth. But those grimaces were not so easily got rid of. It was not until I met Richard Strauss many years later that I profited by his example, for his grimaces were even worse than mine. That is an exceedingly interesting little story which I shall give you in another conversation. No, I sha'n't forget.

My studies at the Conservatory began at once with a disappointment—and a bitter one. Although I was only twelve years old, and up to that time had had no real piano instruction, I already realized, or perhaps I should say sensed, what kind of a teacher I needed. So I went to my first lesson at the Conservatory with an eagerness that would be impossible for me to describe. I feel that emotion still—to this day. It had never occurred to me that I should meet disappointment there, that I should again be defeated in my anxiety to learn how to play. My childish idea was that the Conservatory would solve all my problems—that I should fall into the right hands at once.

But the first teacher I saw was so discouraging and so unpleasant, that I asked at once to be relieved from piano study. He said I had not the hands for piano playing, and many other things as well. So I knew he was not the one for me and the quest still went on. On the other side my teachers in theory were extremely enthusiastic from the start. The theory teacher was a Mr. Studzinski, and in harmony and counterpoint I studied with Roguski. The last named I still remember most gratefully and affectionately.

They one and all agreed that I was to be a composer, not a pianist. I had such great facility in grasping things and learning so quickly, and I had nothing but satisfaction through all my stay in the Conservatory with my studies of theory, harmony, counterpoint and composition. They began immediately on entering.

The second piano teacher I went to was a very emotional man; the first was simply a teacher—a pedagogue, and technique was the thing for him, though he himself had not so very much technique. But the other was an artist, and he admitted and realized at once that I really had something to say with my fingers. "Oh, yes," he said, "you are talented. There is no doubt about that. You have a real and natural gift." But his own piano playing must have been in his youth very much like mine, because he did not pay the necessary attention to the technical difficulties. I came across such teachers all the time. Such cruelty of Fate!

I made some little progress, of course, through hearing, not

At the age of thirteen, with his sister

The youth of fifteen, with his father

through playing myself, and I knew there were certain things which must be played *correctly,* with a correct technique, but I was not yet master of that necessary technique. But in spite of this, I developed a certain repertoire. After two years I could play very acceptably, not perfectly of course, but still with certain accents and emotions that betrayed a natural talent.

At this time it occurred to the Director of the Conservatory that something must be done to attract public attention to the Conservatory, and make it more popular. There were no orchestras in Warsaw, it seems, outside the Opera, only an orchestra from Berlin that came every summer for a short season. So the Director suddenly conceived the great idea of a *Polish* orchestra composed entirely of the students.

Now, while studying harmony and counterpoint, I was very much attracted by various instruments—I wanted to know them well. As it was permitted to every pupil (also encouraged) to join a class of brass, wood and wind instruments, I went first to the teacher of the *flute,* and started my career as a flutist. But there I met again with great discouragement. I could never become a flute player, I was told, because my lips were too thick for the flute. So after a few weeks of hard study I had to give it up, because the teacher insisted upon my leaving his class. Fate again! But, not at all discouraged, I then went to the oboe and clarinet class. There was a very nice teacher there and he liked me personally very much. He gave me the elements of oboe and clarinet playing, but said I had no future with either the clarinet or oboe. I should take up something else, he thought. So I moved on again. To the bassoon next. Yes, I studied the bassoon very seriously. I went from instrument to instrument. From the bassoon I went to the horn and for a few months I really played the horn—and quite acceptably.

Well, after having tried to learn so many instruments, and after having acquired a real knowledge—at least theoretically—of their possibilities, I found that it was necessary to study all the others. So I went on to the class of trumpets and of the trombone. Both instruments were under the same teacher, who immediately saw my remarkable talent for both the trumpet and the trombone, especially the trombone! One day while giving the lesson, he said, "Now, my dear boy, listen to me. You are always trying to play *piano*. But why? Piano is useless for you—you have no future with the piano; your future is here, playing the trombone! You are really remarkably gifted for it, and you will earn your livelihood with the trombone, not with the piano." He was terribly serious about this. "Yes," he repeated, "your future is with the trombone. Mark well my words."

Naturally, his words impressed me very much and although I still held firmly to my faith in my piano playing, I accepted his verdict and worked very hard, and soon acquired (as he prophesied) some reputation with the trombone, to his great delight. In fact when that idea of the symphonic orchestra at the Conservatory matured, I was immediately called upon to take place as first trombone player! I have a photograph of myself with the trombone; it is somewhere about, I think Mrs. Adamowska in Boston still has it. It is a most amusing little picture. I hope you can see it.

Well, the orchestra was organized and rehearsals began at once. I am telling this because it was a very dramatic incident in my student life and gave much concern and sorrow to my poor father. These rehearsals began the end of June and the examinations were also taking place at the same time. This was unfortunate, as I had to pass my examinations, naturally. So I was not very comfortable at these rehearsals, as I was neglecting my school work to attend them. Several times I was sharply reproached by the Director for not going to the rehearsals. He became very angry with me.

"But I cannot rehearse," I protested, "I cannot. It is impossible. I have something more important to do now—my examinations."

"Examinations!" he answered angrily. "Nonsense. There is nothing so important now as these orchestral rehearsals. I order you to attend them." At that moment he was only interested in the orchestra. It was his hobby.

Student Days In Warsaw

Things became more and more difficult until one day I came too late for the rehearsal and was told that I should be punished for it. I should be detained—kept after school. Ah, then I protested violently. "No," I cried defiantly. "No, I shall not be detained. I refuse to remain here. It is impossible." And I was right, because the principal thing was *studying,* not rehearsing for concerts. So I refused to obey. Then they used violence—they actually tried to keep me by force. Then I fought. We had a real encounter, a fight, and even some students took my part—there was a big row. Quite a riot in the Conservatory.

The Director then asked me whether I would at once submit myself to the discipline, or leave the Conservatory altogether. And I said, "I do not acknowledge that the Conservatory has any right to arrest a student for not attending the rehearsals, and I shall not accept that verdict. Please let the door be opened." The Director was amazed at my answer—effrontery he called it. He became very angry. Such independence could not be tolerated. He refused to listen to me. That ended the matter and I was then and there expelled from the Conservatory. I was the only one of all the students to oppose him. But I was always determined to fight for justice. From earliest childhood I had a strong sense of justice and was always trying to use my head—to think things out. So I was left alone.

The rumpus about the orchestra was in the second year of my stay. I started in 1874, and in 1875 happened that unfortunate affair.

At that time, as I have already told you, I lived with the kind Kerntopf family. The eldest son, Edward, was my devoted friend and looked upon me as his protégé. He was a man of thirty or more and I a boy of fifteen. He treated me like a younger brother and had unfailing faith in me. All the people who prophesied that I could never become a pianist, he simply laughed at. He believed in me absolutely, as a pianist, from the very first. That is worth noting. He did everything for me. He took me to all the concerts. For instance, he took me to hear Nicholas Rubinstein (brother of the famous Anton Rubinstein), a very great pianist.

The Paderewski Memoirs

Through Edward Kerntopf I heard all the best musicians who came to Warsaw. From the beginning he was interested in my advancement. He was always trying to educate me—he was my protector and helped me in every way. Without his friendship and interest, that first year at the Conservatory might have been quite different—it would have been much harder. Still I do not think it would have influenced my *inner* being. Even if he had not helped me I know I would have helped myself—I am convinced of that. I had a certain line in my life, at first absolutely unconscious. But I had to reach a certain place. That was destined. But conditions helped me. For instance, that friendship with Edward Kerntopf. He guided me at a crucial moment when I was alone and perfectly helpless, and could not find even a possibility of helping myself.

But I should not be ungrateful to others, and I must say that several times in the student days, I had offers of assistance which, however, I could not accept. I once had an offer from a Polish gentleman in Berlin. He wanted to help me study the piano, and it was a very important offer—to guarantee my studies for several years. But I could not accept it. It was against my feelings. The only one I could accept from was Edward Kerntopf, because I knew I could be of some assistance to him later on— something said that to me—it was an intuition, that I should be able to repay his generosity; that I could acquire some reputation in years to come and be very useful to him.

It was not presumptuous on my part to feel this assurance. It was rather a certain pride. You know that pride permits one to perform an act of humility. It sounds paradoxical, but so it is. It is an act of humility—accepting assistance. All this means that I felt from the beginning a certain line of destiny that must be pursued.

Even being expelled had not much effect on me. Outside things did not influence me very greatly. I said to myself, "It is unpleasant because my father will be very unhappy." Otherwise it did not influence me very much. Even then I had a faith, an inner security of feeling about the *future* that *nothing* could destroy.

Student Days In Warsaw

But my expulsion from the Conservatory did affect the Kerntopf family terribly. They looked upon that as a disgrace. Every one looked upon me after that as some kind of malefactor. "He has been expelled from the Conservatory," they whispered. This hurt me very much. They had been so kind to me, it seemed *ungrateful* to them. But the eldest brother, Edward, always defended me. When they criticised, he would say, "You are stupid, you do not know what you are talking about. It is not a disgrace. He was right. It is an honor really, to be expelled for such a stupid thing."

And I am glad to say it was looked upon in exactly the same way by a majority of teachers at the Conservatory. Although they realized my being so opposed to the discipline of the school was an insult to the institution, they also realized that I was right, and they made some protest to the directors, especially the teacher of harmony and counterpoint, who said, "I protest strongly against all this. It was not right to force that boy to attend the rehearsals when he had his examinations to do. He has been treated unjustly. He should be taken back."

His protest made an impression evidently, for a message was sent from the Conservatory to Edward Kerntopf, which read, "Bring Paderewski back. We will pardon his offense and receive him again in the class." Kerntopf came to me overjoyed and to my amazement said, "Ah, now I have good news for you. You are going back to the Conservatory, for they realize their mistake and you are to return."

"But," I answered, "how is that? I was expelled."

"Oh, never mind that," he said. "That is finished. I have just received word from the Director himself that you are to be received again. They want you to come back at once. They will welcome you."

And so back we went, and I saw again the strong Director with the piercing eyes. He sat at a table surrounded by his professors. He looked keenly at me and said, "Well, Paderewski, you have behaved very badly."

"But," I interrupted, "I still protest against that. I did not behave badly, I was only defending my rights." The Director again bent his searching gaze upon me and continued as though I had not spoken, "But as you have appeared here and performed this act of humility to me, you are forgiven and you may now return and continue your examinations."

Well, it was all so surprising and unexpected, that I really could not say anything. But in my heart I was very glad.

Directly from there I went to the class where the examinations took place, and all the troubles were over, it seemed. Then the orchestra concerts started again. And then a curious thing happened. At that particular moment the newspapers suddenly began to attack the Director. They had only just heard what had happened—that pupils were forced to neglect their studies to attend rehearsals. So the press took up the battle. Various articles were printed in the papers and although the new orchestra was a great success, the public sentiment was against it. The papers continued their attacks until they became so violent that several of the pupils replied and finally sent a protest.

It was a stupid thing to do and it finally became very serious, a great rumpus. I was again drawn into the conflict with the other six signatories and expelled for the second time. This time I left the Conservatory for a year. It was a difficult situation for every one. I then went to a certain professor, the best teacher of piano in the Conservatory, for private lessons. It was all I could do. But I had only three or four lessons with him. He was a very good technician, but he had absolutely no poetry, no emotion. I prepared what he told me to prepare, but it was very deficient. I had had no proper tuition even then after two years at the Conservatory, and he was accustomed to *correct* playing. He cared nothing for playing which was perhaps poetic, but technically incorrect, so naturally he was not interested.

After the fourth lesson, he said, "Now, I'll give you some good advice—do not try to play the piano, because you will *never* be a pianist. Never." And he refused to give me any more lessons. Ah! That was very discouraging. I did not know what to do. So I played by myself, and got on somehow. But I did not yet know *how* to play. There was no real technique. The same cruel Fate pursued me continually.

It took me half my life to realize that there are two ways of using the piano. The one is to play, the other is to *work!* If you use the one, you will never achieve anything. You are carried away with your own emotion and with the emotion of the content of the work you are playing. And you might spend the whole of your life playing without learning anything. You can become drunk in any art on your own emotion—a great many people are wasting their time in that way—arriving at no results at all. While working, of course, you must suffer, you have absolutely no pleasure, only the effort and pain.

You see, all this time I was playing, not working. I only began really working ten years later, and still to this moment I have to fight that inclination to play, because it is so tedious to work. At that time I did not realize, because I did not know *how* to work. But this I did know from the start, that there must be somebody or something which would force one to work, not to play. Well, I found it—but many years later.

II

So I struggled on by myself, and prepared a certain repertoire. I thought I might perhaps give a few concerts. I had that idea. I had already something of a program—Chopin, a few pieces, and Liszt, and so it came about, as such things often do, out of the air, that I started with two companions for a little tour of the Provincial towns. I was nearly sixteen—this was the year after being expelled the second time from the Conservatory. It was a very interesting incident in my life, this first little tour in the north of Poland and Russia. It was, I think, the idea of adventure that really started us off on this perilous trip—adventure—yes, and the need of money. I wanted to earn some money as, in fact, we all did.

I think it was in the beginning the suggestion of the violinist. He hoped in that way to see his family who lived in the north of

Poland and he thought that he at any rate would cover himself with laurels and make a great effect on his family. We started, three pupils of the Conservatory—the cellist, who was the oldest of all—he was about twenty-two—a very well-balanced musician and a very intelligent fellow, very serious in fact. His name was Biernacki. My other colleague was just a lively youth two years older than myself, who played the violin rather well. His name was Cielewicz. I was the Benjamin of the troupe. We got a permit from the Conservatory and it served as a passport as well. I must also add that our parents knew nothing about this great adventure in the beginning.

How different from today! Such a thing probably could not happen in these years of rapid communication with parents in constant touch with pampered children. Although still youths, we were to a great extent "on our own" as you put it, and parental advice was not close at hand. We were completely out of touch with our families. So it was easy for us to keep this great adventure a secret. I knew well enough that my father, had he known, would have no faith in it, nor could he give me any money for such an undertaking. At this time, you must realize, I was earning a little money and helping myself. I was giving lessons then, and these first lessons were paid for at the tremendous sum of twelve cents an hour. At that time I was really very expensive for my father. He had to pay my Conservatory fees, and board, etc., which left no pocket money for me. So I had to earn it myself and I took any pupils that I could get. They came through the good Kerntopf family—of course, mostly children of eight or nine who wanted to play a little. I used to go to their houses and generally gave about two lessons a day—total sum at twelve cents an hour—well, you can easily reckon it.

And so the troupe was organized and we started off, at first very modestly to give concerts only in the summer resorts and watering places. There was quite a series of watering places in that part of the country. We had a very nice little success—we even made a little money, at first, but the 'cellist (who was so serious) suddenly decided to return to the Conservatory. He had

had enough. Our adventure did not appeal to him—at all! But we were ambitious and wanted to go a little further. The 'cellist said, "No, I do not believe in the success of the next concert. I am not as adventurous as you are, I shall leave you now."

So he went home, and we pressed on, but the further we went, the worse it went too. The 'cellist was right. It was all very childish. I was not quite sixteen and my companion eighteen—after all there was not much wisdom in our joint ages. We met with the greatest difficulties, but just when we were in the blackest despair, quite of a sudden would come a little success, which was most unfortunate because we would be so encouraged again, that we would proceed a little further! Yes, these occasional successes of ours proved very disastrous in the end, as you will see.

Our greatest difficulty always was to find a piano—and very rarely could we find a grand piano anywhere. A small square piano, usually hoarse and of terrible tone and seemingly a hundred years old, was the best we could generally find. You can realize that sixty years ago in the small Provincial towns of Poland and Russia, there were not many grand pianos to be had. Naturally, our first necessity in arriving in a town was to search out the musical people of the place, to whom we immediately paid visits. We would present ourselves in some trepidation and ask to have the use of their piano (if they had one) for our concert that night. You can imagine in many cases the surprise which greeted our request. It was unusual, to say the least, but almost everywhere permission was given, and the people consequently became interested in our concert in advance. It was really not such a bad way of advertising, you see, although it was done quite innocently and of great necessity.

Well, after permission to use the piano was granted, the next thing was to carry the piano from the house to the hall where we were to play. Ah! that was an agony! It created a great sensation and great controversy too, because nobody knew how to manage it. To move a piano, like everything else, requires certain knowledge; it is not so simple as you might think. Every one had a different idea, and we would have to go all over the town to gather together enough people to help us. And added to our difficulties, was the great anxiety on the part of the owner of the piano, lest it should be utterly ruined and smashed in transit.

I can say that there was very little time for rest and practice en route. Our entire concert day was spent in finding and then moving the piano. But we were young and it made no difference. The only easy times, I recall, were when we came to a military post, and then the soldiers took a hand. They entered into the spirit of it and were delighted to move the piano for us. But first of all, one of them would try to lift it, and when he found it so terribly heavy, he would begin a great argument that not even four or five men could carry it. Often they would get into quarrels about how many were needed, and sometimes it ended in thirty or forty soldiers coming to carry the piano, and of course they could not do it without shouting and swearing, which, too, proved another advertisement for us! Imagine a squad of soldiers marching through the town shouting, swearing, and carrying on their shoulders—a piano!

When it was finally landed in the hall, I understood how to unwind the piano and put the legs back again, which was naturally an important thing. The piano also had to be tuned and that, too, was my duty. I had an old piano key which served a little, but I must say, a very little. Later on it was our good luck that a man joined our troupe who proved to be a travelling piano tuner. The right man for us! And a great relief to me.

Our soldier piano movers seemed to enjoy the adventure with the piano. We paid them for their work of course, very modestly, for we had so little money, but the principal reward was a little drink of vodka which we offered them after the job was done. Not many of them, I regret to say, came to the concert! Their interest in us ceased with the moving of the piano.

There was another difficult incident during that tour of ours in Russia. We came to a large place where there was a Russian fortress, and we gave a concert. It was not a success. We had no plan where to go next, and while thinking about it, we spent all our money and had absolutely nothing left. What to do? We had a small room at a cheap hotel, but no money at all, even for food.

Fortunately, my companion was more cautious than I and when leaving home had taken with him a little package of tea and sugar. That saved us. With our last few pence we bought a big loaf of bread, and we lived on that tea and bread for about ten days. We had nothing else to eat.

Our landlord (an elderly man who was coughing almost continuously) began to feel anxious about the money due for the room. He asked when we could pay him. It was a bad moment for us, for we did not know. However, we courageously told him, it would be soon.

I was very proud then and did not want to write to my father and ask for help, but the violinist wrote to his people, and thank God! an envelope came shortly which brought him some money. It helped us out of that very bad position and left a little extra that enabled us to reach another place, where we had some prospects of success.

After we received the money, we could pay what we owed at the hotel. It was not very much, but at that time seemed a fabulous sum to us. We felt very much relieved for we could pay the landlord. He was very pleased too, and then started a conversation with us. He suddenly became friendly after receiving the money.

"Well, my young friends," he said, "I understand that you are musicians. I did not hear you play," he turned to me. "But I heard you fiddling, you there," he said, pointing to the violinist. "But you know for me that is not music; all that instrumental music, be it piano or violin, it is really nothing! Nothing!" he shouted. "Piano you play with just the fingers, you know. When you are fiddling you are playing only on animal's intestines! That is all the strings are. It's not music. It means nothing at all." At first I was too amazed to answer.

Then I timidly asked him which kind of music he considered big enough for his tastes.

"Why, *wind* instruments!" he cried, "wind instruments of course—because these instruments are played with the *chest!*" He was very serious. "A man plays with his chest on the wind in-struments—with all his strength, with all his power. And that, I tell you, is something to listen to."

I was greatly puzzled. It took me some time to understand his point of view. But finally I thought it all out. It became very clear. That poor man was coughing all the time, coughing his life away. He was suffering constantly from asthma, and for him the ideal thing, the only thing, was to be able to play with his chest—with his breath—for he hadn't any. It was that strength he ad-mired and longed for, poor man!

Well, that tour lasted for some months, but as we were ex-tremely poor, and had started on our journey in the summer with only summer clothing, we had no overcoats and no furs, and it was a very severe winter. We could not buy clothes, scarcely food. Shoes we did manage to buy because, fortunately, shoes were cheap at the time. But we found one way of protecting ourselves during the journey in snow and frost. We covered ourselves under our vests with newspapers, the best protection and the only one we had. We did not feel the cold at all then, though it was ter-rible. I could not tell you how much it was below zero—I think in some places it was thirty below. This was in the north of Russia —Government of Novgorod. It was remarkable that we survived at all.

Sometimes we saw very sad proofs of the rigors of that climate. I remember so well one bitter morning as we went on our way we saw several soldiers working beside the road. We hailed them as we approached, but they made no response. We hailed them again as we drew nearer but they never moved at all. They were standing very still, so still that they frightened us and then we saw that they were all dead—frozen to death. Six or seven of them frozen to death as they worked. A most terrible picture! Just standing there—frozen to the earth!

There was one incident during this time that was really very dramatic. We kept on somehow through the winter, struggling along, until the snow was already beginning to melt. There was in Russia at that time a large number of military colonies. Enormous acres covered with barracks and inhabited by several regiments. It was at one of these colonies that we decided to give a concert, as there was a large population of these military people with their families. Several regiments were stationed there, of some twelve or fifteen thousand soldiers and the appointed number of officers.

We had great hopes of that place, but when we arrived at the shore of the river, we found we could not cross because the last ferry, the only means of communication, had already left. There was nothing to do but stay in that ferry house until morning. There was no village there—just the cabin of the ferryman.

Then, to pile up the difficulties, I began suddenly to feel very sick. I had a high fever and was simply burning up and very thirsty. The old ferryman took us in, but he had nothing to give us to eat, he said—nothing but tea. So we begged for tea. I was burning up with a dreadful fire. Not only that, but I felt such heat over my face. I could hardly touch it—it was so sore. And we were in complete darkness in the cabin—there were no lamps, no candles even. There was only a torch.

I thought it was my end. My one thought was to reach the opposite shore. Now, I cannot explain this. I have never been able to understand what so suddenly afflicted me. I have never known. Sick as I was, and burning up with a dreadful fever and an unquenchable thirst, I was obsessed with one great longing, a longing for caviar—nothing but caviar. It seemed to me in my madness, for such I believe it was, that only caviar could quench my thirst and make me well. I had not slept one minute, so great was my craving for it.

Finally the ferry came and we crossed to Miedvied, which means in Russian, a bear. That was the name of the colony. There was only one hotel there and when we arrived the proprietor stared at me in astonishment. He exclaimed, "You are not well, sir, you are sick."

I was greatly alarmed at this and said quickly, "Yes, I am well, but very, very hungry, and I am going to eat plenty of caviar. That's what I want."

"Caviar," he said. "Caviar! But you are sick; you are red with fever. You are very sick, sir."

But I insisted that I was quite well and ordered caviar sent to my room and then began eating it. I ate at least two pounds of caviar. Then I took tea to satisfy my burning thirst, and then I slept. Yes, I ate two pounds of caviar and still wanted more. Fresh caviar it was, and delicious! But when I looked at myself in the glass I was horrified, for I was scarlet. I was then highly alarmed and did not know what was wrong with me. I thought perhaps it was scarlet fever, or perhaps the measles. At any rate, I did not dare leave the hotel. I sent for a doctor (a Pole—the majority of physicians in Russia then were Poles), a military doctor, and there was something peculiar about that doctor, which was his name—a strange coincidence, his name was Babianski, the name of my beloved old tutor. This gave me faith in him at once and I felt encouraged.

He examined my pulse and said, "Your pulse is regular, but all you tell me proves that either you have measles, which is dangerous, or you have scarlet fever, which may be still more dangerous. If you pull through, it will be a miracle."

He gave me a little medicine—some powder for my face—and it seemed to relieve me and the pain subsided gradually after my orgy of caviar. After a few days I was all right again. We stayed there a week and I did pull through, as you see. But I must say, with no thanks to the doctor, for I still don't know what was the matter—and I'm sure he didn't.

Then we went on with our tour and had many difficulties, which were constantly increasing. By this time my father had heard of our adventure. I had written him of our troubles, and he sent me a little money then. He was glad to know that I was still alive! He sent me 100 rubles with the idea that I should return home at once. He was anxious about me. The parents of the violinist also told him to return, and he obeyed and left immediately.

So I went on alone with the tour, and was on my way to St. Petersburg, because from there I planned to proceed directly to my father's house. The adventure was over, I thought, and I confess that I was relieved. I was really glad to return to my father's house, for I was tired of it all. I was only seventeen, you know, and I had been gone more than a year.

As I look back upon it all now, I wonder that I managed it at all—only the utter carelessness and confidence of youth made such a tremendous adventure possible.

When I arrived in St. Petersburg, I met a young man I had seen in the Kerntopf family. I was very pleased to see him, for, I suppose, I was a little homesick, and he seemed delighted to see me. He inquired eagerly about my doings, and so on, and so on.

"Well," he said, "where are you going now? What are you intending to do next?" I was only too glad to tell him and explain my plans, delighted at his interest in my welfare.

"Oh," I said, "I am happy to tell you that I am now returning home. I am leaving directly because my father has just sent me the money for the journey." I was so overjoyed at that, that I told him and he too seemed overjoyed to hear about the money, for he immediately borrowed all that money, telling me that he only needed it for a few hours and would bring it back directly. Well, as you have already guessed, the few hours were forever! I never saw him again. He left immediately for Warsaw with my money, and left me penniless in St. Petersburg! He went to his home with the money that was sent me to go to mine. Ah, that was a very painful thing in more ways than one. I believed in him, you see.

To pile up the agony still further, I was not only without a penny in the world, but my luggage and all my possessions were still at the station (where I had met him) because I had planned, you see, to leave St. Petersburg that very day. But when I asked for my luggage, it had been stolen! And I was then left with nothing, literally.

I had noticed when talking with my supposed friend that there was some one with him—a man who did not seem particularly friendly, I thought, and who had a suspicious attitude. Soon after I was left stranded, I met this man again on the street. Perhaps he had been keeping an eye on me. I think that must have been so because he proved to be my guardian angel at that moment. He approached me and said, "What happened between you and that fellow from Warsaw? You have had a long talk. What did he say? Tell me."

"Oh," I answered, "he borrowed money from me."

"And you *gave* him money? That is a pity—a great pity, for he is a rascal!"

"Oh," I interrupted, "but I met him in the house of friends in Warsaw and I believed in him."

The man laughed angrily and said, "You will never see your money again—never! He owes me money, too. He got it in the same way. He is a rascal," he repeated. "A bad fellow."

"What shall I do?" I exclaimed, "I am penniless! I cannot write my father again, because he sent me all he could. It was a large sum for him. He cannot afford to send me any more. There is no one for me to turn to."

"Well," he answered, after a moment, "come to me. I am a very poor man, but I can give you at least a roof to sleep under and a bit of bread to eat." He was a plumber and he was extremely poor, very, very poor. He was just starting to make his living. The only food he could offer me was tea and bread, and a little corner in his poor room. But I was thankful for it. I spent there, I think, about a fortnight, and I did not know what to do. I had tea and bread three times a day. That was all I had to keep me alive, and a corner in which to sleep, and I walked the streets absolutely helpless.

How it happened I do not know, but after a fortnight, the janitor of that house came to me and said, "Have you any relative?"

"Yes," I answered quickly, thinking of my father. "Why?"

"Because there is a letter for you," he said. "A letter."

"A letter for me? Can it be from my father?" I cried.

"What is the name of your father?"

"Jan Paderewski."

Student Days In Warsaw

"Yes, that's right, but the address was wrong so they sent from the post office all over the place to enquire and it has come here."

It was a special letter (what you would call registered) from home. It was a letter from my father with 100 rubles. That was simply a miracle. I was overwhelmed with joy. I got the money and I gave a little to the poor fellow who had kept me alive on bread and tea for a fortnight—and then, I went home. So thankfully.

I reached home safely and there was great rejoicing in our family. It seemed as if I had been gone a century. After a time, when I was alone with my father, I asked him what impulse had prompted him to send me that money the second time, how he knew I was in such dreadful straits.

"Oh, that is easily explained," he answered simply; "I had a dream. I saw you in a desperate position in St. Petersburg, and I immediately sent asking the post office to enquire for you." That was miraculous. My father had found me through a dream. You know I had walked the streets of St. Petersburg day after day, alone with nothing to do. That lodging of the plumber was underground. There was no light there and I could not even read. I could do nothing, absolutely nothing! So I walked the whole day long. After my first tea I went to look at the parks, then I went back home to another cup of tea and then went out on the streets again. And so it went day after day. It seemed an eternity.

And it was then for the first time that I saw Rubinstein, going in a cab through the streets. I knew who it was because I had seen his photographs. If I could have only realized at that moment, that not so very much later I was again to see and actually talk with Rubinstein and even play to him one of my compositions, perhaps my days would not have seemed so desperate then; but such a thing never entered my mind because I was a poor wretch! I was bereft of everything—friends, money, clothes, almost food.

My belongings were lost and I was destitute. How my father's letter reached me I do not know. That was one of the most crucial moments of my life. You know at that time I really had no idea what to do—I was completely crushed, because my only means of joining my family and starting again a normal life were entirely lost. I was left simply like a dead leaf. Many a time I think about that, first of all with infinite gratitude to my dear father, and then to God, too, for having directed my father's hand. That, of course, was destiny—it was the hand of God.

My father did not make one single reproach when I got back —just joy to see me again. That dream made a profound impression on him too.

My heart was filled with gratitude—unspeakable gratitude. And I vowed then to give my father a great happiness. I said to him, "Now I am going to give you a supreme satisfaction. I have given you so much trouble, I shall return now and finish my studies at the Conservatory, and receive my diploma."

"But," he said, "you will have to stay for such a long time. How can you?"

"Well," I replied, "it cannot be helped now, I *must* finish my course and get a diploma. You will see."

So I went back to the Conservatory and I worked very hard, especially on counterpoint and composition, and I worked so hard that in *six months* I finshed my studies of two years. But I worked day and night. I had enormous concentration. They made no difficulties then in taking me back again—they were glad enough to have me.

Then came the finishing act of the school year, and my father came for that occasion and had a tremendous surprise, because I was among those who were going to get their diplomas. You see he never really believed it would happen. And he was standing in that big Hall, the Municipal Hall in Warsaw (I see him still), and he was really frightened. Poor man, he wondered what was going to happen next. Is something wrong again, he thought? But I received that diploma, and he was simply amazed, overwhelmed with joy when the Director read my name in a loud voice. The last one. It was the most brilliant of all, they said. And then I played. How I did, I do not know, as I was deeply moved myself by this great event. A step forward at last! I played the Grieg Concerto with the orchestra. I remember that.

And so it was—I received my diploma and the day ended with happiness in all our hearts. And thus came to an end my studies in the Conservatory at Warsaw.

III

Berlin and the World of Music

I

The rejoicing over the receipt of my diploma was very genuine and continued for some time. First of all, my poor father, whose faith in me had been justified, and the dear, good Kerntopf family, who had befriended me from the first, especially Edward Kerntopf, whose interest and affection never failed, were one and all overjoyed.

After it was all over, I intended, in fact I had great hopes of going somewhere, Berlin or Vienna preferably, to study piano. But alas! I had not the means. My father had done all he could —he could not help me further. In spite of all my efforts, I realized it was impossible—I must remain in Warsaw. So I accepted the post of teacher in the Conservatory there. That offer was made immediately after receiving my diploma, as a result of the brilliant examination I had passed—perhaps a kind of reward after the stormy years there as a student.

And now we come to a great event in my life. I think I shall have to say it very simply—I fell in love. I was only twenty at that time and in spite of the uncertainty of the future, I married. I wanted a home, a personal life of my own—a place and some one that belonged to me. I married in 1880 Antonina Korsak—a young girl who was a student at the Warsaw Conservatory. I had a little home of my own at last and I was happy—but it was a short happiness. A year later my wife died, leaving me alone with our child, a son. I had lived through a brief—a beautiful—experience. Even at twenty, one can plumb the heights and depths and feel the pain and mystery of life. I now faced another change—I must go forward alone. My wife had had some little money of her own, and before her death she asked me to use part of it to continue my musical studies, in which she had the deepest faith. We had in Poland an institution for which I think there is no equivalent in other countries, a very special kind of Trusteeship for orphans, controlled by a number of prominent people, the details of which are of no interest at this moment except that it was in that institution I deposited the money that was to go to my child. It proved to be a tragic choice, for every penny of it was stolen a few years later by certain of these very respectable Trustees, and nothing remained. The little safety that I had then hoped for proved a dream, like so many others.

I have already told you that after the death of my wife, I realized very keenly that there was no future for me there in Warsaw except as a teacher, and so I determined to go to Berlin. I left my child with his grandmother, the mother of my wife, and went directly to Friedrich Kiel, a very famous teacher of that time, to study composition. Everybody said (and I began myself at last almost to believe it) that I could never be a pianist, but that I was very talented for composition. I had already written a few pieces which had been printed in Warsaw, and made quite a little success. So it was very encouraging for me to again study composition—I turned to it naturally.

Now I want to tell you a little about my studies with Kiel in Berlin. . . . You have asked me whether I ever studied the violin among the many instruments that I studied. Yes, and that is rather an amusing story, because in those early days whenever I began my studies, I found myself always learning some instrument other than the piano! And so it happened when I went to Kiel, he too suggested it. He told me that it was absolutely necessary to know the character and possibilities of a *string* instrument, and the violin would be the most practical for me. So I at once got a teacher. Of course, not a teacher of great reputation—I was not ready for that. I had absolutely no knowledge of the first elements of violin playing, so I had a very mediocre teacher—all I could afford.

[57]

But I met again with the same discouragement there, as with the flute, the oboe, and the clarinet! He gave me quite a number of lessons, perhaps ten or twelve, and finally, disgusted, said that I had absolutely no talent for music—none. He did not seem to know that I was a musician, but thought of me simply as a foreigner who wanted to learn a little scratching on the violin, and did not hesitate in discouraging me after a few lessons. "Oh," he said, "why do you study the violin? You will never be a violinist, never. You are not a musician—you have not even a good ear for music, it seems to me. You have absolutely no talent for music. You should stop the lessons now. It's a waste of money."

Well, after that I decided to have a little revenge. The day after this tirade, at my last lesson, I took him into my room where the little piano was and without any preliminaries I began to play for him. He stared at me dumbfounded. The poor fellow was perfectly petrified! (He was a good musician himself though not much of a teacher.) I played one of my latest compositions and then began a Chopin Mazurka, but before I could even finish it he jumped to his feet. "Oh, stop, stop!" he cried, "stop! I have made a fool of myself. A perfect fool! I said you had no talent for music, and you can play like that!" He was pathetic in his embarrassment.

I confess that I enjoyed my little revenge, but I was sorry too, for after that impromptu concert of mine the poor fellow said he would not come again, there was nothing he could do for me, and that was the end of my violin lessons.

Many years afterwards I studied the 'cello with my dear friend Adamowski, which was to my advantage—another string to my bow, so to say. But that story does not belong here at the moment.

Anyhow, with those few lessons of violin and 'cello, I acquired much that has been of great value all my life. I found when making the score of my opera and other works where the orchestra is an important part, that I could play myself, very slowly it is true, but accurately and understandingly, anything that I wrote for the violin and 'cello, etc. All this, as you can easily realize, was invaluable.

Antonina Korsak Paderewska

Paderewski at the time of his marriage

Berlin and the World of Music

At that time, you know, in spite of my unfaltering *inner* conviction of Destiny, I was strongly under the influence of my teachers—that I was *not* going to be, never could be, a successful pianist. That, of course, left its impression. It was an added thing to fight against. From the beginning, even at the Conservatory, everything was against me—discouragement on all sides. Even those who were my intimate friends looked upon virtuosity as something inferior. As I was at that time very fond of composing, and some of my first compositions were rather noteworthy in that little circle of friends, I almost lost myself any hope of becoming a successful pianist. So naturally I turned then to composition. Back of all our actions in life there is usually some strong guiding motive. It may not always appear clearly at the moment, but afterwards one is very keenly aware of it, and so it was in this case. This inner conviction of mine at the time, that there was no future for me in Warsaw except as a teacher, had a tremendous effect upon my whole after life. At that moment I made my decision and turned my face toward another branch of my art.

I left my position at the Conservatory and went straight to Berlin, to that most marvellous man, the greatest pedagogue in the field of composition, Friedrich Kiel, and studied there for seven months. I worked very hard—really too hard, and my nerves gave way. My health broke down completely. I used to work ten or twelve hours a day. I made, of course, very considerable progress, and Kiel looked upon me as a star pupil. He was very proud of my achievements, for I really accomplished much in that comparatively short time. Kiel applauded and encouraged me constantly and told me many times that he had never had a more gifted pupil. All this was very satisfactory, of course. But I must repeat again that Kiel was also deeply interested in my playing (he was one of the few), and whenever I played a composition which I had prepared for him, he would say, "Oh, you must practise your piano more, because you *also* have a remarkable talent for piano playing." He was not like my old teacher of the trumpet and trombone I have told you about—who used to say to me every day, "Look here, my boy, you must devote more time to the *trombone,* because, believe me, the trombone is your future livelihood! With the piano you will never do anything. Never!"

Well, to go on. It was while I was studying in Berlin that I began to meet some famous musicians that were very helpful to me. I met Richard Strauss at the house of my publisher, Bock. It was a very amusing household consisting of his wife, his mother, and several charming children, for whom I used to play, and the children liked me very much consequently. Sometimes we came in the evening, Strauss and myself, and some other musicians of lesser importance than Strauss, and just to amuse the children we played for them, he and I, dance music. On some occasions the company was not only composed of children but of adults too, and the atmosphere was so gay, so intimate, that every one wanted to dance. So we used to play for hours, Strauss and myself, I remember.

Strauss' playing was not very brilliant. He was not a pianist, but he was chiefly a composer all his life. He turned to conducting later on, but he was always very fond of dance music. He adored it and it was delightful to listen to him. But there was one great drawback to the enjoyment of his playing, and that was also a factor which determined me to study the expression of my own face when playing, namely the awful grimaces Strauss made while at the piano. It was too amusing for words to see, but it was also rather painful. One felt almost embarrassed for him. It was really a show in itself—an additional performance.

And now I will say a word about my own habit, already mentioned, of making such unpleasant grimaces, for I was guilty too and was sometimes ridiculed by my colleagues. I had, as a student, to postpone overcoming that, because I never practised long enough to watch myself. But when I arrived in Berlin, and particularly after seeing Strauss at the piano, I knew that it was a grave impediment in the career of an artist, and I then studied all my difficult passages with a mirror before me, and absolutely surmounted that difficulty, but only after months and months of watching myself. It was really very hard because I was already a little over twenty-four and it had become a fixed habit. I surmounted that difficulty to such an extent that I may say now without any exaggeration, I do not know whether there is any other pianist who can keep himself as quiet and as much master of his appearance while playing the most difficult music, as I. But it was a very great effort. And I was never told these things except by my schoolmates at the Conservatory, who made fun of me at the beginning. So I have always been grateful to Strauss for making me realize the importance of overcoming this obnoxious habit.

I am tapping now in this little talk a great reservoir of memories. Those days in Berlin were full of new experiences and contacts. Quite a new life opened its doors to me. I was moving forward, a few groping steps at a time, toward the great world —the great world of art.

There were very many students in Berlin at that time. It was a magic rendezvous for them; the University enjoyed great popularity. There were a number of my own countrymen studying at the University and at the Polytechnic too. I lived in a family by the name of Rohde, a very fine family from Hamburg.

I want to tell you a little about these good people who were so extremely kind and devoted to me. I always remember them with the deepest affection, and their constant care and interest in me. Their house, too, became another home like the Kerntopfs'. How fortunate that was! Things might have been so different.

It was not exactly a student's life that I led in Berlin at that time. I was too serious a man then to join the student group and the people who were so constantly enjoying themselves. I was already considered as a teacher, a former teacher of the Conservatory at Warsaw, and I was the father of a child. Therefore, I did not belong to that gay clique of students and musicians, though occasionally I joined with them in their festivities. Most of them were much older than I, and still studying! In fact I am sure they would always be students! There is a certain type of person, you know, who always remains a student—always studying, but learning nothing.

The Paderewski Memoirs

I was a Pole and very much alone. As I remember it, there were few Polish students there at that time. The Germans were not at all sympathetic to me. That was a time of great persecution of the Poles in Germany and I felt it constantly and deeply. Even in that charming family of my kind publisher, Mr. Bock, I sometimes had to hear very cutting and bitter remarks about my country. And I disliked Berlin very, very much on that account. There were certain political regulations which made me feel rather disgusted with these people and their system. For example, of all the foreign newspapers, only the Polish were prohibited. There was no sale of them at the railway stations (the stations always have foreign papers). Some individuals were very nice, very civilized, but the entire atmosphere was positively antagonistic to Poland.

Berlin was then a very large city with a fine park and a few beautiful buildings. The most beautiful of all was, of course, the Royal Castle, which is an old building dating from the time of the great Elector. Modern buildings, such as the new Parliament (which was burned a few years ago), were not yet in existence when I was a student there. I would not say that the city was beautiful then, but the order and cleanliness of the streets were such as to make an impression of a certain kind of beauty. It was really so perfectly clean that it commanded admiration. In appearance Berlin was rather theatrical. It was all very military. Uniforms were to be seen everywhere. There was even then a certain antagonism between the officers in uniform and the civilians in plain clothes, and one could see always the people stepping humbly aside, even off the sidewalk, to make room for the officers. Marked superiority. It was ridiculous. But the good German people were already accustomed to it. They had got into the habit of acknowledging their inferiority!

Berlin was a city of life and excitement, but little real gaiety. The people did not know at that time how to enjoy themselves, how to amuse themselves. The cafés and Bierkneipen were always full, but although they were very noisy they were not really gay. There was very little laughter in spite of the noise. The

Berlin and the World of Music

German is always serious. All kinds of music was to be heard in Berlin. There were plenty of concerts too, too many. Every day many concerts and very good opera. Wagner then was perfectly established and enjoying tremendous popularity and success, but the Drama was quite mediocre, in my opinion. It was not to be compared with the Burg theatre of Vienna, for instance, one of the most distinguished theatres in Europe.

To continue a little further with the Berlin experiences, I want especially to speak of Mr. Hugo Bock, the publisher. I was introduced to Mr. Bock by a very fine man and good musician who enjoyed much popularity. His name was Moritz Moszkowski, and it was through this introduction of Moszkowski's that my compositions were published, because it was extremely difficult, being young and unknown, to find a publisher. He, Bock, gave me for those first compositions (about nine pieces) the enormous sum of 200 marks, that was about $50. You know I never really expected that—he acted very generously under the circumstances.

In Mr. Bock's house, which was one of the important ones in Berlin, I had the opportunity of meeting many distinguished artists, chiefly musicians, and there I met all the musical celebrities who were living in Berlin or passing through the German capital. Of course, Bock, as a publisher, knew them all.

And first and foremost I should like to mention something which influenced me in my determination to pursue that pianistic career. I was in the office of Bock one day with a new composition, when just as I was leaving, he said to me quite suddenly, "Would you not like to meet Anton Rubinstein?" I was amazed naturally at this, it was quite unexpected. "Of course," I said, "I should be delighted. I—" "Well," he interrupted, "please come then to my house for dinner tonight and you shall see him." So in much excitement I went to dinner and there I met that great, that immense artist. He was most agreeable and gracious and after dinner he came to me and said, "I hear a great deal about your compositions, from Mr. Bock, who speaks highly of them, and I should like to hear some tonight. Will you not play me something?"

I had just finished a set of variations, which I then played for him, and he was very pleased. He listened attentively. "You have a brilliant future," he said when I had finished. "Now play me something more, something else—play some short pieces." I did so, and again he was very complimentary, very kind. "You should compose more," he went on, "more for the piano." "Oh," I protested, "I cannot really do much for the piano, I play so little myself." "Nonsense," he replied, "you should play more, I tell you. You have an inborn technique and you could have, I am sure, a splendid pianistic career." Those fateful words of his left me almost stunned for the moment. I did not know how to answer him—it overwhelmed me. It was such a surprise. This experience with Rubinstein had a tremendous effect. What he said changed my world completely. Of course I was very eager to hear him play but I had not at that moment the courage to ask him. He impressed me from the first as a very noble and good man and an absolutely supreme artist. There was something a little bit uncanny about him too. He had a natural greatness in himself—he was a titanic figure.

Naturally Bock was immensely impressed with Rubinstein's remarks about my compositions. It was a great point in my favor, I could see.

Rubinstein was perfectly enchanting that evening, and after he left, Bock turned to me and said, "Well, is he not wonderful?"

"Yes," I answered, "wonderful." I was still in the grip of this experience. I was greatly excited about it all. "Wonderful, but oh! if I could only hear him play."

"What," shouted Bock, staring at me, "you have not yet heard him play?"

"Never," I answered, "never."

"Then why did you not ask him to play here tonight? He would have done it! He is always very agreeable about it, he would have played for you gladly. You see how he received you —how interested and encouraging, and how pleased he was with your compositions. Oh, what a pity, what a pity!" Bock was walking up and down the room and greatly upset. "Now it is too

late, because tomorrow he leaves for a tour. Still," he added con-
solingly, "you will hear him later—you have plenty of time." But
I never really heard him play until much later in Warsaw.

Among the celebrities then in Berlin, I must put first the
great violinist Joseph Joachim, who was a noble man and an admirable artist. As an interpreter of classical music, especially of
Beethoven, he was absolutely supreme—a highly cultured man
in general. He was not only accessible to younger musicians, but
was always ready to assist them in art, and in other ways too.

On one occasion, following the suggestion of my publisher
(who was not wholly disinterested in the affair naturally), he,
Joachim, invited me to play a few of my own compositions,
which I of course did without hesitation. A small collection of
short piano pieces published under the title, which I never liked,
"Chants du Voyageur," was selected for that purpose. The third
piece in it (in B Major) seemed to impress Joachim quite particularly—and to such an extent that he asked me to repeat it
several times. In general the impression these compositions made
upon him was extremely encouraging to me. I was frequently
invited to the "Musicals" at his house. The people who came
were of local greatness, people holding very high official positions, the professors in the University, the local bigwigs, and so on.

On those occasions I was invited by Joachim repeatedly to
play some of my own compositions, and I considered it as an exceptional favor on his part—a great encouragement.

Then, I am sorry to say, for many years I lost sight of
Joachim, and only about twenty years later I again came into
contact with him. He was a very brilliant technician. He had
absolute command of his instrument. He was a thorough musician and had a great nobility in playing, which was extremely
impressive. An altogether big man, in himself and in his art. The
principal point that impressed every one at first sight and first
hearing of him was a marvellous dignity, which is an extremely
rare quality. Now, if I may be permitted to make an especially
appropriate comparison with another magnificent violinist,
Ysaye, there was always a quality of roughness, or ruggedness if

you like, and just a taint of the comedian at times in Ysaye, which was in great contrast to the dignity that always enveloped Joachim. Ysaye, great artist that he was, was not so supreme as Joachim. Joachim was every inch a giant.

On another occasion at Bock's house I met a German musical writer, Louis Ehlert, whose literary works enjoyed great popularity among German music lovers. He belonged to that little clique of close friends of the immortal composer, Robert Schumann, whom he knew when still a very young man, and of Madame Clara Schumann—the widow of Schumann.

Like Joachim, he was classical and very conservative in his tastes. His admiration for Brahms was not perhaps as absolute and exclusive as that of Joachim. He had perhaps more sensitiveness for modern music than that little musical congregation to which he belonged, which was the adoring group of devotees that always surrounded Madame Clara Schumann. This little band of followers was almost a religious circle. They did not admit anybody else but Schumann and a very few others whom they had canonized—and first and foremost came Brahms.

Ehlert's impressions of my compositions were even more enthusiastic than Joachim's, and his favorite piece among them was again that No. 3 of my "Chants du Voyageur." But he liked as well the variations Op. XI, which did not appeal so strongly to Joachim's more orthodox tastes.

Several years afterwards, he again enquired about my compositions in a letter addressed to Bock, always expressing himself so graciously.

I never met Madame Clara Schumann personally. I saw her only once at an orchestral concert in Frankfurt-am-Main, where I was playing my own Concerto in 1890. She was sitting conspicuously in the first row, and I remember that she was very interested in my Concerto and applauded me loudly, the good old lady! (She was very old then). But, on the contrary, when I came to play my solo, and I had selected as a second number Liszt's Fantasie based upon "Don Juan," she could not refrain from showing her deep disapproval and even, I might say, her disgust! You know in her sacred little clique, Liszt was considered a very devil, and besides he permitted himself such a gross sacrilege as ornaments to Mozart's inspiration. That Fantasie of Liszt's is based upon Mozart's themes taken from the opera "Don Juan," or as better known, "Don Giovanni." Madame Schumann did not conceal her disapproval—she shrugged her shoulders and turned to the lady next to her, talking and expressing with her face her contempt!

Madame Clara Schumann was known chiefly as the wife and survivor of the great, the immortal composer, Robert Schumann. And for that reason, she had many privileges! She played often in England. She had every year a season where she played chamber music, and principally her husband's works; and then she used also to play with Joachim and with Piatti—that was the celebrated trio—in the Popular Concerts organized by Chappell, the publisher, in London. They were called the "Pops" then as now.

Among other artists whom I met at Bock's house was also Pablo de Sarasate, the famous violinist. He was a charming personality and a marvellous artist, with irreproachable technique and the most beautiful violin tone imaginable—more beautiful than Joachim's. He was not to be compared as an interpreter, especially of classical music, with Joachim, but he had much more charm owing to that exceptionally beautiful quality of tone. He had a more beautiful voice, but Joachim was a much greater singer, if you are putting it in terms of singing.

A lovable character too and a loyal friend. Very generous to his colleagues, helping many of them, especially some of the French composers and Spanish too, because he was a Spaniard, though he lived in Paris. Sarasate was a frequent visitor at Warsaw, and I often met him there afterwards, which was always interesting.

In those early years I met and knew almost all the musical giants of the time. It was a glorious period—great composers, pianists, and conductors. These contacts enriched my life. This was true in Warsaw as well as Berlin. At the house of Louis Grossman particularly I had many opportunities of meeting all the artists who came to Warsaw. Grossman was a piano dealer and a very good musician himself. He had written some light operas and had a great interest in music. And this reminds me of an experience in my early musical career that happened in his house. At that time I was rather famous in my little circle in the Conservatory, as a very rapid reader of music. I could read anything and very quickly, at sight. So I was sometimes called upon to play an accompaniment. It so happened that an Italian singer, I do not remember her name for the moment, was giving a concert in Warsaw. She had a very beautiful contralto voice, a very ugly face and the most unpleasant manners (so it is perhaps better that I do not remember her name!). Her husband, who had a glorious baritone voice, was just the opposite—kind and gracious. We made friends from the start. They were giving a concert together and both wanted an accompanist at short notice. Mr. Grossman, who was always trying to help me—it was during the time when I had to struggle for my existence—recommended me highly but, alas, I did not please the lady! She wanted some one else. However, I had to go and make the rehearsal. And she began at once to look for some fault in me. I was a very good accompanist at that time and I did my best for her. But when it came to the final rehearsal, to which she had invited friends, she asked me suddenly to transpose the accompaniment two tones higher. She did not feel in possession of her low notes that day, it seems.

Now, to transpose two tones higher is a terrible task. One tone or half a tone is easy, but two tones cannot be improvised quickly. A string or wind instrument, having to play only one note at a time, can transpose it very easily, but for a pianist it is very difficult and should be prepared beforehand. Well, of course I made a few mistakes. "Oh," she cried, "stop, stop! What an inferior pianist you are; you cannot even transpose—and yet you are attempting to play my accompaniment." It made a very bad impression upon everybody and I suffered very much from that confusion.

At that embarrassing moment the good Mr. Grossman intervened and said in a very loud voice, "But Madame, you have asked him an impossible thing. I do not know whether there is an accompanist anywhere who could transpose two tones *higher* at sight! Impossible—it should have been prepared." That was one of my most unpleasant experiences and I suffered from it at the time, but fortunately it is an attribute of human nature to forget unpleasant experiences, though sometimes they come back and lift their heads—as today.

It was a very touching episode in my relations with Grossman. I always remembered his kind intervention in my favor; he came to my rescue at a bad moment. However, I played at that concert later, when it came off, but it was not necessary to transpose then because the lady had recovered her voice!

On the other hand, to offset this experience, there were moments of very high satisfaction to me as an accompanist. I remember one particularly, the first time Leopold Auer, famous violinist, came to Warsaw; at that time he was at the climax of his career, enjoying enormous success everywhere. He played with the orchestra and also gave a recital, and then he promised to play at the Conservatory. It was in 1878 when I was just finishing my studies there. He had promised to play some new compositions. They were new at that time because they were absolutely unknown in Poland and unknown in Russia. They were the Symphonie Espagnole by Lalo, and a suite for violin by Ferdinand Ries.

He asked for one of the professors of the Conservatory to accompany him. It was difficult and quite modern music. The Director called together all the professors, and asked who could best accompany Auer. No one dared attempt it. So he sent for me. "Paderewski," he said, "we are in a great difficulty and you must help us out. You are the only one who can. You must accompany Leopold Auer this afternoon in his recital. And take care," he warned, anxiously, "because Auer is a splendid artist and must have a fine accompanist. Unfortunately, he has no time for rehearsal and so you must play for him at sight." Well, I was rather overwhelmed at first, but I did it. I had never seen the music before but I read it easily and all went well—to Auer's satisfaction.

[69]

I must confess that I was not deeply concerned, for at that time I did not mind technical difficulties, because I had no technique myself, and the correctness of piano playing was something absolutely indifferent to me. So accompaniments presented no great difficulties. Auer was delighted and said, "The next concert I give, Paderewski, you must play for me again. I do not want any other accompanist." And so I accompanied him on his return. He remembered that even a few years ago, the year before he died, when he was a very old man; in fact, I'm told this little story is in his biography. He was the greatest teacher of the violin ever known. He was for the violin as great a master as Leschetizky for the piano.

I did not mention when speaking about the artists at the house of Grossman that I met there an artist who had been very helpful to me, in fact she was the first pianist to play my compositions, Madame Essipoff. I met her there first in the fall of 1883. I gave her some of my compositions then. She was interested in those Variations in A Minor, and she played them for the first time in Vienna and also played them in her own concerts. I met her later on when I went to Leschetizky. She was very interested and helpful to me always. She was, incidentally, one of the many wives of Leschetizky. He used to say, in fact he frequently said it, and always with great delight, "People call me Bluebeard, and yet, unlike Bluebeard, all my wives are alive! I have had only four wives, and that is not so many when compared to Eugene d'Albert, for instance. D'Albert has had eight. That is surely a record number."

All of which reminds me that d'Albert was another musician I first met at Bock's house in Berlin. He was a pupil of Liszt. He played in Berlin and made a sensation. He was quite a boy still, about eighteen years of age. He was about three years younger than I. He made an immense impression upon me. He played beautifully, with such dash and temperament—a little fellow, very small in stature, not much to look at at the piano, but his playing was remarkable at that time technically and in expression too. But even so there was always something a little unpleasant in his playing—too many mannerisms. It was not reposeful playing. It was much more pleasant to listen to him with one's eyes closed. He was a very good Beethoven player. As a natural gift for piano playing, his was an absolutely remarkable talent.

Unfortunately, he started composing operas. That was a mistake. He expected to make much money with them, and he did make some, but he could have made much more if he had remained a pianist only, because there was not much personality in his compositions while there was great personality in his piano playing. His compositions were mediocre. Also, let me add to all this, he was married every two or three years.

I had known him at that time in Berlin. As a gesture of admiration, my Variations in A Minor were dedicated to him. I do not know whether he ever played them or not. There is a certain etiquette—let us call it—among pianists that they rarely play compositions of *other living pianists*. There are sometimes exceptions of course, though generally they wait until one is dead!

I have not seen d'Albert for thirty years or more. I lost sight of him. The last time I heard him was about three years ago in Geneva. He played well, but in a negligent way, very careless. There were moments of remarkable beauty and there were also moments of very tedious and mediocre playing. It was evident that he did not care for piano playing except just as a means for earning a little money. It was a pity.

Then suddenly about three years ago there came from Evian a letter from one of his daughters, enclosing a note of introduction from him. She wanted very much to meet me. Of course, I wrote at once and asked her to come, and she came with her sister to tea on a Sunday. One of them brought her little child with her, a grandchild of d'Albert.

It was just before my severe illness when I was many years younger than I am now. When I came into the room to greet them, they seemed a little embarrassed; in fact they looked at me in surprise. I noticed it and said at once, "What is the matter? What disturbs you?" They hesitated for a moment and then one of the daughters said, quite seriously, "Well, you see, you surprised me. We understood that you were two or three years older than our father." "I am," I replied, "I am." "But," she continued, "how is that? My father looks so much older than you."

Then I laughed and said, "That is very easily explained. You see it is because I have not been married as many times as your father!"

Well, that was an awful moment, for they, it seems, were the children of his *fourth* wife. They were not at all pleased with my answer. It was a very unfortunate joke.

II

We have again gone far afield with these memories, but they are all very vital to me still. My first years of study in Berlin. This period was with Kiel, you will remember, and I stayed throughout the year studying and then returned to Warsaw for my vacation—a greatly needed vacation, for I had put in a tremendous year of work.

I found upon my return to Warsaw that almost everybody, friends, fellow students, etc., laughed at my intention of going on with my studies. They all said, "Why? You have studied enough, you do not need to study any more." "But," I answered, "I feel I need *still* to study, even composition," though I had already made quite a serious work of that. "No, you know enough already," they argued; "stay here, we need you. The superior class of piano is offered you—stay here in Warsaw." And so it happened I remained there. I listened to them. My funds were very low—so I was obliged to start again as piano teacher. The same old story!

But it was wrong—completely, as I soon found out. There was a very good reason for my fellow students to wish my help at this moment in the Conservatory. There were two factions among the musicians then, one representing the Conservatory and the other a kind of Municipal Society, which was a rival of the Conservatory and a very keen competitor. So a real fight arose between these two institutions. It had assumed very big proportions and naturally the students at the Conservatory wanted some one of their own to help them fight their battles. They felt I was qualified and saw I was in rather a fighting mood on my return. Hence their eagerness to have me abandon my idea of going back to study with Kiel and remain in Warsaw and help them with their fight. I was very interested in this controversy and always ready for a little speech-making. This speech-making in my youth was of great value to me years after in my political career. I must have had a natural inclination, an inborn technique as we say of the piano, for it. So I stayed at the Conservatory, where I was offered a superior class of piano pupils. It was a very great distinction, and I accepted, encouraged, of course, by those false friends. But I was forced then to play myself. I had to show my pupils how to do certain things, which without playing I would not have been able to do. And so I began to practise a little, and my class became very successful, scoring a real triumph at the examinations. Yes, it seems, I was a very good teacher, but I do not like it. I prefer to give ten concerts rather than one lesson! It takes much more of my energy, I assure you. It is a very exhausting profession.

It will not be without interest to know that I worked extremely hard during all that time I was teaching, because I realized that my general education was lacking a great deal. So I then started a course of studies. I was teaching in the daytime, earning my living, and in the evening, from eight to twelve, I had every night my own lessons. I studied Latin, Mathematics, Literature, History. I had four teachers coming every day. It was expensive and I had to give many extra lessons to pay their fees. Sometimes I gave as many as nine or ten piano lessons a day. And I really acquired some serious knowledge. Certain things have been, perhaps, useless, but a great deal was very necessary. Knowledge is the only thing that can enrich but cannot be taken from one.

It was while I was teaching in the Conservatory that I met by chance, at the house of an old friend, the editor of a popular daily newspaper. We had rather a long talk together, I recall, about music, and then, quite suddenly, he said, "Now, I have an idea—what you're saying interests me very much. Why don't you write some articles about music, some criticisms, and so forth? and I will print them."

I was rather surprised at this offer, I must say. It did not tempt me very much at first, but he was very insistent. Then I told him that if I had time I should like to write a few articles because it would be useful, but I had not the leisure then. The newspaper in question belonged to what we call now the "yellow press." It was extremely fond of printing scandals and did not appeal to me at all. And there was still another reason why I could not accept this offer. I did not find myself mature enough then to criticize artists. I could teach pupils at the Conservatory, yes, but to express judgment, to make an opinion (because a critic sometimes *creates* opinion) and to pronounce verdicts upon artists takes an authority, and I did not then consider myself an authority. I knew that from time to time I could have written better criticisms than some experienced writers because I knew music better, and those who write very often cannot judge fairly because they do not know their subject. But at that time I was not ready for making criticism for the simple reason that I had no bitterness in myself. I do not know if critics *must* have bitterness, but generally they have. I must confess I always feel that.

But to go back to that proposition of the editor in question, it happened that I read a few days later in his paper a criticism which made me perfectly wild. It was a severe, unjustified, and violent attack upon a fine artist who made a great impression on me. It was written by somebody who first of all did not know anything about music, and also because he was evidently displeased with the applause and a little ovation that was given to the artist. It was personal spite on his part. That should never enter musical criticism.

Now there is a great deal of that incomprehensible envy which can suddenly move to bitterness and anger even people who do not belong to the profession. Why? I have never been able to understand why. I can understand perfectly well that musicians who are not successful envy colleagues more fortunate than themselves. Yes. I understand that same feeling among literary men, painters, sculptors, etc., but I cannot understand for instance, how a clerk in a business enterprise can bitterly envy an actor or a musician. But that happens. And not only those in an inferior position. I have seen people occupying very high places in society, enjoying all the privileges that such high positions can give, the possession of a fortune and a multitude of friends, and then feeling envious of the admiration that a singer, for instance, enjoys. I never could understand that. It is some strange quality of human nature.

At any rate, when I read that criticism which made me so angry I went directly to the newspaper and asked for the editor. I was in a great state of excitement. "Now," I said, "I am ready. I am going to write for your newspaper. I have decided." I was fired with a holy indignation. The editor, who was a very agreeable man and a very astute one, realized at once that I was in a fighting mood and still he wanted me. "I am delighted," he cried, "for I still want you and will give you a free hand. You can write what you like." And so we made our bargain and I began at once. The editor was true to his word and did give me a free hand.

I think I can say this much for my articles, that never in any other paper in the world have there been, before or since, so many friendly, well-wishing and encouraging criticisms as I was then writing for that paper! Everybody was praised—everybody! That was my reaction—a mighty reaction to those sour critics. I was as violent in my way of feeling as they were in theirs. I had become bitter in a just cause. There is a very charming and appropriate aphorism that I think I may quote here. It applies so well to my own state of mind at that time. It was Heine (unless I am very much mistaken) who said it and probably in one of his numerous essays or criticisms. Heine was witty and very caustic, bitter at times. He coupled words somewhat to this effect:

"The sourest wines make the best of vinegar,
The best musicians, the sourest critics."

Though not exactly quoted, I am sorry to say, that is the sense and gist of it and makes the point of my story.

Well, I enjoyed the work very much. It was a great effort because I was not only teaching, but had my own studies in Latin and history, etc., to prepare. I worked far into the night. I would go to the concert, and after the concert hurry to the newspaper office to write the criticism. It was a heavy burden and I had to economize my sleep, but I managed it somehow and continued the work for a year.

During this period I lived in the Adamowski family, who were my beloved friends, and still are, those that are left. You see, I left the Kerntopf household after I finished my studies at the Conservatory. As long as I was a student, it was quite all right to live in that crowd of children, and the family life was very comfortable and pleasant—but when I grew up and became a teacher myself, I had to have an entirely different way of living. It was a necessity. A little drawing-room where I could teach, and a bedroom, etc. And so it came about that I went to live with the Adamowskis, who arranged a proper place for me. This was a happy time of living and companionship. The two Adamowski boys, Tim and Joseph, were my companions from the very beginning of my student life—my first intimate friends outside the Kerntopf family that I held in the greatest affection. That I still hold through all these years—a friendship that has gone through a life time, although Joseph Adamowski died a few years ago in Boston and only Tim remains.

Well, my life went on along the lines laid down for it. I taught, studied, and wrote. Incessant work. The results at that time seemed rather meagre to me. I was still seeking and longing for my heart's desire. That feeling never left me, and after a year of that pedagogical work I realized absolutely that there was something in me as a pianist. It became a deep conviction. As I look back upon it I think that conviction was always there, in the depths and roots of my being in spite of constant discouragement. It was then that I said, "Now it is enough—enough of teaching!"

Antonina, the sister, as a young woman

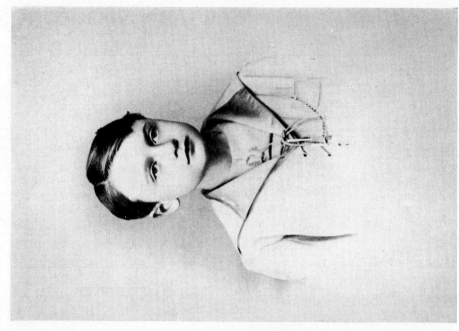

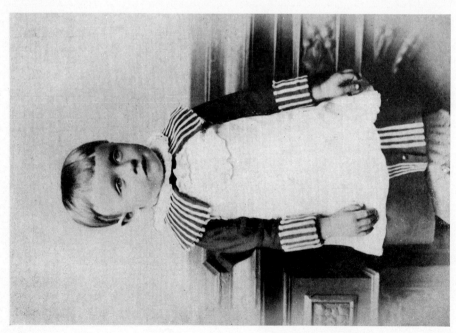

Alfred Paderewski, at three and at eleven years

Berlin and the World of Music

At that moment the inner conviction became a reality never to be shaken again. I was determined then upon a pianistic career, but I realized that first of all I must go away and *finish* my studies of composition, which had been interrupted. So I returned to Berlin. But before going there I had to do something about my poor boy, who had become very ill. I took him to my father because he was living in a place where there was a possibility of having a good physician. He was already showing a serious weakness in walking. It was practically the beginning of infantile paralysis. But in those days they did not know much about that dreadful affliction. The boy was then about four years old. He was very clever and had an unusually high order of intelligence. But his poor frail body made him even then a complete invalid. His illness was progressing very slowly and without possibility of cure. No, I did not realize it then—nobody knew really, even the physicians, and I took him to many. A "weakness in the legs" was the diagnosis of the last physician I consulted. But he did not know. It was a tragedy, a constant anxiety to me.

My return to Berlin the second time was an important step in my musical career. This time I studied with Professor Urban, a very able man who gave me a very sound and solid foundation for my orchestration. Urban was a pupil of the great Kiel, a very special teacher of orchestration. But that knowledge of orchestration was already *in me,* so to speak, on account of having studied and played so many instruments. So I worked on with Urban, but always in the back of my mind was that intention of having a pianistic career. So I continued to play on—by myself.

I want to mention that it was while I was studying orchestration with Urban that I met Alexander Lambert, who was also a pupil of Urban at that time. And that was the beginning of another friendship which lasted for many years. We were both students there together, although he was further advanced in his work than I was. Later on he became a very well-known musician in New York and he was certainly a remarkable teacher. He had a great many pupils all the years of his life and he was a man of exceedingly strong character.

[77]

Although this is not exactly in sequence, I have just now thought of an experience, a very amusing one, I had at a concert. I think it must be included somewhere in these first chapters, so here it is. I was to play in a concert with my friend Gorski, a violinist of some importance, a professor at the Conservatory in Warsaw. I was just beginning my career, but, as I told you, already recognized as a good accompanist. He asked me to go on a short tour with him. We went to a small watering-place. It was just a little Evian in Poland—we have plenty of those water-ing-places in my country and some of them are extremely good, worthy of any Vichy or Spa or Aix-les-Bains, but they lack de-velopment and advertisement.

At one of these places we decided to give our first concert. There were several thousand people there taking the treatment, mostly Jews who were not interested in music, but only interested in their "cure." However, as there were still several hundred cultivated musical people at this particular place, we thought it worth while to give a concert for them. We found on arrival a great discouragement immediately. There was no piano to be had except a very old instrument, the hammers of which were in a pitiable condition. They would respond to the touch by lifting easily, but alas! they would not fall back again—they remained immovable in the air! It is impossible to describe the agony of this. I found I could not play at all. What was to be done with these immovable hammers hanging in the air and the tone still sounding. They would go up, but never, never down! We tried to rehearse our program. I was sure of the accompaniments, that was the most important part as the violinist was the star per-former and an experienced artist. I felt that perhaps I could manage the accompaniments and the violin would somehow carry us through. But my solo pieces, *what* was I to do about them?

Well, I worked over the hammers, trying in every way to fix them, and then I sat down at the piano to play, but it was no use. Up they flew into the air and there they stayed! "This is horrible," I cried to the violinist who was standing by, "we must do something. I can never, never play even one piece on this piano." It was a dreadful moment. I was in a frenzy.

There was with us a young student who had come along on the tour just for fun. He was a pupil of the violinist and fortunately a very good colleague of mine. He was with us at this crucial moment and eager to help. "Wait. I have a plan, an idea. I think I can help you."

"How?" we both shouted. "How? It's impossible."

"Well," he answered, "when you begin to play, I will stand close to the piano and push the hammers down just as quickly as they go up. I can easily do that and you will then be able to play and I don't think the audience will really notice—I can do it so quickly." Well, it was certainly an ingenuous idea and our last resort, and we had to do something, so we agreed to it and hoped for some good results.

The concert started but it started with an incident, a very unusual one and very amusing. The Prefect of the place decided to come to the concert. He was a Russian General, as the country was ruled by Russia then. He arrived in a great carriage, very showy and dashing, and was attended by several tall Cossacks. He was the master of the entire district and declared that he would not only like to listen to the concert, but he even would pay for his tickets, which was most magnanimous on his part. But although he would gladly pay admission he said he would not mingle with the public! He was far above that! So he continued, "I can only come on one condition, and that is that you open wide the windows and I myself, my wife and all my children will listen to your concert—but from the *outside!*"

So, after these arrangements were made we began the concert, my friend standing close to the piano pushing down the hammers as quickly as they flew up into the air. The accompaniments for the violinist were not so bad—there were little chords, etc., at first and then some arpeggios, so our young helper had not to work so very hard, and of course not all the hammers were defective. But when it came to my solos, ah! then you should have seen him. His hands went like lightning. They flew like birds from side to side. He had to lean way across the piano—back and forth he weaved and darted in constant motion. He worked much harder than I. I was simply playing, but he had to do all the work, pushing those unruly hammers back into place continually. What an experience! It was a race between us, and try as he would he could never quite keep up with me—the piano always came out victor.

Some of the audience finally caught on, and even rose in their seats to look. They could not understand what was happening, and it must have been a strange sight. After the concert was over I hurried out and mingled with the crowd, for I was, I confess, curious to hear their comments. They did not notice me as they were all talking so busily together. I could hear what some of them were saying, which was just what I wanted. It was most interesting. They gathered in groups, excitedly discussing the concert. "And how," one asked, "did you like that young pianist?" "Oh, very well. He was all right, but the other one, you know, the second pianist who was playing at the back of the piano, he was the best, I think, and he worked much harder than the other! He was the *real* artist, make no mistake!"

IV

Vienna: Leschetizky and Rubinstein

I

Now to turn back for a moment to my decision to have a pianistic career, a resolve that came to me when I was finishing my studies in orchestration with Urban in Berlin. It was about this time I went for a short vacation to Poland to a place in the Tatra Mountains to work on the native music of the peasants, and there I met Madame Modjeska, the famous Polish actress. She was still very beautiful. I had seen her before but only on the stage. She was considered the most admirable artist in our dramatic theatre.

She was distinguished in every way and had a specially beautiful speaking voice. She had a graceful figure, too, but still there was something in her movements on the stage that perhaps was, shall we say, not so elastic, not so abandoned as Bernhardt, for instance. Modjeska was of the classical school of acting. Acting at that time was very different from nowadays. It was more eloquent, more studied—"the grand manner," as we call it, prevailed. It called for more oratory in those days. There was a style of acting, especially in the great classic dramas, that is completely lost now. That is why there are no longer actors who can play Shakespeare, or the great Greek dramas, and this is especially true, too, of stylized plays like "The School for Scandal" and "She Stoops to Conquer." But this is a theme that one can elaborate endlessly.

To speak further of Modjeska, her name is graven deeply on the scroll of honor among actresses. She was very popular in America, too, and there are still many people who speak of her enthusiastically. My meeting with her in Zakopane when I was a poor unknown student proved a real turning point among the many turning points in my career. I had already acquired some little reputation in that country, as professor at the Conservatory, and for having published already thirty or more pieces for piano, which were very well received. So I was considered even then as somebody. Modjeska was extremely kind to me, as was her husband, and I was a frequent visitor in their house. She talked to me a great deal about my plans and my future, and said, "Now you must start your career as a pianist, you must not wait any longer—I am convinced of that."

"Yes," I said, "that is my intention, but I haven't a repertoire, and I am not yet ready for that career."

"But why not, why not?" she cried impatiently.

Then I explained still further to them my difficulties, and obstacles. But they were very optimistic, and were so impressed with my playing that they seemed not to believe that I needed more study. My friends, you see, were always against my studying, against my *working!* That was really tragic! So we talked more and more on the subject. I said I should like to go to Leschetizky, who was the greatest teacher of that time and who had produced many pupils who played really beautifully. And then I said I must give a concert before leaving, in Cracow, which was not very far distant from the place we were in.

Cracow is a university town. One of the oldest universities in the world is there, founded in 1364. It is our Oxford, you know—has the same kind of atmosphere and is a charming and interesting place, one of the most beautiful on the Continent. It is the ancient capital of Poland, full of beautiful monuments and very ancient and interesting houses.

Cracow was a fascinating place to me and I was anxious to give a concert there. When I told Modjeska how much I wanted this, she was very enthusiastic. "Ah," she said, "that is splendid. You must give a concert in Cracow and I will help you. I will help you gladly."

Well, I was really touched and overcome at her kindness. I could not refuse that gracious offer because it meant for me a *sold out house!* With my poor little following I could not have

Madame Modjeska in Sardou's "Odette" in 1882

Vienna: Leschetizky and Rubinstein

filled a small hall. So Modjeska came to Cracow and helped me with that concert. Her name on the program was magic. She recited a few poems and created, as always, a furore. The house was crowded and it brought over 400 gulden. At that time that was about $200, but it was an enormous sum to me! It permitted me to go to Vienna and study with Leschetizky for two or three months. And it was Modjeska who gave the final help to my dream.

So I went to Vienna and Leschetizky with all speed—Leschetizky, the lode star of my early years, the greatest teacher of his generation. I do not know of any one who approaches him now or then. There is absolutely none who can compare with him. He was in that respect a giant—all those I know at the present moment are pygmies, measured by his standards.

I studied with him for a few months. I had some nine or ten lessons but, I repeat, he was not very encouraging. First of all I was already a musician, with my studies as composer completed, and I was already a musical personality, and he did not feel very comfortable about explaining to me, for instance, the sense and style of a composition, because in that respect perhaps I knew even a little more than he himself. He recognized this immediately. He gave me very *much encouragement* as a *composer,* but *discouraged* me positively as a *pianist,* saying that it was too late! I was at that time twenty-four and I had to start from the beginning—finger exercises! I had to make up for all the years lost when nobody showed me how to work. I was already dancing, without having learned to walk.

But Leschetizky was kind and generous; he never charged me anything for the lessons—never; he gave me freely and generously of his time and knowledge. But from the very first moment he said I could have become a great pianist if only I had begun to study earlier. This was heart-breaking, you know. If he had simply said to me, "You have *no talent* for piano playing," I could have borne it. I was accustomed to that opinion, and I would not have had to regret the past. But when he said that I *could have* become . . . ! Ah, that was terrible!

Well, in spite of the verdict, I began studying with him. I knew how to interpret—to make an effect, that I was always sure of. But before I came to Leschetizky I had not the slightest idea of how to proceed with work, and he gave me that help. He talked a great deal—he showed me the way—he explained. That is the way he used to teach. He opened up another world to me in my art. After those groping, struggling years, even in a few lessons things became clear. I began to see, to understand, to find my way, to know how to work. And my thankfulness to Leschetizky is as great today as it was then. I cannot overestimate what he did for me in his indication of the way to work. It was masterly.

Later, at the beginning of my success, he did not believe it! He could not really understand it because, you see, he did not know that I was so persistent, so energetic, and so physically enduring that I could make good all those losses of my early youth. So at first he did not acknowledge me as a representative of his school of playing. I was not an exponent of the famous Leschetizky method which had produced the greatest players of that time. He did not believe that it was legitimate—my success. I did not find it very legitimate myself at the beginning, because the success came before I was ready to enjoy it. I could not fully enjoy it, because in my opinion I was not yet deserving it.

And there was still another thing in our relationship that was difficult. I came to him already with a certain small reputation as a pianist and he, therefore, had a somewhat different attitude toward me than toward the usual student. I was already a composer of promise who deeply wanted to learn from him, it is true, but one he could not teach anything concerning interpretation for instance, and that was very embarrassing, awkward for him, and it was perhaps for that reason that he did not encourage me. I was embarrassing him. He was extremely kind and good, and liked me personally very much indeed. Still, he did not feel quite comfortable when I was taking my lesson.

He was a wonderful man, of great brilliance. He taught me more in those few lessons than I had learned during the whole twenty-four years preceding that time. What was interesting in him was first of all the tone production, then there was his attention to rhythm. That singing tone of his was really remarkable, and there was also a certain brilliancy which was not always in the best taste perhaps, because it was sometimes a little bit decorative, a little superficial, a little flamboyant. He, I repeat, never considered me an exponent of his school—and I'll explain this more fully later on.

I think we may here enlarge a little particularly on my first impression of meeting Leschetizky. When I went to Vienna I had no letters of introduction to him. I had never met him before and I was really rather apprehensive of my first visit to him. I had to wait for a long time after reaching his house, because he was not an early riser.

His habit was to enjoy himself after his lessons very late in the evening. He had his dinner rather late, and when he used to go to concerts or opera, his supper was after that, which was contrary to the tradition of all the Viennese people. As you know, in Vienna theatrical performances (especially the opera) began very early, usually before seven, but by ten o'clock everything was over and every man was armed with a key to his house; otherwise he would have to pay a little sum to the janitor to get in! So people were orderly, conservative, and economical, and came provided with a key. But such was not the case with Leschetizky. He lived in his own villa, and he used to take his meals as most artists do, very late in the evening, and then he sat till three or four o'clock playing cards, or for preference billiards, because it gave him a little exercise, after which he used to go for a walk. Consequently he got up very late and his day always began after eleven. I came well before eleven for my first appointment and I had to wait for a long time. A very long time it seemed to me in my anxiety.

When he finally received me, I was delighted to notice that my name was familiar to him. It was already familiar on account of those Variations in A Minor which his wife, Madame Essipoff-Leschetizky, had played almost everywhere. I owe a great debt of gratitude to her for having been the first pianist to play my compositions before a large and cultured public.

So he received me very cordially and talked about compositions, and about modern music. Then he sat down at the piano and played for me, with notes, of course, some of the Viennese composers, who paid him the tribute of their admiration by offering him their own compositions.

He did not know in those first few moments that it was my intention to *play* for him. He really thought I just came to present some compositions. When I told him that my intention was to have some piano lessons with him, he was very much surprised, amazed in fact.

"But," he exclaimed, "have you not already played in public?"

"Yes," I said, "but not in very important places. I have given a number of concerts but I played mostly my own compositions, because I have no repertoire as yet."

Then he was frightened!—disturbed, upset! "And you intend to make a repertoire, to start study now as a virtuoso, at your age? Do you realize what you are saying? It is impossible, I tell you." He became greatly agitated then and walked about the room nervous and irritated. It was evident that he was at a complete loss to know what to say to me. In this moment of suspense I felt completely at his mercy—there was nothing I could say or do. My world crumbled into ruins in those few moments. Finally he stopped his walk, pulled himself together and said, "Well, at any rate play me something—play something for me now, it does not matter what."

So I played; of course, my own compositions. He listened very attentively—quietly—then he said, "You have a great many qualities as a pianist. You have a *natural* technique, but it lacks so very much. But still you have the *principal* quality, that is *tone*. Without having studied, you already know how to vary that tone, how to give different expressions with your fingers alone, and there is still something else which is quite remarkable, and that is —your pedalling! That is perhaps the most extraordinary thing, that any one who has not seriously studied the piano can realize the enormous importance of pedalling. But you are a musician, I see, and it is that musical instinct that leads you in using so properly the principal means of expression—the pedal. But, I am afraid there will be too much to do with your fingers, because they lack *absolutely discipline!*" He was so positive, so sure, an almost infallible judgment.

"I am afraid you do not know *how to work!*" He put his finger on it immediately. My tragedy! My heart almost lost a beat at these fateful words. I was fearful that he would not accept me as a pupil.

"If I decide to give you a few lessons," he continued, "you must start with *finger exercises* and some Czerny studies." A pupil again!

I confess I was not prepared for that! I knew Czerny—master of finger exercises, of course, because I myself was teaching my own pupils Czerny, but it is quite a different thing to *teach* somebody, than to do it yourself. There is almost as much difference as between preaching and acting. But I took these studies, and according to his instructions I started with finger exercises. Of course, I could not improve in a few weeks or months even, because bad habits were already deeply rooted in me, an amateurish way of treating the piano, just playing the piano, fingering—*anyhow!* Just as anybody does who is a good reader at sight, who does not care for technique and only cares for notes. It did not matter to me with what finger I played the notes, the principal thing was to play them—to produce the sound.

So after the first few lessons, Leschetizky, who did not usually prepare pupils himself (he had many fine pupils who did the preparatory work), got discouraged, and even extremely nervous. If he had sent me to one of these teachers first, it would have been easier for him, much simpler, because he would not then have had the annoyance and bother of listening to finger exercises. He was too much of an artist to watch my progress. But he did it—he endured that boredom like a great dancing master who has to teach some one how to walk!

It was out of his great kindness, his generosity, that he thought it could be done in a few days, and for several weeks I was really making mistakes like a small child, because I had never been taught how to use my fingers. He made this great exception in my favor out of consideration for me, and the realization too that I had passed far beyond the pupil stage. It was a difficult position for him and for me too.

There lies the principal reason why he discouraged me so many times. "It is too late! too late!" he would say. "You cannot become a great pianist because you have wasted your time in studying perhaps more pleasant things for yourself, such as counterpoint, the orchestration, and so on." There was always a kind of reproach in his attitude—that I knew too much! Not friction exactly, but that was his little revenge. He wanted to put the piano playing always on a higher level even than composition.

But in spite of all this, I learnt a few pieces with him. I learnt a Concerto of Saint-Saëns well enough to play it a year later at Strasbourg with the orchestra, so you see I made great progress. Before, I would never have been able to play in such a way, and with the consciousness that it was well done. I played, also, a few pieces by Bach, one Sonata of Beethoven, one of the easiest, and then one by Schumann, and a few short pieces. That was all I played with him during my first three or four months' study. There were some nine or ten lessons altogether. This was my first visit with Leschetizky—I went back again later, as you will see.

Although my student life was a happy one in Vienna, I worked very hard. I had absolutely no relaxation—it was work, work, work. The conditions were such that I had to take advantage of every moment to repair what the past had so burdened me with. I had to—there was not a moment to lose. I had nothing else than an absolute devotion to my work. I used to practise seven hours a day during all that stay in Vienna—and my recreation and amusement? Well, my lessons with Leschetizky filled my horizon, for that was study and recreation and inspiration at the same time. But I did read a great deal and not only newspapers. I was already very much interested in politics and read many different books. I read too much, perhaps.

Vienna: Leschetizky and Rubinstein

I lived then in two very humble rooms not far from Leschetizky's villa. For many years I had them, and into these little rooms were crowded all the memories of my struggles and disappointments—the years of hard unceasing work—my first début in Vienna and my first composition of a large form (my Concerto was written there, you know). In these two little rooms, so small you could have put them into this one, all these poignant memories were crowded. From them I went forth to meet life, and out of that sentiment I was very much attached to them and kept them for many years after I became a successful pianist.

When I left Vienna and established myself in '89 in Paris, I still kept those rooms, although I rarely went there, especially after my long American tours. I even offered to buy the house when the owner sold it. But I learned too late about the sale. When I applied for it the house was gone. Those little rooms were very precious to me. I am sorry I could not buy the house. But perhaps it was a kind Fate after all! It would have been a great burden to me now.

Another souvenir of those cherished rooms was a spider. I have not yet told you the story of the spider—my spider. That is such a charming story of my youth. One day I was practising in my little room in Vienna. Among the pieces I was then studying, and which I had to play every day as a finger exercise, was a certain study by Chopin, a study in thirds. I was just starting to work—I lit the candles and sat down at the piano. The room was very dark, you know, there were so many tall shrubs growing close to the window. Then, suddenly in the midst of my playing, there came down from the ceiling right on to the piano desk, something like a tiny silver thread. It attracted my attention and I looked a little closer, and then I saw—a spider attached to it. He hung there motionless and appeared to be listening to my playing, and as long as I played that particular study in *thirds,* the little spider remained there perfectly still on his line.

And now comes the interesting thing. After finishing the study in thirds, I went on to another study—in sixths this time, and the moment I began it, the spider turned himself quickly about, and hurried up to the ceiling. Well, it struck me at the moment as very funny, and I was interested and deeply intrigued. I said to myself, "Now, I must see whether that spider is really musical or not—whether he meant to come down to listen on purpose, or by accident." So I suddenly stopped my study in *sixths,* and quickly started again the one in *thirds.* Instantly, down came the little spider! He seemed to slide down his line, and this time to the very end, and sat on the piano desk and listened. He did not seem at all frightened, only deeply interested in the music.

He had aroused my interest greatly and I wondered if he would appear the next morning. I was very curious about him—I felt sure I should see him again. Well, he did appear the moment I began my day's work with the thirds. That little thread still hung from the ceiling, and down he came the moment I touched the piano, and this same thing continued all that day, and the next day and for many weeks he came—he was a faithful companion. Whenever I started the study in thirds, the little spider came quickly to the piano desk and listened. After a time I arrived so far as to be able to see his eyes—so brilliant, like tiny, shining diamonds. He would sit immovable, or hang immovable I should say, during that Chopin Etude, perfectly content and perfectly quiet. But the moment I stopped that particular study, back he went quickly to the ceiling and disappeared. Sometimes, I used to think, quite angrily.

When the vacation time came I confess I felt strangely anxious about the spider. What would become of him, I wondered. "Shall I find him when I return?" I asked myself. He had become a part of my daily practice, a kind of companion, and I knew I should miss him. When I returned in September, I looked for him everywhere. I looked for the little line, but it no longer hung from the ceiling. I played my study in thirds, again and again I played it, but I could not find my spider friend. The room seemed empty and lonely without him. What had happened to him? Had some careless housemaid crushed out his little life, or had he, lonely and discouraged with the closed piano and silent room, gone elsewhere? I could only hope so. But the days went on, and I never saw my spider friend again.

During my time of study with Leschetizky, there happened something of real interest and importance. Certain musicians of Vienna decided to establish a club of their own, and a circular was sent to all teachers and music students inviting them to join. The club was organized by Leschetizky and it was at the first meeting that I was introduced by Leschetizky himself. It was on that occasion, too, that I met for the first time Johannes Brahms, among the most famous of the musicians in Vienna.

It was a very nice and intimate gathering of musicians just among themselves, and I was invited, with some other young pianist, to play a few pieces of my own, and Brahms listened and expressed himself very graciously and favorably to me afterwards.

I remember well the opinion that he expressed about the Sonata for piano and violin which was played at a later meeting of that club. When he heard it he listened attentively as always, and then he said, "Well, Paderewski, it is very effective, very fine, but it is not chamber music; it is a concert Sonata." That was a little criticism and a valuable one, I thought. At the same time it was also a kind of appreciation.

Then many gatherings followed the establishment of the club and I attended them all and had plenty of opportunities of seeing Brahms and talking with him. Brahms was rather a silent person. I cannot say otherwise. Even when I visited Brahms alone on one occasion, to hear his opinion of one of my compositions, I had not the impression that he was a very communicative or a very learned man. But he knew a great deal in many ways, I think. He was not a very highly educated man and I don't believe that he ever had time to take much interest in things aside from music. But I think he was interested in politics. I had that impression, although I had no opportunity of approaching the subject with him. I wish I had, because politics even then interested me tremendously.

Brahms lived in Vienna and I saw him very often during my stay there. He was unfailingly kind to me. But he was not usually very kind—he had the reputation of being rather brutal at times and he was *fond* of being brutal—or shall we say brusque—he enjoyed it, though I don't feel that by nature he was really brutal —it was just a kind of pose, a protection to hide his great sensitiveness. No one could have written like Brahms who was not highly sensitive. He was short, very stout, with a tremendous belly and a great beard. Rather a caricature of Jupiter, because the face was that of Jupiter. A fine head, a very fine head, short legs and very small feet. Brahms never taught. I approached him on one occasion with the purpose of asking him whether he would perhaps give me a few lessons. But he would not consider it. "No," he said. "No. I never teach. I have no time. And besides, you do not need any further tuition. You can become your own teacher now. You do not need me." His refusal, however, was a very real disappointment to me.

There were two men then reigning alternatively in the field of music. On one side there was a very big camp of Wagnerians, and on the other there were the followers of the old classical masters, who worshipped Brahms. The official musicians, I mean the Academy of Music and all the Conservatories (there were a number of them in Berlin), were of course all for Brahms. But the *public* was for Wagner, and the attraction of Wagner was still enhanced by the fact that it was connected with entertainment, that is the opera. The opera is really entertainment, you know. So Brahms had a rather restricted number of followers. But, as in Germany there is always a necessity for at least one great composer of symphonies (to satisfy the traditions of Beethoven, Schumann, and Mendelssohn, etc.), and Brahms was a very great exponent of symphonic music, of pure music, the press as well as all real music lovers always spoke in highest terms of enthusiasm and admiration for Brahms. For instance, Joachim was very much against Wagner, though he admired his cleverness. But he was personally greatly attached to Brahms, and particularly as Brahms was recommended to the musical world by Schumann, whom Joachim adored.

You remember perhaps reading that when Brahms first appeared before Robert Schumann, he made such a deep impression upon him that he wrote and published in his musical newspapers in Leipsig, an article about Brahms which opened with these challenging words, "Gentlemen! Hats off! A genius!" Schumann actually called him a genius. It was perhaps excessive because Brahms was not such a genius, he was a great master, a really wonderful composer, especially of chamber music, but he could not be compared with Bach and not even with Schumann himself.

While I was in Vienna, I enjoyed very much the operatic performances, but still more the theatrical performances, the dramas, the comedies especially. I had very definite ideas about the theatre even then. Of course, the theatre in Vienna was on a much higher plane than in Berlin. There was a stamp of officialdom in everything in Berlin, owing to that military system and the strong iron hand of the Government. In Vienna there was much more freedom, much more possibility for the display of personalities. There was a charm and sparkle in the very atmosphere there—a charm in the people, charm in everything! Vienna was a city of charm, and I am still very fond of it. It is the city of my heart.

Yes, Vienna, which is one of the most beautiful and sympathetic cities on the Continent, was at that time a very gay place. It reflected the mood of the people. There was much splendid music, the orchestra, the Philharmonic, being one of the finest in the world (much finer than the Berlin Philharmonic). There was only one orchestra which could be compared to it, even in some ways superior, the orchestra of the Conservatory of Paris. The violins were better in Vienna, but the wind instruments of the Paris orchestra were superior to those of any other orchestra in the world.

These remarks about the orchestras are a little digression on my part, I know, from our main theme, but it is an unusual story and it may be of some interest to use it here. That Paris orchestra was a little republic in itself which, unlike any other orchestra, always selected its own conductor, the conductor most agreeable to them and one who did not make them work too much. Yet in spite of that very dangerous policy, it remained a great orchestra. True, they lacked discipline on that account because the conductor was not in absolute authority. But the players of the wind instruments were the greatest virtuosi, and it was those very men who made the superiority of that orchestra, because nobody could have been compared with those marvellous players of the flute, clarinet, oboe, and so forth.

The Vienna Opera, too, was the first Opera of all the German-speaking countries. Besides, they had the finest dramatic theatre in the world. The cycles of Schiller and Shakespeare which were given every year were really of absolute perfection. They had a tradition to follow, you see, and the Court supported all these theatres very munificently.

Life in Vienna, as I said, was very intense and very gay. The impression it made upon me was a deep one, although it was not the first great city in which I had lived—because I had already spent two years in Berlin.

But the temperament of the Viennese was quite different, very sympathetic. There was a great variety in that population. While the German capital was purely German, Vienna was a conglomerate of many nationalities from which the Austrian Empire was built. There were Hungarians, there were Serbs, Bohemians, Slovenes, and Ruthenians. There were, of course, a great many Poles, and Poles played quite an important part in the political administration of the country. There were a great many representatives of the Polish people in both the Lower and Upper Houses. Some Polish gentlemen were occupying the highest positions in the Empire. Even the heads of the Government were Poles, and in that respect it was specially sympathetic to me. The Minister of Finance and the Minister of Communications, people whom I knew, were occupying those foremost positions.

The Court of Vienna was guided by one of the most severe etiquettes in the world, so the Court did not mingle at all. It was all so different, Berlin and Vienna—ah! there could have been no greater contrast than those two cities.

In those poor student days I was too young and too insignificant to have access to any of those high places. That came much later. But I am convinced that I never would have enjoyed the privilege of being at the Court of Germany, or even at the Court of Austria, because I considered those Courts—as well as that of Russia—as my oppressors, the oppressors of Poland.

In Vienna, Leschetizky was a vital part of the musical life. His influence upon his students was profound, an influence that never died. My thoughts turn back to those days with him very often, even now, and I want to tell you that although his remarks were not always encouraging for me—in spite of his almost systematic discouragement, telling me constantly that I came too late and so on—I must admit that he treated me with an exceptional favor. He always showed me a certain consideration that was very kind. Once a week there was a large gathering of his most advanced pupils who enjoyed private lessons with him, and they played before all the students. It was really a kind of concert but was generaly spoken of as the "class." This "class" was greatly dreaded by the pupils as the standard of playing was very high, and Leschetizky sat at the piano ready to pour out his wrath and fury upon any pupil who failed to measure up to this high standard of his. He showed no mercy. He would at times stop a pupil and practically give a lesson then and there. Sometimes it was short, the correction; but often the remarks were not only long but accompanied by angry words! He would storm and shout and become really violent. He would lose his temper, and sometimes he would be most unpleasant, but after his class, he would be the first one to go to that pupil and say, "Well, well, it was not so bad after all." He was kind, good and really very generous at heart. But as a teacher he was implacable.

Now he never asked me to play in the class. There was a certain sparing of my feelings in that, and of my position, because he felt perhaps that I could not be compared then with all those young musicians who were studying with him and playing in the classes. He knew from the start that I belonged in a different place and that he could not put me among that crowd of pupils. It was very kind. It was thoughtful and very considerate. It touched me deeply.

Leschetizky was not precisely a beautiful man in appearance, but he had a noble impressive head. And there was a great deal of magnetism about him, an extraordinary intelligence, and he was a very highly educated man. His German was perfect, of course, because he made all his studies in Vienna, though he was born in Poland of a purely Polish mother—which is not generally remembered. As to the nationality of his father, I could not really tell you what it was. It was not German anyhow; the name itself proves that. I think it was Slavonic, perhaps Ruthenian, or Bohemian. But his father used the Polish language; he had lived in Poland almost all his life. Leschetizky's French was very good too. He spoke excellent French.

The percentage of his pupils who were interesting was enormous. They all had a certain stamp of Leschetizky. All his pupils could get some beauty of tone. That applies to every one. Every one of his pupils could handle the piano in a musical way, *i.e.*, produce a pleasing tone. They all had a singing tone. That was very, very important. Just as important also was the rhythm. They all, even those who had no sense of rhythm, played rhythmically after studying with him. The number of his pupils already possessing a certain name, and having a certain success in public, is very great.

I had my separate lessons with Leschetizky once a fortnight, but after every class he always asked me to come to him because he wanted always to be surrounded by young people—who could amuse him and whom he could enjoy—and as I could play cards, billiards, and so on, I was a very welcome companion.

I had about nine or ten lessons the *first time* in Vienna, and sixteen the second time. And that was not all. I had afterwards some extra lessons in spite of my having already played in concert. I found that I could still learn something and I really learned from Leschetizky *how to work*. That is the greatest thing for any artist to know, how to work. I came to the conclusion—I must express it rather paradoxically—that if one wishes to derive pleasure from the piano for himself he should just *play*. If he wishes that *other* people have pleasure from his playing, he must *work!* I had just begun to realize that. I needed baptizing by fire by very large crowds of people—audiences, and I had not yet had that baptism —the baptism of Fire!

II

After these first few months with Leschetizky I felt that I had learnt a great deal, and then just at that moment of accomplishment I was obliged to return to Warsaw again. It was absolutely necessary, as my savings were exhausted and I needed money. I had already quite a number of compositions published and still in manuscript, so I went on composing. I wrote a violin sonata and a few songs, then I decided to give a concert—my own compositions—in Warsaw, in 1885. It was right after this concert that I heard Rubinstein play for the first time. I had already met him, you will remember, at the house of Bock, in Berlin, when he was so encouraging about my compositions. This time in Warsaw, I heard him play (he gave several concerts there) and it made a tremendous impression on me. He was the greatest artist of the time. I heard four of his concerts. The first time it was really overwhelming—impossible to describe! He played a Concerto with orchestra, and then a few small pieces, and he played wonderfully—particularly his own Concerto. I did not know that Concerto then and I was not an expert judge. I only knew there were in his playing great elemental strength and moments of remarkable beauty.

Then in the short pieces which he played, there were a really profound emotion and great poetry. There again I had also the impression of elemental force and barbarism at the same time. But he was not always correct in his playing. His playing revealed a remarkable command of the instrument, and at the same time shortcomings in memory and in technique as well. His technique at moments was simply dazzling, and at other moments he became quite the amateur. But he had that *natural* technique. That served him and saved him many a time. To be a great artist one must always have that *inborn* quality. There were, for instance, moments in the Schumann Sonatas and Beethoven Sonatas when he just played anything! It made a tremendous difference *what* he played. When he came to melody, to something lyric, ah! it was compensation indeed for the minutes of defective playing. There were some places which he even omitted—he lost himself completely and played instead of the real text anything that just accidently came under his fingers. It could be dreadful—dreadful!

But on the other hand, the few short pieces of Chopin, especially the mazurkas, preludes, and nocturnes, he played divinely. Yes, he played certain things divinely, others atrociously. There were whole pages where I could not distinguish one single correct phrase. He forgot! For instance I remember well when he played the Schumann Sonata, the First Sonata, Opus 11, in F Sharp Minor, it was frightful. But when it came to the aria (there is a part of that Sonata which contains a beautiful aria), a short piece of some three minutes duration, that was beautifully done with an atmosphere of really heavenly serenity. Then came the finale, and it was again incorrect, chaotic. But there were always moments of genius in his playing.

That was a very curious contrast between him and his brother, Nicholas, who was also a very famous pianist. When he played a Concerto with orchestra, it was magnificent, really splendid, so academic and so correct and big too. His tone was extremely beautiful, perhaps because of those wonderful fat fingers of his. He had, you know, fat hands with fat finger tips which always produce a most beautiful tone. I have certain things of interest to say about these fat finger tips and their importance in piano playing. I think we will find just the right place for that in another part of my story and it is an interesting topic of discussion, but this is not the moment. Now we must go on with Rubinstein. There is still so much to say.

When Nicholas Rubinstein attacked a small piece, he was just a dancing bear! But ah! Anton Rubinstein, when he played short pieces, he was, I repeat, really divine. They were jewels—perfect in every respect. Those which he had learnt as a youth he played always exquisitely because those things remained with him, but things which he learnt as a grown-up man, he did not practise suf-

ficiently, because he was always composing. *That* was his real
love, and he was very unfortunate because it was not always
reciprocated!

I heard him play many small pieces by Chopin. Those nocturnes, preludes, and mazurkas were divinely played. Then I
heard him twice in private houses, once at the house of the
Director of the Conservatory in Warsaw, and then in the house
of a friend, and it was frightful. He had evidently not practised
at all. It was lamentable.

I should like with your permission to talk still a little more
about Rubinstein, particularly his personality and appearance,
especially on the platform. First of all, he had a tremendous frame.
He was not very tall but powerfully built and his head was remarkably interesting with a mass of dark unruly hair. It was a
Beethoven head. He could not see very clearly (he was nearly
blind) and that expression of his eyes, which were always half
closed (because he could not bear the light) added still more to
the impression of a powerful but rather mysterious being.

He spoke excellent French and German too, and Russian
naturally. He was not a cultivated man. He was the son of a
Jewish merchant but there was absolutely nothing about him
which was Jewish in appearance and nothing in his way of talking. He had none of the mannerisms of his race. His brother
Nicholas, however, was just the opposite—of fair complexion and
looked like his race.

Of course, I had heard so much as a child about Rubinstein
and his wonderful successes, his magnificent playing and about
his compositions too, that hearing him not only made a great
impression upon me but was the fulfillment of a dream, let us say,
of what I had imagined his greatness to be. It was a lesson to me
in many ways, a lesson and a warning, the combination of his
greatness and of his utter carelessness. His compositions, for example, were rather carelessly made. Almost every one starts with
a beautiful idea, but it is not worked out. He had not the necessary concentration or patience for a composer.

His negligence in his piano work was probably due to the fact that his chief object was always composing, and playing was just a necessity of life. Whenever he went on tour, he always returned with a trunk full of manuscripts. Hundreds and hundreds of his compositions have been published. He produced many operas, he wrote six or seven symphonies, six piano concertos and also a concerto for the violin. In chamber music he wrote trios, quartets with piano, quartets for strings—oh! innumerable works—but everything begins finely and then, alas! leaves a great deal to be desired.

He was a stormy character—torn by many things. He was in constant conflict with himself and the necessity for piano playing, while he was always longing to compose. That enormous driving power of his, and his ambition too, drove him on—and on—in his consuming hope for immortality.

I suppose I am one of the few pianists who still play Rubinstein's music. All the others neglect him completely, with the exception of the Concerto in D Minor. That is still played by some pianists, but his simple pieces are absolutely forgotten. The Barcarolles, they are beautiful, some of the songs too. The Valse Caprice is extremely brilliant and effective and many others are beautiful and poetic. His Concerto in D Minor, as I've already said, is a great favorite on account of its first movement, which is a wonder. The whole of the first movement is a masterpiece. It is just as if it had been born, like Minerva from the brain of Jupiter, perfect. The second movement contains some very fine music too, but it is not to be compared in workmanship or inspiration with the first movement. The finale is weak, but still on account of that superb first movement the Concerto pleases enormously both the player and the listener. It is still being played, and I think that it will be his only composition of large dimension that will remain alive.

Rubinstein was a titanic figure, and I repeat again that at that time his playing was of the greatest encouragement in my career. It fanned the fires of my ambition. But in spite of the inspiration of Rubinstein's playing, my own problems remained unsolved. I was very poor—I had no money. The concert that I'd just given so successfully was not a great help financially. I did not know what to do next—and then suddenly, a few weeks after this, came a little ray of light. I received a letter from Leschetizky telling me that he had heard from the Conservatory in Strasbourg asking him to recommend a professor for that institution.

Leschetizky wrote enthusiastically and said, "I have an interesting proposition from the Strasbourg Conservatory. They ask for a musician, a professor of harmony and counterpoint and at the same time a professor of piano playing for the upper class of pupils. I have recommended you particularly. I strongly advise you to accept this offer. You are in a position to be useful to them and to make a good living, because Strasbourg is a very wealthy place. There are many people there who are interested in music. The Conservatory has a high standing, and as you know both German and French, you will be able to teach in both languages, which is very important indeed in that particular city."

Leschetizky recommended me very strongly to accept that position which was, to a certain extent, a confirmation of what he had already said about my playing—too late, too late for me ever to become a pianist!

Well, I thought it over. Although I bitterly rebelled against it, I realized all his kindness in trying to help me—there seemed to be only one thing to do. I had no money, so I accepted the inevitable. I went to Strasbourg. Again a teacher! I went there in July, 1885 —I was not yet twenty-five—and I was obliged to pass an examination, which was very funny to me at this stage of my career, to be examined and judged by amateurs.

The Conservatory, you see, was controlled by two factions, the City, which was municipal, and the Trustees, who were all amateurs. They gathered together upon my arrival to listen to my playing and pass judgment upon me. I played for them not only solos but performed some chamber music also. The professors of violin and 'cello were summoned to play with me to try me out. We played, and evidently I pleased all these serious gentlemen, because they immediately signed the contract. I was to receive 2400 marks a year, about $600—which was a big sum for that time. But the conditions were that during the year I had to play in a subscription concert, a concerto with orchestra, two chamber music concerts, and give a piano recital besides! A formidable program.

Oh, yes, it was very hard work. I had twenty-four hours a week of teaching, and it was not very much, that little sum of money, you know. There was hardly anything left beyond my living expenses, so I was forced to give private lessons to eke out a meagre livelihood. And with all this I was constantly studying and practising myself.

What years of labor I look back upon! As we talk about it now, I really do not understand how I could have withstood all the work of my life. Year after year from boyhood until now, incessant, unending work, both physical and mental. I must have had a magnificent constitution—of iron. I am still thankful for it.

While teaching at the Conservatory the work was very hard, because I had only a few talented pupils. Although there was quite a large class, it was the usual thing, young girls without any particular gift who were studying just for a diploma, nothing else. You know how it is in schools—everywhere the same the world over.

But the good thing at the Strasbourg Conservatory was my playing in public, difficult as it was. It kept my buried hopes alive. At the first concert I played the Saint-Saëns Concerto which I had studied with Leschetizky, and then several solo pieces. Then I played the chamber music concert—and after that I gave a recital. It was again a real success. My playing in public caused me, of course, a great deal of excitement—of suffering too, to put it plainly—but was always rewarded with a positive success. I was progressing.

I was also asked to go to Karlsruhe to play in a concert there. Then I played in some of the small provincial towns of Alsace. I was becoming known, you see, and that was the most encouraging thing at that moment. There were many important French people in Alsace whom I met then and saw afterwards in Paris. And in particular I am grateful to the famous statesman Jules Ferry, and Charles Floquet, president of the Chamber of Deputies. And there was another house at which I was made most welcome, the home of Monsieur Scheurer-Kestner, a Senator who had a great influence in Paris at that time. These kind people encouraged me, in fact urged me to go to Paris and play there. Their enthusiasm again gave me a fresh impetus. They thought I was quite ready for a Paris début. Their interest was so keen and sincere—they crossed my path at another psychological moment.

At this time I began to realize that the way was opening. In spite of all everybody had said, I knew now that I was going to be a pianist. I realized after those first appearances in Alsace that the public was very gracious and kind to me. I said to myself, "I have now the possibility of playing in Paris, perhaps even a real success awaits me there, I must not miss it. I must go forward." This conviction fortified my faith in myself—upheld me in the terrible labor I was undergoing.

The feeling I had after hearing Rubinstein play came back again and again and sustained me. My year in the Strasbourg Conservatory, though very difficult, and strenuous, in regard to my teaching, was, nevertheless, something of a harvest time in other ways. Many new friends came into my life, and again I had the great pleasure of seeing Rubinstein once more.

It happened that he was passing through Strasbourg on his way to Paris for his farewell concerts. He called them historical concerts, because he presented in seven programs almost all the masterpieces of piano literature. He gave these concerts in all the great capitals of Europe, in Vienna, Paris, Berlin, and London too, and of course in his own country, St. Petersburg and Moscow.

He was going to pass through Strasbourg and telegraphed to Franz Stockhausen, Director of the Conservatory, that he would pass at such and such a time and would stay at the station about two hours. The trains were not very quick in those days and there were always long stops in important stations. He invited the Director to lunch at the station, and said, "Bring Paderewski with you." It was a very great compliment that he even remembered me and knew I was there. So we went. He was very nice—

inquired about my life in Strasbourg, then about my compositions, which he remembered. "I hope to meet you in Paris when I play there shortly. You must surely come, I shall expect you," he said. This invitation enchanted me and I made up my mind to go to Paris and hear him once more. I made great efforts for that—great sacrifices, for a trip to Paris was expensive and hard for me to manage in my poverty.

And now we come to one of the most painful moments of my life. After weeks of careful planning and saving, I went to Paris. You know, having only some 2400 marks a year ($600) I could not afford much luxury. But I went there, and stayed in a very modest hotel. I inquired for Rubinstein on arrival, and learnt that he was living in the Hotel du Helder. So I went at once to see him. He was giving his seven recitals in the Salle Erard, which held only about 700 people. Of course the house was sold out long in advance, but I knew there was somewhere a place to squeeze me in—there is always room to put somebody in a corner or behind the platform—some place, no matter how small the hall. So when I went to see him he was very cordial and he retained me to luncheon with some other people. After lunch I approached him very timidly, but joyously, and told him that I had come to Paris especially to hear one of his concerts, and asked him about getting a ticket. Now I do not know why that kind and really very generous man should have answered me as he did, for he had, as you remember, already invited me to this concert a few weeks before. But, instead of saying, "Yes, there is a ticket at your disposal," he answered very abruptly, "Oh, that is not my business. Don't bother me. You must apply to Wolff." Wolff was his agent, his manager, and was travelling with him all over Europe. He was a very important man in the musical world because he had a famous agency that practically monopolized the entire artistic enterprises of Europe. Wolff was the agent for Rubinstein, for Joachim and all the great stars of the time.

So I went to Mr. Wolff, of whom I shall say more later, in my own connection. He was living in the same hotel, and I repeated my request for a ticket and mentioned that Rubinstein

Johannes Brahms

Photograph by Ella Barnett

Anton Rubinstein

Photograph by Brown Brothers

Hans von Bülow

Paderewski at the time of his début

had invited me. But Mr. Wolff was still more drastic! He laughed and said, "Ticket! Oh, my dear sir, it is ridiculous! There are hundreds like you who would like a ticket! There is no possibility of your hearing the Master. None! None!"

But I was not to be put aside so easily—the thing meant too much to me. So I tried again, and said to Wolff, "Can I not *stand* somewhere in the hall, then—near the door or perhaps back of the stage? Surely," I pleaded, "there must be some corner where you can put me—it does not matter, so long as I hear him play again." At this Wolff became very impatient, quite angry, and pushed me aside. "Oh, no, no, no," he cried. "I have already told you there are hundreds of people who would like to have that same privilege. It is impossible—I have no place for you, sir." And he turned abruptly and left me without another word. And that was the same man that only a few years later begged me to become one of his artists!

I remember that I stood perfectly still where he left me. I was so shocked. I could not realize at that instant that my trip was in vain, for I had come to Paris only for that. It was one of the greatest disappointments of my life. I was overwhelmed.

Now I have always wondered, I still do as we talk about it, at Rubinstein's attitude in this affair. On the face of it, it was incomprehensible to me, but there is something in every human creature that we must call the spirit of *perversity*. When that spirit of perversity suddenly appears, you do things which are contrary to your liking, contrary to your nature. Nobody knows why—least of all yourself. For instance, that spirit sometimes shows itself in exaggerating things, not exactly lying, but saying something which is not corresponding to the real truth. That same spirit will also make promises, false promises, just for the sake of being agreeable—the jolly-good-fellow sort of attitude— the thing you mean for a moment and forget in an hour. Ah, we all have such moments. I have had them with the rest of mankind. I have said things which I did not like, which I did not mean, did not think, which came just through an accident in the functioning of my faculties—like the trembling of wires through a storm which makes the light flicker. That happens with human nerves very often. Some wire is crossed—there is an explosion! And even the lights may go out—for a moment. So I think it must have been with Rubinstein—there was an explosion! And certainly there was with Mr. Wolff!

At any rate my sacrifice was in vain. At this distance of years, it is hard to realize how I had saved and struggled to make that trip to Paris. My salary was so small at the time that I had barely enough to live on. It was real poverty. I ground myself down to the barest necessities. It was about the time of the Rubinstein adventure that I was obliged to buy a pair of new shoes, ready-made of course. They proved to be too small, and hurt my feet so cruelly that I had to go to the Conservatory in my very badly worn slippers. I could not afford to buy another pair of shoes—everything was being saved and put aside then for that great trip to Paris! It was an enormous enterprise for me, and I had to refuse myself a great many things after that, as well as before, and still I did not hear him! I never heard him play again.

That disappointment was very deeply felt. It may surprise you to know that even now, from time to time, I think about it, and always at each time when some one applies for tickets to my own recitals. I have never refused anybody and I have often had to pay for the tickets myself. Although I never heard Rubinstein play again, this episode taught me a very great lesson. I repeat, I have never refused anybody who wanted to hear me, never during the thousands of concerts I have given. I always gave to those who applied to me personally for a ticket. If there was no seat possible, I saw to it that any one who expressed the wish to hear me should be, somehow, somewhere, put behind the platform, or in a corner, on a stool, a chair, but somewhere, if there was no room left in the hall.

It is extremely difficult for a person living in prosperity and luxury to realize that some one else may be in want. It requires a great deal of imagination. Would that such imagination were oftener used!

Vienna: Leschetizky and Rubinstein

But we must go on with my own story. I taught in the Strasbourg Conservatory for nearly a year and all was well. My pupils were admitted as the best pupils because I was rather a good teacher, it seems. I had planned to spend my vacation in Poland, of course. But when I approached the directors, they absolutely refused to pay me for my two months' vacation.

I was amazed at their refusal. But when I protested at such injustice they only replied that I had a contract for a year, which evidently, in their opinion, did not include a vacation. They wished to make an economy of $80 at my expense, and so without further argument I left the Conservatory. I was so disgusted with that treatment that I left immediately and went back to Poland, not knowing at that moment what to do next.

That was a very difficult period—the more difficult because I left that job which meant a certain security. I could, of course, re-enter the Conservatory of Warsaw and teach there again, but that I was determined not to do. At this time I was convinced of two things—they were very clear in my mind. I was determined upon a pianistic career, and also determined never to teach again. Never! I stood at another parting of the ways. If I failed now to establish myself as a pianist and carry out my convictions, it would be too late. There was only one straight course ahead— I must go back to Leschetizky again and study. It was the great objective of my life at that moment. Nothing else really mattered. With all my powers of knowing, I knew this. But how to manage it? My father could do nothing more—there was nobody. So I started giving a few little concerts, but they were not a financial success. It was very pleasant from the artistic point of view because people recognized that I was much better than before, and that was of some little encouragement, but still I had no money. The grim facts confronted me at every turn, but my determination never failed. No matter what happened, even if I starved, *I was determined to go back to Leschetizky again.*

When I arrived in Warsaw, my dear friend Edward Kerntopf came to me at once and begged me to play for him, he was so anxious to hear me again. He was delighted. "Oh, but you play wonderfully, now," he said, "wonderfully. You must continue to study. If you do, you can have a big career. I am convinced of it."

"But," I replied, "how can that be? How is it possible—I have not the money."

Now it happened that at that very moment there was an exhibition of industrial products going on in Warsaw and the Kerntopf pianos were being exhibited. Edward Kerntopf was, naturally, very interested in this, and suggested that, as an advertisement for both the pianos and myself, I play them. So I played several times with great success, and he was so happy. Immediately after my last playing he came to me and said, "Well, I have something to tell you. Good news. I see the way now. It's all clear. My mind is made up that you must go back to Leschetizky at once."

"But," I interrupted, "I have no money."

"Never mind, never mind," he answered, "you shall have the money. I shall give it to you!"

Ah, he was a friend—a true, understanding friend. He loaned me the money then and for nearly a year he sent it regularly every month. He never failed me.

So I went back to Vienna, and presented myself at once to Leschetizky. He was very pleased to see me again and said, "It must have helped you, then—your lessons with me—I hear you have played in public and I know you made quite a good impression. Well, I am very glad to see you back, very glad. Now we shall work again." That was very nice—like the sun shining through the black clouds, so charming. It was a happy time and Leschetizky was pleased. I composed a few pieces and played them for him, and they pleased him, but they were perhaps a little too heavy for him—he always had that point of view of the *effect* produced upon an audience. These pieces impressed him very seriously—he was quite surprised to hear such good music —but he said, "Yes, it is very good, still it is very *heavy* and the public won't like it! Have you anything else? Something lighter?"

Vienna: Leschetizky and Rubinstein

Then I played the third piece, the Minuet. That was a revelation to him. "Now this," he said, "is going to be a tremendous success. My wife, Madame Essipoff, must play it in her concerts." And two days later she did play it marvellously well. She was a wonderful pianist, a fine artist. She was the first one to play it in public, and she made it popular almost instantaneously.

There is rather a pretty little story connected with the Minuet and how I happened to write it. It grew out of a little joke, and again, with your permission, I will add this story, which has been told before, I know, but this is the true one.

There was in Warsaw a very distinguished physician (a genius of a physician), Professor Chalubinski, whom I had met in the mountains. He took a fancy to me because I wrote something about music that pleased him. He was an old man then, about seventy, and I was a youth of twenty-six. He wanted me to come to his house as often as possible, as he was very fond of music. I was not very well at that time, I was rather delicate, always under a strain, but I enjoyed going to his house—there was a certain relaxation and happiness there. I often played to the old man. On one occasion there was a distinguished writer there, a friend of his, Alexander Swietochowski, and both these gentlemen were very enthusiastic about Mozart. They worshipped Mozart, and always asked me to play something of his—it was their greatest happiness.

At that time my Mozart was very limited. I played only three or four pieces, and so I was obliged to repeat them very often. But each time I played my little Mozart repertory the old gentlemen began shouting with delight, "Oh, Mozart—what a wonderful genius. No one can write such music as Mozart. What style! What purity! There is no one in the world to compare with Mozart. He stands alone." There was no end to their enthusiasm.

Well, this would go on as long as I played for them. Mozart was their God and they would listen to nothing else. Finally I got tired of it and I determined to put an end to it. I had an idea.

One day returning to the house of Kerntopf, where I stayed in Warsaw, I sat down at the piano and improvised a minuet! Just for fun. This minuet was rather in the style of Mozart. I improvised it, repeated the melody several times, and put it into shape of composition. I said to myself, "Now, the next time I go to Professor Chalubinski and he calls for his Mozart, I shall play this and see what he says then." Of course the Minuet was quite different then from what it is now, it was far simpler. It was devoid of any ornament, purely Mozart in style, without the ending cadenza. That was added later.

I must confess that I presented myself the next evening at the house of Chalubinski with keen anticipation. I was all ready for him. The good doctor! He was eagerly awaiting my arrival and asked as usual for some music, would I not play a little Mozart for him? So I agreed and played at once my new composition, the Minuet. Almost before I had finished the last bar the dear old man was on his feet. "Oh, Mozart," he cried. "What a wonderful piece! Tell me, Paderewski, is there any one now alive who could write such music?" I looked at him, and then I laughed and said, "Yes, there is such a person. *I* have!" "What," he cried. "*You*—impossible! Nonsense; you are making a joke." "No," I answered, "it is possible, for I have done it. You have just listened to it."

Oh, these poor old men! They simply stared at me. "What are you saying?" they cried. "What do you mean? Surely we have been listening to Mozart—no other. You cannot write like Mozart. No!"

Now I must admit that I had a few seconds of pity for them, but I went on, nevertheless, and said, "Yes, it is possible, because I now confess to you, my dear sirs, that I composed that piece myself a few days ago. *I* composed it, not Mozart! I did it just to surprise you—to see if I could! A little joke, that's all."

The poor doctor was overcome. "No, no," he exclaimed, "that is impossible—you are telling us a story—it is not true." "Yes," I answered, "I assure you I did it. Coming from your house the other evening I had the idea and I improvised it and wrote it in the style of Mozart. I will show you the composition if you do not believe me. But it is quite true."

Vienna: Leschetizky and Rubinstein

It was a terrible blow to them and they were very angry at first at being so misled. Naturally, it ended our Mozart for that evening, but a few nights later I was asked to play the real Mozart, which I did with pleasure and a good deal of remorse. And then they asked very politely afterwards to hear the Minuet. Ah! It was a touching moment for us all. I played it for them, feeling very penitent by that time, and they expressed themselves as liking it very much. In fact, they became so fond of it that I always had to play it for them, and then I realized that this piece was going to make my name popular—it will help me in my career, I thought. And such was the case, for it was that same Minuet that so pleased Leschetizky when I returned for the second time to Vienna. It was a revelation to him.

As I remember it, at this period I had about sixteen lessons with him. I found that I had learned a great deal from him—he fulfilled my heart's desire. I had learned how to *work*. Yes, I repeat to you, *how to work,* and this is of the utmost importance. I have said this before, but in the career of every artist, no matter what his profession, the knowledge of *how to work* is his greatest asset. I practised eight or nine hours a day and was composing also, so you see I labored tremendously.

During this time I published the Minuet, which became very popular with all the Leschetizky pupils too, thanks to Madame Essipoff's playing. I did not want to publish the Minuet alone, a short piece like that, so I composed two others and published them together, and received for them the enormous sum of 600 marks—that is about $150 in your money, but it was a fortune to me then.

One day my practice was interrupted by the arrival of Leschetizky. He came to my little rooms at the cottage, and I could see from his expression that he had something of importance to tell me. He began at once and said, "Now I have a suggestion to make to you. Would you not like to make your first appearance here in Vienna? There is an excellent opportunity now. Pauline Lucca (who is a very great singer, a beautiful artist) is giving a charity concert and she wants to have a pianist also, because she cannot fill the whole program. Will you play? I think it is a very good chance! I believe you should do it," he went on before I could answer.

I was immediately struck with the idea, and felt that Leschetizky really wanted me to play, so I answered, "Yes, I should be very glad to play." And so it was arranged. It was a very fine concert under fashionable patronage and there was a full house. I played and made a real impression. I played some Beethoven and Chopin, and some of my own compositions. Although I was absolutely unknown as a pianist on the eve of the concert, I was already looked upon as a personality. That was another little encouragement. And it helped me.

It was just a few weeks before this concert that a rather interesting and unexpected thing befell me. That story and Leschetizky's famous remark have followed me through the years. It happened only a few weeks before the concert. There was a great gathering of musicians and some rather important critics in a restaurant in Vienna, and Leschetizky invited me to join him, and introduced me to that important group. But he introduced me simply as "my young friend." He did not mention my name or even say I was a pupil. He drew me forward and said, "Now this young friend of mine is a composer. Do any of you know his compositions? Have you heard him play them?" Of course every one said he had not (the Minuet had not then become popular). "Ah, that is a pity," he laughed, "because you soon will hear them and, moreover, let me tell you to watch his career. Watch it well, because you will soon have to hear a very great deal about this young man!"

V

The Success That Came Too Soon

I

The concert with Madame Lucca was my first appearance before a large audience. Leschetizky was present and greatly pleased at my reception. After the concert he came to me and said, "Well, Paderewski, now I believe if you acquire a large repertoire, you may still have some real success. After hearing you tonight I feel convinced of it." As I have already told you, he did not consider me a representative of his school of playing because I had my own readings, etc., which were not according to his ideas. For instance I could not play pieces, especially Chopin, which he edited and revised with certain little differences. I could not admit that! Chopin needed no change. I never played them—I could not—and he never proposed that to me. There was always a little friction, not visible, but under the surface, between us from time to time on that score.

But as I have said, Leschetizky was undoubtedly pleased with that first appearance of mine and his approval gave me immense encouragement. It was very advantageous—that début. I was nervous, yes, of course. I do not know whether it is the same thing with other people, but I have a theory myself that I should like to speak about now. A theory about nervousness.

For many years in my career I had that terrible pain before playing—that anguish which is not to be described. It takes not only all your courage, but all your strength. It is agonizing, frightful. My theory was and still is that that fright, that terrible inside nervousness, practically fear of everything, of the public, of the piano, of the conditions and of the memory too, was nothing else but a bad conscience. For years and years I had it. I was continually analyzing myself, and it took me a very long time before I discovered that it was, I repeat, a bad conscience, which meant there was something in my program which I had *not yet completely* mastered, a difficulty which was above me, *I* was not above the difficulty. There was still some weak point in my program, something I had not conquered. And this is always the case. Fright is only the sense of insecurity, and it may be insecurity of only one passage or phrase. For instance, you may play ten pieces on a program perfectly, without a blunder, they are absolutely under your control, but if the eleventh is not in perfect condition, let us say, and even one little phrase or a few bars of a great composition remain unconquered, and elude the fingers, it is quite enough to upset your whole inner being—if those few bars absolutely evade you. One passage can torture you with unspeakable anguish, and that is what disturbs and frightens you to such an extent.

When I realized this and came to more mature years, I practised quite differently. I found the right way. Of course, in any public appearance, there is always the usual nervousness, but that is quite a different thing. And you know in a repertory which contains fifteen, eighteen, and sometimes twenty or more pieces, it is enough to have only a single piece, one little phrase, that you have not mastered, to completely unnerve you, and beget the most dreadful fear.

Well, after that début at the Lucca concert, I was somewhat encouraged. First of all, I had one program absolutely ready. I said, "Perhaps I may now venture to go to Paris to play that one concert." Of that particular program I felt absolutely sure. Also, I had just received from my friends in Strasbourg a letter inviting me to come there and give a recital, and the added good news that other friends (in Paris) were even ready to assist me in arranging my first concert there. I felt myself then at the turning point, a high moment. The way seemed open at last, and I determined to hesitate no longer but try at least one recital. So I went to Paris.

First of all it was arranged that certain people were to hear me in private homes. My first appearance was in the house of

The Success That Came Too Soon

the kind Senator, already mentioned, Monsieur Scheurer-Kestner. Both he and his wife, who was a charming amateur singer, I knew in Alsace. They were very important people and there were many notables of the Paris world in their house that night. Later on I also played at the home of a very great physician whose wife was a singer of remarkable ability—a very great artist, Madame Trélat, one of the greatest singers I ever heard. They were all so very enthusiastic that I could not understand how, with that modest equipment of mine, I could produce such an impression. I played also to the Director of the House of Erard (the house of the great Erard pianos), who was also extremely enthusiastic, and became one of my dearest friends from that moment of meeting, Monsieur Albert Blondel.

It happened that Madame Essipoff was concertizing in France at that time, and came to Paris just before my concert, and introduced me to Monsieur Blondel. It was one of the memorable happenings of my career, for he became a devoted friend—a friendship that lasted through all his life. His loving interest in my career never ceased. I played for him, and he immediately offered me the Salle Erard for my concert, and there my début in Paris took place.

So it all happened quite simply, despite all my doubts. I gave my first recital in Paris, in the Salle Erard, with great hope. It was in March, 1888. It was an extremely brilliant audience. Perhaps one of the reasons for that particularly brilliant audience, so often remarked, was that there was quite a large colony of Polish people in Paris at that time, aristocrats, highly cultured and very musical, and they all attended this concert and brought their friends of the French aristocracy. That explains the "brilliance" of the attendance. I was unknown. It was my nationality that helped me a great deal in gathering together these distinguished folk. Besides the notables already mentioned, there were many prominent French people present, foreigners and some famous musicians as well. Tschaikowsky, the great Russian composer, who was then in Paris, was there. Then there were the two famous orchestra conductors—Colonne and Lamoureux, and of

course Madame Essipoff and my dear friend, Princess Brancovan, and Madame Trélat, Madame Dubois, the last pupil of
Chopin, and so many others. In fact, most of the prominent musicians of the time were there.

The hall was crowded. They were so enthusiastic that I had
to play for another hour after the concert. It was all very exciting
and I think I may say it was really a tremendous success. I could
hardly believe it—after all my doubts and fears.

Immediately after that recital every one rushed back to the
dressing-room, including the two conductors, Lamoureux and
Colonne—but the first to reach me was Lamoureux—Colonne
came a few minutes afterward—and so it was Lamoureux who
then engaged me on the spot for an orchestra concert. I knew that
I played rather acceptably, that it had made a sensation, but I also
knew perfectly well that I was *not* equipped for a *number* of
concerts. I intended to play one recital only, and now Lamoureux
wanted me to play with the orchestra, and also arrange for several other concerts immediately. I was aghast. I had nothing to
play—only the one program that I had already given! Was it not
terrible? That was a tragedy indeed! Only one program—one!
When I remember that, I am shivering to this day. I should not
like to go through it another time in my life, that experience.

Yes, of course I was nervous. My nervousness at that concert
was extreme; it even increased after the recital when I realized
what was in store for me. The sense of responsibility dominated
me throughout. I was overwhelmed with a great fear for the
future. Although there were many incidents during that recital
showing that I pleased the audience and that I was scoring a
great success, I did not pay any particular attention to them because I was already overtaken with terror of what lay ahead.
What shall I do? What shall I do? The words kept racing
through my mind, for my reception that night had exceeded my
expectations immeasurably. I could not realize it at all. I thought
I was gradually working up to a career, and then, in a moment,
came this success in all its surprising greatness. I was overcome
completely with joy and with a sense of triumph too, but I was

The Success That Came Too Soon

not drunk, as we say, with this success. Ah! No. Not at all. I was extremely sober, too sober even, because it spoiled all my joy, this sense of responsibility.

But it had to be so, otherwise I should not have accomplished anything if I had felt satisfied then. It gave me of course that stimulus to work, and not only encouraged me, but more than that it *forced* me to work.

The reaction of the audience that night came toward the middle of the program, I remember. I had to begin with some classical, rather austere numbers; the thirty-two variations in C Minor by Beethoven I played for the first number. Then I played a few shorter pieces; then the Sixth Rhapsody of Liszt. The reception was very noisy, especially of the last numbers.

Yes, that was the beginning of a career which I was not foreseeing, and in fact did not expect so suddenly. It surprised me, it even frightened me, and imposed upon me the terrible work of preparing myself to a degree that would justify that unexpected, tremendous success and make it legitimate. Why? That is easily answered. Because it came too soon. I was *not* ready. No. I was not ready to enjoy it, and not ripe enough to deserve it. I was so occupied with my playing, with my effort, that I could not think about the consequences at that moment. Only afterwards, when the concert was finished, when the people came with their demonstration of approval, appreciation, and encouragement—then it was overwhelming. It was a landslide of applause, a landslide of success if you like—and a catastrophe, the responsibility! It was something I did not look for; it was not only unexpected but totally undeserved. I have never been modest, no, because modesty is undervaluation. But I was humble, and I am still humble. My art—that was the important thing—not my personality. But when I realized the effect of that personality, I knew instantly what was in store for me—how much responsibility, how much suffering. "Now I am entering into an inferno," I said to myself. "This is not heaven, it is hell." I had played already in Strasbourg and elsewhere—but this was Paris, Paris! And of course then began the years and years of labor, beyond my strength even, and of suffering. Yes, that was what I realized after my concert. Like a bolt of lightning there followed immediately, in the wake of my début, a great public demand for a second concert. And I had nothing! I had no other program.

The Paris press, too, was very enthusiastic and helped increase the public demand for a second concert immediately. And I repeat I had nothing.

"But you must give a second concert," all my friends said. "You must, otherwise your first concert will be useless, because it would seem to the public that you have no more programs, and that you are a failure. That must not be." Alas! I realized this only too well—far more deeply than any one else. There was only one thing to do. So I had to prepare very quickly a second program. I began to work immediately. There was no other way. I was three weeks working on the second program. How did I ever do it! Even now I cannot tell how. It was colossal. The first program took eight months. Imagine what one could do in three weeks!

But—I did the impossible! I prepared it somehow. It was not perfect academically, but I got it into shape. I met the challenge. With my towering ambition and youth—and youth is a tremendous force. And then I played with great success in the first orchestral concert—the Saint-Saëns Concerto in C Minor. I played in the second a Hungarian Fantasia by Liszt. I earned some money. It was all very satisfactory to me. But I lived as in a dream —a dream fulfilled above my most daring expectations. At my second recital I made a little more money, and I was then invited to play in private homes and at the Lyons Philharmonic Society. They gave only chamber music fortunately, and chamber music was much easier. I was invited to play at Brussels, too, and made quite a little success there. In fact, my playing was the sensation of the season, I think I may safely say at this date.

The line of my life was extending, but I knew well that I was not yet ready for the big concert career I wanted. There is nothing more terrible than to meet a good success for which one is not ready or ripe. It is an agony. Nothing can describe the feeling of an honest heart. Perhaps had I been less conscientious, with smaller aspirations, I might have been pleased and even satisfied with the Paris début, but at that moment, when it came to me so unexpectedly, it was overwhelming! Why does it come now when I am not ready and cannot take full advantage of it? Over and over again I was tortured by this thought. You can imagine what this realization meant, with only one program really ready to meet the situation. I saw the danger ahead and knew that I must face it. The necessity of having several programs ready immediately made me determine then and there to return to Vienna and Leschetizky as quickly as possible.

II

So I went back to Vienna and began to prepare a large repertory, and I prepared two programs, but mostly by myself, for Leschetizky was not there when I arrived and when he came back he could not give me as many lessons as I wanted. But he did give me some lessons, and the principal pieces I had to play in my programs I played to him and he approved them. It was a time of intensive work—and Leschetizky was very generous. But I was already working more and more according to my own judgment and views. And there was a certain little friction on account of that. He saw that I was too emancipated then for him.

Then came another great event for me—I had a real début in Vienna, in 1889, and that was an immense, an immediate success.

It was my first recital in Vienna. It took place in the Bösendorfer Hall. Bösendorfer was a famous piano maker in Vienna and he had a very large concert hall in his piano house. Bösendorfer was a charming gentleman, very friendly with artists, and he treated me with special kindness and cordiality. That concert attracted a very large audience, and I even then in Vienna made quite a nice little sum of money with my recital. The critics of Vienna received me with great enthusiasm. Here is perhaps the moment that I may say they hailed me as "a great star." My career as a pianist was then launched. There was solid ground under my feet at last. I could now return to Paris and give three concerts instead of one. I prepared two concertos then, and I also wrote my own concerto. I had started·writing that concerto in '88. After the first season in Paris I wrote it, in a very short time. I scored it in '89 in Paris and wanted to play it myself, but Madame Essipoff said, as she had introduced some of my compositions already in Vienna, she would like to do this concerto too. As Leschetizky had invited the great conductor, Hans Richter, to hear this composition, she was naturally anxious to play it. I must add here that Madame Essipoff was Leschetizky's wife at this moment. I say this advisedly, because there were several Mesdames Leschetizky—all musical—all charming! The Richter episode was very interesting and important to me. I shall tell you a little about it later. Richter was one of the great conductors of the moment.

It was an age of great conductors and I had the rare good fortune of meeting many of them. Leschetizky's influence was always tremendous, and at his house—well, the whole world, we may say, passed through it—the whole world of music at any rate.

I should like now to answer a question of yours and tell you something about the importance of orchestras in Europe, their great number, and also about the very great conductors in those days. Some of those conductors I met while in Vienna. Hans Richter was then at the summit of his reputation. He was already recognized as a classical exponent of the Wagnerian art. He used to go every year to Bayreuth to prepare and conduct the performance of Wagnerian operas. He was the head of the very famous Court Opera in Vienna. Besides, he conducted the Philharmonic concerts, which enjoyed at that time such a universal reputation. It was considered by composers as by virtuosi, a great honor to have their names associated with that institution.

Leschetizky, who was alive to everything of importance connected with the life of a musical student, realizing the prestige of having my concerto played in those concerts under Richter, invited him one Sunday to his house and asked me to play the concerto while Richter read the score. Well, Richter sat by the piano and read the score while I played it in Leschetizky's music room. The performance met with immediate success, for Richter said very encouraging and flattering words, and asked me to play that concerto in one of his forthcoming concerts.

I realized that it was a mark of the highest distinction for any composition, and for any artist to play at a Richter concert, but Madame Essipoff-Leschetizky, who was present, said, "Oh, *I* must play that concerto. I have been studying it for several weeks and I claim the privilege of being the Godmother of that work." And then Leschetizky took it up and insisted upon it too. Although Richter suggested my playing it myself, I really think he would not have encouraged me and he probably felt that Madame Essipoff would make a greater appeal than I would. As a matter of fact I was glad to have her do it, because I had not studied the concerto sufficiently for a great public performance.

It was really a good fortune, although I felt disappointed at the time. She was a charming pianist and very successful. Her playing in many ways was perfect, except when it came to strong, effective pieces—then she was lacking in real force, as women pianists usually are. Quite different. from Madame Teresa Carreño, who was a very, shall I say, strong pianist, even too strong for a woman. Carreño was one of the women pianists who had a very big tone, but it was not a beautiful tone because beautiful tone must include tenderness, and she had none of that, just brilliance. Essipoff, on the contrary, was quite the opposite. She was very feminine in her playing, and small poetic pieces she could play admirably. She was an intelligent woman with evident culture, attractive to look at, and with a very pleasing personality altogether, which was a great asset to her on the concert platform.

So it was Madame Essipoff who played my concerto for the first time a few days after Richter read the score, and it had an immediate success. I am so sorry I cannot find another word for that because it seems to me the word success is becoming very frequent in our conversation. At any rate, it was favorably received, not only by the audience but by the critics as well. Hans Richter had great faith in my compositions, as he proved by giving a masterly performance of my symphony in London some years later. I was there and enjoyed it very much. That first performance was a great emotion for me.

Now, Richter was extremely kind, amiable, and a thoroughly good man. He was very much acclaimed wherever he appeared, but he remained all through his life a modest, accessible artist, and ready to assist a young musician in every way he could. He was not a linguist. The only language he used, and used very well indeed, was his mother tongue. In spite of his long career in England, where he used to spend several months every year, he never learned to speak correct English. There are many amusing stories based upon that defective English of his. I may be permitted to quote one of them which was very characteristic.

He was invited once for a week-end to a friend, living some distance from London. His wife was going to stay on there, for some time, but he had to return to London on the Sunday night, for his rehearsals. So when he got to the station, he asked for two tickets and then said to the agent, "Please give me two tickets, one for me to come back to London, and one for my wife *not* to come back!"

Yes, it is quite true, Richter was among the most eminent and finest interpreters of Wagner, and not only of Wagner, but of all classical music. He never tried to make extraordinary effects and give sensational readings of Beethoven and the other Masters. He just gave a solid, sound and yet very refined performance of every work he conducted. He ranked among the first. I remember seeing some of his early photographs which were very popular at that time and had a great sale in Germany and England. There was one in particular, representing him sitting between Wagner and Liszt, reading a score. It was certainly very interesting. To see a picture means often much more than to read a chapter. The picture tells its story so quickly. It appeals to that element of childhood, perhaps, which remains with so many people through life—mercifully.

You asked me a moment ago to speak of the other great German conductors at the time I was beginning my career. Well, one of the most popular was Hans von Bülow, who was extremely erratic in everything, and so he was in his career. His performances were sensational, but they were perfect in every way. He was one of the greatest conductors. In speaking of von Bülow one always thinks of his connection with Liszt and the effects of his marriage to Liszt's daughter, Cosima. It is a long story, and had, we might say, great importance and publicity at the time—and still has for some people. Cosima was married to von Bülow, and after some years left him and married Wagner.

All this was of tremendous interest to musicians and brought about the great rupture between Liszt and Wagner. It has been the cause of much controversy and explanations, which will go on as long as stories about Wagner are being written.

Although I knew von Bülow well later on in my career, this story has no special place in my own biography. Just a bit of the panorama of the doings of those tremendous musical days. Yes, I agree with you and bow to your wishes that every biography should tell its own story and reflect the doings of the times, which, you must admit, is something of a colossal task. We are indebted to the little photograph of von Bülow sitting so contentedly between Liszt and Wagner for this extra bit of musical history.

Hans von Bülow was very sarcastic, and sometimes even unjust on account of his being so witty—that is a quality which is always rather dangerous. He simply could not abstain from making witty remarks about people. He thoroughly enjoyed it. I recall a most amusing thing he said about a well-known conductor of popular concerts at the Crystal Palace in London. Some one said to von Bülow, "Well, how do you like our English conductors?" "What conductors?" asked von Bülow. "Well, Sir Charles Hallé, for instance." "Oh," with a shrug, "he is quite good—he is a good musician." "Then, what do you think about X?" "Oh," von Bülow laughed, "he is a bus conductor!" "Why?" "Why!" said von Bülow, "because he is always *behind!*" Great laughter! Prolonged laughter. Rather cruel but, unfortunately, it contained a grain of truth which makes the point of the story.

Yes, I had several particular contacts with von Bülow, one a very unpleasant one in Berlin. But that comes later on. It's a long and still painful story.

There were, besides von Bülow, other very important conductors in Germany. For instance, Schuch, who was at Dresden. He was a man of genius. Remarkable, subtle, tender, and powerful. He had all the qualities. A wonderful man. I knew him well.

Then, too, there was Levi, but I never heard him conduct. He was a contemporary of Hans Richter. He, too, enjoyed a tremendous reputation in Germany and Bayreuth.

Then Mottl, another great Wagnerian conductor, made a large reputation in Germany and in other countries. He was most successful in Paris and London. It was an age of great orchestras and great conductors, but in my opinion there are few giants now, if I may use such an expression, although there are many fine conductors at this moment who enjoy tremendous favor, and great reputation. For instance, you have in America now as leader of the Boston Symphony, Serge Koussevitzky, a Russian. I have never heard him but he is highly esteemed. And there is Stokowski, head of the great Philadelphia orchestra, and Bruno Walter of Munich, for instance, who seems also to have been most successful in America of late years. But when all is said and done, there is nobody—nobody to be compared with Toscanini, for he is a transcendent genius—a genius of the first order. One cannot speak in any ordinary terms of Toscanini.

It is quite true, those men are tremendous powers in the musical life of the community. In America, for instance, certain conductors, like Theodore Thomas, were not only pioneers in symphonic music, but musical conductors of the nation as well. They were builders of orchestras. Leopold Damrosch was another great pioneer. He formed the first Symphony Orchestra in New York. Anton Seidl came later and should be mentioned here, as a great conductor but not as a pioneer, not in that class.

You must realize that in every capital of a kingdom or a grand dukedom and of every principality in Germany, they had a Court Theatre. Everywhere. In some places, like Cologne and

The Success That Came Too Soon

Düsseldorf and Hanover after the annexation of these Rhenish Provinces and of the Hanover kingdom of Prussia, the Diet of the provinces considered it their duty toward the public to keep a permanent theatre and subsidize the theatre and the orchestra. And the free cities, such as Hamburg, Bremen, and Frankfurt-am-Main, all had fine orchestras, and opera, consequently.

I think that these remarks, though not strictly in chronological order, will perhaps be of some interest here.

After that début in Vienna, my *real* début as I always call it, I felt my career had already begun and I was fully prepared now to give three programs in Paris, the result of my final work with Leschetizky. So I returned to Paris at once, ready and eager.

It was at the time of the Exhibition in 1889 and I was asked to give a concert at the Exhibition, which I gladly did. And then I had the supreme satisfaction of being useful to my dear friend, Edward Kerntopf, because I encouraged him to send to Paris, for the Exhibition, his own pianos. And he sent them and through my influence was fortunate enough to obtain a gold medal for them. That was the happiest moment of his life, and a very happy moment in my existence, too. At last I could show him a little gratitude for all his benefits to me.

I was then getting many engagements. My reputation was growing more and more. I played many times in Brussels, Liège, Antwerp and so on, and then in the provincial towns of France. I played in Lyons, Bordeaux and Nantes, and also several times in Nancy, concerts and chamber music. I gave recitals in Lyons, but I could not give any recitals in Bordeaux because Bordeaux is, perhaps, the most unmusical city in the whole world, and I do not hesitate at all to put it in my memoirs. The people are absolutely wooden. They do not care for music and yet it is one of the richest cities in France. From the sales of the famous Bordeaux wines they were simply rolling in prosperity. Lyons, on the contrary, is really musical. There are many adherents there of serious music and they are all very cultured and enthusiastic. In Bordeaux, they are absolutely nothing. It is quite extraordinary. Nantes is musical, Nancy is musical, Toulouse is also musical, but Bordeaux—!! Ah!

The people of France are very fond of opera. On the whole, one must say they are more fond of opera than of anything else. But for pure, classical music, devoid of any glittering accessories, I must say they are not yet prepared. In Lyons and Nantes, there are conservatories; in Bordeaux, there is nothing of the kind. The only attempt in Bordeaux, for example, for a musical season were three or four concerts which were very pompously called Philharmonic Concerts. They were ridiculous.

I was engaged to play at one of these Philharmonic Concerts, as they were so ambitiously called. Through all these years, during my entire career, it is interesting to note that I have given only three concerts in Bordeaux, and the very first concert there, in 1889, was with the Philharmonic Orchestra just mentioned. It was an absurd affair and very funny. I think I must tell you about it.

The program was practically endless! It began at half past eight o'clock and we were all still there at one in the morning! The program consisted of the orchestra, which played three or four numbers; a 'cellist, who played a concerto and a group of solos; two singers, one of them a lady and a charming singer, too, who sang two long arias and a group of songs; there was also a baritone, who sang two long arias and another group of songs; there were two groups of violin numbers—and myself! I played one long concerto and two groups of solos. Whoever heard of such a program! Incredible!

The concert was well attended and attentively listened to for the first few hours, but when, about midnight, a few of the weary people tried to leave the hall, they found they were unable to do so. Why? you ask. Because the President of the Society had locked all doors and put the keys into his own pocket! He did not wish any one to miss one single note of that program. The President of the Society was very nice-looking and evidently a very agreeable gentleman. He managed everything in his own way like a general, including the artists as well as the program, for we, too, were locked in! He was with us most of the evening, only going out occasionally to gaze at the audience from the wings to see that all

The Success That Came Too Soon

was well. Of course we artists were all put together, as is the custom, in one room. The room was comfortable, but not big enough for such a company for that length of time. There were, in addition to the artists, their accompanists, too, as each performer had his own accompanist. The 'cellist had his; the lady singer had hers; the baritone had his, and the violinist too had his, and so on and on. We were as endless in numbers as the program!

The lady singer was also accompanied by her husband, a rather jovial Frenchman, and I mention him because he played an amusing rôle in our comedy that evening. After the concert, when at last everything was over, the President of the Society appeared in the artists' room to congratulate us. He made the most cordial compliments to every one. He was overflowing with delight and praise for us all. When he approached the singer to offer her his heartfelt thanks, her husband, the jovial Frenchman I have just spoken of, quickly stepped forward, extended his hand and said, "Well, how are you? I am very glad to see you, my dear *cousin!*" The President stopped short in amazement and stared at the man. "Cousin," he repeated, *"cousin!* What do you mean by calling me your cousin. I have never seen you before in my life, sir!" "Oh, well," the other answered with a laugh, "when one is obliged to remain so long together as we have done this evening, one naturally feels a member of the family, and since we have been locked up all these hours, I must, therefore, regard you now as a *relative!*"

Well, it was very amusing. The poor President was overwhelmed for a moment, but he rallied like the good general he was. The door was unlocked and we were released, and it all ended very satisfactorily.

Among the musicians of the orchestra (it was half amateur and half professional) there was a young fellow playing, I think, in the second violins, who came back to the artists' room to speak to me. He approached me rather hesitatingly at first. After a few compliments he said, "I should like so much to see you again, Monsieur Paderewski. Would you not be kind enough to dine with me tomorrow?" "Tomorrow," I answered, "Why, it is *already tomorrow!* You mean *today!*" "Well, yes," he laughed, "today. Will you come and dine with me today?"

It was a Sunday and I had to remain in Bordeaux that day, so I accepted his invitation. But, of course, it was a trap. He had invited many guests, it seemed, and he really wanted me to play for them after the dinner. I noticed on my arrival, the piano was open and a rather large number of people present, so I was quite cautious and ate very little. I played, naturally; there was no other way out of it and at that moment in my career I was only too glad to have an opportunity to play certain pieces of which I was not sure. To "try them on the dog," as we say. So I played several things very willingly, and the young gentleman said before I began, "Oh, if you will only play for us today, if you will just play *one* solo, I will send you a fine barrel of wine, in token of my gratitude, and thanks."

Well, I played as I have told you, not because he offered me the barrel of wine, but I had agreed to and it was agreeable to me. He thanked me most profusely when I finished and said, "You must leave me your address. You will get that wine very soon in token of my appreciation. The finest wine I can buy, I shall send you." Need I add that I never got that barrel of wine?

Well, there was another amusing incident in my artistic career in France. I was engaged to take part in a Philharmonic concert in another provincial city. It was in Tours in 1890. Tours is a charming place, but you know the number of people fond of real musical art is extremely small. But that is again an illustration of that provincial musical sentiment in France. They engaged me. They knew that I was rather a success in Paris, and that newspapers spoke very favorably about me, and so they thought it was absolutely indispensable for them to have me play there, once at least. So I accepted the engagement—it was a very nice fee—and I went to Tours. I always detested those miscellaneous concerts, because, you know, one is, so to say, charged with a certain electricity for playing, and, as long as one plays, that electricity works—it renews itself. But when one has to stop continually and

The Success That Came Too Soon

wait for half an hour between numbers, one has to recharge one-self all over again, and sometimes it does not work at all. It is very difficult.

Well, at this concert at Tours, first some one sang, a baritone I think, and then I had to play. I played, and the audience was very much pleased, and I was glad, though I did not expect much enthusiasm there. Then a lady singer sang. Then came Galipaux. He was an actor of great talent, and very popular then. He recited one of his amusing monologues, and he absolutely changed the atmosphere. It became then quite a different thing. Next came a tenor, I do not remember the name. He was rather a mediocre singer, but he had the most marvellous high notes. Those top notes of his sent his audience quite crazy with delight. You know "ut de poitrine," as it used to be called in French, and he sang with that "ut de poitrine." Well, that was the climax. That was the end of the rest of us! It was in the very middle of the concert that he produced those top notes that won all hearts. I had to play after him! And nobody listened to me—nobody! I came after the immense excitement of the top notes, and I came only with a Nocturne of Chopin. What a tedious thing for that audience! They did not even listen to me. I might as well not have been there.

But I played then just as I usually played, not a bit worse—but no top notes—therefore, no applause! No excitement! They were bored, they wanted more top notes. Well, I did not feel happy at that moment. Then the lady singer came again—again great success. She sang, I think, some coloratura with many trills and cadenzas.

Then again came Galipaux, the actor—another success and then the tenor—the tenor with the top notes. This time he was simply a furore. The audience went wild! So wild that when I appeared right after his number, to play my last group of solos, well, this time nobody listened to me at all—they simply began talking. They paid no attention to me whatever. I thanked God when it was finished.

It was all very funny, of course, but also very painful. Such a thing had never happened to me before. I had only one thought in my mind, to get the next train out of Tours.

When the concert was over, all the other artists expressed to me their deep condolences and regret that I was such a failure. I can assure you it was very unpleasant. The only bright moment was the arrival of a little gentleman of the name of Mame, a charming man and the publisher of holy books. At Tours, there is that famous publishing house, Mame. He was very musical and had real musical culture, too. He came to the artists' room to speak to me. He was quite furious and expressed his regrets and deep apologies, and said he was disgusted with the behavior of the audience, who proved themselves to be only a lot of barbarians. He was quite upset. He felt the musical integrity of Tours was at stake. He could not understand, he said, why that wretched singer who had a very bad voice and only a few top notes, had made such a sensation, why the audience had gone crazy over that mediocre performance, and had not paid any attention to real art, and so on.

I suppose it was a little balm to my feelings at that moment. At any rate, it started a friendship that lasted for years. Yes, for years and years that dear good man came to every one of my recitals in Paris. Was that not charming of him? And always after each concert he would hurry back to greet me, and his first words were always the same—"Well, my friend, this is a little different from Tours, is it not?"

These are two amusing stories to our credit. That is good measure. We must be serious again, and we now come to a moment in my career—it was in '90—when I had to prepare on short notice, just out of gratitude for my French colleague, a program of French composition exclusively. I had two concertos and some twelve or more short pieces, and I learned all that within a fortnight! It was a charity concert for some institution. I was obliged to do it.

I mention this program of French composition which I had to learn so rapidly, because it is connected with an experience that will be useful to others. I learned these pieces in a fortnight and

The Success That Came Too Soon

played them all, and played them well too! Technically well, I mean—not a single slip! But I was not sure of my memory even ten minutes before the concert. It was an agony! I had to look at the music—the concertos especially—just before I went on to the platform. Up to the last minute I was memorizing continuously. I went through the concert—I pulled through my program to the satisfaction of the audience and the composers who were present. I played several compositions by unknown composers that day. But here is the interesting part of my story and the reason for it. Three days later, I did not know one bit of it, and could not repeat one single piece. Not one! It was gone. All this shows that nothing can be accomplished through one big effort of *forced* memory. I crammed and I stuffed myself literally like one of the famous Strasbourg geese! Every student should realize that good and enduring results are obtainable only through a series of small but *continuous daily* efforts, but a single effort is absolutely sterile. Knowledge, whether in science or in art, or in any human occupation, can be achieved only through *daily* toil and effort. That is absolutely true.

As it is with many people, so it is with students who are taking examinations—they enjoy themselves for a whole year until the time comes for the examination, then they make a supreme effort and acquire superficial, but brilliant, knowledge for the moment. After that, the same thing happens to them as happened to me with my program of fifteen pieces learned in a fortnight—nothing left of it—nothing!

"Time is very vindictive and takes a cruel revenge on everything accomplished without its co-operation."

VI

Paris and a Dutch Supper Tour

I

My life in Paris is a big chapter in itself. It was one of the richest periods of my career—the beginning of my real artist life. It is difficult to recapture, in a fleeting moment, the feelings of that time, and to recreate for you the mental and spiritual dimension I lived in. To tell the story of those days so long ago in which I must necessarily play the leading rôle and become the Hero of the drama—of my difficulties and disappointments, my mistakes and hopes and high ambitions, and then the fun and the luck and the work—that is the task before us, to which we must address ourselves.

So perhaps we should turn now to the chronological order, for there are certain moments of the Paris life which are of great interest, and will add a kind of seasoning to the story. So many touching and interesting things I remember in connection with the great personalities of that time—things that are perhaps not generally known, or that may have been forgotten. In Paris, as in London, I met all the famous figures of the day in music, society, and politics. A great regiment—alas, we must now say of ghosts, for they are all dead.

It was at this time that I brought my son, that poor sick child, to Paris that he might be near me. My friends, Mr. and Mrs. Gorski, took care of him then. He lived with them, in fact. It was all very difficult and his condition was a great tragedy. I could not go to Poland for him, owing to the great difficulty of passports, so Edward Kerntopf brought him to Vienna, and Mr. Stowiowski's father brought him to me in Paris. He had incredible difficulty even then in walking. He was about nine years old. It was very hard, this constant anxiety in the background of my life, my work increasing and absorbing every moment of my time, my career, for what else can I call it, surging and pushing on, demanding all my powers, time and force—and my poor boy to be cared for, to be cured, as I hoped for many years. I had to go on with my work, I had to follow my destiny. I was not yet thirty and every hour was precious. But always in the foreground was the menace of his illness, a constantly increasing problem to be met. He had his tutors at this time and he was intelligent and gifted; he had a brilliant clear mind; he loved music too. It was difficult to take him to concerts, but he often went to recitals at the Salle Erard which we could manage easily and he was very happy to go, and touchingly proud of me at these concerts. It was a great excitement to him, a stimulant to his mind. Poor child, he was completely cut off from everything in life except intellectual things, by his great infirmity.

I had three seasons in Paris before appearing in London and the contacts and friends made then continued through the years. I decided to make Paris my headquarters and took a small apartment in the Avenue Victor Hugo—a very small and modest one it was, but still, I had to get my roots, so to speak, into the ground.

That little apartment was very dear to my heart. Just as the two little rooms in Vienna, it became a part of my life and, as in Vienna, I kept the Paris apartment for many years, until 1906 in fact. It was all connected with my work, a little world of my own—a world of work, of increasing work, a work that never stopped. And I know as absolutely today as then that I was always struggling for perfection, pushing on and on to that ever-receding, faraway peak of attainment. All work is like that. Immensities increase as we progress and the summit of the mountain is always farther and farther away.

My greatest anxiety in those years was learning new programs and giving them to the audiences. My thoughts and my work became the world I lived in, the only occupation of my heart and life. The career filled everything—it was over and above everything. This building period, as I call it, hard as it was, was gloriously rich in other ways and exerted a great deal of influence, naturally, and was tremendously stimulating. It was then that I began to meet many people in all walks of life, important people, and through them I glimpsed another world. I knew all the great musicians of the hour. Their doors opened to me, and Charles Gounod was among the first. His was a wonderful personality. There was something in his appearance which gave you the impression of a High Priest. Gounod was very stately, with a beautiful white beard, wonderfully expressive eyes, and with a facility of speech that was perhaps a little ecclesiastical at times, because it was so unctuous; every sentence was perfect when he spoke—a voice always harmonious and never excessive in intonation. Kind and benevolent in every way, a beautiful man really. He was not only the master of a school (because all modern French operas proceed from Charles Gounod) but there was something I dare say pontifical in his ways and in his influence over younger musicians. It was a very marked characteristic of his.

Gounod was not only a composer, but a very learned man. He knew many things, but never wrote about them, as did some of his colleagues. He preferred to write nothing but music. He was not as fond of writing, of putting his knowledge into print as was, for instance, Camille Saint-Saëns, though he was just as versatile. He just kept within the limits of his art. He was an enthusiastic admirer of Mozart and considered him as his ideal. This is even noticeable to a certain extent in some of his compositions, because they are essentially simple, with the sincere and frank predominance of melody.

In my opinion, certain parts of his "Faust" are as beautiful as anything written in music. For instance, the love scene, the middle part of the waltz (which is of rare beauty), the prelude and the serenade. There are pages of supreme inspiration.

There is an opera of his which is a comedy, "Le Médecin

Charles François Gounod

From the painting by Benjamin Constant

Camille Saint-Saëns

Jules Massenet

malgré lui," based on Molière's comedy, which is a chef-d'œuvre. There is "Mireille," another opera, based upon a poem by Mistral, one of the greatest French poets.

Now there is something still little known about Gounod which is of great interest, I think. That was his singing at the piano. He sang French songs sometimes, quite often in fact, at the house of the old Madame Marchesi, the renowned singing teacher, and it was supremely beautiful. He had a poor, thin little voice, but he could do anything with that voice. He had a rare gift for singing. He sang with great emotion and style. I used to go to his house very often. He was a charming companion. It was always a joy to me to be with him and it was an added joy for me to see him at my concerts and hear him applauding and shouting his approval, "Bravo! Paderewski, bravo!" He always came. I loved him very much.

Gounod had a tremendous knowledge of affairs, but he never tried to appear brilliant. He was a simple, natural kind of man and sometimes very jovial in his wit.

The next greatest French musician, after Gounod, who became my friend was Camille Saint-Saëns. He was an extraordinary man because he knew so many things. His knowledge was very wide. He wrote philosophical books. He wrote even a book on astronomy. He was a member of the Institute of France. He was elected as a musician, but he used very often to go to sittings in any department of the Institute, to the department of archæology, for instance, where he would read an interesting memorandum on that subject, or to the department of mathematics, where he would read something about astronomy. A most erudite and unusual man.

There was at that time, when I was in Paris, a singer of great reputation and of marvellous baritone voice, whose name was Faure. His elocution and his masterly use of the remnant of his voice, for he was then really an old man, were just as remarkable and even more refined than the now almost forgotten (except by musicians) Battistini. Battistini was one of the greatest baritone singers of our time, one of the greatest of any time.

I once played in a concert when Faure sang. I noticed only one fault with him. That was, he used to hold certain notes very long—he would make a tremendous retard if they were beautiful, and hang on to them forever. The prolongation of those notes was sometimes extremely painful, even to his admirers.

On one occasion it was in the house of an aristocratic lady who gave fashionable musicals quite frequently. Charles Gounod was present and Faure was about to sing certain songs of Gounod. It was an occasion, and every one quite conscious of it. The charming lady of the house suggested that perhaps it would please Gounod to accompany Monsieur Faure himself. Would he?

"Oh, no, Madame," he replied quickly. "Why should I? I cannot sit down in *every* corner." Gounod was not easy of approach, as you see, and this was a characteristic answer.

Saint-Saëns was unfailingly kind to me. He came to my concerts when I played his own Concerto in C Minor and was perfectly enthusiastic, and after that never missed an opportunity to show his good feelings. I still have some photographs of him with his expression of gratitude and affection and so on, which I prize very highly because he was a man who never showed any sentiment. It was a well-known fact that he was neither amiable nor accessible—always extremely difficult to approach, but I can only say that to me he was always kind and considerate.

In connection with this, I remember an incident with him in 1888. I had finished the orchestration of my own concerto for piano. It was in the summer of that year. I had been already introduced to Saint-Saëns. When I finished that concerto, I was still lacking in experience. I had not even heard it performed— it was something I was longing for. I wanted to have the opinion then of a really great orchestral composer. I needed it. So without further thought I took my score and went directly to Saint-Saëns. But I was rather timid, though I already knew him personally, and he had heard my playing of his concerto. But I realized on second thought that it was, perhaps, presumption on my part to go to him. Still I went to his house nevertheless. I was so anxious for his opinion.

He opened the door himself. "Oh, Paderewski, it's you. Come in," he said. "Come in. What do you want?" I realized even before he spoke that he was in a great hurry and irritable, probably writing something as usual and not wanting to be interrupted. "What can I do for you? What do you want?"

"Oh," I hesitated what to answer. I knew he was annoyed. I had come at the wrong moment. "I came to ask your opinion about my piano concerto," I said very timidly. "I——"

"My dear Paderewski," he cried, "I have not the time. I cannot talk to you today. I cannot."

"I am sorry," I said, starting to leave. "Perhaps—perhaps—I may come another time," I ventured, still hopeful.

"Oh," he cried. "Another time may be even worse than today. I have no time—ever." He took a few steps impatiently about the room. "Well, you are here, so I suppose I must receive you. Let me hear your concerto. Will you play it for me?"

"Yes," I answered. "And I have the score for you also to read."

He took the score and read it as I played. He listened very attentively. At the Andante he stopped me, saying, "What a delightful Andante! Will you kindly repeat that?" I repeated it. I began to feel encouraged. He was really interested. Finally he said, "There is nothing to be changed. You may play it whenever you like. It will please the people. It's quite ready. You needn't be afraid of it, I assure you."

So the interview turned out very happily after all and he sent me off with high hopes and renewed courage. At that moment in my career, his assurance that the concerto was ready made me feel a certain faith in my work that I might otherwise not have had then.

I met him many times after that, at certain concerts where I played some of his own works. But the most pleasant experience with him was in Geneva, Switzerland, many, many years afterwards. I think it was in 1911. There was a festival of his works given by Gustave Doret, who was the conductor. He invited Saint-Saëns to come and told him I was going to play his concerto; whereupon Saint-Saëns immediately wrote back, saying, "Perhaps I may be able to induce Paderewski to play my Polonaise also, which I wrote years ago for two pianos. Ask him if he will play it with me." Of course I accepted with great pleasure, and so we played together that Polonaise. He was really delighted. It was a most touching occasion. Although Saint-Saëns had intended to stay only for his own concerto, when he heard that my Symphony was to be performed at the last concert, he insisted on staying another day for that. That was very kind of him, a gracious gesture.

A big banquet was offered in his honor after the festival and I was asked to say a few words and I made an address which pleased and moved him very much. It made me happy, too. It was a charming reunion altogether.

The third interesting musician I met in those early days in Paris was Massenet, a man of great talent; a great faculty for writing, very successful and very rich, too. I think he was the richest among French musicians. He liked very much to go on the day of the performance of his opera—whether at the Grand Opéra or at the Opéra Comique and personally inquire at the box office about the sale of the seats. "How are the tickets selling?" he would ask. "Is the house sold out tonight? I hope so."

Even when he was quite ill, in spite of physical difficulties he would get up in the morning, read in the journal that his opera was to be performed that evening, and then off he would go to the box office. It was a little mania, of course. I think it was not wholly a financial interest. He really wanted to know how the public was feeling towards him, whether he was still popular or not. It was a mixture of feelings, like most things. I did not find him very witty personally. He was, of course, not a man of such tremendous interest as Saint-Saëns, or Gounod. He was a musician and somewhat imbued with his personal greatness.

Massenet wrote a number of operas and two especially found great favor with the public. "Manon" was his first great success and then, of course, "Thaïs," which is still performed. I saw the first performance of "Thaïs" with Sybil Sanderson, a young American soprano from California, a sort of protégée of Massenet. She made a great furore in Paris for a time. "Thaïs" became a great sensation of the opera season through Mary Garden's beautiful interpretation. Massenet wrote many lovely songs too, which had a vogue at that time.

I also knew Vincent d'Indy, who was a great musician. He was already, to a certain extent, under the influence of the new currents in German music. There was some little Wagnerian streak in his art. It was not by any means an imitation, but he was just betraying that atmospheric influence. He was the first Frenchman who did, and it was, of course, long before the real or ultra modern French music made its appearance, Debussy, Ravel, and so on. D'Indy wrote some delightful things for the orchestra, several symphonic poems, operas, and chamber music, but his masterpiece of great dimension still remains "Le Chant de la Cloche," based upon the famous Schiller poem.

I knew Charles-Marie Widor, who was an organist and a composer and a professor of composition in the Paris Conservatory, especially of orchestration, a very learned, tactful and clever man. He played quite an important part, not only in the musical world of Paris at that time, but as Permanent Secretary of the Institute of France, which is a very high position, indeed, and a very influential one. In spite of his being now ninety-three years of age he still continues to work, and work well. He is a man of remarkable ability and a wonderful character altogether.

Yes, I knew him well. I saw him here in Paris a few years ago—two years ago I think, and we talked about various things of great interest to us both. I asked him, I remember, if he knew anything concerning the interest Charles the Great took in music. "Well," he said, "I know a little—I know that he was very much interested in music and that he was surrounded by musicians of that time (eighth century) but I shall look up some documents to enlighten you." And he did. Just two days afterwards I received a little book where all the works of the composers (of plain-chant) were mentioned. Yes, he sent me that book. He had thought about it, and found it. He had taken that trouble—a man over ninety. That gives you some idea of the quality of the man—does it not?

Widor was also the organist of the Church of St. Sulpice. The organ of St. Sulpice was a remarkably beautiful one and Widor's famous organ recital every Sunday morning was a rendezvous of the whole aristocratic and artistic Paris world. The church was always crowded with the most brilliant gathering of beautiful and fashionable ladies. I think there is an interesting comment to be made here when speaking about a church, for the church, it seems to me, is almost exclusively a feminist institution. I have always felt this to be so, and in this particular instance it certainly was, for there were only the most influential, fashionable ladies present and it was always the same audience. All the beautiful ladies of Paris were present; there were even some foreign ladies of great distinction and especial brilliance always to be found there on Sunday, as near to the organ and Widor as they could possibly get. And of course, naturally, it was very agreeable to him, for it is very pleasant to anybody to look at beautiful faces and charming dresses, and so on. To hear Widor on Sunday morning at St. Sulpice became a habit and a fashion that lasted many years.

These gatherings could only be compared to certain lectures, for instance, of Professor Caro at the Sorbonne, when, for that rather heavy subject of philosophy, an audience of the fashionable ladies of Paris was gathered together and the hall was not half large enough to contain them all! Such was his popularity. Professor Caro was a real celebrity, a very brilliant and interesting man, but he does not belong in my musical memories.

I think right here in this list of famous musicians there should certainly be added the name of Edouard Lalo. I used to see him very frequently in the house of Sarasate, the great violinist. They were very close friends and I was often admitted into their stimulating and delightful atmosphere. Lalo wrote several concertos for the violin, chamber music, some beautiful songs, and toward the end of his career he had the joy of seeing his opera "Le Roi d'Ys" performed. It was, so far as I know, the only opera he wrote and it was a very beautiful thing.

In this increasingly long list Gabriel Fauré has his special place. Fauré was a great composer of songs. They used to call him, rather pretentiously, the French Schumann. The comparison was not very much justified, I must say, because the range of Schumann was so very much higher and very much wider, and of course his genius is unquestionable. But Fauré wrote many beautiful and poetic songs. His chamber music, though enjoying some popularity, was not as profound nor as perfect as to form. One piece, however, seems to me to be a wonderful addition to the comparatively poor literature for the 'cello. That is his Elégie. That is a gem.

The only great French composer of noble and lofty inspiration who has almost created a school among modern musicians of France and Belgium was César Franck. He was a Walloon —French language, but Flemish origin. He was the only one whom I did not meet personally. He was never to be seen in concerts. He was living like a monk, seeing only his pupils, and it is generally believed that he was actually afraid of new acquaintances. He retired absolutely from life. So I never tried to approach him, but I admired him very deeply. Certain things, for instance, that symphony of his (in D minor) and his violin sonata—beautiful, very noble music—a master work.

But aside from musicians, I had opportunities to meet the greatest painters, sculptors, and even poets of France. In fact, I knew many of them well. It was a brilliant society. These opportunities came at first through a talented French painter in Strasbourg. His name was Schutzenberger. When I came to Paris, he gave several receptions for me, and I had the privilege of seeing the studios of almost all the important painters of that time. Gérome, Benjamin-Constant, Bouguereau, Bonnat, Puvis de Chavannes, and Detaille, etc. But Rodin, the sculptor, I never met. He was not at all accessible.

Naturally, I knew some artists who were not French; for instance, Munkacsy, the great Hungarian painter. I played several times in his studio, to which the best society of Paris was always very eager to go.

There were some salons in Paris where music was considered almost as a religion. Several ladies of the highest society played the piano themselves and rather well, and devoted to that art much energy and labor. They were pupils of a Madame Dubois. and Madame Dubois was the *last pupil of Chopin*. She must have been in her youth extremely beautiful, because when I was introduced to her for the first time, she was already a very old lady but of exceptionally attractive features and wonderfully beautiful expression.

I heard from her certain interesting remarks as they were made by the great Master himself, and I cannot deny that I derived some benefit from them, even at second hand. She told me many things of interest.

I remember once when I was playing the 17th Prelude of Chopin, Madame Dubois said that Chopin himself used to play that bass note in the final section (in spite of playing everything else diminuendo) with great strength. He always *struck* that note in the same way and with the *same* strength, because of the meaning he attached to it. He accentuated that bass note— he proclaimed it, because the idea of that Prelude is based on the sound of an old clock in the castle which strikes the *eleventh* hour. Madame Dubois told me that I should *not* make that note diminuendo as I intended, in accordance with the right hand which plays diminuendo continually, but said that Chopin always insisted the bass note should be struck with the *same* strength —no diminuendo, because the clock knows no diminuendo. That bass note was the clock speaking. I have always played it since then as I was told Chopin wanted it to be.

Madame Dubois was the mother of all the pianists in the best Parisian society! She was beloved of all these ladies. Whenever there was a little reception at Madame Dubois', you would meet there the most eminent, the most illustrious families of France.

Among her pupils there was an exceptionally talented lady,

Paris and a Dutch Supper Tour

Princesse de Brancovan, whose salon had the reputation of being the most musical and exclusive in Paris. The Princess was of Greek origin, married to a Roumanian prince by the name of Bibesco, a former reigning dynasty in Roumania, a very ancient dynasty. There were several brothers Bibesco and she was the widow of the eldest brother who had inherited the ancient title of Bessaraba of Brancovan.

I played many times in her distinguished home.

Another salon was at the house of Princess Alexandra Bibesco, who was married to the brother of the Prince de Brancovan, but bearing another title. The Princess Bibesco was a good pianist herself too, and there was a great deal of rivalry between the two princesses on account of their piano playing.

I knew them both, but I must acknowledge that the art of the Princesse de Brancovan was much more perfect. She had a beautiful tone, but was extremely nervous and always frightened when asked to play. She used to say, "I am afraid of being afraid," but when she played Mozart, it was really beautiful, admirable.

I think this is the place where I should mention her daughters, particularly the poetess, the Comtesse de Noailles. The other daughter was a very gifted sculptress who married Prince de Caraman Chimay. Of her three children there is only her son Prince de Brancovan who remains, and who lives in Roumania. But it is of Anna, the Comtesse de Noailles, that I now wish to speak. She was considered one of the real, perhaps I may even say great, poets. I knew her when she was twelve years of age, when I visited them near Evian. They had a villa in a suburb of Evian, a very beautiful villa on the lake. I first heard that little child playing exercises. She was very fond of music, and practised faithfully. But she was rather fragile and always suffering. Her nervous constitution was extremely delicate and she had not the strength to become a pianist in spite of her determined efforts. I think that hearing my playing so often, she finally got rather discouraged, poor child, and abandoned the piano. But she expressed herself in poetry and some of her poems rank among the masterpieces of modern French poetry. They were mostly lyrical. She was a very highly educated person with a fine and inquiring mind and had a great inclination toward philosophy. She knew practically all the schools of philosophy, beginning with the Greek and ending with the modern ones. She was really extraordinary, and especially in conversation; her erudition was surprising because she took interest in everything that was new and important. She understood Einstein, for instance, and she studied the works of Einstein and could discuss them like a specialist. A wonderful mind. She wrote many poems treating of music; she wrote poems on Chopin, Liszt, Mozart, and Schubert. One of her favorite composers was Schubert.

She recited her poems delightfully and very willingly. She was always pleased to see that people were interested; in fact, she "took" the stage, as they say. That was the eternal feminine —the woman in her. She liked to be the center of interest. Her reciting of her own poems was extremely interesting. She had an amazing personality, and a very beautiful, vivid face and marvellous eyes, but she was very delicate and extremely small—a fragile creature of nerves and fire. I can think of no other words in describing her sensitive and flaming personality.

She died when I was crossing the ocean on my return from America in 1933. I was returning home on the *Ile de France* and Monsieur Herriot, the Premier of France, who was on board, first brought me the news of her death. He came to my cabin in the early morning the day before landing and said, "Our dear friend, Comtesse de Noailles, has just died. I have received a radio message."

She died one of the greatest poets of the time. She published a book entitled *The Book of My Life* and there is in it a chapter in which she has written about me, so beautifully, so touchingly that I cannot do less, and alas I cannot do more, than acknowledge now my gratitude for the long years of our friendship and my devotion to her.

Her funeral was a very special occasion and naturally received great publicity. As one of her closest and oldest friends,

Paris and a Dutch Supper Tour

I was invited to speak. It was a poignant occasion for me. I had many beautiful souvenirs of friendship and memories concerning her, but they all fell so far short in expression of all that I felt that day. She too, with her wonderful mother, and so many other cherished friends, had passed from my life forever. I could only express then my devotion to her shadow.

And now we turn back again to my early Paris days. It was at that time that Wagner's star was rising formidably on the musical horizon of Paris. His music had already raised a terrible controversy. It was a burning topic. On the part of musicians, though, there was little opposition. They soon began to bow their heads before Wagner's genius. Although "Lohengrin" was the first of his operas that actually launched him in Paris, it must not be forgotten that "Tannhäuser" had already been produced thirty years before, in 1861, in a storm of fury and resentment on the part of the musicians. It was given for three performances only, I believe. At the first performance of "Tannhäuser," the audience went wild, perfectly mad, and to the accompaniment of howls, hisses, booing and whistling on keys, the poor singers and orchestra fought their way. It was Pandemonium and to a degree unimaginable. The audience was absolutely out of hand and outraged, and with the exception of the Pilgrims' Chorus, to which they listened with some tolerance and faint applause, the catastrophe was complete. All this is common knowledge, I know, although many may have forgotten it at the moment, as "Lohengrin" is generally spoken of as the first Wagnerian opera to be produced in Paris. It, too, had a stormy reception both inside and outside the Opera House.

The première of "Lohengrin" took place at the Grand Opéra in Paris in 1891, three years after my début there, and there was a violent demonstration, an actual riot in fact which occurred in front of the Opera House. Several people were injured and a number killed, and it was some time before the police could control the furious mob. The Parisians were outraged at the performances of Wagner, a German, in their city. It was on account of his attitude after the Franco-Prussian war, when he was triumphantly hailing the victory of the Prussians over France. It was sheer patriotism on their part.

But, unlike "Tannhäuser," "Lohengrin" was produced many times that season at the Opéra and was the first real recognition of Wagner's genius and final acceptance by the Parisian public. "The music of the future," as it was called, had won its place to a certain extent.

Gounod, for instance, felt rather strongly about Wagner. I once heard him discussing the Wagner operas and I remember well something he said then about them, a criticism that is often used and credited to various people. But I, myself, heard Gounod say these very words, more than forty-five years ago. "Yes" said Gounod laughingly, but oh so sarcastically, "I agree—certainly there are delightful moments in Wagner's operas, but *awful quarters of an hour.*" (Il y a des délicieux moments, mais des fichus quarts d'heure.)

I remember also that Gounod said on another occasion that Wagner was a monster!—but "un monstre puissant." Wagner's operas were all so much against the Italian and French tradition of the continuous singing of beautiful arias and the beautiful singing tone. In the Wagner operas the orchestral music predominates. That was hard to understand for a people educated in a quite different atmosphere and accustomed to different formulas and different traditions altogether.

Of course all these happenings and contacts made a new life —a new world for me, in great contrast and quite different from Berlin and Vienna. The French society at that time was particularly brilliant and the Paris world rich in musicians, sculptors, and poets. I entered into an atmosphere that surpassed anything I had dreamed—anything I had imagined, even the imagination of youth.

One of my most charming souvenirs was meeting, at the house of my dear friend, Princesse de Brancovan, the poet, Frédéric Mistral, the greatest poet of France. He spoke the most beautiful French but with the most unbearable accent. It was really painful to listen to him when reciting his poems in French, for instance, which he often did. The first few lines were dreadful—a different language altogether. But gradually his enthusiasm and his masterly elocution made you forget that shortcoming, that little drawback of accent, and you were compelled to listen, and with keen enjoyment.

The great particular furore of that season, was, of course, Sarah Bernhardt, "The Divine Sarah" she was called. I was playing in Budapest many years ago and she was performing there at the same time. After her performance all the aristocracy of Budapest organized a banquet in her honor. I think she would not have paid much attention to me then because there were a great many people gathered in that Hotel Hungaria, but one of the gentlemen present, Count C., said, "Somebody must say a few words tonight, and I do not know anybody here who will have the courage to speak French before the Divine Sarah." Then he turned suddenly to me, why I don't know, and said, "Ah, you must be very familiar with French, Monsieur Paderewski, perhaps you will say a few words for us." So I made a little address. Fortunately it pleased her very much, it seems, and she thanked me and asked me to call upon her in her home in Paris, which unfortunately I could never do, because whenever I intended to do so, some engagement interfered. So I was never in her house, which was rather famous and something of a menagerie, if report was true. She was said to have a lion cub as a pet and there was even a rumor that she kept a snake or two. However, the house of such a woman could not fail to be an interesting reflection of her own personality. She had many gifts other than her acting. She fancied herself a sculptress and worked at it and did a number of things. She was a person of tremendous vitality, a kind of special force that created sparks wherever she went. All this, I think we may safely say, was in addition to her extraordinary talent for acting. She was a brilliantly clever woman in many ways—a child of the limelight. She created a world of her own and reigned over it as long as she lived.

She was a marvellous actress, who always made upon me the same impression as the great French orator, Jaurès. There was the same lack of material strength. She had a very limited voice in spite of her power. In moments of calm recitation it was incomparable. When she became very dramatic, on profoundly emotional moments, the voice became shrill and harsh and even hoarse. She was unable to speak in a very loud tone. I could never understand why they spoke of her voice as "golden." In my opinion it seemed to be exactly the opposite of golden.

And so it was with Jaurès. Jaurès was a well-known Socialist, a teacher of philosophy and a lecturer. He ardently championed the cause of Socialism and had an active career in French politics. He was famous as an orator and later was one of the most energetic defenders of Dreyfus. I heard him several times and always with the same feeling, his voice was so painful to listen to, and each time I said to myself, "Now I shall enjoy him to-morrow, when I can read his address in the newspaper!" Because there was so much thought, such co-ordination, such artistic climaxes in his speeches which his voice could not give. His voice and his gesture were absolutely inadequate to his emotion. He had peculiar hands too; hands which appeared to be lifeless, and his sleeves hung down over them. There was always a certain awkwardness in his hands; his gestures were feeble and impotent. His voice was exactly the same as Sarah Bernhardt's—when it came to the necessity of using a powerful tone, it was inadequate. But he had power nevertheless, though he completely lacked magnetism.

But Sarah Bernhardt had enormous magnetism. It drew and held in complete thraldom her audience, wherever it was. In that respect she was impeccable. A divine gift of the gods!

Sir Henry Irving, too, had that same inadequate voice, but he realized his shortcomings and knew how to manage his voice so it never offended your ear. Voices always affect me deeply and a poor, rasping tone always sets up nervous irritation. It seemed to me that there was an aureole round Irving's head whenever he appeared on the stage. He always created quite a different atmosphere in whatever rôle he played. He raised the whole tone.

But if Irving's voice was unsatisfactory, certainly the adored

Paris and a Dutch Supper Tour

Ellen Terry's, who always played with him, was just opposite. That was a marvellous voice. Rich and powerful. It still lingers in my ears, so noble and harmonious. It was like beautiful music.

Actors are always dear to the heart of the public. They excite the imagination, it seems to me, more than any other artist. There were several famous actresses that were idols in my Paris days—the lovely Jane Hading and that enormous favorite, Réjane, the finest comedian of her time. And there was another great actress, long dead, whose fame still rings round the world —Rachel. She was a great tragedienne—according to many people, perhaps the greatest actress that ever lived, certainly the greatest French actress. I heard constantly about her gifts from very old French people whom I knew in Paris. They still talked, and I may say even wept, at their memories of Rachel. She was an undying figure and later on, curiously enough, and from an American by adoption, Carl Schurz, I again listened to rhapsodies about this amazing creature. Carl Schurz spoke of her as a divinity; he said he had never in his life had an impression comparable to that he obtained from seeing Rachel act. Schurz spoke about Rachel, not only with eloquence, but with the warmth and emotion and tenderness of a very young man. She still filled his mind as a thing apart. When talking with him, Rachel became alive to me—I could almost imagine that I, too, had seen her.

And Monet Sully, too, and the brothers Coquelin. Of course I knew them and enjoyed them like all the great Paris world.

It is true, I saw and met them all and they enriched and enlarged my vision. They made their impress at the time and have left their charming memories with me. But life was a stern, grim business then—nothing really mattered but work. The career was being built step by step—slow, painful stages.

II

There is a little episode that I recall at this moment in connection with my first season in Paris. It is rather amusing to look back upon, but it was most painful at the time. I will offer it as a little diversion from too many celebrities.

One day early in the spring, in May I think, in 1889, there appeared at my little apartment in the Avenue Victor Hugo, a gentleman—no, I will not give his name—who offered me a tour in Holland. I was rather surprised at this and said it was too late, that the season was over in May.

"Oh, never mind, that does not matter at all," he said, "we can still have a very successful tour, and here is my contract for you to look at. I had it all ready, you see. Read it and see whether the conditions are agreeable to you or not. I shall be very glad to arrange this tour. I'm very anxious to, in fact."

Well, I looked at the contract and, as he said, it was quite favorable. There was a very acceptable fee, and also the obligation on the part of the gentleman to pay me on the evening of each performance, either after or before the concert. It was all very clear. Nothing to find fault with.

"But," he said, after we had discussed the contract, "you must realize that Holland is a very peculiar country. A recital alone will not appeal to the public. They are especially fond of chamber music and if we could arrange a trio, for instance, it would be very advantageous to us all. You naturally will be the principal figure, but a trio will increase the sale of tickets."

I had no objection to this and said, "Well, that is your business. I accept either recitals or chamber music concerts, whatever you wish and think best. But a group of my solos after playing chamber music from notes (which is very hard work) would be too fatiguing. There must be something to change the mood, a short piece for the violin or 'cello, or something like that."

Well, we talked it over, and the gentleman (who must still be nameless) was quite agreeable to this suggestion and engaged a 'cellist and a violinist, whom I knew very well and with whom I had frequently played in Paris. So all was well, and we began our tour.

On our way to Holland we stopped at Rheims, and played in the circus there because there was no hall available. There was a very poor attendance, first, because Rheims is a very small place, and secondly, it was too late, and thirdly, because we played in a circus!

So, as I've just said, the attendance was poor. The impresario commented upon this and seemed disappointed, but said, "Never mind, I have the envelope here with your fee, and I beg you to accept it now." "Oh," I replied, "this concert was not a success, the audience was very small. I cannot accept that fee. I must first look at the receipts. Have you got them?"

"No, not yet," he answered. "The receipts are not yet prepared. You will have them tomorrow morning."

"Then tomorrow morning," I said, "we will decide about my fee, because I never accept money which I have not earned." That has been throughout my whole career a principle that I have never changed.

After the concert we went out as usual for a little supper. You know Rheims is the capital of Champagne. We had supper in a little restaurant opposite the cathedral and it was an excellent supper. There were six of us—the trio, the accompanist, the impresario, and the secretary. We had exceptionally good food, and we drank six bottles of champagne! All very agreeable. It was really a little banquet in the capital of Champagne, and I remember it very well because when the bill came it was only frs. 37. They gave us an excellent supper at frs. 3 each, and six bottles of champagne also frs. 3 each! The champagne was light, just like water, otherwise we should not have been able to drink so much of it. So in spite of our poor receipts, the evening ended happily and we went on our way to The Hague, with high hopes and in good spirits. There we played two concerts. They, too, were badly attended. It was too late—the season was over and almost every one was in the country.

But in spite of this we continued the tour and went on to Utrecht. Again, this concert was poorly attended, and so it was during the whole tour. Everywhere we met with the same disappointment—everywhere poor houses, very small indeed. It was always the same. I never received one single rupee for my work during all that tour. But that comes later in my story. The impresario provided the railway tickets; that was his sole contribution to the trip. Mine, in addition to my services, was to provide the suppers, the suppers that took place every night after our disastrous concerts! And let me add that suppers in Holland were rather expensive. It seems that because I gave the first supper, I was expected to continue them all through the tour. Fortunately, I had left France with several thousand francs in my possession, so I devoted this money entirely to that laudable purpose!

The final concert of this unfortunate trip was in a small place where only retired functionaries from the Colonies lived. The name of that place is Arnheim. This concert was the poorest of the lot, the hall practically empty—our swan song! Before we left the hall our impresario paid the accompanist, the 'cellist and the violinist, but to me he only said that he would settle everything on our return to Paris the next day. I did not believe it, of course, but there was nothing to do but accept the situation.

And now for the grand finale! After the concert at Arnheim came the most dramatic moment of the whole Dutch tour. Directly the concert was over, a gentleman came to the artists' room and said to me in much distress, "Ah, Monsieur Paderewski, I am quite ashamed of this little place; you have had such a poor attendance. I feel very badly about it. But you must not blame us, the citizens of Arnheim, because it is really too late in the season. Nobody could attract an audience now, no matter how brilliant, how well known. There are no musical people here now —it is summer. So only the impresario should be blamed, that he selected this time of the year for a concert tour! I am extremely sorry," he went on, "I feel it very keenly and so I beg you to forget this unfortunate experience, please, and accept my regards and compliments and come to supper with me tonight, all of you, as my guests. We will have a fine supper together before you go."

Well, I hesitated. I did not know the kind gentleman, but just at that moment the impresario came to me and whispered, "Oh, Monsieur Paderewski, do accept this invitation. Why should *you* always treat us? Let our good friend buy the supper and be our host tonight. He is a nice man, well known here, and he is very anxious to entertain us. His carriage is waiting. Let us go."

So I accepted and it was a very fine supper indeed; in fact, it was the best of all the suppers we had during the tour; exquisite cooking; many choice wines, for which I did not care very much, but which my companions liked immensely—I cared for only a little champagne. During my entire career I have had that preference for only a little champagne after a concert.

So our kind host really entertained us, I may say, royally. It was splendid! We ate and drank our fill—then he ordered expensive cigars. I do not smoke cigars but all the members of the little troupe accepted with delight. And then came the liqueurs, which I did not touch. I never drink liqueurs. Then our kind and solicitous host bade us good night and went away after much hand-shaking and further expressions of good will.

The next morning we had to leave early, to return after all these triumphs, to Paris. I asked for my bill. It was brought to me. I looked at it and stood aghast! I was petrified—I could not believe my eyes. It was ten times more than my usual bill during the tour and then I saw that every item of that great supper of the night before was on my bill.

"What is this?" I cried, "why, this is a mistake. I did not order this supper. I was invited. The gentleman who was our host last night invited us. But perhaps you have charged twice. This is not right. It is a mistake."

"No," the clerk answered, "Oh no, that is not a mistake. The gentleman who invited you was the hotel proprietor, the owner. He was your host."

"He was my host?" I interrupted.

"Oh, yes," answered the clerk, "he was your host, but you pay for the supper!"

There was nothing I could do, literally, but give him everything I had left; my last francs went over the counter. And so, on that high note, the tour came to an end and we took leave of each other, my companions and I. As we left the train upon arrival in Paris, the impresario said, "You understand, of course, Monsieur Paderewski, that tomorrow I shall come early in the day and settle in full all your concert fees." Then he smilingly extended his hand and—we parted. I never saw him again, needless to say.

Twenty years later he published his memoirs. He quite forgot to speak about those sad experiences, but he did say that I was a "very nice" fellow, and that he liked me very much. Oh, no, I shall not tell you his name.

Nothing of that kind has ever happened to me since. It was a good lesson. I tried to find an explanation of the motive which prompted him in engaging me for that season, which was not a season for concerts at all, and obviously a bad business enterprise. But it was not until a year later that I met a gentleman from Holland who told me how it happened. It seems the impresario had engaged the famous Lamoureux Orchestra of Paris for a series of concerts in those same cities, and being, let us say, rather an opponent of absolute truth, he made promises which he could not fulfill. Lamoureux, a keen business man, naturally looked for some guarantees. He said he could *not* go to Holland with his 100 musicians without having some *positive* assurance that the money would be paid, whatever the results of the concerts.

Well, of course, the impresario made all kinds of big promises and advertised his concerts well in advance. Then, seeing that he could not get the required guarantee, he abandoned his project. But as he had already advertised himself and his concerts in all those places, and knew it would be a very serious blow to his reputation if he failed in his agreements, he tried to arrange at once something else, just in order to save his face. "Well," he explained to a friend, "it is very easy. Instead of Lamoureux who has been prevented from coming to Holland by unforeseen circumstances, I shall offer the public at once the opportunity of listening to the brilliant young Polish pianist who has made such a furore in Paris." And so, without the slightest hesitation, knowing that the season was over and that he had no money at all, he arranged our unfortunate tour, and I was caught in his trap. He was saved—but

Paris and a Dutch Supper Tour

I—well, I had the tour and had also the opportunity in addition of giving many splendid suppers, especially the last one, which was a triumph. That was the extent of my profits. Although this was an expensive trip, I learned something from it and gained further and deeper insight into human nature.

VII

England and a Berlin Enigma

I

And now to the next great step—London. A London season was filling my thoughts—I had made up my mind to go there next. I had had three really successful seasons in Paris and at this moment London was my goal. I had my feet on the ground, as we say. I felt sure of myself—I was moving steadily on in my career, and I want to say here that a London success would mean far more in a solid sense than any success in either Paris or Germany, German opinion to the contrary, of course—and on this subject I have a most interesting story to tell you later on. So London it was.

I arrived in England after those successful seasons in Paris, and announced three recitals in London at the old St. James's Hall, May, 1890. I was then already sure of my pianistic equipment. Pianistic equipment means armor and weapons—my experience was my armor and technical skill my weapons. I had a large experience then. I had already played my programs many times and with a certain effect, rather favorable. So I approached London with confidence and a great eagerness and hope. I had as a part of my equipment, let me call it, a few good friends there whom I had met before in Paris. I counted their interest also as part of my stock in trade. But in spite of this, there were very few people at my first London recital—it was a very small audience and little money in the box office. Although it was a keen disappointment, still I could not expect more because I realized that I was unknown and just starting my career there. How could it be different? I asked myself. Naturally, I was beset with misgivings and painful reactions after that first recital, and then—just as I was recovering from this depression—came the newspapers! I was criticized frightfully in the press. There were few good words for me. This attack was probably due, to a certain extent, to the very tactless advertising of my concert. Daniel Mayer, the manager, was very eager to make me not only a great but an immediate success—to attract at once a very large audience, to make a sensation! And so he opened my season with the brilliant idea of advertising me as "Paderewski, the Lion of Paris!" He plastered all London with the advertisement of the arrival of the "Lion of Paris." It was his firm conviction that this inspiration on his part would attract the attention of all London. It did! It made me ridiculous! And I suffered very much from it.

In England it was considered very bad taste. Such things do not please the English people. It was in my opinion a lamentable and tragic mistake. When I saw that awful advertisement upon my arrival in London two days before my recital, I was deeply distressed. I knew it would have just the opposite effect from what was intended, and I immediately sent for Mayer and asked him to change it at once; in fact, I demanded that he change it, and after much violent argument and great agony, I succeeded. The last two advertisements of my concerts were without that additional attribute, may I say!

There is something to be said now about Daniel Mayer. He came to me really through my devoted friend, Monsieur Blondel. I had never been in London, and Blondel, who was also director of the House of Erard in London, said, "Now, Paderewski, this is the time for you to go to London and try your luck, and achieve with the great English public what you have already achieved here in Paris. I am sure you will succeed. But don't delay."

"But," I hesitated, "I do not know any one in London; it will be very difficult."

"True," Blondel replied, "but we have many acquaintances there who can be useful and your reputation has already gone across the Channel. I will write to Chappell, head of the great publishing house, about you. He can be very helpful."

He was true to his word and did so, but Chappell, unfortunately, did not consider that it was wise for him to introduce a new artist. He had had his regular clients for many years, he was an elderly man and perfectly satisfied with what he had, and absolutely declined to undertake the management of my concerts. It may be of interest to know that Chappell was then organizing the Saturday popular concerts, the "Pops," as they are now known. But Chappell did not completely abandon me. On the contrary, he said, "I think I may be of some use to you, Paderewski. We have a young impresario here, Daniel Mayer, who is a very capable man, and I recommend him to you as a manager."

Chappell then wrote to Mayer personally, proposing that he manage my concerts, and so it came about that he became my manager, and it was his own, I must say, funny idea of attracting the attention of the public by his fantastic advertisement of the arrival of the "Lion of Paris"!

I had had great successes in Paris and my concerts were so well attended then that I was playing almost everywhere. So my arrangements were made with Mayer for the London season. We had happy relations for many years after, but we began our partnership rather disastrously. That ridiculous advertisement was his own responsibility, and it was both tactless and in very bad taste and he quite overstepped the mark in his efforts to exploit me.

The press took up the matter also, and not one, but quite a few, of the newspapers spoke extremely badly about me, saying, "So, this is the 'Lion of Paris'! Well, we shall soon hear him roar! A Lion from Paris!" etc. And so they played upon the theme. It was a good one and they all attacked it. I had then a tremendous head of hair, very reddish and very thick, so I displeased the majority of the critics on that ground, and further added to the annoyance of the advertisement, which was very great. There was one exception, however, the critic of *The Times*. He wrote beautifully, but he did not agree with my playing of Schumann, of course, because he belonged to Madame Clara Schumann's congregation. So my playing of Schumann displeased him very much. It was revolutionary for him, he was accustomed to that modest and very restrained Schumann-playing as performed by that very old lady! It was a tradition, and I was destroying, or disturbing, that tradition. I played it exactly as Schumann wanted it played—I mean not as to perfection, but as to the dynamics of the composition. When it was *fortissimo,* I played *fortissimo,* which Madame Schumann, poor lady, could not produce. Therefore, in all these works, which were played in public by her, and which had established a certain tradition, I surprised the audience, and audiences do not like. surprises.

But in spite of these poor criticisms, my second concert was better attended, and evidently those opponents saw that their remarks had but little effect upon the audience. They grew considerably, so the critics changed a little bit their opinions, as the audiences increased.

When the third recital came, it was extremely well attended. They began even to find some fine qualities in my playing, and so it grew, continuously. Then I played with the Philharmonic Orchestra, and I played at various other concerts, and they gradually changed all around, except Mr. Fuller Maitland, the critic of *The Times,* one of the greatest critics of the world and an excellent musician himself, a real artist. Whatever he wrote was just. He criticized me sometimes, but justly, and everything was so pure, honest, and really not only genuine, but based upon some solid foundation and reason. So I have always been grateful to him, as he helped me.

I was then offered—it was the summer season—a series of recitals in the Provinces, and then came my little revenge, because when that first provincial tour in England in the fall of 1890 was advertised, a pamphlet was prepared by my manager, Daniel Mayer, to be distributed in the form of a circular, to all the music lovers in every place we were to visit. He had his representatives everywhere and they all had a list of the people who went to concerts, and they sent these circulars to all their clientele.

By then I was aware of the dangers and pitfalls in advertising, so I asked to see the pamphlet. First there was a little biographical sketch; then my compositions were mentioned and the critics quoted and excerpts given from their criticisms. You know how it is usually done by managers—a few *good* criticisms, then a series of *dots,* then again a *nice* little phrase, a plum, more *dots,* and so on. I read the pamphlet, and then said to my manager, "Now, this is quite wrong. It won't do at all. You must put it exactly as it was—exactly."

"But I cannot," he cried, "I cannot. It would be madness! Ruin!!"

"Never mind. I am not going to cheat the public. You must put in, in full, every criticism that was written about my playing."

Mayer became perfectly furious at this, for it was the most dreadful collection of criticism. "Impossible," he cried. "I won't do it. I won't do it! It would be ridiculous. We should be ruined!"

"Then I shall go to another agent. You must do it."

"But people won't come," he cried. "It's suicide!"

"If they are intelligent they will come," I said. "They will say to themselves, "This is very strange. How is it possible for an artist, capable of giving such a fine program, to be so *badly* criticized? They will be curious. Then you must give them gradually all these *improvements* in the opinions." This was my idea. It was first of all honest, and then, too, a little revenge.

Well, after much agony and arguing it was done and I must say it read *horribly!* Mayer was still in despair when he brought it to me for approval.

"What artist," he said, "who even pretends to give a concert comes with such dreadful recommendations? We are ruined! I repeat, ruined."

However, in spite of his prophecies the tour was a success from the start. Poor Mayer! He made that first mistake with the "Lion of Paris" and then he almost made a second mistake when he did not at once agree with my opinion—it was something so unusual. But in the end he realized it and was astonished when he saw that first provincial concert, I think it was either Birmingham or Edinburgh, and the hall more than half full. For a first concert in the Provinces, that was remarkable. By the end of the season the houses were full everywhere, and in London the same.

I had about forty concerts that season in London. I do not mean my own recitals, but appearances in public, including various clubs, etc., where I played. There were also a few orchestral concerts. In Manchester, I remember, I played with the then famous and good old Sir Charles Hallé, and in Liverpool with him too. Sir Charles Hallé was the conductor of the Manchester Orchestra, the Liverpool Orchestra and Choral Society as well. He took his orchestra to various places, including London, where he made a very strong and brave effort to advance the music of Berlioz at that time. These concerts did not have enormous success, but in spite of that he was a well-known figure in music. He enjoyed unusual advantages too in his early days. He knew well that famous group in Paris in the '40's. He was a friend of Chopin, of the great Liszt and Thalberg, and many other giants of that time. He was a very good musician and a very solid and sure conductor.

Altogether the London season was a successful one—a full one. I played in addition to my recitals, etc., in private houses as well, because at that time it was the biggest money to be earned and it was also the fashion. In Paris, for instance, I had mostly private houses in the beginning, to provide me material gains, and as a result, even before my first American tour, I had some little money saved.

The London season left me with a greater security—security in myself and my art. The ground was stronger and firmer under my feet. The first season had been a success in spite of the disastrous opening and a bad press. I had, to a certain extent, conquered London. The audiences increased, the press was enthusiastic—it was all growing and going forward and onward.

You ask me if it was at that time that Bernard Shaw was writing his musical criticisms which were so startling to the staid English public. I do not remember exactly as to that, but it was during my first season in London in 1890 that he wrote his famous criticisms in a periodical which was called *The World,* a fashionable weekly edited by Edmund Yates, the novelist. Shaw's criticism, or perhaps I might say, his attack upon me was almost as violent as he declared my attack was upon the piano! It was his criticism of my first concert and he said among other devastating things that I was a harmonious blacksmith who laid a concerto on the piano as upon an anvil, and hammered it out with exuberant enjoyment—words not easily forgotten! Later on he was more merciful, shall I say, and praised my playing of Schumann's Sonata, and even went so far once as to mention my name in the same sentence with Rubinstein—though not flatteringly.

If, as you say, he is one of my greatest admirers now, I am thankful for that, but, nevertheless, he was already writing unfavorable criticisms when the press and the public were of a different opinion. He could never be with the crowd. He wrote, perhaps, not so much as my opponent, but as an opponent of *public opinion.* That, I think, was more in accordance with his character, and he treated me not only severely but, I may say, ridiculously. No, we have never met. In all my visits to London this has never come about and it would be interesting after all these years for us to speak together.

The criticisms at that time I was very eager to read and, naturally, they made me unhappy and, I must admit, a trifle nervous. But after I had read a few of the first criticisms, I found it perfectly useless to make myself needlessly nervous with such reading. It affected me too deeply.

These criticisms of the London press recall to my mind very vividly my first disastrous appearance in Berlin and the press, and the consequences of that affair, which have gone through my lifetime, more or less.

It was in that same year, 1890, I think, that I played an extensive tour in Germany. I had already played in Germany the year before for a few concerts, but this other tour was much more extensive. I gave a concert at Frankfurt-am-Main, and I played several times in Hamburg. I derived a great deal of satisfaction from all these concerts, not only on account of being well received by the audiences, but because the playing with those German orchestras was highly satisfactory. I think I played four or five times in Hamburg at that time and enjoyed it.

I remember well the director of the orchestral concerts in Hamburg—a kind and amiable man and a very excellent musician who was, unfortunately, afflicted with Beethoven's infirmity—he was almost entirely deaf. But he could conduct in spite of it, because the orchestra knew his shortcomings and they worked well together.

I had also, at that time, a pleasant experience in Schwerin at an orchestral concert, after which I was invited to the Court of the Grand Duchess to play at a private reunion for the Grand Ducal family. The greatest impression of that event was not the concert, but the remarkable beauty of the castle, which is one of the finest in Germany, dating back to the sixteenth century.

In that same season I played also concerts in Dresden, which were extremely pleasant to me. Of course, at that time I had not yet the reputation to attract large audiences, and my concerts were given in smaller halls; but they were well attended and there was a great deal of enthusiasm which I felt to be very genuine and, therefore, of great satisfaction to me. My musical world was growing.

In that same year, a queen, a very picturesque and romantic one, Carmen Sylva, Queen of Roumania, rose on my musical horizon. I was introduced to her by the Princess Bibesco and was received at the castle in Bucharest and played several times for the Queen. I found her an interesting and artistic person. She wrote many poems under the name of Carmen Sylva, which in her Court circles were taken rather seriously.

I never saw the King of Roumania. He did not care for music and "made no bones" about it, but the heir was a decidedly musical young man. Quite beautiful to look at at that time, and very much in love with a young Roumanian poet by the name of Mademoiselle Helene Vacaresco. Dynastic interests did not permit of a marriage between the two, so the young heir promptly married the daughter of a duke, and Mademoiselle Vacaresco turned her attention to literature and politics, in which she is still very active and is the permanent delegate of Roumania to the League of Nations. The young prince married a year or two later a princess whom I knew as a child—a child that grew up to be a world figure. She was the daughter of the Duke of Edinburgh of England, and became afterwards Queen Marie of Roumania, whom we all know—a very beautiful woman and a great personality, which she used in many ways. She has had a stormy career. The King was rather quiet, rather timid, and did not like public appearances. She was just the contrary. During the war she was the leader. She did everything—went everywhere. She was untiring. She even went to the camps and addressed the soldiers in stirring tones. She "wore the pants," as I think you sometimes say so expressively in your very strong English, as well as the crown! But again we're out of our order. It is so easy to ramble and digress. We must pick up the biographical thread again.

II

My appearances before German audiences were almost always a source of great artistic satisfaction to me. And that may be applied to every place I have ever appeared in that musical country, except Berlin. Before telling you about that, there is something I should like now to mention, a small matter that was just a disappointment at the time, but which had a very far-reaching and, to my way of thinking, very subtle effect upon the Berlin fiasco which was to come.

I had gone to see Wolff, the famous agent in Berlin, the year before, in the autumn of 1889. I realized then the necessity of having an agent for the Continent. This you will remember was before Daniel Mayer became my manager and before my first London concert. Wolff's agency was the most powerful in Europe—a medium of the utmost importance. To appear under the Wolff banner meant assured success for an artist, and so on my way to Hamburg, I stopped in Berlin and visited Wolff and asked him to take the management of my concerts in Germany into his hands. And—well, he flatly refused! You will remember that this is the same Wolff who was Rubinstein's manager and the man who so absolutely refused to even let me stand in the hall at Rubinstein's Paris concert years before. Wolff had tremendous influence in the concert field in Europe at that time and his refusal to accept me was a great blow. But an artist must always be prepared for any emergency. I was beginning to learn that the path of a pianist, particularly when he is blazing a trail, is beset with difficulties, to put it mildly. How true I found this to be in the Berlin concert! I came to Berlin in the fall of 1890. I was engaged for a Philharmonic concert under the conductorship of Hans von Bülow. I had been told that von Bülow had read my piano concerto and wanted me to play it with him. According to my publisher, Hugo Bock, he was extremely anxious to have me play that concerto with the Philharmonic Orchestra. Von Bülow was exceedingly enthusiastic about this work and came to the hotel to see me immediately upon arrival and said that he was looking forward with sincere joy to our performance next day. He could not say enough. It was all very gratifying to me. I was to play my concerto and then after that a group of solos. I presented my programs for his choice. I had arranged them very carefully—in such a way as to appeal particularly to a large audience because these subscription concerts of the Philharmonic had very large audiences.

Von Bülow selected a group of solos which, however, did not altogether please me. I thought that he could have made a happier selection and in that moment I felt in his choice a certain, shall I say, eccentricity. However, I had to abide by it as his was the final word.

Two days later came the first concert, an afternoon concert known then as a "public rehearsal" which always took place the day before the evening concert. The hall was crowded and the reception the audience granted me was so spontaneous and so cordial that I was delighted. I had never experienced anything like it before. It was something amazing in its immensity. Von Bülow, after the rehearsal, said to me, but in a rather angry tone, I thought, "Do you know that I have never seen anything like it before? Your reception today was colossal." While I was rather flattered by that remark, I noticed, at the same time, in his tone something that hurt me. I felt it.

A few minutes later, during the intermission, there hurried into the hall the gentleman who was the head of the great musical agency. This man, as you may surmise, was the same Mr. Wolff that I had encountered the year before when I had gone to him and asked to be taken under his management. The same Mr. Wolff that refused to accept me as one of his artists, just as he had refused years before to give me even standing room at the Rubinstein concert. The same great Mr. Wolff! He came directly to the artists' room and was most agreeable and rather excited. He pretended, of course, not to have met me before. "Well, Mr. Paderewski," he said at once, "you have had an exceptional reception today. It is most unusual at a début and you are going to have, without doubt, a phenomenal success tomorrow. You will now make a splendid career. I have never before seen a pianist receiving such an ovation in Berlin, such a unanimous recognition and applause on a first appearance. I'm delighted. And now I have a proposition to make to you."

He paused and we looked at each other—it was a dramatic moment. I knew perfectly what was coming and it was a thing of vast importance to the rest of my career. You will realize that at this time Daniel Mayer was my manager. He was a kind and honest man whom I liked very much, but he was in a very modest position then—not to be compared with Wolff. He had not the same connections or the reputation. The other was a power in himself, having his representatives in every country. Wolff was the sole representative then for the whole world. He had a fine mind; he was clever. He was not only an exceptionally brilliant business man, but a highly educated man, and musical. He was a real connaisseur in art. When he offered, for instance, to launch an artist, it represented a great deal, because his assets were formidable, while the position of my own agent, Daniel Mayer, was not to be compared with his in any way. I realized this only too well, but my mind was already made up. I think Wolff realized this too, but he went on very suavely and repeated his proposition. He said, "I am sincerely overjoyed at your success and I now propose to you that under my management you will have similar success everywhere, not only in Germany, but in every country in the world. I am sure of it." He still ignored, you see, completely our previous meetings. But I could not allow that and I answered, "When I was in Berlin last year, Mr. Wolff, before I had my present manager, Daniel Mayer, I approached you on several occasions and asked whether you could arrange some concerts for me in Germany and you absolutely refused. You made it very clear to me, saying that you only accepted those pianists who had already made successful débuts, and artists of a certain reputation. Although I had had successes in Paris, Vienna, and even in London, still you had no faith in me, you would have none of me. It was not until this very minute after the great ovation just given me, that you wish to enroll me under your banner. And so it is to your interest and your pleasure to come to me now and offer, so graciously, your management. You ask me to betray Daniel Mayer, who has worked for me so honestly, so devotedly these past months, and to whom I owe a certain gratitude for that work. Do you think it would be honest on my part to leave him, because you are now pleased to offer me some successes in a future of which you are so sure?"

"Oh, well," he laughed, "that is business, my dear sir— business! Don't regard it so seriously. Join me now and you will be very glad you have done it. You will never regret it, never, if you come to me."

"No," I answered. "No, no!"

For just a second he seemed taken aback, but he gathered himself together quickly and said, "But that is nonsense, Mr. Paderewski. Surely you do not mean it. This is a business proposition I make you, of the utmost importance to your career.

Sentiment should not interfere with it. Surely 'no' is not your final answer."

Again we measured each other with our eyes, and I replied as before, "No, Mr. Wolff. I shall not change my answer. It is no, and it is final."

Wolff simply stared at me a second, then shrugged his shoulders and said, "Well, it seems impossible, but if 'no' is your answer, I must tell you very frankly that you will regret it."

Again we looked into each other's eyes, then Wolff turned and left the room.

At the moment I did not pay much attention to what he said. I only wished to be rid of him then. It was a very disagreeable encounter. But the next day, during the concert (my second appearance), I noticed that I *had* to regret it, as he said. A strange and unbelievable thing happened. The playing of the concerto by the orchestra was simply abominable. It was a catastrophe. My performance was ruined. Why? Alas! Who can say? I do not say that Wolff was responsible in any way for it, but it happened so.

First of all, when I came to the hall to play, I found von Bülow in a great state of nervousness, even of anger. That upset me immediately. I could not understand how a man who was so enthusiastic as he was the day before, and who was so overjoyed at my success then, assuring me over and over again that he had never seen any reception as enthusiastic as mine, could so suddenly change overnight. We were playing the same program that had gone so magnificently the day before. How was this possible? What had happened? I was overwhelmed and terribly hurt. I felt completely in the dark. I could not understand his actions. First he said that I was late, which was ridiculous, because I arrived just before he had to conduct his first number. Altogether his attitude toward me was very strange, and his anger and displeasure unmistakable. It affected me deeply and although it made me more nervous than usual, I cannot say that his temper actually influenced my playing, no, but—it certainly added greatly to my discomfort.

England and a Berlin Enigma

I was not afraid of my concerto. I was perfectly prepared and, after all, I was playing my own composition and, therefore, I had not to be frightened about the opinion of my interpretation—but I was nervous naturally and it was all very disagreeable and unhappy. But I was totally unprepared for the dreadful things that began to happen the moment I started to play. How I went through that concerto I really do not understand to this day, because there were so many mistakes, so many errors on the part of the orchestra and the conductor, von Bülow. It was frightful! It was a nightmare! The whole performance an agony. Everything was absolutely wrong on the part of von Bülow and the orchestra. It was a massacre. But bad as that was, I still had another ordeal to go through. When I began my group of solos in the second half of the program, and started to play the Hungarian March by Schubert-Liszt, von Bülow, who had elected to sit beside the piano that day, suddenly jumped up, pushed his chair back, and ran quickly off the stage and disappeared! Of course, it caused a stir in the audience. People began immediately to whisper and every one became very restless and uneasy. The atmosphere was charged with wonder and a certain amusement. Von Bülow had completely destroyed the mood. It was almost impossible to finish the number. The audience ceased to listen; they were thinking of von Bülow. I realized all that had happened and still played on, but it was an agony indescribable to me.

Von Bülow, it seems, was famous for his ability to provide surprises for his listeners and to attract attention to himself—and in that way hold the constant interest of his audience. It was regarded in Berlin, to a certain extent, with amusement and tolerance, and even in his own recitals people used to say, "What is he going to do now? What next?" That was a deliberate well-known attitude on his part.

Unfortunately his antics, if I may use that word, did not always have very happy results, and certainly in my case it was a tragedy. So when, to cap the climax, he suddenly sprang from his chair and literally ran from the platform during my playing, I realized that it was my doom then and there before the Berlin audience. It was a fatal moment and was regarded by them as a gesture against me. He did not care to listen. That is what his going and his way of going conveyed to every one. The program finished—a perfect fiasco! The catastrophe was complete!

And the cause of all this? Was he in league with Wolff? Ah, that is a question I cannot answer. I do not know. I shall never know. Probably, yes, but I cannot say. I have no proof, but I cannot make any other deduction because the facts are there.

You ask if it was personal jealousy on von Bülow's part. Perhaps, but I do not seriously so think, because he was a man of rather broad mind and of naturally generous inclinations. Still, jealousy is a strange thing, you know, and strange things and deeds are committed in its name. Why he treated me as he did, I shall never know. I can only state the fact that the concert was considered a complete fiasco. As a result of his leaving in the middle of my solo, some of the critics said that my composition was worthless; some others said that I played very beautifully the Nocturne of Chopin which was the first number among my solos, then expressed deep regret that I played such a thing as that Schubert Hungarian Funeral March! It was, indeed, a funeral march to my début in Berlin!

But some other newspapers treated me from a political point of view. They really attacked me and wrote most sarcastically. "Why does this Pole come here?" wrote one journal. "What does he want from an audience like our Philharmonic Society? He has no place with us. Because he wrote that little Minuet does he think he can impose upon us that tedious, abominable, dull concerto of his? How ridiculous!"

Well, I was terribly chagrined and angered, too, at these unwarranted criticisms. I wanted to leave Berlin altogether, but my agent had made contracts for another orchestral concert at the Academy, and two recitals, and I had to play them. I had no choice. The audiences in all these other concerts behaved beautifully. There was great enthusiasm and I had to play many encores. But the *critics* continued their attacks, political and musical—it was absolutely disgraceful. They had nothing to say for me, not a single good word. The mischief was complete.

My publisher, Bock, was so unhappy about it. It affected him deeply. He said, "I cannot understand it. I cannot. I do not know what it means. Have you done anything here to be so viciously treated? Did you offend anybody? What has happened? There must be some reason."

"No," I answered, "no. I am incapable of offending any one. I treat every one with due respect, because, first of all, I respect myself."

After my last recital I saw Bock again and he still spoke of it with great bitterness. "Well, it is all a great mystery," he said, "a great pity, but never mind, we must forget it—perhaps in a year or two, when you come again, everything will be changed. It will all be forgotten then. The same people will perhaps no longer write in the newspapers. Then you will have your revenge, later on."

"No," I said. "I shall never have my revenge because I shall never come back, never. I shall never play in Berlin again." And I have never done so. I have had offers which were just as brilliant and flattering as in America, from Berlin. I have been invited even by the Court, which was a tremendous distinction considering the German spirit. I have played in almost all other cities of Germany, always with pleasure and success, but I never played in Berlin again. In spite of all my political activity: for instance, even up to three years ago, I still had offers from Berlin, invitations from the Government even, to play, with the assurance that I would be received with all the acclaim and honors due to me not only as an artist, but as a statesman. I have always declined, and I am not sorry for it.

A few weeks after the Berlin fiasco I received a charming letter from von Bülow reminding me that I had yet to come to Hamburg to play with the orchestra, because he was conducting these orchestra concerts also. I had to go to Hamburg, because there was a contract already made. So I fulfilled my obligation. I went. He received me as a brother. There was much warmth and cordiality in his manner and in his words. He said, at once, "Now you must come to me, to my house, and have all your meals with us. We will entertain you. You know my wife is a Pole. She will be so delighted to have an opportunity to speak Polish with you, and I shall be very glad, indeed, to have you as my guest." So it was arranged that I was to go to luncheon after the rehearsal. Even the menu was to be specially ordered for me. "Tell me, Paderewski, what you best like to eat. Is there any dish you especially prefer? If so, we shall prepare it, with pleasure."

"Oh," I replied, most tactfully I thought, "at luncheon I must tell you that I prefer your company above all else!"

"Oh, cannibal," he cried, "cannibal!"

Yes, von Bülow was delightful during that Hamburg engagement and I had no more bitterness towards him—it was all wiped away at that meeting, which proved to be the last. I never saw him again.

At the time of my Berlin concert the whole of the German press were convinced that whatever was approved by the German *press* must be recognized by the whole world. They had a great animosity against me, from the start of my career (all this naturally applies chiefly to Berlin), because I had made a success *first* in Paris and London and in several other countries, without having had that stamp of perfection given me by the Berlin press. So they had to treat me to a great extent as an intruder, as some one who had won a certain place in the world, but illegitimately.

VIII

London Memories

I

My first season in London, preceding the Berlin fiasco, had proved a beautiful reality in many ways. Friendships were established then that went on through my life. And first of all in the place of honor, and in my heart, I put my two godmothers, Lady Barrington and her sister, Mrs. Yorke. I met them through those two Roumanian princesses, those rare friends who were of such great assistance to me. I already have spoken about the musical receptions at the house of Princesse de Brancovan in Paris, those splendid gatherings of the aristocracy and artists, and the opportunities I had then to meet people who contributed to the success of my career, which is not to be forgotten even now.

Mrs. Yorke was a most distinguished person. She was the mother of the present Duchess of Portland. Some members of her family were very prominent in British diplomatic circles. The family held a position of great distinction. It was her sister, Lady Barrington, who, thank God, is still alive though she is eighty-seven years old, who gave me constant opportunities to meet British statesmen, as well as many members of the English artistocracy.* Her husband, Sir Eric Barrington, was secretary to Lord Salisbury, the then Prime Minister. She and her sister, Mrs. Yorke, were practically my godmothers, the godmothers of my career as they called themselves, during my first recitals in London. Their efforts and enthusiasms were unceasing. It was a social basis—the springboard of my artistic life in the British capital.

For years and years I used to go, when Sir Eric was alive,

*Lady Barrington died in 1937.

to their house at least once a week. They were dear and wonderful friends. I see Lady Barrington now whenever I am in London. She is old and frail, but she still upholds the tradition of going to my concerts. She never fails to go. That is so touching.

It was through her that something happened which was of vast consequence to the welfare of my country a few years afterward. That was my meeting in her house with Lord Balfour, one of the noblest and loftiest souls I have ever known. At a later moment in my life he played a tremendous rôle. In an age of wise and splendid men he stood apart. And it was a wonderful age, a golden era. Life was at its richest and highest then. It was a great flowering of that English civilization. That I had some little part of that life and great enjoyment in it, is still a spiritual solace to me.

It was at Lady Barrington's house too that I met Henry James many times—the famous American author who was a notable figure in the literary world of London. I liked Henry James immensely from the moment I met him, but there was something that always appeared a bit artificial in his speech. Whether he spoke English, which he spoke beautifully, or French—and his French was perfect—there was something a little too academic for intimate conversation. His turn of mind was always literary. There was always a charming and perfectly rounded sentence ready about everything and everybody. His mind worked liked that. He did not shine in conversation, I remember, but he was a literary giant nevertheless. I feel that I can say here that I loved that man. He was a remarkable person, so cultured, so elegant. He was a distinguished figure in every gathering. After our first meeting at Lady Barrington's house I used to see him very often and we had many long conversations together. We talked about everything under the sun, as Henry James was interested in everything. At that time my English was not my strong point, so we often spoke French together, and his French was a delight. I admired his writings enormously, though I do not think I will go as far as you do in saying that he was the greatest writer of his time, the subtlest and most profound.

I agree with your admiration of the *way* he used, manipulated *words;* it was masterly. I remember that he did not seem as American to me as certain Bostonians or other Americans I had met, although he was truly, deeply American in spite of his having taken up his life in London. There are many stories about his weighty conversations, the slowness and hesitation of his speech when trying to find just the right word to express himself, and the great dignity and solemnity that he exercised upon every one who came near him. That is probably all true during the end of his life when his writing and speech became more and more involved, but when I knew him those talks with him linger in my mind still as of indescribable charm and vivid interest.

I remember that voice of his too. It also had a tremendous charm for me. It was so quiet, so benevolent, so profound, if I may use that word to describe a voice, so *good,* for Henry James was first and foremost a good man—a noble character. And no virtue, in my opinion, is as exhilarating as *goodness.*

Among the many outstanding figures in the musical world of London there was a remarkably gifted man—a good conductor, a brilliant accompanist and a fine teacher, whose chief occupation, however, was singing. His name was Georg Henschel. With the mere shadow of a voice, an ugly, small voice in fact, he could produce the greatest emotional effects. He would completely enthrall his audience and hold them under his spell because he was such a consummate artist. He was a charming fellow too, an extremely enjoyable person, highly intelligent and capable of talking about many things. He and his gifted wife were great favorites in America as in London in those years.

During the season he gave frequent receptions, always with music. At one of these soirées I met H. R. H. Princess Louise, then Marchioness of Lorne, now Duchess of Argyll, an artistic lady of great charm and grace, a painter as well, which I did not know at that time but was to be made aware of in a rather amusing way shortly after. That story comes later.

Then there were Edward Burne-Jones (later knighted) and Sir Laurence Alma-Tadema, the sculptor Gilbert, and many,

many others, all of whom I knew well and who became my friends.

I saw Burne-Jones from a cab before I had the honor of meeting him. His personality impressed me deeply and moved me. I was driving gaily along in a hansom cab one day on my way to St. John's Wood, when suddenly I saw a gentleman approaching. He was walking slowly along and even at that distance he radiated an unusual kind of power and nobility. He had the expression of an apostle, I thought. Instinctively I raised my hat from the depths of my hansom cab and saluted his dignity. I did not know then that it was Burne-Jones, the great portrait painter. A few days later I was taken by a friend to his studio when he made four or five sketches of me, one of which acquired a very wide popularity. It was done in two hours—it was marvellous. I remember that he drew very rapidly, even violently. It became one of his most famous drawings and was known everywhere. The original is here in my house—he was gracious enough to give it to me. A princely gift.

But you are protesting this story I see. You want the Archangel part. I thought so. Mrs. Gaskell, a close friend of Burne-Jones, has told it frequently, I hear, and it has already been written in a book of memoirs including certain stories about Burne-Jones. But you tell me it was from neither of these sources, but from Lady Maude Warrender, that you heard it a short time ago. Ah, that was charming of her. I knew Lady Maude Warrender very well as a delightful hostess, but she comes into my story many years later when I was entertained at her London house. So she is reviving the Archangel story.

Yes, I accept your reproach that you had to hear it first from her, but perhaps you will credit me with a little modesty even at this late day and a certain sensitiveness about my hair, which was very real in those days. Well, you shall have the story: Burne-Jones, it seems, passed me while walking serenely along the street one day and after a moment of swift and astonished contemplation, of which I was quite unconscious, he walked on a few steps, then hurried back and passed me a second time for another swift look, then turned abruptly and returned to his

The Burne-Jones drawing

From a drawing by P. Rajon

Sir Laurence Alma-Tadema

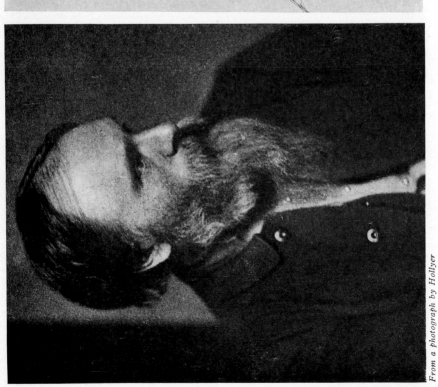

From a photograph by Hollyer

Edward Burne-Jones, 1885

studio in hot haste proclaiming upon his arrival that he had seen an Archangel—an Archangel with a splendid halo of golden hair, treading the London pavements! That he must put his Archangel on paper at once; that he must draw that halo from memory before the image faded. Ah, that was my hair, you see, for there were quantities of it in those youthful days and it looked then exactly as it does in his famous drawing.

And now for the dénouement, the climax of the story. When I was taken to his studio a complete stranger, a few days afterward, he was so surprised at the sight of me on his threshold, that he greeted me with a shout of delight—"My Archangel," he cried, and without another word set to work immediately to complete his drawing, while I stood silent and mystified until it was explained to me later on.

And now you have the story—both stories, but the only thing that really matters is that Burne-Jones honored me by making his masterly silver-point drawing, which is considered one of the finest portraits of the kind ever made.

Naturally we became close friends after that and I met him frequently at the house of my dear friend Lady Lewis, and at Sir Laurence Alma-Tadema's as well; they were all close friends. Burne-Jones, contrary to his appearance (I told you he looked like an apostle), was full of humor. He was really an extremely amusing and lively man. Although he went to all my concerts, I never played for him privately, but I did play for Alma-Tadema, who had a most wonderful piano on which I played many times. The piano was unique in its way and became quite famous through the years. I can almost say, as my host at the hotel in Moscow said of his piano, that it was "not a piano, but a gold mine."

The Tadema piano, too, was more than a piano, it was an autograph album! It was a grand piano, most beautifully inlaid with silver, colored woods and mother of pearl, a kind of mosaic with set-in panels of parchment paper which served for the autographs I have just spoken of. These panels were completely covered with the autographs of the hundreds of distinguished celebrities from all parts of the world who came to the Alma-Tadema house. They became so crowded with signatures that new panels had frequently to be added. I think my name, too, can still be seen on one of the old panels. They were always an object of keen interest to visitors.

This fine piano was built by Broadwood, a famous English firm, and cost two thousand pounds. There is a picture of it which might be of interest to use, although it gives no adequate idea of its exceptional beauty. After Alma-Tadema's death there seemed no one ready to take it and it found its way, as is usually the case, to the great sales room of Christie's in London. It makes one sad to think that it was not rescued by some old friend of those days or by a museum. It was finally bought by Maples', the well-known department store in London, and put on view in one of their departments.

The story and fame of the piano still live somehow, for only two years ago its picture appeared in *The London Telegraph,* and the little story with it. There it still is at Maples' great shop, which has given it sanctuary—I think I may use that term in memory of its distinguished friends. A piano can be a very personal possession, a beloved friend, and sometimes, even an enemy.

There are one or two experiences to relate on this subject, stories that at the time had rather tragic import for me—when my piano became my enemy. I have had many and royal battles with my pianos during my career, battles that had to be fought to the bitter end. But all this belongs in another talk for another day.

To go back now to our original theme.

At this time I was seeing a great deal of Alma-Tadema and I was asked to sit for a portrait by him. I agreed, of course. It was an honor. It was probably the most exacting and elaborate posing for a picture that has ever been done, because at the first sitting I found, to my surprise, that there were three people making my portrait! There were the Princess Louise, Sir Laurence himself, and Lady Alma-Tadema, and all three were furiously painting me at the same time. Each one was constantly begging me to turn *his* way! It was an amazing ordeal; it was not sitting, it was moving all the time, incessant moving. It continued several days and each day was more "moving" than the last. However, the three pictures were finally completed. Lady Alma-Tadema, who was a very gifted painter herself, had made a very small picture of me. Alma-Tadema made quite a masterpiece as far as painting is concerned. The picture painted by the Princess Louise is still in her possession at Kensington Palace. It was quite good but not so successful as to the likeness because, quite evidently, I was not turning enough *her* way! It is very important to have a good light, and they could not all have a good light, hence the constant turning this way and that. It was a most amusing experience, but somewhat of a strain while it lasted.

There was one person in the room that day who did not ask me to turn her way, and for the reason that she was not a painter, but the young daughter of the Alma-Tademas, Miss Laurence Alma-Tadema. She was audience that day and seemed highly amused, I thought, at the predicament I was in. She was my friend through all those years and her unfailing friendship to me and my family and her loving service to Poland during the war are something that I want to speak particularly about. Such friendships are cherished possessions. As I talk of those wonderful days, I feel that perhaps I was specially blessed in that respect. Again we must reserve for a later chapter Miss Alma-Tadema's efforts for Poland during the war.

The Alma-Tadema household was very artistic—all that was of importance in the world of art was to be found in their beautiful home. The whole London world came there. He was a very brilliant and amusing person, and full of kindness.

He was one of the picturesque and famous characters of that time, a wonderful artist and very much the vogue. His famous receptions were, I think, on Monday every week, when the best and most fashionable society of London, and I may say of all the world, gathered there. There was always a musical program and a charming little supper afterward. I often played on these occasions and it always gave me great happiness to do so.

Alma-Tadema was very fond of entertaining and he did it with extreme kindness and tact. He was a princely host. He always had the proper word for everybody—he was so fond of the *ceremony* of receiving. He was a person of most refined taste and of very sure judgment. It was always something extraordinary to me

ST. JAMES'S HALL.

M. PADEREWSKI'S

FIRST & SECOND

Pianoforte Recitals,

Tuesday, June 16, & Tuesday, June 23, 1891,

AT THREE O'CLOCK.

Under the direction of Mr. DANIEL MAYER, 180, New Bond Street, W.

STALLS, 10s. 6d   BALCONY, 3s.   ADMISSION, 1s.

Tickets may be obtained of the usual Agents, and at BASIL TREE's Ticket Office, St .James's Hall.

A. S, MALLETT, ALLEN & Co., Printers, 68—70, Wardour Street, London, W.

The restrained advertisement announcing the second London season

how well he understood music, and how he spoke about it—always with real sentiment and a profound knowledge. Alma-Tadema was one of my very first and best friends in London.

At that time it was the custom for great actors, especially those who had their own theatres, to give receptions after the performance. It was a charming orgy of night life. At 12 or 12:30 you would go to the Haymarket Theatre where Tree was performing, then sometimes to the Lyceum where Irving was playing. I was young, eager to enter into everything and fascinated by the richness of the London life at that time. I accepted many times the invitations of Beerbohm Tree especially, and I was also frequently a guest at supper with Sir Henry Irving. These supper parties were indescribably, delightful.

It was all so gay and charming. A vanished world.

My first London seasons were extremely successful. I was well launched then and the audiences had grown steadily. There was reason to feel that London had now become a part of my regular musical season. It was during my second tour in 1891 that I was invited to play before Queen Victoria. This gratified me very much, for I had an enormous admiration for her. But before I tell you about my concert at Windsor, there is something to be said about the fashion then of playing in private houses in London.

The "at homes" were very popular and played rather an important part in the season of every artist who came to London. Although they were financially satisfactory, or I should say became so, they were not altogether an unmixed blessing. I had countless propositions to play in private houses in London, so many that it even became a difficulty to decide which to accept. I played in several places, but it was very hard, I found, because it was a form of entertainment that was not considered very seriously by the guests. Alas, even the charming hostesses did not regard the event as a concert. I used to feel that they just engaged the artists to permit the company to talk—to hold conversations that were not too attentively listened to. It was really dreadful and I suffered agonies. I resented it to such a degree that on several occasions I was bold enough, and rude enough, to stop playing entirely and then apologize to those engaged in lively conversation for having interrupted them! At first I feared my sarcasm was too subtle for them but, after several experiences, it had its effect.

No, there was no actual dramatic incident, nothing really happened. The guests were more surprised than resentful, but there came a slight improvement in conditions whenever I played, after having reprimanded them. I established a certain standard of behavior that, during my playing at least, there must be no conversation. I would not allow that. When they began to talk —I would stop. And as I was not very well acquainted with the language—I was then just starting my studies in English—I usually spoke to them in French. I would say, "I am very sorry to interrupt your conversation. I deeply regret that I am obliged to disturb you, so I am going to stop for a while now and allow you to continue talking." You can imagine the effect it had! However, it did some good. In certain concerts even, I did it several times, and with remarkable results.

I actually accomplished two things then, and I claim the credit for it. First of all, I educated those fashionable audiences in *how* to listen to music, and the proper attitude toward an artist. Many of them afterward said, "What a change in the audiences now at the 'at homes'! No more talking, thank God."

Secondly, I accomplished another thing for the benefit of my colleagues, because I raised the prices for these private appearances everywhere.

In London at that time, a fee of sixty guineas was the highest price paid for an "at home." I am not speaking, of course, of Adelina Patti, who often sang privately. She always had a really tremendous fee. People would pay simply anything to get her. There was also another popular singer, Madame Albani, a Canadian by birth, who was greatly loved by the English people. She received the unusual sum of one hundred guineas. Albani was a beautiful singer and great favorite and friend of Queen Victoria, which added to her enormous popularity.

Well, I played the first season for sixty guineas. Then I asked two hundred guineas after that, and for several years I received it. But as my concerts increased I was not in such need of earning extra money and could, therefore, dispense with the "at homes" and I was only too thankful to be able to refuse them. It was not much of a pleasure even under the best conditions. There was always noise, certain moving of chairs, and little irritations that were impossible to avoid in a house, and quite understandable. On some rare occasions, yes, it was a pleasure; but in many cases it was really a kind of slavery—to play just because one is paid for it, and then to have to be disturbed by somebody who is entering or leaving the room. On certain occasions, when Royalty came during my playing, the whole audience stood up, of course, and I had to stop, and I also had to bow before the King or Queen, or whoever it was that entered. So I then raised my price to five hundred guineas to make it practically impossible to engage me. That was unheard of and made a certain sensation, but gradually every artist raised his price so that rich people who had to entertain distinguished society, and who engaged great artists, had to pay very large sums for them, which was just and right.

The conditions were such then that, for instance, even in America, when an artist was engaged, he was not allowed to enter by the principal entrance, the front door, but had to go to the side door like the grocery boy. I had that experience myself once in New York. On arrival I was led by the servants to the back entrance. After I had recovered from my amazement, I refused to go through the back door and returned to my hotel. Of course, immediately somebody was sent to me with humble apologies and explanations and I returned and found a small regiment of servants at the front door to usher me in and up the staircase, where the lady of the house was waiting to receive me, overcome with embarrassment and full of futile explanations. How absurd it all seems when one looks back upon it now, and how very funny!

It was in 1891 that Queen Victoria had expressed a desire to hear me play. I think I have already told you that she made a very deep impression upon me then. This statement will bear repetition. She always impressed me as long as she lived.

I was notified by some of the officials of her household that her Majesty wished to hear me. So I went to Windsor. The beauty of that castle, that ancient style of life, impressed me very deeply indeed. It was really an admirable evening. It happened that the Queen was not feeling very well, so she arrived in the hall in an invalid chair. I was then presented to her. She addressed me in beautiful French and impressed me as being a queen in every sense of that often misused word. There was such a majesty about that little woman; although she was very small in size, the feeling about her was one of bigness. She had great nobility.

I was surprised to find that she knew so much about music. Whatever she said was just to the point. Her taste and education were classical, of course. She had studied, among other things, the piano and was said to be one of the few pupils of Mendelssohn—such is the legend—so her favorite composers were either before or during the period of Mendelssohn's life. I had to arrange my program accordingly, and it was very graciously and kindly approved. She expressed the wish to hear me some time again, and often, she said, and her evident pleasure and kindness added something special to the evening that has always lingered in my memory.

The atmosphere at Windsor was rather solemn, if not austere. But after her disappearance that evening—she had to go early to bed—her three daughters came in looking like the three graces, Princess Christian, Princess Beatrice, and Princess Louise. The two last were beautiful at that time. Princess Christian was not as beautiful. She was much older, but was extremely amiable and had a lively and gracious manner, I recall. I had quite a long conversation with them which I enjoyed.

A year or two afterward, I was again invited to Windsor and received still more kindly and graciously than before by the Queen. On that occasion she presented me with her picture. She seemed older and feebler but still a sovereign in every way. She was a wise queen—wise and fortunate. She knew how to select her advisers, and being a woman of vision and astuteness, she accomplished a long and glorious reign. Her hold or influence on her people was tremendous and never lessened. She reigned so long that the people used to say, "She is like the weather in Scotland; it rains and rains and never gives a chance to the sun." There was a certain truth in that saying. Edward came to the throne late in life. He too was a wise sovereign. His great popularity as the Prince of Wales reached to every corner of the world and held to the end of his life. Yes, he was a wise ruler for England. He had a very rare tact and diplomacy and accomplished much good for his people. I met King Edward VII only once, I regret to say. It was at a private musical I was giving. He was not very musical himself; he did not share his mother's fondness for it.

In fact the only musical person in the royal family after Queen Victoria was Queen Alexandra, who was deaf. She had great difficulty in listening to music. I met her first through your beautiful American Lady Randolph Churchill. She was then living opposite Hyde Park, and as I had often met her and her sister, Lady Leslie, in Paris, of course I was invited to visit them in London. Lady Randolph Churchill asked me to a luncheon and then told me that the Princess of Wales was coming specially to hear me play. There I met this charming lady who afterward became Queen of England. Beautiful as she was, she talked to me in such a way as to make me actually shiver with fright, because I did not understand one single word she said. Like most deaf people, she whispered very softly and it was impossible to hear her murmurs. This, added to my inability to understand English (I was just beginning to speak English at that time), made a conversation with her—an agony. She was evidently pleased with my playing because she expressed her pleasure by asking me to go to see her very soon, which, of course, I did and then I played to her again. I played a long program, I remember, consequently our conversation together was short, which was all to my advantage at that moment of my deficient English. The Princess of Wales was the most beautiful creature imaginable. One I shall never forget.

Twenty years later, after the death of the King, I saw her once more. She was then living at Marlborough House, and she invited me, as before, to go and see her. Again I went and again I played for her. She listened most attentively and heard me, it seemed, better than some years before. I had a most pleasant conversation with her before my playing and afterwards, in which the Marquis of Soveral, former personal friend of King Edward, also took a very lively part.

He was a very kind man, charming in manner, highly educated but looking almost like an Oriental, so dark was his complexion. To him is attributed the following witty remark, which went the rounds of London. He once accompanied King Edward to the theatre where a play by Oscar Wilde was being performed. It was having great success—"The Importance of Being Earnest." After the performance the King went with his suite to a supper at the house of Sir Ernest Cassel. Cassel was a very powerful and rich banker at that time, a Jew, and it was a rumor in London that he had the honor and constant privilege of assisting the King in his financial embarrassments. In the course of that supper, King Edward said, "Well, Soveral, what do you think about 'The Importance of Being Earnest'?" And Soveral, with a slightly amused laugh and a quick glance at Sir Ernest Cassel, instantly replied, "What I am thinking just now, Sire, is about the importance of being Ernest—Cassel!" A quick answer! A *double entendre* that, shall we say, hit the proverbial nail on the head. Soveral was famous for his witty quips.

One of the really remarkable men in England at that period was Alfred Harmsworth, who later became Lord Northcliffe and created what is known as the modern newspaper. He played a conspicuous rôle in English affairs, particularly political affairs, later on in his career. Eventually he owned many newspapers and periodicals. In fact, his first publication as a very young man was a periodical called *Answers to Correspondents.* I think that is correct. After that, *The Evening News,* and *The Daily Mail* passed into his hands and in later years he climbed to the very highest point in English journalism when he became owner of that great newspaper, *The London Times.* He was still firmly established on that throne when he died many years later. His was a long and amazing career.

Although this is destroying the whole chronological order of events (because I met Harmsworth in 1895), perhaps it is as well that I again make one of those little detours of which you are so fond. Our meeting came about rather interestingly. There was a gathering of the representatives of the Dominions. Prime Ministers and special delegates of all these Dominions were in London, and Alfred Harmsworth, who was then living in Berkeley Square, invited me to play for this very distinguished company. He at once made a tremendous impression upon me by his temperament, his brilliant way of talking, and by his aristocratic manners in spite of his rather humble origin. He did not belong to the aristocracy, but came from the middle classes. He made in a few years a big fortune through his newspapers, and already then, though a young man, was occupying an exceptionally powerful position. The best evidence of it was in the fact that at his invitation all the delegates of the Dominions, all the dignitaries of those far-away countries, were only too glad to accept his hospitality.

I was fortunate enough to make a favorable impression upon him, because from that day on a friendship began which lasted until his death. On many occasions his generosity and kindness to me have been of great service to my country. Whenever I asked him to take up some problem concerning Poland—I am speaking now about later years, of course—it was done without hesitation and in strict conformity with my request. He had a great influence then. He had contacts with all the newspapers of the world and above all, he controlled, in fact owned, those two tremendous organs, *The London Times* and *The Daily Mail,* one paper appealing to the refined and dignified intellectual public, and the other appealing to the whole of the country practically, and to the younger generation.

His premature death, which ended his great usefulness to the public, has been not only a severe loss to me personally, but to my country as well. Since then *The Times* has completely changed, and even *The Daily Mail* is not the same; it, too, seems to have changed its sentiments towards Poland.

I have lost several of these cherished friends in recent years, Lord Balfour among others. The part they played in my life, the value of their interest and companionship from the very begin-

ning of my first going to London, was of an importance that cannot be measured by any words of mine at this time. Would that
it could, and that I could find adequate expression for my memories of these great men. But time presses. I can only mention
a few of them now, for we must go back to the early struggling days of my career and speak of the next great event,
perhaps the greatest, that brought me to America, the country
of my heart, my second home. This was of colossal importance
and I felt at that time ready for the great undertaking. I was
ready to face even the terrors of the Atlantic, the bridge to the
New World. America, then as now, was a "promised land" to
all European artists, a land of fantastic and fabulous legend,
with money and appreciation flowing out to meet the artist from
the great and lively and generous American public.

IX

America

In the year 1891, Daniel Mayer secured an engagement for me in the United States. The tour was arranged under the auspices of the house of Steinway, the great piano manufacturers who offered me a contract for the first American tour which was to be managed by a member of that famous firm, Charles F. Tretbar. Before going there I had to prepare a very large repertoire. I was aware of the fact that I should have to play many recitals in New York, Boston, and Chicago and several orchestral concerts too. I was asked by Mr. Tretbar, who was arranging my tour of eighty concerts in America, to submit to him a list of all my repertoire. Fortunately, it was already large, but I had to work very hard for several months to refresh my memory and consolidate my fingers. The list I sent Mr. Tretbar contained quite a number of pieces of which I was not so absolutely sure at that moment, and quite especially of the *concertos* with the orchestra, hence this extra work.

Anyhow, I started my preparations for the American tour and for several months (three practically) I practised more than ever before. I realized very clearly that it was the moment to make quite a little fortune. But it was also a very risky step. A certain guarantee, $30,000, was offered for the eighty concerts, by the house of Steinway, and Tretbar had already sold many of these concerts in advance. He did not really expect a great success on this, my first tour, as he explained when we met. He was simply trying to "cover himself" as they say. You know the house of Steinway was not a concert agency, but a great piano firm, and they had no intention of making money with my concerts; their object was the advertisement of the Steinway piano. So it was stipulated in the contract that whatever I might earn over and above the figure mentioned would belong entirely to me. It was a charming, generous contract.

Well, I started off bravely, not doubting for a moment that I should be able to surmount all the difficulties of the enterprise. Before my departure, I had to play a few concerts in England, but those few concerts turned out to be quite a large tour of thirty-eight piano recitals given in a little over six weeks because I was then en route for America. I was not pleased with that but the tour was advertised and I had to keep my engagements, naturally, though it was an extra burden and strain.

Therefore, I was a little tired when I started the voyage on a small inexpensive steamer with the insignificant name of *The Spray,* as I recall it. I sailed on the 3d of November, 1891, and the journey was frightful. It was my first experience as a sailor and even with visions of a promised land luring me on, it was lamentable. There were moments when I wished I had not undertaken it. I was in agony most of the voyage, which seemed endless.

When I finally landed in New York, New York was far from being that land of mountains and shooting towers illuminated so brilliantly and making such an overwhelming impression as now. There were only small, dirty, low buildings near the wharf in those days. We arrived at night. There were hardly any lights and the impression was rather sordid and depressing. Darkness everywhere. How different now! A few people only at the dock as the steamer was not an important one. The night was gloomy and rainy and cold. It was a very ugly atmosphere altogether and added to my depression.

Mr. Tretbar, of Steinway's, came to greet me, but his greeting was in accord with the weather, not very cordial! In fact, he too was rather cold and severe. After the customary greetings, he said a few words which actually made me shiver. "Well," he began, "we hear you have had brilliant successes in London and

America

Paris, but let me tell you, Mr. Paderewski, you need not expect anything like that here in America. We have heard them all, all the pianists, all the great ones, and our demands are very exacting. We are not easily pleased here. Having heard all the best artists in the world every season, we have a certain standard which is very difficult to overcome. We are exacting, I repeat to you, and you must not imagine that you can achieve here a tremendous success at all! So, as a beginning I want to warn you now that we already have heard the greatest virtuosi, Rubinstein, von Bülow, etc., and we also have here pianists of big reputation and remarkable talent and importance. Their demands are modest because they know that piano music is not as well rewarded as singing or even violin playing. So you should not, I repeat, expect extraordinary houses. Although I have done my best for you, it is nothing very remarkable."

Well, that was a blow to me. Before I had been in America ten minutes, I was met by discouragement on every side. Mr. Tretbar's fateful words destroyed my last faint hopes. There was to be nothing left then for me over and above my guarantee, and I had dreamed of a richer harvest. But there was nothing to be done about it. I was under contract, my expenses were paid, and at least there was the guarantee of $30,000 (which at that time was a very large sum of money) to be depended upon. But at this first moment of arrival, when Mr. Tretbar was so graciously welcoming me, I was so depressed, so discouraged, that I asked immediately when the next steamer would leave for Europe. My one thought then was to return instantly. I did not ask Mr. Tretbar naturally, but inquired through my secretary, who also felt very strongly these discouraging words of Tretbar.

Immediately upon arrival we went to the Union Square Hotel, and that first night I intended to run away from the hotel. It was full of insects. Wherever I looked, in every corner, there were spots black with a mass of insects. I did not know what they were, I had never seen anything like them before. Then, there were mice in the hotel too. I spent a dreadful night. Mr. Tretbar, it seems, naturally wanted to make the expenses as small as possible, in order to save money, and that was why I was sent to that awful hotel.

Early the next day I sent Goerlitz, my secretary, to Steinway's to tell them that I could not live in that hotel another hour, and to ask where there was a decent hotel I could move to, because I could not remain longer in that horrible place filled with noisy commercial travellers, and so forth, not to mention mice and bugs!

The Steinways were very agreeable and said at once, "Of course if Paderewski is not comfortable there he must go to another hotel." So my secretary replied, "Mr. Paderewski says that if a better hotel is too expensive, he will gladly pay the bill himself, but he cannot stay where he is."

"No," they said. "Oh, no, we have made our contract and we must abide by it and provide him with every comfort." They were really fine people, the Steinways, with a high degree of honor and justice.

So Goerlitz secured rooms for me at the old Windsor Hotel. It was then one of the biggest buildings in New York. It was four stories high! A very old-fashioned but comfortable hotel with good food. It was on Fifth Avenue and 46th Street.

The largest monument of the city at that time on Fifth Avenue was the old reservoir at 42d Street. I must confess that that was the most impressive thing about New York, after the Cathedral, in those days, because it had such a huge imposing form. There was not very much imagination about the building, but it appealed to one as an old fortress, something from the remote past, something like a medieval castle. I was delighted always to stop and look at it because it was such an enjoyment for my eyes. It gave me pleasure. It was not even, but narrower at the top. It was really beautiful. Now there is the Library standing there, which is not as beautiful as that citadel was, in my opinion.

After settling myself in the old Windsor Hotel, I immediately began arrangements for the coming tour.

But discouraging as my greetings were at the pier on arrival,

America

they were nothing compared to what I learned when I got the plan of the tour. I had imagined that it would be graduated, at first starting with a few concerts, then a little rest, then more concerts, etc. But, no, nothing of the sort, it was concert after concert with only a day or two between: a continuous tour, and I had to begin in New York with *three orchestral* concerts, at which I had to play *six* piano concertos in one week and a group of solos. It was incredible! Six piano concertos in one week! I found myself repeating it over and over again, "six piano concertos—six piano concertos"! When Mr. Tretbar told me that unbelievable truth, I was simply stunned. At first I could only stare at him. I could not believe he was in earnest. But I soon found out that he was, and it was six concertos or nothing! True, I had four of them ready, but the other two, although I had played them once or twice, were not in my opinion yet ready for public performance. Why, in Europe, I might not have an opportunity of playing six concertos in one season. In one entire season, six concertos would be tremendous. But in New York, I was expected to play six concertos in one week!

I was completely dazed at first. The dreadful knowledge of what faced me had a paralyzing effect. At that moment I longed for the earth to open and swallow me up. It was superhuman. Perhaps now, after all these years, I should be able to accomplish such a colossal thing after a long preparation, but then, at the begining of my career, with my small experience and at such short notice, it was really something terrific. I said to myself, "Perhaps I shall not be able to survive it, perhaps I will only be able to play five concertos, perhaps"—oh, it was a kind of madness.

But somehow, I gathered my courage together and started practising. I must add here that after the week of six concertos (already advertised) I had in addition to play six recitals. These recitals were scheduled for the following two weeks, which meant practically a concert every other day and a different program each time. That was again Mr. Tretbar's doings, it seems, and one of the reasons, as he told me afterwards (because we later became good friends), was this: he had a particular friend then, a pianist, whom he adored, and he did not want anybody to make a bigger success than that pianist, and especially me. A strange reason.

Well, I started my work. If I had to do it again, probably I should run away somewhere, to Alaska, or Patagonia, but very far away from mankind.

I played the first time at Carnegie Hall. Walter Damrosch was the conductor. He was a very young man at that time and he gave me a great deal of pleasure as a conductor and as an accompanist. As an organizer and a progressive figure in the musical world, Damrosch has contributed since then very much to the progress of music in the United States, and up to this moment his activities, both musical and civic, are outstanding. He comes again into our story at a later moment. Our friendship began when I made my début forty-six years ago, and still lives on. I made my début in New York under his baton. Many people came to that first concert from outside. There were two concertos and a group of solos at that first concert. It was very well received, but not yet any kind of sensation. I was severely criticized in some papers; in some others, very highly praised, but altogether it was not a phenomenal success, no.

They waited for the second concert. But for the second concert I had to make the rehearsal the morning after the first one, and I was not yet prepared.

I want now, even at the risk of repeating myself, to say that the average person, or the great public, let me say, has no idea of the amount of practice necessary, absolutely necessary, in the presentation of a concert. It is not sufficient to know and to play well (or even beautifully) the numbers arranged. It is not sufficient to have played the same program the week before (and even to repeat it the next day) without incredible hours of practice and concentration. And so it is with every performance, hours of practice and mental work, and all this *in addition* to the never-ending finger practice—shall I call it—the technique. That is why it is so necessary for sufficient time *between* concerts for

FIRST CONCERT,

TUESDAY EV'G, NOVEMBER 17TH. 1891,

AT 8.15 O'CLOCK.

PROGRAMME.

---

1. OVERTURE—*In Springtime,* ....GOLDMARK

   ORCHESTRA.

2. CONCERTO—No. 2, in G minor, ...CAMILLE SAINT-SAËNS

   Andante sostenuto.   Allegro scherzando.   Presto.

   IGNACE J. PADEREWSKI.

3. AIRS DE BALLET from *Iphigenie en Aulide,*...........GLUCK

   ORCHESTRA.

4. PIANO SOLI—*a,* Nocturne,
   b, Prelude,
   c, Valse,   } .... FRED. CHOPIN
   d, Etude,
   e, Ballade,

   IGNACE J. PADEREWSKI.

INTERMISSION.

---

5. CONCERTO—No. 1, Op. 17,..........IGNACE J. PADEREWSKI

   Allegro.   Romanza.   Allegro molto vivace.

   IGNACE J. PADEREWSKI.

6. "RIDE OF THE VALKYRIES," ....WAGNER

   ORCHESTRA.

Steinway & Sons' Pianos used at these Concerts.

The first New York appearance, at Carnegie Hall, with
Walter Damrosch conducting

preparation of each program as you play it. This lack of time, the rush of one concert after another upon my arrival in New York, was something unheard of to me, something I was utterly unprepared to face, and I was overwhelmed with the sheer physical aspect of the task before me. But youth was on my side, and an unbounded ambition and will to conquer—though the labor involved was superhuman. I am still paying in flesh and blood for my first New York season, and you shall soon see why.

When I was told that the rehearsal for my next concert was to take place directly after my first one, it is not an exaggeration to say that I was really overcome. I was frightfully exhausted from the first, and knew that I must be up and ready in the morning for the colossal task of an orchestral rehearsal. Then the trouble began—more trouble. I found that I could not practise in the Hotel Windsor, because it was full of very old people, residents, who would not tolerate music at night, the only time I could work. So I went to 14th Street, to the piano warehouse of the Steinways. It was the only solution. I could not, naturally, go in the middle of the night to practise in a hotel or a house, so Steinways' piano room was my only hope.

I remember when I appeared at the door, how startled the night watchman looked, and I must have presented a strange appearance. The watchman, however, opened the room where the pianos were stored, and there, in that cold and gloomy loft, I began my practising. There were no lights except the two candles on the piano. It must have been a strange sight as I think back upon it—the empty room, with two fluttering candles and the two men, the night watchman and my secretary, each snoring loudly in his corner as I worked on until morning. That was all I had for inspiration! I would not like to go through that experience again.

I practised five hours that night, after my concert, remember, and I prepared the concerto and was ready the next morning for rehearsal at ten o'clock. After the rehearsal, I practised again all day for the concert. How did I do it? Ah, I cannot tell you how I endured it, but the second concert, in spite of my fatigue, was much better than my first one. There was a larger attendance (again at Carnegie Hall) and some real demonstration of public favor that day which gave me still more courage to help the dreadful fatigue. It was a little ray of hope, without which I do not know whether I would have been able to go again that night to the old Steinway warehouse and prepare for the *third* rehearsal. I had to play the Rubinstein Concerto and the Chopin E Minor Concerto, and some important solo numbers. It was an afternoon concert and it had taken me seventeen hours of the one day to practise. My arms were dropping off. But I could not have rest. I could not cancel or postpone the concert—it was impossible. So I played that Rubinstein Concerto, and the reception was really remarkable, tremendous. That was the real beginning of my career in America.

There was a very large sum in the box office, too; for that time it was phenomenal. Mr. Tretbar came and congratulated me and said, "Well, it is surprising what you have made in this concert." There was, I think, about $3000. They had never had that sum before—never.

Two days later I gave my first recital. Preoccupied with the responsibility of my concerts and incessant work, I had really no idea *where* my first recital would take place—in Carnegie Hall I supposed—and only on the day of the concert was I told by my secretary that it was in the *small* hall at the Madison Square Garden.

"A small hall," I cried; "what does this mean, what small hall?"

"Oh," Goerlitz answered, "it is the little hall in Madison Square."

"But," I said, "this is impossible. It cannot be. There is some mistake. Why, I have just filled Carnegie Hall, why am I put in this small hall now?"

Goerlitz simply shrugged his shoulders and said, "Mr. Tretbar has arranged it."

I was terribly upset. I felt the deep injustice of this. "But," I said to Goerlitz, "this is wrong, absolutely wrong. There must be a certain force that is working against me. I have just had great progress in my three concerts, each one being larger in receipts and better in appreciation and now after all that success—after having filled Carnegie Hall to capacity, I am sent to a small hall for my first recital." I was indignant. I was outraged. It was wrong, illogical, unfair, and so I expressed myself.

Tretbar got the full blast of this, and came at once to see me and I told him exactly what I thought about it all and expressed myself in terms that were quite justified. I may add that they were very strong! Of course, he had many explanations and excuses, but I cut them short once and for all when I said, "It is unworthy of a firm like the Steinways to treat me in this way."

At that time there was nobody except William Steinway, the head of the firm, to decide things. His was the final voice. There were many subordinates, of course, but no one with real authority. Unfortunately for me, William Steinway was very ill at that moment. He was suffering from a severe attack of rheumatism and there was no one to whom I could appeal. Mr. Tretbar was unable and unwilling to assume responsibility and simply said, "Well, we have our policy and we cannot change it at a moment's notice. You are under contract and you will have to play in the hall that we have already arranged for." So there was nothing to be done. I was caught in a trap and in the small hall I must play.

I gave my first recital there. I think it went very well. I had arranged my program very carefully I felt, reserving the very best and most brilliant pieces of my repertoire for the last three recitals, which I was very sure I could arrange to have in Carnegie Hall in spite of Mr. Tretbar and other difficulties.

At that first recital, I looked out at the hall very particularly. It was not full, but that did not disturb me in spite of the fact that Mr. Tretbar came to the dressing room to see me, smiling rather sarcastically I thought, even triumphantly. "Well," he cried, rubbing his hands nervously together, "you see this small hall is quite large enough for you. I told you how it would be and you must realize now that you were mistaken." It was his moment of triumph and he was all smiles. But I said nothing. I bided my time.

The second recital was much better attended. The public, especially those who were at the orchestral concert at Carnegie Hall, when seeing the announcement that my first recital was to be in a small hall, had the impression that the management had no great faith in me—letting me play in a second-rate hall. So they did not come. Such was and still is my belief.

But the first recital made rather a favorable impression. I was then quite alone, with no orchestra. Many more people came to the second, and the third recital on Saturday in the afternoon was crowded, "packed full" as you say—there were not even seats enough for those who wanted to get in. People were turned away. After this concert I may add that Tretbar did not have any comments to make about the size of the audience!

It was a great triumph and I felt myself on solid ground at last. I was determined to have no more small halls; my mind was made up. I said to Goerlitz, "Now, this is the end. I am not going to play any more. I shall break the contract. They may make a lawsuit, they may do anything they please, I will not play again in that small hall. I shall go back to Carnegie Hall or I shall not play in New York again."

Well, Goerlitz realized my determination and the importance of all this, and the message was taken to William Steinway himself, and by my secretary. This time there were no negotiations with Mr. Tretbar. William Steinway put an end to all the trouble, and he decided at once that all my concerts thereafter should be given in Carnegie Hall.

You can imagine my relief, and my appreciation, too, of Mr. Steinway's decision. It showed his clear-sightedness and his acumen, also his great sense of justice. Good man—a splendid man, one so easy to deal with, so clear of vision—a loyal friend to the end of his life.

My last three recitals were at Carnegie Hall and were a great success artistically and financially. The last two were completely "sold out." I should have been very happy then because it was a great victory, and all those efforts and labors crowned by success, but I was then suffering so terribly from overwork, I was so exhausted and in such cruel pain that every concert was an agony for me.

II

I must not forget to tell you now that directly after my first appearance I had the opportunity of meeting most of the critics of New York, Boston, and Philadelphia, and all this was arranged by Mr. Tretbar, who looked after everything. On the night after my first concert in New York, Tretbar invited all the critics to a big supper at which I was to make the personal acquaintance of these gentlemen of the press. I still preserve very pleasant recollections of that meeting. For instance, William J. Henderson—he was a very cultured and able critic, with whom I had many occasions to talk. Sometimes he did not agree with my interpretation, but that is quite natural. He was always very fair and sincere, I felt, in what he said.

I also met a great many times, in Boston, Mr. Philip Hale, of *The Boston Herald*. He was a highly educated man of great culture and he knew many things besides music. But his criticisms were sometimes—I would not say adverse, but so sardonic, in their suggestion as to be unmistakable. There was always some little personal remark. He was witty, and wit is a very dangerous weapon in a critic, and in any one practically, because witty people cannot refrain from making witty remarks, and witty remarks are not always amusing when they are a little bit ironical. But my recollections of Philip Hale, in spite of this, are very sympathetic. There was something in me though, which always shocked him—I cannot find another word for it—and that was my hair! He apparently could never get accustomed to it, nor could he resist certain facetious allusions to it. I must confess it was always a question in my mind whether Hale was envious of my hair, or simply disturbed by the sight of it. At any rate he always had to overcome to a certain extent his feeling and his annoyance, though it often trickled through into some rather caustic remarks in his notices, which was natural enough, feeling as he did.

Richard Aldrich, on the contrary, did not mind my hair at all. He was a splendid man—just, intelligent, and always impartial, and wrote very beautiful English. Henderson, of whom I have just spoken, and whom I knew at the beginning of my career when Tretbar had my management completely in his hands, was one of the New York critics and one of the best, and his criticisms in *The New York Sun* carried great weight with music lovers. There were so many critics at that time that I knew throughout the country that were kind to me and whom I should like to mention now.

In Boston, for instance, there was William Apthorp, of *The Transcript*. And Reginald De Koven in New York, a very delightful fellow. "Reggie," as we called him, became one of my personal friends later on, though he started with very adverse criticisms of my concerts which continued for some time.

In Chicago there was another very charming fellow, a critic on *The Tribune,* William Hubbard. He was an admirer from the start, but he was almost as dangerous as Finck in his admiration. Henry T. Finck, take him all in all, was a very fine critic. He wrote for that distinguished paper, *The Evening Post,* which stood high in public opinion and journalism in those days. Finck was a lovable man and a faithful friend and gave me many proofs of the warmth of his personal devotion. And of James Huneker, that brilliant, versatile writer and man, there is a great deal to say, but he and Finck, too, come in another chapter, where they can receive more than a mention.

The job of critic is an arduous and at the same time a delicate one, and a great responsibility must always be theirs. Every artist realizes this and their enormous influence on the public. Those were the days when I knew the critics personally and met them frequently on my first tour in America. Of the present day critics, I know very few. My relationships with the American critics, unfortunately, since the war have not been renewed (with the exception of Olin Downes, who has been at Morges to see me).

The Paderewski Memoirs

Many years ago I gave up forever reading notices of my concerts. This was a luxury that I allowed myself after a certain period. There were many reasons for it which are too personal and involved to interest you, but my appreciation of their criticisms is none the less sincere because I do not happen to know them personally.

During that first American tour I was completely in the hands of Mr. Tretbar. He arranged everything, but there is still something I wish to add to this now that is of some interest and certainly of some amusement. He managed all the concerts, acting somewhat as a great Field Marshal, sending out his orders and directions through the country, but never moving from New York himself. The General in command, however, was quite another affair. He was a man appointed by Tretbar, hired by him to execute his orders, an Englishman, a very fine, charming old fellow by the name of C. T. Fryer. He was the practical manager and travelled continually and was present at all my concerts. In other words, to put it simply, he did the work.

After the first season, on my return, Mr. Tretbar satisfied himself with the rôle of Supreme Council. Mr. Fryer was again the manager, acting with complete understanding of my secretary, Mr. Hugo Goerlitz, whose position had, shall we say, perhaps just a little bit "turned" his head, because he believed then that he was really the boss! That is an American expression which I think particularly fits the case. Goerlitz was a German and a fairly educated man. He belonged to a good family. His brother was a general and I knew his father and mother very well. They were such nice old people. But Goerlitz was certainly an adventurous character. And now I want to correct an impression, which at the time caused some considerable misunderstanding. Goerlitz was never my manager. He liked to feel that he was and that, of course, came through his ambition. He wanted to be something higher, more powerful, than a secretary. Being a secretary, he was a subordinate; as manager, he could quite a little lord it over me. But, contrary to all impressions, he was never my manager, never. He was my secretary, and a very efficient one, for about nine years, from 1891 to 1900, and he travelled everywhere with me during that period, which, with all its success, was an adventurous and stormy one.

The position of manager is quite a curious one psychologically. You know in some cases, and it is natural enough, a manager often actually becomes the artist, at least in his own mind. He is so used to arranging and managing affairs in speaking *for* the artist, that he even in his telegrams, also in conversation, sometimes speaks of himself *as* the artist! I will give you a very amusing little comment on this. Telegrams used often to come to me signed with my manager's name, C. T. Fryer, saying, "I refuse to play on such and such a date," or "Yes, I accept. I will play at such and such a concert." Even the secretary did it after a time. It was very contagious, you see. When I first saw one of these strange telegrams, I was dumbfounded. Fryer brought me the first one and I asked him what it meant. "Oh," he said, "that is just a custom; we all do it. It means nothing. Your secretary has simply signed this with his own name. All managers do that." Fryer went on, "It is a kind of habit they get into. They sign their own name for the artist. You know we managers get to feel that we own the artist, and sometimes," he said laughingly, "some of us even think we *are* the artist! Why, I have often heard managers say, 'Well, I played the other day to a very full house,' or 'I sang beautifully at the opera last night. Did you hear me?'"

Well, this was my first experience in such tactics and it certainly had a very ludicrous side. Afterwards I became a bit more accustomed to the idea, but I think I always resented it a little. But it always amused me in spite of that. The attitude of Goerlitz reminded me very much of my good old friend Stengel (the husband of Madame Sembrich, and her manager), who was a great offender in this respect. I heard him many times, when Sembrich had to appear, or refuse to appear, say, "Oh yes, I am going to sing tonight," or, "I have a cold tonight and have refused to sing at the opera," or, "We are singing next Monday in 'The Barber.'" It always made me laugh, it was so strange! So absurd! I remember one particular occasion—the great celebration of Sembrich's thirty years or so in the opera. There was a supper in her honor and many distinguished people made addresses. I was asked to speak, too, so I thought, now is the time to make a little facetious comment on this strange managerial habit of actually becoming the artist. After opening my speech with the usual introductions, I said that it was with special pleasure I found that Madame Sembrich herself was singing, and *not* her husband, as I had been led to believe, when I heard him a few days before say to a comrade, *"We* are singing at the great banquet tomorrow night," and added, "I have decided to sing Schumann's 'Nussbaum.' It is such a favorite." Of course, this created great laughter and Stengel himself was delighted. I then went on and elaborated my theme. I said, "I have heard him so many, many times say, 'I am not going to sing tonight,' or, 'Yes, I am singing tonight' that I can only say I came in great trepidation fearing that he actually *would* sing tonight!" More laughter. "But," I added, turning to Madame Sembrich, "thank God, he is *not* going to sing tonight—it is Madame Sembrich herself who is to appear." The audience quickly caught on and burst into roars of laughter. So the whole occasion ended very happily and even had some little notice in the press.

But times have changed and I think it was only the managers of that period who indulged in that way of talking. They owned the artist—simply owned him.

Mr. Charles Ellis of Boston, a most accomplished gentleman, followed Fryer and Tretbar. Since then I have had absolutely no trouble or annoyance of any kind, and I may add, *sotto voce,* he, Ellis, never played himself. No, he never refused, or played— for me! Nor does Mr. George Engles, my present manager.

These comments, I see, amuse you—well, they amuse me still.

Life has a way of repeating itself, and in America, as in London and Paris, every one was very kind to me, and I was immensely struck then, and I still am, with the constant hospitality and friendly feeling of the American people. I was everywhere received with touching evidences of their interest and friendship. The whole American "scene," as your Henry James called it, was of a vitality and freshness unlike anything I had ever known. The names of hundreds of interested and kindly people flock to my mind—charming acquaintances interested in my career, and all a part of the audiences that I found to welcome me throughout the land. Many of them became close friends as years went on, and Richard Watson Gilder was one of the first who crossed my path and became a staunch friend and supporter in those early days.

The Gilder family was unique, even in New York. It was the most charming household imaginable—he, a real poet, and she an angel! He was the editor of *The Century Magazine,* a distinguished literary magazine then, but now no longer in existence. The Gilders held an exceptional position in New York society —they had then what was perhaps the only thing approaching the so-called "literary salon," so popular in Europe. In their interesting old house in Eighth Street gathered all the great visiting artists, musicians, distinguished writers, sculptors, painters, and politicians who came to America. Gilder also held a unique position in the literary world then. He was a connaisseur of art and of life. He appreciated and recognized at once the unusual in everything—in people as well. He was a most loyal friend and beautiful character. There are many interesting things to say about the quality of his friendship, his loyalty to your great President, Grover Cleveland, his warm devotion to Eleanora Duse, the great Italian actress, for it was he who first recognized her talents and hailed her as the supreme genius when she came, poor and unknown, to America.

Mark Twain, another great American who was a friend and neighbor, was a very vital part of the Gilder household. I met him there, and the beautiful impression he made upon me abides with me still. He was a purely American product, some one that only America could have produced, in the quality of his mind, his humor and character. I think he remains an undimmed figure in your history. The years will not diminish his towering qualities and virtues. I spent many happy hours with them there—so many joyous occasions, they crowd my memory and still warm my heart. The Gilder house was a kind of home to me, a real home during those first years in America. I always looked forward to going there, it was such relaxation and happiness to be with them and participate in the life of that delightful family. There were charming children and it was so warm and friendly. One of the children, Francesca, now married to a New York doctor, then a very little girl, was a great favorite of mine. She was always very serious about everything she did and was also very shy. There is rather a nice little story that has followed me down through the years in connection with Francesca. It happened during my second tour, when everything was going at top speed and my concerts were crowded and enthusiasm was at its highest pinnacle.

I remember going to the Gilder house one afternoon and finding Mrs. Gilder alone in the drawing room with the little Francesca, who it seems was waiting for her governess to arrive and show her mother a new dance she had learned. Mrs. Gilder conceived the idea that I, too, would enjoy the dance and asked me to remain. Well, to make the proverbial long story short, the governess did not appear, much to the distress of little Francesca. It was then that I met my first, shall we say, Waterloo, for I offered to play for Francesca to dance—offered to take the place of the English governess who always played her dance music. In fact, I was so vain, or perhaps I may say courageous, as to insist upon playing for Francesca, much to Mrs. Gilder's delight, but apparently not to Francesca's! Mrs. Gilder, I remember, jumped from her chair and said, "Oh, Francesca, how delightful, how kind of Mr. Paderewski! Think, darling, how wonderful it will be when he plays for you. That will be something for you to remember all your life; it will be something you can tell your own little girls when you grow up—that Mr. Paderewski once played for you to dance." And so forth, and so on.

Still Francesca remained silent, but neither her mother nor I perceived her doubts, for at once I sat down at the piano and made two or three preliminary notes and learned that it was a kind of minuet that Francesca was to dance. I tried several things and finally, with her mother applauding and smiling and encouraging, Francesca unwillingly began. We went on for a few moments and it seemed to me that everything was quite all right. But not so Francesca. After various attempts and a few false starts, she stopped suddenly and refused to take another step! Mrs. Gilder's consternation was pathetic. "Oh, Francesca," she cried, "what is it? What is the matter? Why don't you go on with your dance?" But Francesca only shook her head; she said nothing. I hopefully continued to play, but not another step would she take, and then the dreadful thing happened. "Francesca," Mrs. Gilder cried, "what is the matter? Don't you *like* Mr. Paderewski's beautiful playing?" We both waited in a dreadful silence for the answer. It came! With tears running down her poor little face, in a husky and frightened voice Francesca said, "Oh, no, no, Mama. I cannot dance when Mr. Paderewski plays, I cannot. I'd rather have my governess. *She* knows how to play for me."

Mr. Gilder died many years ago and Mrs. Gilder's death followed not long after. The old house in Eighth Street is no longer a rendezvous. The curtain has rung down forever on those loyal, devoted friends. A lovely household of early America.

Andrew Carnegie was one of the prominent and extremely picturesque figures in America when I arrived there. I think perhaps in the parlance of the day you would count him among your first citizens. He was a man of vast wealth. He had an extraordinary business career and his name was known throughout the world. It was on the occasion of my first concert in America that I met him and I saw him afterward in England and Scotland very often. We became good friends and I played for him, and visited him often during the early American days. He did not live then in the great house where his wife now lives, but somewhere much more humble in 56th or 57th Street. He was a remarkable person, and while he was not in any sense of the word a patron of the arts, he was very fond of music, and especially fond of his native bagpipes—a true Scotsman.

Years later I used to visit him at Skibo Castle, and how well I remember those bagpipes! When there were guests in the castle, every morning without fail, and early too, there came an orchestra of pipes and they played before the rooms of every guest to awaken them for breakfast. The intention was charming but the experience was not always agreeable.

Carnegie was a Laird and he wore the costume too. He delighted in that, but I think he never wore it in New York. Before dinner there was again a procession of those bagpipes which led the guests into the dining room. He had many musical customs, shall I say, for after luncheon and again after dinner, there was an organist at hand who gave a real program of music for the entertainment of guests. So I think we are safe in saying that he was very fond of music. I did not notice any trace of a higher musical culture, but he certainly liked the bagpipes and his organ recitals.

Of his charities I cannot speak except, of course, his libraries. His donation of libraries throughout the United States (I don't know how many) was phenomenal. There are libraries everywhere, in almost every town, I think I may safely say. He was always a good friend to me and later on I shall speak of something that he once offered to do for me. That story does not belong here.

Now let us pick up again the thread of my first American season. The recital, or "at home," in private houses was not so popular in New York as it was in London. I had only a few engagements, but there was one special arrangement, I recollect, when four recitals were organized at the studio of a famous painter who had at that time a big reputation in New York, Mr. William Chase. At the Chase studio I gave four concerts, and all were crowded to such an extent that people were actually sitting next to me, so close they almost prevented me from playing. I felt suffocated. Although it was a gracious and very flattering tribute on the part of these devoted friends, the performance was nevertheless an ordeal.

A committee of my New York friends was formed to organize these concerts, of most distinguished musical people headed by Mrs. William H. Draper. There were also Miss Etta Dunham, Miss Eleanor Blodgett, the Gilders, Miss Arnold, Mrs. Charles Ditson, wife of the well-known music publisher, a popular hostess of those early days, and many others. Mr. George Vanderbilt, too (a delightful fellow), I remember among the men.

But all these names are not important now. The interesting thing is that these recitals at the Chase studio made something of a sensation. They were fashionable and most exclusive. While the studio was big enough for its own purposes, it was not agreeable when some three or four hundred people were crowded into it. In fact it was dreadful. I do not think that at that time studio music was much in vogue. It was just a lionizing idea—a stunt (I think that is the proper word for it) so often indulged in by ladies in search of celebrities.

The most agreeable and enjoyable private house in which I played in America was that of Mrs. Bliss in Santa Barbara, and I played there a number of times. Whenever I was in California, she asked me to play for her and I always did it gladly, for her love and appreciation of music were very rare. To play in her house was an experience unlike anything else I found—it was like celebrating a mass. The atmosphere of silence was like that of a temple. It was beautiful and inspiring.

There was still one other house where I played with particular pleasure, yes, with affection, and that was the house of Joshua Montgomery Sears, a distinguished Bostonian. They were my beloved friends from the beginning and it was a delight to go there, and their beautiful house in Boston was a haven of hospitality. That house was a landmark in my artistic career. Sears was a perfectly delightful fellow, cultivated, interesting and amusing, and I always looked forward to being under his roof because, among other pleasures, he had a most beautiful room built especially for music. On one occasion—it was his birthday—I came down from Portland, Maine, to play in that beautiful room with the entire Boston Symphony Orchestra, which will give you some idea of its size. This was a little birthday surprise for him and it was a gala occasion—everything on a grand scale.

There was another concert that season with the Boston Orchestra which was specially noteworthy. It was given to raise funds for the Washington Arch in Washington Square, New York. The Arch was not yet finished, and it was Mr. Gilder who arranged the concert and asked me whether I would be willing to play. Of course I was very glad to. It was my first concert for a public benefit and Major Higginson, of Boston, hearing about it, suggested, with his usual generosity, that in addition to my program I play a concerto or two with orchestra. He followed up his suggestion with the princely offer of sending the Boston Symphony Orchestra to New York for that purpose. So it developed into a great affair. The concert was given at the Metropolitan Opera House and there was a very large attendance and a big sum was collected, and Gilder was the chief spirit of the occasion. I think we must try to find one of the old programs.

III

All this was adding to the popularity and establishment of my name in America. After the first New York season I went to Boston, where I had at once a great success. Perhaps it was due to the fact that I already had friends in the Boston Symphony Orchestra, Timothy and Joseph Adamowski and some others. Then, too, the conductor of the Boston Symphony, Arthur Nikisch, whom I had met before in Europe, was my good friend, and all that made my first appearance there much easier than in New York. I was among friends. And the Boston Orchestra was magnificent.

Yes, I was among friends and I was happy at the thought of being with the Adamowskis again—Tim and Joseph—and they were delighted that I was coming. It was all a great contrast to the New York début, where I was entirely alone and knew nobody. Both the Adamowski boys were members of the orchestra —Tim was the first violin and Joseph the 'cellist—and they were both members of the famous Tavern Club of Boston, which had a most distinguished membership and was the rendezvous of the wittiest and most prominent professional men in all walks of life. It was all very delightful and I have cherished memories of my connection with the Tavern Club, which continue up to the

METROPOLITAN OPERA HOUSE.

Sunday Evening, March 27th, 1892,

AT 8.15 O'CLOCK.

FOR THE BENEFIT OF THE WASHINGTON ARCH FUND.

LAST APPEARANCE OF

PADEREWSKI,

(Leaving for Europe on March 29th, 1892,)

AND THE ENTIRE

Boston Symphony Orchestra,

GENEROUSLY OFFERED TO MR. PADEREWSKI FOR THIS OCCASION BY COL. HIGGINSON.

ARTHUR NIKISCH, ... **Conductor.**

PROGRAMME.

OVERTURE—*Tannhäuser,*...RICHARD WAGNER

ORCHESTRA.

CONCERTO in A minor,.....................................ROBERT SCHUMANN

Allegro affettuoso.   Intermezzo: Andantino grazioso.   Allegro Vivace.

PADEREWSKI.

OVERTURE—*Benvenuto Cellini,*................................HECTOR BERLIOZ

ORCHESTRA.

CONCERTO—Op. 17,..PADEREWSKI

Allegro.   Romanza.   Allegro molto vivace.

PADEREWSKI.

POËME SYMPHONIQUE—*Le Rouet d'Omphale,*...........CAMILLE SAINT-SAËNS

ORCHESTRA.

HUNGARIAN FANTASIA,.......................................FRANZ LISZT

PADEREWSKI.

STEINWAY & SONS' PIANO USED AT THIS CONCERT.

present, for I never fail to go there when I play in Boston, and there is always a royal welcome awaiting me.

There is an old, in fact very old, but still amusing anecdote connected with my first appearance at the Tavern Club which followed directly after my début in Boston, forty-six long years ago. I played there for the first time with the Boston Symphony, as I have already mentioned, and it was all very exciting, and I remember so well to this day the public rehearsal in the afternoon (which was really my début), and the concert the following evening.

Directly after the rehearsal, which took place in the old Music Hall of Boston, Joseph Adamowski took me immediately on to the Tavern Club. My playing had been a great success that afternoon and the audience was most enthusiastic, in fact wildly so, perhaps I may tell you, and it was altogether a tremendous kind of an ovation. So as I entered the big library at the Tavern Club with Joseph Adamowski, the whole room broke into applause and greetings in the most touching and spontaneous manner. It was all very thrilling, I must admit, and the men crowded excitedly around me. It was a great hubbub! Every one asking questions at once, every one being introduced and I was completely surrounded with these kindly well-wishers and friends shaking hands right and left, but alas, being unable myself to say anything. I spoke very little English at that time and felt greatly handicapped in expressing myself. Suddenly in the midst of all the excitement, when the noise was at its height, Tim Adamowski rushed into the room in a blaze of exaltation and pride over his Polish countryman. He was breathless and inarticulate, but so profoundly moved and happy that it was really touching. He was bursting with his desire to acclaim me not only before the Tavern Club but before the whole city of Boston! He wanted to shout my success to the whole world at that moment. He struggled to make himself heard above all the din and racket, but he too was sadly handicapped. His English was not as good as it might have been. He spoke it, yes, well enough, but he very often used quite the wrong words, and words that expressed just the opposite of what he meant, and on this occasion he certainly outdid himself!

He pushed his way to my side and, waving his arms high above his head, he shouted out the great and familiar quotation from Julius Cæsar, but not quite, not quite, "he came, he saw, he conquered." Adamowski held up his hand and with an enormous voice cried out, to the whole assembly, who suddenly became silent, "Gentlemen—Look—look—here he is—Paderewski, the first and greatest of all pianists. He came," cried Adamowski, "he saw," his voice soaring still higher and louder, "he inquired!"

There was an awful, a blank moment and then, of course, the uproar was deafening. I was completely in the dark, for I had no idea what he was saying. My English, as I have already said, was conspicuous by its absence. But that whole crowd burst into a prodigious roar of laughter that went on and on and on until it seemed to me it would never end, and still I did not know what it was all about.

That little story has kept itself alive, though with many variations, through all these years, so I feel that it is perhaps still worth the telling.

The magnificence and beauty of tone, in fact, the great perfection of the Boston Symphony Orchestra, was a constant source of wonder to me. I had not expected anything so fine; in fact, it surprised and interested me extremely to find three great orchestras in America. Perhaps we should say four, including the Chicago Orchestra. But the Boston Symphony must always be mentioned particularly and first, because it was one of the greatest orchestras in the whole world, and it played such an important part in the musical life in the United States. It was founded by Major Henry L. Higginson of Boston. He was its patron saint and he supported it like a prince until his death.

A further word is due here about Major Higginson—a personal word. He was a very generous citizen; he created the Boston Symphony Orchestra and he rendered very noble, exceptionally important service to the musical culture of the United States. Yes, I knew him well. He was a very fine man; he was a protector of music in America and he accomplished wonderful things.

But he was a banker too, and had a peculiar and particular way of combining the two which is quite understandable, for it takes the riches of a bank or banker to support a great orchestra. An orchestra, some one very correctly said, is the plaything of a king, and to become the patron saint of the Boston Symphony Orchestra made enormous demands upon Mr. Higginson's purse and generosity. He deserves all the affection and respect that he enjoyed. The Boston Symphony is a great legacy to America.

Yes, he loved music and he knew a great deal about it. For one single man to do what he did was a miracle. It was said he went even beyond his means in promoting that orchestra. Enthusiasm made him do it, and his sense of civic duty. The very first conductor of the Boston Symphony was Georg Henschel of England, but the real foundation work was done after that by Gericke. He was the most perfect driller (there is no better word for it) of that orchestra. He demanded perfection. He made it such a homogeneous body through that constant drilling and unceasing work. That fact was fully acknowledged and appreciated by Higginson himself and the entire Boston public. Arthur Nikisch followed him. He was one of the greatest conductors of the time. I cannot indulge in too much praise when speaking about him. I have known many splendid conductors, but the closest to my heart was Arthur Nikisch, whom I first met in Europe. Nikisch was the conductor of the Boston Symphony when I came to America. His was a most sympathetic personality, a strong emotional interpreter for every kind of music. He was not a specialist, he was an all-round great musician. One could not always agree with him, but one was bound to recognize his absolute authority, sincerity, and brilliancy, in whatever he was performing.

It was a pity that he had to leave the Boston Symphony, which was so successful under his baton. He diasgreed in some respects with Major Higginson, and that was most unfortunate. He, Higginson, made great sacrifices to establish and maintain that orchestra. For many years he paid all the deficits. He stood by it until the end of his life, but he and Nikisch had some difference. I never could learn what it was, there was some serious misunderstanding and as a consequence, Nikisch left, and was immediately invited to Budapest as a director of the Opera in the Hungarian capital. It was the greatest enjoyment for me to play with him at the Boston Symphony concerts, and I had that enjoyment again in Leipzig, where I played with him several times in later years.

To be quite frank, I must add here that the very highest satisfaction I derived when playing with the orchestra was when I played with Karl Muck. He followed Nikisch as conductor of the Boston Symphony. He was an ideal accompanist. It was simply indescribable, the perfection of his accompaniment. It was something quite exceptional. He had such sympathy with the soloist, and he always tried first of all to give the soloist the fullest satisfaction. When the war came, and America entered it, there was great criticism of Muck and he was finally put in some prison or concentration camp until the close of the war. He could not hide his feelings then, which were pro-German naturally. I don't think this belongs here, still . . .

As my first American tour drew to a close I was more and more fatigued, and anxious to get home. My one idea was to give as soon as possible the eighty recitals and return to Europe.

I suffered so much through overwork and in consequence an unbearable pain in my arm, and then, there were other things, too, that came to torment me. The whole business and financial side of my tour was very difficult. Mr. Tretbar had sold a great many of the concerts to various agents throughout the country, but not to my advantage, decidedly not. When I looked through the list of all the concerts he had arranged, I saw among them recitals and even orchestral appearances sold at only $200 each. I was appalled! How was it possible for me to make any additional money through such an unfair arrangement? But there it was. The contracts were already made. I had to accept them. Nevertheless, it was an added discouragement.

I played in Philadelphia for the small sum of $300, an orchestral concert with the hall packed. Such a small sum was unheard of even for an unknown artist, and I was not unknown then. In fact, it was on the strength of my reputation and those great successes in Paris and London that I was engaged to come to America. But to repeat, I was under contract—there was nothing I could do. Nothing.

I had to go to Chicago for two concerts. I played in the Auditorium on the New Year's Eve 1891–1892, and on New Year's Day, before a packed house, all for the same ridiculous sum. Theodore Thomas was the conductor of the orchestra.

That was a very impressive concert for me, because I had heard so much about Thomas and his activities in America. I looked forward with eagerness to playing with him, but my time, owing to the contracts made by Tretbar for so many concerts in quick succession, was so taken up that I did not arrive in time even to rehearse with Thomas. I reached Chicago in the morning, and at 2:30 that same day had to play with the orchestra— another terrible experience and strain added to the long list of them. I had never seen the hall, never heard the orchestra, and had never even seen Thomas himself, and it was my first appearance in Chicago. However, all went well. Just before the concert, I was closeted in my dressing room, alone and anxious. Thomas began the concert with the usual symphony, and after it was finished, as I stood awaiting my entrance, I saw a gentleman with a little wig hurrying from the platform, looking eagerly around him. "Paderewski! Where is Paderewski?" he cried. "Where is Paderewski?"

"Here I am," I answered and stepped forward to meet him.

"Well," he said, "I am very glad to know you."

We shook hands. "And I am delighted to see you, Mr. Thomas." Then, without further ado or delay, he put his hand on my shoulder and said, "Well, come, let's go and play," and he turned quickly and we walked on to the platform together. That was all. It was really remarkable—no fuss, no delay, just "Let's go and play." Nothing more. But one had immediate confidence in him. He was a splendid conductor, with authority and refinement and intuition. A real musician, a musician by the grace of God. It was a tremendous impression he made upon me.

SIXTEENTH CONCERT.

(SYMPHONY.)

SOLOIST: IGNACE J. PADEREWSKI.

PROGRAM.

SYMPHONY No. 5, E. Minor, op. 64.   ·   ·   ·   ·   *Tschaikowsky*
ANDANTE—ALLEGRO CON ANIMA.
ANDANTE CANTABILE.
VALSE—ALLEGRO MODERATO.   FINALE.

CONCERTO, for Piano, A Minor, op. 17,   ·   ·   ·   ·   *Paderewski*
ALLEGRO, A Minor, 3–4.
ROMANZA ANDANTE, C Major, 2–4.
ALLEGRO MOLTO VIVACE, A Major, 2–4.

Intermission.

BACCHANALE, TANNHAEUSER.   ·   ·   ·   ·   ·   ·   ·   *Wagner*

PIANO SOLO, { NOCTURNE,   ·   ·   ·   ·   ·   ·   ·   *Chopin*
{ VALSE,   "
{ RHAPSODY,   ·   ·   ·   ·   ·   ·   ·   *Liszt*

SLAVONIC DANCE,   ·   ·   ·   ·   ·   ·   ·   *Dvorak*

THE STEINWAY PIANO IS USED.

Program of one of the early appearances with Theodore Thomas and
his orchestra, March 4, 1893

The audience was huge—4000 people filled the hall. At that time it was the largest audience I had ever had. Since then I have had audiences perhaps three or four times that size before me, but at that time it made a stupendous impression. It was a great thrill.

Well, after the concert, we spoke together, Thomas and I, in the dressing room, and I must say that Thomas loved me at once. It was love at first sight on the part of both of us. He had been a wonderful support and friend to me that day. He asked me afterwards *how* I dared risk my appearance at a first concert without a rehearsal, without even knowing him or what he would do. How had I the faith and courage to attempt it? I answered him straight from the heart the only answer I could give. "It was simply an instinct," I said, "I knew, absolutely knew, it would be all right. Although I had never seen you I knew I could trust you."

He was greatly touched, I saw, and pleased. "I shall never forget that," he said, putting his hand on my shoulder. "I shall never forget it."

Thomas was another real friend from that moment, another friend to count on. It was a high-water mark in my American experiences, and as far as the public and the press were concerned it was a success. That made me very happy, too, for Thomas as well as myself.

After Chicago I went to Milwaukee and played my first two recitals there. Again it was the same old story. I received only $200 for each recital. But there was something still worse to come. I had to return to Chicago, where I was booked for three recitals in one week and each one sold for $500. These recitals were extremely well attended, the house sold for at least $3000! Why? It is very easy to understand, because the local agent in Chicago, who shall be nameless, a man who had heard me in both Paris and London, came to Tretbar even before I arrived in New York, and secured these three recitals for this ridiculous sum. It was altogether a disastrous and shocking experience to me at that time. It distressed me deeply. It was especially hard at that moment because I suffered dreadfully in addition with my arms,

Walter Damrosch—the young conductor

Theodore Thomas—an informal photograph

Pages from an announcement of Boston recitals in Paderewski's first season in America

and my hands were so tired—and getting more so all the time. Only a pianist with a large reputation can realize what it means to play, for instance, eight performances in three weeks. When one is just beginning his career, the academic side of the performance must be absolutely correct, and that correctness is very dearly bought always, because it means continuous practice. At that time I often worked seventeen hours a day. I allowed myself just an hour for my meals and only six hours for sleep. Ah, that was hard labor and I felt it, not only then and immediately, but forty years afterwards, and I can say now that I am still feeling the effects of those superhuman efforts.

I had already played in all the important cities, but in many of the smaller places my first appearance, naturally, was not attended by large audiences. Suddenly there came a change. It happened in Portland, Maine. Although it was my first appearance, I saw, to my amazement, the hall completely filled. There was actually a demonstration, up to that moment unknown by me. Practically the entire audience rushed behind the platform to shake hands with me. It was a crowd of about 1000 people, and every one shook hands so cordially that after that experience my right hand was swollen twice its size.

I was greatly surprised at all this, and when I inquired the cause of such a reception and such a large audience at my first appearance, I was told that it was due to an extraordinary publicity I had just received through the *Century Magazine,* at that time edited by my friend Richard Watson Gilder. In the last issue there had been a poem by him called, "How Paderewski Plays." It made quite a sensation. There was also a long article by the eminent pianist and teacher, Doctor William Mason, who was at that time recognized as the first pedagogue in America.

But, however pleasant and gratifying (and they were gratifying) those little progresses of my career, I have, unfortunately, to confess that it did not make me feel very happy at that moment, as I was suffering too much. The pain in my right hand and arm was increasing. There was a reason for this. Steinway pianos, universally recognized as the most marvellous instruments in the world, had a certain peculiarity which was rather dangerous for concert players. Their action at that time was extremely heavy and fatiguing. I realized this must be changed. The Steinways were willing to do everything in their power to comply with my wishes, but their *workmen,* who already had a certain routine, were the decided enemies of any change or any innovation. They fought it.

I immediately complained of this fault to the Steinways and they said it would be changed at once. But it was *not* changed because the workmen refused to accept my criticism. Every one of those workmen, the regulators especially, was an expert and an authority in his own way. They were convinced that what they were doing must be accepted as perfection; that they had not to adapt themselves to the wishes of a mere artist, but that the artist should adapt himself to the piano. They respected my criticism—and ignored it.

That was very hard because the actual physical strength required to produce a very big tone from a Steinway piano, as it was then, was almost beyond the power of any artist. The strain was terrific. I realized early in my tour that something had to be done, and so the controversy began and it meant continual fighting. But finally I had my way and the action was changed on the pianos used by me only. It was a great victory in the end, but what a struggle to attain! My piano then, with all its beauty and power, became gradually quite docile, and my intimate relation to the instrument was most enjoyable. It was no longer my enemy; I no longer had to fight with it—we were friends.

This change was made during my tour and the relief afforded me was tremendous. Then, suddenly, shortly after the settlement of our difficulties, disaster befell me through an accident from which I am still suffering to this day. I remember that just before my recital in Rochester there was an interim of four or five days when there were no concerts at all. It was a blessing. Then came the Rochester recital on a bitter cold night in midwinter.

I had to go directly from the train to the hall and start my recital. As usual, I struck two or three opening chords,—when suddenly, something broke in my arm! A terrific pain—an agony —followed. I had the feeling that I must run from the platform, that I would never be able to play again. Of course, I mastered the feeling in a second, because I realized that it would be disastrous for me to do such a thing. But in such dreadful moments one sees everything black. I thought it was the end of everything —that my career was over, because something very serious, I knew, had happened to my arm. It became suddenly very stiff and the pain was indescribable. But somehow I held myself together and began the playing of Beethoven's Appassionata. How I got through it I shall never be able to tell you. It was one of the miracles that an artist is sometimes able to perform. I had ceased to be able to think; I could only feel the pain which gripped me completely, and to add to it all was a great bewilderment. What had happened? I could not understand. It was one of my excellent pianos that I was playing; there was nothing wrong with it until this accident. But there was a reason, as I soon found out. The piano, it seems, had been sent to the factory for several days, and one of the regulators, not aware of the importance of the action agreeable to me, changed that action completely, restored it to its former stiffness, and the piano was put *back,* I may say, into its original condition—just as it was before I won my fight to have this fault remedied. The regulator, poor man, thought it was all for the best. He could not realize that what he so carelessly did might have cost me my career.

After the concert I went immediately to a physician. He said I had torn and strained some tendons in my arm and injured seriously my finger, and the condition was extremely grave. "There is nothing I can do for you," he said. "You must rest. There is nothing else that will help you—nothing."

"But I cannot rest. I have still many more concerts," I answered. I was in despair. I had concerts to give almost every day and on some occasions concerts in the afternoon and evening. So I could not rest; I could not stop. I must go on like one in a trap—on and on.

The Paderewski Memoirs

In every place I went I had first of all to find a physician to treat my finger just before the concert because by then, it would not move at all. The agony was indescribable. It was a great danger that I risked in playing, a risk that every physician warned me against. But I took it, because out of all that blackness there was just one ray of light to sustain me—I was nearing the end of my tour. I thought of only one thing then, to be able to finish the tour. That I must do.

By that time I had become accustomed to the constant and terrific pain in my arm and I had also learned to play with four fingers only, of my right hand, and to adjust my will and nerves to the ordeal of going through an almost daily public performance, with the knowledge that each concert brought me nearer my release.

Upon my return to New York I had to give a group of recitals with some new programs. Then came numerous demands from various cities for additional recitals. Mr. William Steinway, realizing that through the sale of my concerts at a very cheap price a great wrong had been done me, said, "Now, Paderewski, you are going to give these extra concerts and we will pay all expenses—everything. It shall be clear gain for you. That will be our small contribution to reward you for what was, I am sorry to say, badly managed at the beginning of your tour."

Well, that was noble and very beautiful. Old William Steinway was a wonderful man. This unexpected offer at that moment seemed to me the kind hand of Fate. I realized fully the seriousness of my condition. I felt, as did the physicians, that I might never play again. Perhaps it was the end of my career. In those black moments life seemed to have stopped. What was I to do? I was defenseless. These extra concerts (at least if I could give them) meant something to help my incapacity. I made up my mind to go through with it. I do not know how I did it. I used hot water, massage, electricity, and everything to nurse and galvanize into life my dead finger. After the electricity, the finger would move very slightly, but I was not in command of it. It was always an agony. But I gave the concerts, nevertheless (about twenty-seven in all), and I made much more than in all the preceding ones. I made a very large sum of money and I was thankful.

And then an important, touching thing happened. After the last recital, Mr. Tretbar came to me and said, "Well, Paderewski, before we say good-by, I must apologize for everything I have done which was wrong. I see my mistake now. I admire you and I love you, and I am your loyal friend." And so he remained, until his last days, devoted and helpful and so affectionate to me. Later on, when I had a little misunderstanding with one of the members of the Steinway family, it was Tretbar who was the first one to protest. He was my good friend.

My first tour became a long series of concerts, 107 in all, and before it was over I was asked to return the following season.

So it all ended very happily, and I looked forward with great hope to my return to America. But it was a hope that wavered and sometimes went out in the face of my disaster. I knew that I faced a difficult recovery, but how slow and how difficult I did not fully realize, fortunately, at that moment. The work was over, the harness dropped from my shoulders, and I rejoiced at my success and the thought of returning. It made me very happy. I already loved America.

There is a great deal that I would say about those early days, almost fifty years ago. America made a profound impression upon me then, though a bewildering one at first. The United States is a country of immense, unimaginable richness and variety. There is so much natural beauty; the country contains wonders of nature and practically an unlimited number of attractions: mountains, valleys, bays, harbors, canyons—its beauties and wonders are really countless. And yet, to a foreigner travelling in America forty or fifty years ago, who confined himself to visiting only cities and towns, it would appear a very ugly country, indeed.

The change is now something glorious. But at that time, when I first came to America, outside of a few cities like Boston, for instance, and beautiful cities like Washington, with those splendid monuments, those wide, open streets—it is one of the most beautiful places on earth—the whole country was dirty and disorderly. Wherever you went, the places were dirty. There was so much carelessness. The people's minds were preoccupied with other things. On the railway lines, the landscape, when it was not strikingly beautiful by the will of God, was absolutely exasperating and disgraceful by the awkwardness of man. Not the mining camps, but the farms. There were many large cities then, and the villages were not villages in our European sense of the word; they were towns, or small cities perhaps I should say.

There is no peasant class in America, but there are many foreigners, and the foreigners were thinking only about making money, and did not care at all about beautifying their homes or doing anything, apparently, to improve what they had received. In America, the foreigner does not do what he is obliged to do in his own country. He has little respect for the privileges allowed him. From the moment he touches American shores he feels himself "free," and often with very tragic results to the country that has opened its doors to him. This is a deep subject which we can only touch upon, but the contrasts in America, as I first saw it, were very striking—beauties of nature and the hideousness of man, so to speak, side by side. There was never anything done to beautify the places people lived in; no flowers in the windows, few gardens, even in the towns where there was plenty of room for gardens. But now it is quite changed. For instance, such places as Springfield, Massachusetts, which I knew as a small unattractive place at the beginning of my career in 1892, is now a lovely city with beautiful buildings. Northampton, too, is a charming place. Another town, St. Joseph, Missouri, which I knew in 1892 as an ugly village, is now a perfectly charming residential city, and many other places I could mention have been completely transformed.

Upon arrival, the country impressed me as being gigantic, of colossal resources, with enormous possibilities and with an energetic, enterprising, and laborious population. Every one seemed to be thinking of nothing else but enriching himself. It was an

America

atmosphere of intense competition, of continuous effort, and of speed—speed, speed, even then. Nearly every one was thinking and speaking about money. And yet, at the same time—so generous! I know it better perhaps than many other people.

Naturally, that ambition exercised a strong influence upon me. I wanted to make money, too, and I had some excuse. I was not rich myself, my family was poor, and my country was poor. I wanted to help them all, especially my country, and in a certain way, very modestly, I did, years later.

But it would be very wrong to draw out of my words the conclusion that the United States is a materialistic country. Of course, many people are convinced that Americans are interested only in money, and that the cost of a thing impresses them much more than its beauty, that the money value is the note to stress with Americans, that the dollar is the one thing they worship— the thing they most want to hear about. Like the guide at St. Peter's Basilica in Rome, who, when showing American visitors the beauty of the place, felt constrained to say every few minutes, "That, ladies and gentlemen, cost so many thousands of dollars." I protest this,—really, nothing can be more unfair, although there is a certain amount of truth in it, just enough to make the point of argument.

Of course, there are some people for whom the value of a thing is to be expressed only in figures, but that quality is not confined to Americans alone. My experience has taught me that there is more idealism in America than anywhere else on the globe. I have known people who spent all their lives making a fortune, and after years of effort and privation, when they reached their aim, spent in one moment all the fruits of a long and laborious life for an *ideal*. That is perfectly true, and I have not found in any other country such an enormous percentage of people who, through their individual gifts, advanced progress and culture or supported charitable institutions, as in America.

One has only to think of those marvellous institutions established by such men as Andrew Carnegie and Rockefeller to realize this glorious truth. The universities that have been established by Stanford, Hopkins, and Eastman and many other institutions endowed by private individuals; the Morgan Library and the marvellous museums—all through America they are scattered with amazing lavishness. But the institutions of Carnegie and Rockefeller deserve especial mention, for they are really colossal in their wealth and importance and benefit to mankind, not only in America, but throughout the entire world.

I never met Rockefeller the senior, but I did know his son, John D., Jr., who is carrying on with princely magnificence and vision the great work of the Rockefeller Foundation, started by his father. But I knew personally and intimately Andrew Carnegie, whom I have already talked about. I was with him a great many times, not only in New York, but in Scotland and in a place near Tunbridge Wells, where he had hired a beautiful old estate, and I spent vacations there for several years. He was stimulating mentally and I was constantly struck with his quickness and ingenuity and shrewdness in seeing so clearly every side of a situation. He used to ask me repeatedly then to make him my banker. He wanted to help me safeguard my earnings, but I was a little too proud. Had I been older and wiser, I should have accepted his offer. I am sorry now I did not do it, because I should have been much better off if I had.

The progress accomplished in the United States in a very short time in the way of art and science is chiefly due to the munificence of those American millionaires—those pioneers of progress, shall we call them? In many places, orchestral concerts were established only by that means, not only in Boston, Chicago and Philadelphia, but in many less important cities like Pittsburgh, St. Louis, Cleveland, Detroit, Los Angeles, and San Francisco. Baltimore is now going to have a permanent orchestra, I hear. And Rochester, too, has a small, admirable one, owing to the generosity of Eastman. He built a conservatory for music there which is excellent in all its departments, I understand.

Bok, who founded the Curtis Institute in Philadelphia, where Madame Sembrich taught the last years of her life and Josef

America

Hofmann is now teaching, and the Juilliard Institute in New York, a great musical institution—such magnificent giving is typically American. That kind of public spirit is to be found in some places in England, but very rarely on the European continent, extremely rarely. Rich people in Europe generally keep their money without much thought of the community. There is less of this particular kind of civic duty and responsibility.

I was always told before coming to the United States that the American public was very fickle. That is the expression they used. But I did not find it so myself. In my own experience I found a certain fidelity and attachment from the beginning. All my American friends have remained true to me and have never changed. They form some of the strongest ties of my life.

Munificent giving has become almost an institution in America, which seems to be a country of institutions. There are a great many, and some of them are quite unique. The bootblacks, for instance—they also are an institution. We have nothing like them in all Europe. They are characteristic of the American people, who, in my opinion, in spite of their great energy, are not fond of manual work. Perhaps that explains why they develop machinery to such an extent. There is practically no servant class in America in the sense that we have servants in Europe, also due to the democratic spirit. The best servants in the rich American families are Europeans.

Still, in spite of your marvellous mechanical inventions and luxuries, one misses very much certain little comforts and conveniences that are part of every-day life in Europe. One cannot have service (in the sense I mean) in America, but although one easily gets accustomed to it, one never ceases to miss it.

Although you have so little service, you still have a certain chivalrous attitude toward women. When one enters a lift, for instance, and there are only men, suddenly a woman, maybe a cook, appears, and every man takes off his hat. That is very nice, I think; it always pleased me greatly.

But perhaps I must now qualify this statement, I am sorry to say. Years ago this was almost universally true, but now there is, indeed, a marked change in the attitude of men toward women, and I must say of women toward men. Yes, a great change, and it is universal, though perhaps more noticeable in America, that land of violent contrasts, than anywhere else. It is felt that this has come about since general suffrage and since the war. Woman appears now as a competitor, taking away man's occupations but at the same time wanting the same privileges and consideration as before. And there is the trouble.

X

Audiences, and a Political Detour

I

As you see, America made a profound impression on me, and I
was already looking forward eagerly to my return the following
season. I sailed for Europe at the end of my first tour prepared
to rest and find myself again, to cure the fourth finger, if possible,
and be rid of the agonizing pain. I confidently expected that the
rest would permit me to recuperate all my forces and be ready
for the second tour at the end of September, 1892. Unfortunately,
that was an illusion because the pain in my arm and fourth
finger continued with increasing intensity. I was still under contract for two concerts in London, and although I knew the risk
was very great, and against all doctors' advice, I played these
concerts in spite of the danger. Necessity and ambition carried
me through somehow, with the assistance of youth.

I went to London and gave a recital there and was also
engaged by Mr. William Waldorf Astor for two big "at homes."
He had taken a beautiful house in London and moved permanently to England. These musicals of his were always the sensation of the London season. The most celebrated artists were
engaged. It must have cost him an enormous sum of money and,
of course, the most aristocratic society and the most distinguished
visitors were invited to attend these functions. Members of the
royal family and foreign sovereigns were frequently among the
guests. The particularity of these events (as regards myself) was
that all the other artists were changed every year, but for eight
or nine years I was engaged each season.

Mr. Astor was a prince among hosts, and I preserve a truly

affectionate memory of his personality, and of his family, too. In his house the guests were always quiet, and as attentive as in a concert hall. It was a joy to play there. That happens so rarely and only a few times has it been my privilege to have such an experience in a private house.

I have already told you of that lovely house in Santa Barbara, Mrs. Bliss's, where the atmosphere was so beautiful. There was always absolute silence and the audience really enjoyed the music—they came for that purpose and showed it and I felt it. And it was the same with those tremendous gatherings in Mr. Astor's house in London, in Carlton House Terrace. He received the people at the top of the staircase, and remained behind the audience watching carefully whether they behaved well or not. He *imposed* silence on his audiences, and I found it so remarkable. He did not invite people to come for pleasant little conversations with each other—but to hear music. Neither did he allow the artist disturbed and the program interrupted as so frequently happens in a private house. Gracious host that he was, this rule was absolute, and I can only find myself repeating that he imposed silence upon his guests. So gradually by this method he educated at least those who were constant guests in his house, to listen to music with some concentration of mind and courtesy to the artist. As to the foreigners, they, too, had to learn. It is unusual for a host to do that. It was a delight to me always to play for Mr. Astor. You cannot say this of playing in many private houses. It is agonizing to play when nobody seems to listen, and many times in the beginning of my career I have had that humiliating experience.

I have in connection with this theme several more variations to offer you, one which we shall take time to tell now. A very interesting story, but it happened almost twenty years later. I was in South America. I played first in Rio de Janeiro, where I had very pleasant experiences. The concerts were good. They were well attended. There was a group of people in Rio and Sao Paulo who were attentive, cultured, and enthusiastic. This would have given me complete satisfaction ordinarily, but I was not feeling well at that time. I was rather nervously exhausted, and when I reached Buenos Aires I had to remain there for several weeks. During that time I went to several concerts. In each of these concerts I, to my surprise and horror, noticed something which made me think that I could not really stay there. I could not play there, I felt, because at every concert I had been to, the whole audience talked—talked aloud and incessantly! And do you know why? Why this rude, incessant conversation was allowed during a concert? Why this continuous talking? The answer from their point of view is very simple. It is a Spanish tradition!—not to be questioned or criticized. Just accepted.

In Spain, society life *begins* in concerts or at the opera, it seems. They do not give receptions, but they receive in their boxes! All the richest and most fashionable people of the city go from box to box, greeting each other, having conversations and holding little soirées, while the performance is going on.

It was so terrifying to me that I said to myself, "No, I cannot play here. It is impossible." I was about to cancel my concerts when by some accident I met a most charming lady, Madame de Castex, in Buenos Aires. A beautiful person. These people in South America, especially in the Argentine, are more exclusive than any aristocracy in the world, and consequently they think that an artist is just a hired entertainer, who should be treated kindly, of course, but just as a paid servant. So they were greatly surprised and not at all pleased to meet me in society at first. It happened in this way. No one came to pay me a visit (which was unusual) or paid the slightest attention to me, except this charming Madame de Castex, who very graciously invited me to a luncheon. I accepted, of course, and realized on arrival that it was a decided surprise to the other guests to find me there. They could think of me only at the piano! But they had to accept me, naturally, and follow the lead of the popular hostess, who said very graciously, "Oh, Mr. Paderewski, it is a great honor to have you with us, and we rejoice so much to know that you are giving six recitals here. That is delightful," she smiled at me— "and we are all anticipating the event keenly."

"Ah, Madame," I answered quickly, "you are very kind, but I do not know positively yet whether you will hear me in those six recitals. Probably you will not hear me in even one recital! Yes, it is quite likely that you will not hear me at all."

She stared at me in astonishment. "Oh, Mr. Paderewski, why do you say that? What do you mean?"

"I mean, Madame," I answered, "that I do not know whether I shall be able to play in your beautiful city or not." Great sensation among those present. Absolute silence!

"But you surely don't mean that. Why? Why? Tell me. I insist." Madame de Castex fairly hurled her questions at me.

"Because," I said very quietly, "I would not be able to accept your way of treating artists, and concerts in general." Consternation among the guests! After a moment Madame de Castex recovered herself and said, "But Mr. Paderewski, I do not understand. What do you mean by that? We *adore* music. We go to every concert. You surely must have some good reason for making such a statement."

"I have. A very good reason—the best of reasons. I do not play when the audience is talking."

She turned absolutely pale. "Oh," she said, "you mean you—" she could not go on, so I continued this painful dialogue.

"If any one talked during the first piece I played I should simply bow to the audience and leave the stage. If I am asked why I do not play, I shall simply answer 'I play only before audiences who *listen* to music and not to their own talking.'"

There were a few minutes then of absolute silence; no one seemed to breathe. The air was heavy with horror! Then suddenly Madame de Castex rose and in a very loud and excited voice said, "Well, you are going to play here, Mr. Paderewski, and you will enjoy your playing here too, because we want to hear you. It is an honor to have you, and we shall respect your wishes. I promise you that."

That was a reassuring moment for me, and I was naturally much affected by it, and gratified too. The luncheon was in a perfect hubbub instantly, all talking at once.

Audiences, and a Political Detour

Although I had great faith in my hostess, I did not feel so very sure that she would be able to do all she had promised. A few days later came my first concert. With a feeling of uncertainty and great apprehension, I appeared on the platform. I was greeted most graciously, even enthusiastically, and I said to myself, "So far all's well, but will they talk or not? My decision is made, however. I shall stop if they begin to talk. Perhaps I shall not actually leave the platform, but I shall at least stop playing at once."

Well, I had not to stop! I played my entire concert through in complete silence. Not even a whisper was to be heard. It was a marvellous audience. I do not know whether I have ever had a better one in that respect. I played eight concerts instead of six, and every one was a real enjoyment. That is still a great memory for me. And Madame de Castex was responsible for it all. She, herself, went from house to house literally. She made a regular campaign of it. I heard afterward from one of her friends whom she attacked on the subject, that Madame de Castex assured her that if any one talked during the concert, the whole contract would be cancelled immediately, and worse still, it would appear as an absolute scandal in Buenos Aires. "Why," she said, "we shall be the laughing-stock of the whole musical world. Telegrams will be sent abroad that Buenos Aires is such an unmusical community and so stupid and impolite that Paderewski was unable to play his concerts there. He was actually obliged to leave the platform because the audience talked incessantly through his playing. Can we let such a thing as that," she cried, "happen here? Impossible. We must show Mr. Paderewski that we are really the most attentive and courteous audience in the whole world." That was the edict that went forth. It was masterly.

The only place, I think, where people were not brought to silence (even in spite of my frequent interrupting of their conversation) was in Paris. They were really the most unruly audiences of all. I do not know whether it was due to the fact that in Paris these "at homes" were so cosmopolitan, or whether they were specially unmusical; but whatever the reason, it was very unpleasant for the artist. So I stopped early in my career playing in private houses. In the beginning it was necessary, but as soon as I could do without them, I was glad to stop.

II

And now I am going to make an abrupt change of subject. I hope these many and devious detours will add a little color and charm to the musical part of our narrative. It is of politics that I want to speak at the moment. As you know, I have always been deeply interested in politics and welcomed every occasion that brought me in contact with English statesmen, and I met then most of the distinguished and important men in the political life of England. This began even with my second London season. They remain a vivid strand through the years. Later on, when war rocked the world, their friendship was a bulwark. They belong to this period of my life and I must speak about them now—as I knew them in the beginning.

And first of all, let me tell you a little about Asquith. I knew him well. I went frequently to his house to dine and lunch. Asquith was a very highly educated man, a man evidently with a brilliant future ahead of him. When I first knew him he was a member of Parliament and he was, of course, a Liberal. He was very intriguing to me, perhaps for the reason that my interest in politics was very keen, even then. I was always studying the conditions of my own country, and consequently of other countries in relation to mine. What impressed me very greatly then was the fact that when I was in the society of Liberals, for instance, I usually met, among the guests, Conservatives, living on friendly terms and even displaying friendship and affection for each other. I was not accustomed to see such things on the Continent. Quite the contrary. For instance, one of the guests whom I saw several times at Mr. Asquith's house was Arthur James Balfour, who was the head of the Opposition each time that Asquith was Prime Minister.

Balfour—what precious memories Balfour and his unfailing

Lord Balfour

At the turn of the century

Audiences, and a Political Detour

friendship stir in me. I met him first years before the war, and I found him one of the most remarkable and charming of men, of the very highest culture, a gifted writer, a brilliant conversationalist, and so cultivated in his opinions and tastes. He had an interest in everything—in painting, in writing, in music, and was universally informed about many things, which very frequently is not the case with political men. One of the traits of his character that was so sympathetic to everybody was his extreme generosity and his sense of justice. I can only say that he was the first man during the Great War from whose lips I heard encouraging words concerning my own country.

I visited him several times. I was invited to luncheons and dinners with him at his London house. We had many serious conversations and we talked of all the things under the sun, including politics, of course, and he was a most informing and erudite man. Often we talked philosophy, too, which has always interested me enormously. I was surprised then at his intimate knowledge of different philosophical schools, especially of certain German philosophers. Shortly after one of these discussions, he sent me his own remarkable little book—*The Foundations of Belief*. I still have it in my possession.

His philosophy of life? you ask. It is difficult to put it in a few words. I would not say he was a pessimist; far from it, for being so just, and many-sided, and clear, he never rejected anything without first studying it, and he always tried to discover something *good* in everything. That was the most pronounced manifestation of his sense of justice. I agree to the desire of the human heart to find good in every one. But one cannot fail to realize in the course of generations, that humanity is not progressing all the time—far from it. In spite of all our great inventions and discoveries, I do not think precisely that we are progressing now. We are not in the Dark Ages, in the sense of the Middle Ages (after the downfall of the Roman Empire) when a great darkness came; still, we are certainly declining at this moment. This period is, to a certain extent, decadence.

Balfour and I frequently had long talks on this subject. And I must repeat, his sense of justice was always his dominant note. It is also a strong English characteristic. I always feel the English quite different from other peoples, markedly different. It is strange how that little strip of water separating them from the Continent makes all that difference. They are different in every respect. In clothes, for instance, to start with. And it is not only human beings. Animals are different, horses are different, dogs are different, all kinds of domestic animals are different. You can see in England dogs which you never see except on rare occasions on the Continent—of better breed and sounder. Well-fed, and much better taken care of. Wonderful horses and wonderful cows—those Jersey cows, those Shorthorn cows for example. And then other animals too—even pigs are cleaner and in better condition. And Southdown sheep—and poultry. Everything is different—in many respects better.

You can travel from Calais to Moscow without seeing very much difference in the countryside, except in cleanliness. The further East you go, the dirtier and more squalid things are, not only human beings, but everything. But the moment you have crossed the English Channel, you find quite different conditions —the aspect of everything changes completely.

Yes, I agree when you tell me you have a feeling of security in England, particularly now when all Europe is walking a tight rope. It is quite understandable that you should feel that, because you are also of the English race and speak the English language. But that feeling of security is felt by every one who goes there, irrespective of nationality. It is quite true, yes, there is law and order, there is a quiet order—they *obey* in England. There is no obedience in America, none—with its vast, mixed population and its seething cauldron of restless people from every country in the world. The English, on the contrary, are a law-abiding people and not only law-abiding, but there is something in England and the English character which is above even that, and that is the social instinct. They realize and practise civic duty. Wherever there are English people, there order is preserved. They respect the law.

The English have still another marked characteristic—once

your friend, always your friend. They may be longer in accepting you, but once you are accepted you remain forever installed in their hearts. How true this is! I think at this moment particularly of two dear friends, Sir George and Lady Lewis. Their friendship lasted from the beginning of my knowing them to the very end. Theirs was one of the most hospitable houses in London. She was very artistic in her tastes, and there was always a great gathering there of artists, especially musicians, because she belonged herself to a very musical family. Their house was the constant meeting place of the most distinguished personalities. A little world of its own in the heart of London. It seemed to me that I entered another dimension whenever I passed through its welcoming doors. Political men of national importance, scientists, painters, writers, as well as all the great musicians of the time, came there eagerly and gave of their best, of their talk, of their music, their wit, their ideas, hopes and beliefs. It was a rare mingling of high and kindred personalities, over which presided those gracious, incomparable hosts, Sir George and Lady Lewis. That house does not exist any more. Another bulwark, another landmark gone. The lights are out, the curtain down.

The passing of that great period, the nineties, brought to a close a tremendous era, a flowering of all that was most beautiful and elegant in life. We shall not see its like again. The actual closing, I think, began with the death of Queen Victoria. As long as she lived, all her governments tried to avoid any trouble, to let her enjoy, to the end, that prosperous and happy reign. It was a mighty one, and her Jubilee in 1897 was a tremendous outpouring of expression of affection and magnificence.

I was at the Queen's Jubilee and it was a wonderful sight— of a splendor hardly to be imagined. I saw the great pageant, that procession of all the vassals of the Empire, the Maharajahs, the Governors of Dominions, and Prime Ministers, all following the carriage of the Queen. One of the greatest impressions I ever experienced was when I saw that magnificent display of riches, especially on the part of the Indian Maharajahs. It was marvellous. They wore all their jewels—they seemed clothed in jewels.

Such gorgeous emeralds of a fire and brilliance that was simply dazzling even in that procession of blazing gems.

The Maharajahs at the Queen's Jubilee were certainly a high point of that impressive occasion. The Queen, herself, rode in an open carriage; she looked so small, so frail, so tired, but still very majestic—that was one of her qualities. Little and old as she was then, the power and majesty of Queen Victoria was unquestionable. It seemed even to increase with her years. She rode in her golden coach that day and wore her crown. The coach was open so that every one of her loyal subjects could see her. It was a touching occasion, and the memory of it still is.

I viewed the whole glittering pageant from the balcony of a friend in St. James's Street. After the Queen and the Maharajahs, the thing that impressed me most was the bagpipe player marching in the very front of the whole tremendous procession. He practically opened the parade. Nothing could have been more beautiful and more picturesque. The leader of those Scotsmen was a giant—he was nearly seven feet tall and was especially selected for that occasion. In spite of that huge body, he was graceful in form and had remarkable beauty. That splendid vital figure is still before me, perhaps even more than those gorgeously dressed Maharajahs, adorned with their priceless jewels. I see him —more beautiful than the others—walking ahead and playing his pipes. It was thrilling!

The Queen's Jubilee was a great gesture on the part of her subjects at the rounding out of her reign. She was always a potent figure to me from the first time I had the honor of meeting her. A year before her death she sent for me and I played again at Windsor. She comes before my eyes and I can see and hear her at this moment, now as then, after all these years. Again I see the splendid room and the old figure in the wheel chair—so old and tired. She was as gracious and friendly as when I first played for her, and her smile was always so charming. I have a picture here that she gave me on that occasion that is very like her, except for her transforming smile—no camera could capture that. Physically she was short, stout and unromantic in appearance—morally she was a tremendous figure of dignity and beauty. And she still lives on in all her glory. Lives on, reborn in book, play and films. This mighty little figure still holds her place among us, and we continue to bow to her sovereign qualities.

That was an age of great figures in England. During these extraordinary years I met most of them. Many of them entered the drama of my life—many of them became my devoted friends.

The Duke of Connaught was one of the people of whom I have such charming recollections still. I met him first in Dublin— he was then the Governor-General of Ireland. He was a man of marked courtesy and consideration, which he showed me very unexpectedly at that time. He was attending my concert in Dublin, and during the interval sent one of his aides-de-camp to ask me to come to his box. Such an invitation, as you realize, was not only an invitation, but a command as well. Although it is against my custom ever to speak with any one during my concerts, I was, naturally enough, delighted to go to him. Unfortunately, the theatre was constructed in such a way that I could not possibly reach his box except by marching down the center aisle of the theatre, through the whole audience. Of course this I could not do, and begged to be excused on that account. A few minutes later the aide-de-camp came hurrying back and said, "Oh, Mr. Paderewski, we are sorry to have disturbed you, but his Royal Highness understands the situation perfectly and will go up for a few minutes to another box nearer the stage, and he can speak to you there at your convenience."

Ah, that was a great courtesy on his part. You see the graciousness and simplicity of the man. I was deeply touched by his consideration. I saw him many times after that and the last time was at the unveiling of the Lincoln Monument in London in 1920. It was a very wet day, and just as the addresses began it suddenly poured in torrents. The Duke of Connaught, who was standing near me, was kind enough to say, "Ah, Paderewski, come here, come nearer to me. You see I have a very large umbrella and we can both stand under it, I'm sure."

Lloyd George spoke at the unveiling and as usual he made a

very fine speech. He was extremely witty. I don't think I enjoyed him as much as usual that day, because only a few hours earlier I had visited him, and asked him for something that he had refused absolutely, and it was a very important matter to me. I was then the delegate of Poland to the Conference of Ambassadors in Paris, where a very serious problem was being solved. That problem concerned my country and the verdict was very much against Poland. After that verdict I went directly to London and asked Lloyd George to change it, and he had told me very kindly and in a very friendly manner that it was absolutely impossible. His answer so depressed me that I think I was not in a very receptive mood for his speech a few hours later. But his speeches generally disarmed and charmed one because, as I have said, he was always very witty. There is an amusing story about something that happened during the great suffragette movement, when Mrs. Pankhurst and her daughter were at the helm. Lloyd George was very much opposed to suffrage and he fought that movement constantly and with some success. On one occasion there was a great meeting organized by those valiant ladies and he made a speech, and evidently his arguments were so vigorous that one of the women shouted angrily, "If you were my husband, Mr. Lloyd George, I would give you *poison!*" And he, quite undisturbed, said, "My good lady, if I were your husband, I would *take* poison myself!"

I saw Lloyd George very often during and after the war, but that is another moment in my memoirs and comes many years later. I still turn back to those early days because of the many important men that I met in England then. The contact with such statesmen was of vital interest to me over and above everything else, for there was always the hope at the back of my mind that I could sometime be useful to my country. Friendships with these eminent men enlarged and enriched my vision and knowledge of political affairs. It has been my very good fortune to meet such men in many countries, particularly in England, before and during the war.

Lord Rosebery was a man of whom I have pleasant and

grateful memories. I knew him slightly at first, but it was later, during the war, that I approached him on a certain occasion. He was already old and tired, but he received me so kindly and, of course, agreed to what I asked. I invited him then to become a member of the Polish Relief Committee during the war, and he immediately consented. He said he would be very glad to serve, but I must excuse him if he did not attend all the meetings on account of his health and of his advanced years. He was most gracious. We talked about Napoleon a great deal (you know his hobby was Napoleon) and he had many interesting souvenirs of Napoleon in his house. He was very well informed on that subject. He wrote a book about Napoleon which is valuable to students.

Both Lord Morley and Lord Haldane I met first in the early years. Lord Morley was another distinguished figure of that time. But I saw him only twice and both times at luncheon with Mr. Herbert Asquith, who was then Prime Minister of England. There is a story connected with this luncheon to come later on.

But Lord Haldane I knew better and he was a man that I liked very much. He was, I think, very unjustly treated by some of his contemporaries after the war. Some of them considered him too pro-German, which was not true. He was a good Englishman of Scottish origin. In a way, every person, American or Englishman, educated in Germany, is pro-German. They, the Germans, have that peculiar talent for capturing souls! I made my studies in Berlin as a youth, and I still preserve very pleasant memories of my life there—memories of the character of the people, of certain of their customs, habits, kindnesses, etc., but as to their politics—no! I am decidedly anti-German. But even when pronouncing those words, I am not precisely correct, because it is not anti-*German* that I am, but anti-Prussian, because all that is now in Germany so unpleasant, so brutal, so presumptuous, so impertinent and so arrogant and so ruthless, is *Prussian*. It has been imposed upon Germany.

So, in speaking about Lord Haldane, he, too, had the same experiences. He had friends in the Universities where he had studied, and he preserved those happy memories of his professors. He was fond of German science, of German philosophy, of Hegel quite especially; he wrote certain books on Hegel which he sent me and which I still read with great interest. I cannot say anything else but that I enjoyed very much all my meetings with Lord Haldane and found them of the greatest interest.

I cannot speak of these men except in terms of the highest admiration. One after another they come to mind as we talk and it is always the same thing. They were splendid men and shed a great light and influence on the times. The interest of such men of integrity in the political life of the country was very inspiring to me. They were not politicians, they were statesmen, keen of vision and of great character. In this day of politicians only, the comparison is inevitable.

Lord Charles Stuart of Wortley was a friend at whose house I met many of these statesmen. He became a very dear friend. He died a few years ago. There is still his widow, who was the daughter of Sir John Millais, the famous English painter. She is now like a bird with one wing since the death of her distinguished husband. Lord Stuart of Wortley had been several times a member of the Cabinet. It was always interesting to me to talk politics with him. I had the good luck to meet, in every country I visited, the foremost men in the political world. It made my life very rich and was a preparation for something that was to come later, much later. But all that belongs to another part of my memoirs, with which I am not yet ready to treat.

Now, there is a very important man who also does not belong in this period, but I shall tell my little story about him nevertheless, because he was a very important man and it is a very charming story, I think, and I am glad you agree that this is the place to tell it.

It all happened years before the war. It was in Lyons; I used to go there every season on a concert tour and generally stayed for a length of time because I had there many warm friends. In the house of one of these friends I met on a special occasion the Prefect of Lyons. Now there are many prefects in France, but very few, if any, arrived at such a distinguished position as did this particular one. He was Jules Cambon, French Ambassador to Germany in 1914, the year of the war.

At the moment of our first meeting, it was just an agreeable occasion among friends. Many years later, however, that early meeting took on a greater significance. We need not go into the history of Cambon here; all the world knows now his great services to France during the war, and all that he stood for then, and all his memory now stands for. The point of our story is, that many years later, thirty to be exact, when I arrived in Paris in 1919, during the Peace Conference, some one from the Polish delegation, meeting me in the house of X, said, "Oh, Mr. Paderewski, this is indeed an opportune moment. Will you not come with me? I want to introduce you to a very important person." I agreed and he then took me into another room and there stood—Cambon. He went quickly towards him and without further preliminaries said, "May I introduce to you, sir, our Prime Minister, Monsieur Paderewski?" And Cambon, with a look of quick recognition, said immediately, "Ah, but you have come thirty years too late. Paderewski and I have known each other for more than thirty years."

Well, it was a momentous time for all of us. Cambon was a great figure in the Peace Conference. He was a tremendous character. He was a true friend to me. I had known him, since '88, and I loved that man. He was a helpful supporter to me all through the Peace Conference. Three years ago, when I saw him for the last time, he was still a young and ardent man in spirit. At ninety-one, although he showed in many ways his great age, his spirit was still undaunted and beautiful. Cambon is now dead. I paid him my last respects only a few weeks ago in Vevey, where he died.

What a blessing that I was permitted, while travelling over the whole world, to know these great statesmen. It was a destiny over which I had no control, but it helped in so many unexpected ways later on in that war that changed all the continent of

Europe and the destiny of my own country. The war that was to come! And which, even forty years before, had been a topic of discussion and prophecy by a few wise and farseeing men. I myself heard it frequently mentioned in different Englishmen's houses. Lord Roberts, the great military man of England, predicted it constantly years before it happened. I never knew Lord Roberts. How I wish I had!

Lord Roberts was always keenly interested in French military science and appreciated it very highly, and, consequently, was greatly beloved by the French people. He went frequently to France, and some five or six years before the war he visited France for the last time. On his return to England he had a great deal to say about military and political affairs. It was then he predicted the war. He was one of the very few who predicted it at that time and he said very emphatically, "France will win, but not alone. A coalition will be formed against the two Central Powers, who will also have some allies. But," he added, "final victory will come under the leadership of an unknown general. He is now a director of the Military Academy at St. Cyr and his name is Foch. I believe Foch the greatest military genius of the present time." Prophetic words!

I, too, very modestly predicted the war before it happened. I remember the incident perfectly. It was at the house of my close friend, Lord Stuart of Wortley, in 1908. There were only a few people there for dinner and afterwards we all talked together rather intimately. It was a brilliant evening. It is sad to think they are all gone. There was Lord Charles himself, Lord Beresford and Lord Northcliffe, though he was not Lord Northcliffe at that time. We were all in intimate conversation together and I said, "A war, I think, is in store for you in a very few years."

"War, what war?" they asked almost in one voice.

"With the Germans, of course," I answered. "None other."

Lord Charles was very vehement—he did not believe it at all. But Northcliffe did and was the first one to say, "Yes, you undoubtedly are right, and they are already preparing for it, though no one believes it."

Audiences, and a Political Detour

And then Lord Beresford, who was a sailor, said, "Yes, I agree; it is absolutely true, they are now preparing a tremendous navy."

It was a most interesting conversation. Beresford was of the opinion (just as was Lord Northcliffe) that there was absolutely no possibility of any defeat of the British nation. But, and I remember this so well, Lord Charles was of the opinion that there was still a possibility of arranging all these delicate problems between the two countries. I must add that he gradually, later on, changed his mind.

What prophetic moments come to us. A new acquaintance, a chance conversation, and one has glimpsed forward through the years. Such a moment arrived once at the house of Asquith. He was then Prime Minister of England, many years after I had first met him. I was invited to a luncheon, which was rather a large affair. It was all most agreeable and there were many distinguished people invited. Among them there was a certain Russian gentleman, who must have been of much importance from the deference paid him. But, unfortunately, I did not catch his name when we were presented—not until the end of the luncheon. When the ladies had left the table and we sat smoking, Lord Morley came to my side and began a little conversation with me. "Well, Mr. Paderewski," he said, "we are all political men here today, as you see, and some of us are naturally very eager to be always in the limelight of public favor, to be always in power. Tell me, now, is there any one here with whom you would exchange your power over the public at this moment of your great popularity?"

"Yes," I answered quickly. "Yes, but not forever! For a certain time, I would, for instance, exchange now my power with that of—Stolypin," who was then the Russian Prime Minister.

"But why?" Lord Morley looked at me for a moment in astonishment. "But why? Why?"

"For the simple reason that, having his power, I would be able to make for my own people some changes for the betterment of their condition and existence altogether."

"Well, yes, of course," he said slowly, "but you could not hold it, that power."

"Ah, that is another question. I do not know if circumstances would enable me to hold that power indefinitely, but I should be glad to have it even for a short time."

At that moment the guests got up and Mr. Asquith led us into another room. When we reached the door, Lord Morley suddenly stopped Asquith and said, laughingly, "Look here, Asquith, I have something very interesting to tell you. Mr. Paderewski has just told me he would gladly exchange his power over the public—well, for that of Stolypin."

"Why?" said Asquith shortly. "Why?" He was sometimes very dry, very abrupt. He had evidently been talking with the Russian gentleman in question and was still in the mood of that conversation.

"Why? Because he would like to have such a power as Stolypin's to help his own country, Poland."

And Asquith, very pompous as he sometimes could be, simply said, "There is no hope for your country, sir, none!"

For a tense moment those words of his hung on the air. Then I replied, "Ah, Mr. Asquith, there are certain things under the sun which even a Prime Minister of England cannot foresee and foretell!"

XI

Second American Visit

Well, enough of statesmen and politicians. These remembrances are taking us far afield and years ahead of the period of career building. But one can talk best when one follows one's mood, and our mood, or inclination, has led us here. And all this has its place—an important place—in this story of my life, a variation on the main theme. To make use of that homely old proverb "too many cooks spoil the broth," we may easily find that too many concerts will have the same effect. Nevertheless, we must return to our concerts, our main theme, and speak about my second American season—and my fourth finger! I fulfilled those engagements in London in spite of that dreadful finger and the always increasing pain in my arm, the result of terrible overwork in my first American tour.

But, once all these engagements in France and England were fulfilled, I looked for help, consulting various and famous physicians. They advised numerous ways of treating it, but gave me very little hope of a complete recovery, and the second American tour was approaching. I was in despair.

Of course, I had also to prepare some new programs. So a complete rest was absolutely impossible; there was necessary work to do at once. After having spent considerable time in following the different treatments prescribed, I saw with terror that the end of September was approaching, and there was not only no improvement in the condition of my right arm and hand, but even a decided inability to continue my practising. I was worse, and I had to face it. So I had to postpone the American tour until the end of December of that year.

During my rest I was treated by a masseur in Paris, who gave me the first real assistance. He restored a certain strength in the arm, but my fourth finger still refused to move. So then I decided to exercise it myself, and very systematically, very slowly, after many weeks, I arrived at being able to move it, which was due to that particular masseur, who was not a physician, but just a bone-setter. It was he who found the sore spot in my arm. I continued to practise in this way, and there was every day a little improvement. But that finger has remained for over thirty years weaker than any of the others.

That was a dreadful time. It was marvellous that I preserved my nerves, that they did not give way completely under the strain. It happened, too, just when I was reaching my goal and on my way to earn large sums of money. I had already acquired quite a reputation, and then came that catastrophe. I was not quite thirty-two, and was already, to a certain extent, crippled.

But still I kept a little courage and began to notice considerable improvement. I dared to start preparing two new programs, and finally found myself able to begin my American tour. That second tour, in spite of the condition of my finger and my partial inability to play with assurance and authority, was a brilliant success. It was a triumph over conditions that seems now, as I look back through the years, a kind of miracle.

My habit is to try out the pianos (as well as the programs) in small places where I have absolutely no friends, no social relations, etc., in order to be perfectly sure that I shall not see a familiar face in the audience which would prevent me from an absolute concentration of mind. I usually play three or four times in various small places before going to important cities like Boston, New York, or Chicago.

The second tour opened auspiciously, and the Steinway pianos I found in marvellous condition upon my return. They were then prepared with such care and affection that I had nothing to say, but to play and praise the instruments. They were beautiful.

Second American Visit

The Steinway pianos deserve a special mention here, I think. They are the greatest pianos in the world. The finest piano before the Steinway was the Erard. Erard was the creator of the piano, and the action as made by Erard is applied to every piano in the world. Technically, the Erard action is the most perfect in existence. Perhaps, to be just, I should say that up to this moment it was the most perfect. But now the Steinway is equally good. The quality of the tone of the Steinway is supreme. The quality of tone in the Erard is not as beautiful, not as pleasing to the ear, because it is too clear; it reflects, so to say, the character of the French race. It has precision, clarity, elegance and technical perfection, but it takes a real master of the Erard to make the Erard piano sing. While a Steinway, with its beautiful tone, is always singing, no matter who plays it.

My season began with the greatest satisfaction, and I played everywhere to enthusiastic houses. My return to America was a happiness to me. I already felt I was a part of the life there and I felt a real affection for the country and the American people, an affection that has lasted through all these years. There were many recitals in New York at the beginning of that season, and in Philadelphia, too. In connection with the Philadelphia concerts I had another mishap, or I should say experience, that almost ended my tour and actually prevented me from playing for several days. I think with your permission we will include the story here.

There was an opening of the new Steinway piano premises in Philadelphia, which was something of an occasion, and I was asked to be present. Naturally, I accepted, and I remember that I went directly from my recital to the reception hall. Now you must realize that giving a recital is a tremendous ordeal, a great strain on mind, nerves, and body; all one's powers are taxed to the utmost. A recital is not a time for personal enjoyment—it is not, as you say in America, a picnic. This particular recital was a very arduous one. I had played a program of some two and a half hours with many encores and was extremely exhausted and in no condition to further tax my strength. Fortunately, I did not realize what was in store for me at the reception; otherwise I think I should never have had the courage to go in spite of my promise. When I reached the reception, I found, to my amazement, practically the whole of my audience waiting to speak to me and I was obliged to stand in line and shake hands with everybody. It was a ghastly ordeal, and finally my right hand became so swollen and inflamed that I had to offer my left hand. There were about 1000 people there and each one shook hands twice. It was a dreadful experience. I said to myself, "Another reception like this, and I shall not be able to play ever any more."

I played frequently in Philadelphia and always with success and enjoyment on my part. Philadelphia recalls to my mind another hand-shaking story, and the most amusing little adventure that also happened back in the early days. It was my habit always to return to New York immediately after my concerts there. On this particular occasion I had ordered at the famous old Delmonico restaurant, then at Broadway and 26th Street, a nice little dinner for a few intimate friends which I was looking forward to with great pleasure. I arrived in good season and saw, to my amazement, an unusually large crowd of people talking and laughing together in the reception room. It was evidently an important affair. Some association (I think it was the Jewelers' Association of New York) were having their annual banquet. My own dinner was already ordered in a private dining room, and before going to greet my friends, I went to the dressing room. While I was removing my coat, a gentleman came in in great haste, apparently looking for some one, and when he saw me he stopped absolutely short and stared at me. Then he came a few steps nearer, very slowly, still staring at me open-eyed, and I may say open-mouthed.

"Well," he exclaimed, after a moment. "That's strange. Very strange."

I looked at him in amazement. "Yes," he continued, still staring at me, "this is the strangest thing I ever saw." He seemed hypnotized at the sight of me. His expression was so startled that I was forced to say, "But, what is so strange?"

"Why," he answered, "because you remind me of that piano-playing fellow Padrooski—same hair, same necktie, same shoes, same coat. Never saw anything like it, never. You're just like him. Say, who are you anyhow?"

"Well," I answered smiling, "I am Paderewski."

"What," he shouted, "*you* are Padrooski? You? You don't mean it. You're Padrooski, really, seriously? You tell me you're Padrooski? No!"

"Yes," I answered. "I am Paderewski and no other."

"My God," and without another word he rushed to the door, flung it wide open and shouted, "Boys, boys—Mr. Johnson, Mr. Smith, Mr. Jones, come on up here quick, all of you, come in here and let me introduce you to my friend, Mr. Padrooski."

Well, they rushed in from all sides; they flowed in like the waves of the sea, and I was soon completely surrounded with what seemed to me an unruly mob of unknown faces, and then while my own guests were waiting I was actually obliged to shake hands with about 200 people, while my newfound friend of the dressing room, shouting and gesticulating with delight interspersed with frequent embraces and slaps on the shoulder, introduced me. It was amazing.

After this experience I began to feel that I must be known everywhere in America even in that short time, and that my hair, which I think I told you Mr. Philip Hale, the eminent critic of Boston, so seriously objected to, was a mark of identification from which there was no escape.

· The critics in America, of whom Mr. Philip Hale was one of the most prominent, were extremely nice. But the man who wrote the first kind words about me, and until his last criticism spoke so well, was Henry T. Finck. In every criticism of his there was perhaps much more affection than impartial judgment. He praised me always, even when my playing was inferior, as inevitably had to happen considering my physical condition at that time. Some others were also very kind and enthusiastic, and still others were perhaps not quite so admiring.

James Huneker was also a very great enthusiast. I speak specially of him because he was such a remarkable man and critic, and he knew a great deal about the piano. He was an excellent musician. He had studied the piano in Paris and used to play well. At first he was perhaps the most enthusiastic of all the critics, but when he adopted the policy of a certain musical periodical (he belonged to the staff) and had to write according to the spirit of that paper—which at that time was run on rather commercial lines—his criticism somewhat changed. But I cannot complain about that. It was natural. But I suffered some very unpleasant moments.

Ah! Why? Well, that is a long story. Now I do not like to remember and speak about people who have perhaps not acted quite fairly in the past. I do not mean in regard to myself, but all in all. The musical journal in question acted in a very unfair way. I prefer not to speak of the actual causes now, for it all ended after a time with apologies made to me in a way that was really touching. For instance, the principal offender, the editor himself, who had attacked me in an outrageous way, came shortly before he died to apologize personally. At the time, though, it caused me great unhappiness and I know that a great many people knew about it and will still remember it. Huneker's name brings back to me the memory of this unhappy episode, although he was not connected with it—far from it.

Finck, I repeat, was a fine critic with great musical knowledge. But, like most of us, he had some preferences and also some *prejudices,* but the difference between Finck and many other critics was that Finck was sincere, while the others were continually changing their prejudices and preferences, sometimes even during a season! Finck, however, was always the same. He was a rare character, and was a very interesting man, and a good man. He died only a few years ago after a long and eminent career. As long as he lived I saw him frequently, and several times he came to visit us at Morges with his wife, a most sympathetic and intelligent woman for whom I also had a very sincere friendship.

That second American tour was suddenly interrupted amidst a phenomenal financial success by another disastrous occurrence. Fate had still another blow in store for me. Yes, my hands. Another accident to my hands. I was invited to a dinner at the house of a famous hostess in New York with Jean and Edouard de Reszke, and some other eminent artists. The dinner was good, the company charming, and to crown it all, the hostess a most gracious and brilliant woman. The "stage," shall we say, was charmingly "set," and the atmosphere after dinner was so sympathetic that, though I *never* play after having enjoyed a meal, I could not resist the wish of the hostess to play "just a few little pieces." Contrary to the well-known story about Chopin, who, once invited to play after dinner, answered quickly, "Oh, but Madame, I have eaten so little!" Well, I felt that in this instance I had to play because I had eaten so *much!*

No one else wanted to contribute to the recreation of the assembly, so it seemed inevitable that I should do it myself. As I'd just given a recital, my fingers were very tired, and evidently there was some little scratch on my skin which I had not noticed. I felt it at once upon touching the piano; it was very unpleasant, but the consequences were perfectly disastrous, because my finger became infected. This was a dreadful misfortune. At that particular moment, there was a chamber music concert approaching. I had promised the Adamowski Quartette to take part in their concert. This I did very gladly through my lifelong friendship for them. Every ticket had been sold, and, as I was the fashion just then, my name on the program had meant a "full house." So, under no circumstances could I fail them. I could not possibly withdraw; I had to play.

On the eve of the concert I was in such frightful pain that I was in absolute despair as to whether I should be able even to sit at the piano. If it had been my own concert I should have cancelled it immediately, but for the Adamowskis—impossible! I had had no sleep. The finger was swollen beyond belief. It all happened very quickly after the dinner, just a few hours. And the only doctor I could get at that time of night evidently was unable to help me, as the swelling continued.

Very early in the morning I went to Doctor Lange, a German physician who was highly recommended. I went to him in great agony. He looked at my finger and said, "This is very, *very* serious. It must be operated upon immediately." "But," I cried, "do you know that I have to *play* this afternoon—I must play." "Play?" he cried, "you are crazy! That is impossible. You will see how serious it is when I perform the operation."

"Do anything you like," I answered, "but I must play. Do anything, but stop this pain. Use an anæsthetic to make me feel as little as possible, but I must play."

"But it is madness," he said, "madness! You cannot play. You take a great risk. Greater than you know."

"Even so," I answered, "I must play. I beg of you to do all you can. Surely your science must be sufficient to help me a little for this one occasion. I will stop playing then."

"For how long?" he growled. "How long?"

"Well," I hesitated. "A fortnight."

"Not long enough. Not *half* long enough."

"Then three weeks," I cried. "Yes, three weeks. I promise you."

The doctor laughed. "That is better. Then I shall try to do my best for you now."

Well, he performed the operation. It was something frightful. Then he put a little bandage around the finger and used some anæsthetics in order to make me feel as little pain as possible. I was stupid enough to let my secretary carry out his wish to print some circulars and have one put on each chair at the concert, to say that I had just been operated on for a felon and that I apologized in advance for my playing. That was a mistake.

I played. I played with those four fingers. I had to play a Beethoven trio and a Brahms quartet with the Adamowskis. Fortunately, I was playing only a few solos which were very familiar to me, some Schubert and a little Chopin. But even so, the pain was a torture. During the playing all the effects of the anæsthetic gradually disappeared, and I was then facing reality—the most agonizing pain that could be imagined, because all the time I was hurting that fresh wound.

The next day every one (except Finck, who wrote that I was

playing under such tragic circumstances) criticized me most severely without mentioning that I had just been operated on. The doctor was right. I had to stop playing entirely after that concert. I gave up some seven or eight recitals and just nursed my finger. I still had some twenty or more concerts to give.

When I started to play again, weeks later, there was still a bandage around the finger and my doctor still protested that I was beginning too soon. He was quite right, because each time I played, in spite of the bandage, I reopened the wound and, in consequence, at the end of every concert the keyboard was covered with blood! The first time it made a terrific impression on me. It was an ugly sight. I could scarcely go on playing, but I soon got accustomed to it, I must admit, and during the rest of that tour of twenty-two concerts, I played each one with a bandaged finger and the keyboard was always red when I finished.

How did I dare to take such a risk? You may well ask that. And I can only make you the same answer that I have made before —necessity and ambition and, of course, the all-conquering disregard of youth.

But Fate was good to me, and considering the amount of work and the number of concerts I have given in my long life, I have been well treated, indeed, by my guardian angels.

On both the first and second American tours, I stopped at the old Windsor Hotel when in New York, where I lived most comfortably. I always stayed there until it was destroyed by fire in 1899. It happened on St. Patrick's Day when a great parade was passing and the hotel was filled with watching guests. Suddenly without warning, the whole great place burst into flames. The fire was caused by a lighted match thrown carelessly through a window which set fire to one of the lace curtains. Many lives were lost and it was a dreadful catastrophe. It was the destruction of this famous hotel that caused a wave of reform in all hotel construction because while it was considered the best hotel in New York, it was in reality a huge fire-trap.

During its long life the Windsor Hotel was a homelike sort of place and a great many old people lived there permanently. One distinguished old couple I remember particularly, a Mr. and Mrs. Sanford, who were the parents of a gentleman who became a very true friend of mine, one of the most gifted amateur pianists I have ever known. Sam Sanford was his name. He was professor of music at a university, a remarkable musician. He came to my first concert and attended them all. He was a delightful companion, musically and otherwise. We met first at a billiard table. I was playing billiards. There was a billiard room at the Windsor Hotel, and as I was rather a good player, especially of pool, I used to go there often for a little rest and exercise with my secretary.

Whenever I went there, as my reputation as a pool player was then well established, many interested people gathered about and watched the game. One of the frequent onlookers I noticed was a big silent man with a strong, Napoleonic face. He stood out somewhat from the others. This gentleman was Mr. William McKinley, future President of the United States. He always came in very quietly and watched my playing with the keenest interest, but he never spoke a word to anybody. He just came and looked and smiled quietly to himself now and then, but never spoke. His silence was rather marked, I remember, in that group of eager and sometimes excited watchers. It was during one of these times that Sam Sanford appeared and we became friends across the billiard table.

Sometimes he invited me to dinner at his club, and one evening I met there three very amusing old men whose entire interest in life appeared to be in the aristocracy of Europe! Their three daughters, it seems, had all married titles and the old gentlemen were so delighted that they never lost an opportunity to mention the fact—it proved, alas, to be their only topic of conversation, and their pride and satisfaction in their titled sons-in-law was unbounded. An amusing comment on democratic America! The three old men always sat somewhat apart in the most comfortable corner of the Club—always talking together about their titled daughters, and their husbands. There was great rivalry between them. They enchanted me and I never tired of hearing them talk, although I always knew exactly what was coming. The story never varied.

Second American Visit

The first one began thus: "Well," he would say with great pride, "I am delighted to tell you that I have just had a letter this morning from my daughter, the Countess X——. She writes to tell me that her husband, the Count, is suffering dreadfully from the unusually cold weather.'

At this the second would quietly lean forward and say "How strange. You must be mistaken, for my son-in-law, the Marquis, says quite the contrary. He writes me that the weather on the Continent is unusually warm and beautiful."

And then, very impatiently, the eldest of the three old gentlemen would rise from his chair and interrupt quite angrily with, "Oh, nonsense, my daughter, the Duchess, has just written me from her palace in Florence that the weather is not at all good there and she and the Duke are leaving immediately for the Riviera. The Duke is very delicate, you know," the old gentleman would add, glaring at the other two, who quickly subsided. Ah, he was the strongest of them all. His daughter was a Duchess —his son-in-law, a Duke!

After that little outburst, which happened whenever they were together, they all sank peacefully back in their chairs and sat in silence for some time.

The people I met during that first American tour were of great interest to me. There were many distinguished American men at that moment who were greatly in the public eye. I knew most of them and some of them became my warm friends. The American man was a very different product from the European and I found all these contacts stimulating. In fact everything in America was stimulating. There was a sense of adventure in the air. I think one always feels that upon arrival in the United States, no matter how often one goes there.

Joseph Choate was one of the many distinguished men that I talked with several times at the house of my dear valued friend, Miss Eleanor Blodgett. He was a famous lawyer and later on became Ambassador to England. Choate was a very able and brilliant man, and very lovable. He was extremely witty and always had just the right answer for every occasion.

[257]

And I met, during those early American days, Mr. Charles Eliot, former president of Harvard, a splendid man. And General Horace Porter, too, another ambassador, and that famous American figure and after-dinner speaker, Mr. Chauncey Depew. I must say Senator Depew. He was most picturesque, and typically American. It was at a dinner at the Pulitzers' that I first met Mr. Depew.

Joseph Pulitzer was a most gracious host, and at that particular dinner quite a little flurry of surprise was caused by the charming speech of Mr. Depew when he rose and proposed my health and gave the toast "To the King!" For just a second every one, even Pulitzer himself, was slightly bewildered. In that democratic country, a toast to the King was unheard of, but in a second or two Depew in his charming and inimitable way explained the mystery, and it was altogether a most happy and friendly occasion.

Joseph Pulitzer was editor of *The New York World,* a great newspaper of enormous influence while he lived. He was a very remarkable man in his way. I met him in Paris in 1889. It was during the Exposition I met him for the first time and he took rather a fancy to me and I liked him, too, very much. The feeling was mutual from the moment of meeting.

Even then he was losing his sight and finally became entirely blind, perhaps the greatest tragedy that could have befallen him. In the midst of his great activities and the gravest responsibilities, at the very pinnacle of his career, he was struck down. Pulitzer was in certain ways an extremely brilliant man. He knew a great deal about law and many other things, and he was a very great journalist—one of the greatest. He was very fond of music too. He was a Jew of Hungarian extraction and naturally loved very much his Hungarian music. Whenever I was in New York I used to go to his house and I greatly enjoyed their family life for the first few years, when I saw him often. When he became blind I used to go and play for him—a little recital in a way. I would play for several hours the things he loved most, and I was so happy to give him this pleasure—to lift a little the curtain of his dark days.

Second American Visit

Those hours with Pulitzer were very rewarding in spite of their sadness. He was so grateful—it was heart-breaking. He could find no way of expressing his thanks and always said the same thing over and over again. "What can I do to show you my gratitude?" he would cry. "Tell me—what can I do?"

He always had several secretaries, cultivated and interesting young men, close at hand. One of them I recall was a musician; he had to play for him every day for some hours, not to amuse him, but simply to give him a certain rest after the others had done their work, for Pulitzer, in spite of his blindness, did an immense amount of work each day on his paper, *The New York World*—that great newspaper which, like its founder, is now no more.

All those secretaries were completely worn out after a short time. He was so exacting, so eager, so interested in everything and so full of a passionate energy, that he drew from each and every one of them all they could give him—their brains, their vitality, their sympathies—everything. He paid them, of course, very generously, but several of them told me it was a fearful drain upon them, and absolutely exhausting. And what money can pay such a toll?

In general knowledge Pulitzer was rather deficient. There were a great many things he did not know, along with the things he did. He was educated, but not cultivated. In music, he liked Beethoven and Liszt—such a contrast! I always played for him a Beethoven Sonata and a Liszt Rhapsody and he was always quite wild and enchanted.

Under the circumstances of our close friendship and his great admiration for my playing, it was strange and amusing too, that *his* newspaper was the only one in which I used to read invariably adverse criticisms of my playing. The music critic then was Reginald deKoven. The good "Reggie," as all his friends called him, later on became my warm friend. But after every New York recital during my first seasons there came a very bad criticism. It always amused me. If I had wished for a little revenge, I would have said to Pulitzer when he asked what he could do to show his gratitude, "You may tell your music critic of the *World* to treat me a little more justly—even a little more kindly in his criticism." But I never did, for I realized that Pulitzer probably gave very little thought to musical criticisms and besides, what editor would dare interfere with his music critic, who is king in his own domain? At any rate, whatever the reason, Pulitzer's newspaper rarely had a good word to say for me.

Pulitzer used to come to every recital of mine as long as he was able, led in by his secretary. He generally occupied the same seat near the front and I always knew that he would be there. It was very pathetic. He never failed to come until his health became so broken he could no longer go out. He was a tragic figure—vital to the end. The last time I saw him was on his yacht at Mentone, and I felt then that we should never meet again. His death ended a very vivid and interesting friendship that I always valued and whose memory I still cherish. It is an abundant memory and as we talk about him many sides of his truly extraordinary character and versatile mind still occur to me, for we had many things in common besides music. Our talks together ranged from subject to subject, and the Bible was often one of them.

The Bible was frequently read to him by one of his secretaries and I remember hearing that on one occasion when he came to a particularly drastic part of a story, Pulitzer stopped him abruptly and protested with great violence and excitement, "What dreadful people! What a tribe! If they lived today they would be arrested. We'd call the police!"

You may accept this story or not just as you please, but I find myself in complete sympathy with Pulitzer's views. Although I doubt if he knew the Bible as well as I knew it, for example almost by heart since I was fifteen, I, too, even at that early age, when I read certain passages of that great Book, felt like shouting out my protest. Yes, it shocked me frequently and gave me certain ideas which were not very orthodox. It brought great inquiries and certain doubts to my mind which I have kept, and not lost as the years have gone on.

This is a deeply interesting, but rather delicate, subject and perhaps I may shock some one's religious feelings, but nevertheless, I had the impression, even then, as a boy that the Bible was not a holy book and that it had very little to do with our Christian religion. The Old Testament is absolutely un-Christian and anti-Christian. But the founders of the Church looked upon the Old Testament as something which had a very strong connecting link with the Gospel on account of the prophets. And that is, to a certain degree, justified. The Old Testament contains great prophecies. It has a great wisdom, too, but it is not, in my opinion, the inspired word of God. But what is so inspiring and so lofty, and will be forever one of the most magnificent expressions of lyric beauty, is the Gospel (the Gospels of Matthew, Mark, Luke and John). It has a musical beauty that is beyond compare and must so appeal to every sensitive nature. From my youth it has thrilled and sustained me and will remain with me forever in its serene loftiness and beauty.

These views of mine have perhaps no special reason here at this moment of my history, but they are still of some concern to me and add another thread, a certain interest, to our story, I think.

You are quite right when you say that a biography must run the gamut, not only of the times in which one lives and their great changes, but of the people and the events which are a part of them. A biography must reveal one's feelings and one's emotions, the growth of the brain and spirit as one goes on from childhood to old age. All—all contribute to the great pattern of one's life.

A wonderful story of your great Henry James bears a title that fits our case, I think. It is called "The Figure in the Carpet." The Figure which starts in the beginning with a few simple threads, and goes on gathering more and more threads and colors until the end, when the final complete pattern is revealed. It is formed and woven as we go, but we can see only the particular bit that we are weaving at the moment. Bright threads, black threads, the good strong threads, and the tangled broken ones all go into the making. And so it must be.

II

And now we shall pick up again the dropped thread of my second American tour which brings us to an important event in the American scene—the World's Fair which took place in Chicago. That was a tremendous happening and drew people not only from all parts of the country, but from all over the world.

I received an invitation from the Committee of the World's Fair to appear there with Theodore Thomas's Orchestra in the concert hall especially built for musical productions at the Exposition. This was to take place in May, 1893, towards the end of my tour.

I was very much interested in the World's Fair because it was an opportunity to see those energetic and ambitious leaders of Chicago at their best. Chicago already had impressed me more than any other city in America. As I have already mentioned, when I first arrived in New York, forty-five years ago, one of the largest buildings at that time was the Windsor Hotel. Chicago already had several skyscrapers, as they are so admirably and aptly called. They had the first skyscrapers, although many people, particularly foreigners, do not know this and think that New York built the first ones. But to Chicago must go the credit for that amazing development. It was the "Windy City" (by no means a misnomer) that was the very first to introduce these huge buildings in America. There was already a perfectly tremendous building, I think the Masonic Temple, which was nineteen or twenty stories high. The appearance of that building was extremely impressive after all the large, but low, buildings in New York. There was also a huge hotel called The Auditorium, which contained the concert hall in which I made my first appearance, the largest hall at that time in the entire country.

Everywhere there was to be noted a strong movement towards the beautifying of the city. Several parks had already been started. There has always been a strong civic feeling in Chicago, and the Exposition gave a still greater emphasis to that collective activity.

AUDITORIUM,

. . . CHICAGO . . .

Wednesday Afternoon, March 8th, 1893, at 2 o'clock.

PADEREWSKI'S

PIANO RECITAL.

PROGRAMME.

FANTAISIE ET FUGUE, A minor,	*Bach-Liszt*
SONATA, Op. 31, E flat,	*Beethoven*
Allegro, Scherzo, Menuet con Trio, Presto con Fusco.	
NACHTSTUECK,	*Schumann*
ETUDE,	*Paganini-Schumann*
IMPROMPTU,	*Schubert*
SOIREE DE VIENNE,	*Schubert-Liszt*
BARCAROLLE,	
ETUDE,	
BERCEUSE,	*Chopin*
POLONAISE,	
MELODIE,	*Paderewski*
CAPRICE, "SPRING DAWN,"	*William Mason*
RHAPSODIE HONGROISE,	*Liszt*

At that time there were in my mind three things of colossal dimensions in America which impressed me as being objects of condensed immensity. I find no other way to express it. Niagara Falls, the City of Chicago, and the Grand Canyon.

Niagara Falls has that condensed immensity—although it is comparatively small, yet it impresses one as a world in itself, and terrific—of indescribable power and beauty.

The Grand Canyon, which I saw a few years later, gave me again that impression of a colossal strength concentrated in one considerable area; and Chicago, with that stupendous driving force which was pushing those eager millions of population towards their goal, gave me again the impression of that concentrated immensity similar to those two cataclysms of nature.

But while Niagara Falls and the Grand Canyon were the results of brutal forces of nature, Chicago appealed to me then as being the result of all the tremendous, but intelligent, forces of mankind.

There was a large group of men, leaders in that activity, whom I had the opportunity of meeting upon my arrival. The grounds of the World's Fair were like a huge camp. It was a strange sight. All the men who were directing those colossal preparations were practically living (really camping) there on the spot. We spent there, before the official opening of the Fair and the concerts, about a fortnight, living in rooms which were not yet even finished. We lived and slept there. It was most uncomfortable but exciting. Everything was in great disorder. The plaster covering the walls was not yet dry. Everything had been put up in a hurry. There was humidity everywhere, coming not only from the neighboring lake, but from the dampness of the buildings.

The committee invited me to stay there and it was certainly a unique experience. Had I realized what was in store for me I probably should never have accepted the invitation. It was something fantastic in its discomfort. But the strangeness and adventure of it all appealed to me. Like everything in America on my arrival, it filled me with a great wonder and excitement. America

William Steinway

A PEACEFUL SOLUTION.

AT THE NEXT WORLD'S FAIR PADEREWSKI WILL PLAY ON ALL THE PIANOS AT ONCE.

From a photograph by the Culver Service

The cartoonist Keppler's view of Paderewski's difficulties with the piano makers at the Chicago World's Fair

was a land of miracles—performed "overnight" as you say. Among the outstanding figures in this enterprise, there was a man of actual genius by the name of Daniel Burnham, who was practically the creator of all that was beautiful in Chicago then. He was probably the greatest architect of that time, a beautiful man, full of imagination, of high culture, and above all a man always thinking about the good of his fellow citizens, and devoting to it all his energy and strength. Burnham was really the constructive genius of the World's Fair. It was his driving force that carried the enterprise through triumphantly.

So many of Chicago's important men were active and creative in the great World's Fair. It was a tremendous outpouring of civic pride and feeling on the part of every one concerned. I knew only a few of them at that time, but I remember particularly the Deering brothers, Cyrus McCormick and Charles Atwood, the architect. Theodore Thomas was conducting all the orchestral and choral performances during the Exposition.

Grover Cleveland, then President of the United States, formally opened the Chicago Fair, in the presence of at least half a million people. It was something really gorgeous. He made on that occasion a beautiful, impressive address. I met him only once, and I never saw him again, but one knows of him as one of America's greatest Presidents.

The concerts were most successful, but the pleasure I had was not without certain unpleasant surprises. I was then playing everywhere the Steinway piano, and the House of Steinway, for some reason best known to themselves, did not wish to exhibit at the Fair. The competitors of that illustrious firm started an opposition and wanted me to be prevented from playing, at the Exposition, an instrument which was not exhibited. It took all the energy and skill and tact of Theodore Thomas and all his friends to obtain the agreement of the committee to my playing on a Steinway piano.

It was a very bad situation, but finally I was allowed to play the Steinway, without, however, having been able to stop the bitter controversy which was going on at that time and which still went on for months in the newspapers, because every one of those competitors had their supporters, and they were fighting on legal grounds.

I do not know now and did not know then why the Steinways did not exhibit there, but they must have had some very important reasons, I'm sure.

There was no accident, no mutilation to the piano during this quarrel, as sometimes happens. The strings of my piano were never cut in America, as the people in charge were very attentive and vigilant and watched the piano constantly. I had no complaint to make of the condition of the pianos and their fitness for the concerts, as in some countries where I had certain experiences which bordered on actual catastrophe. For instance, in St. Petersburg there was naturally no Steinway piano to be had when I played there. As I had been accustomed for several years (when not in America) to play the Erard piano, I asked my good friend Monsieur Blondel to send two Erard concert grands for the Russian tour in 1899. He did so. They were beautiful and I was delighted, but when I came to the concert hall in St. Petersburg, half an hour before the arrival of the orchestra, I found, to my horror, that one of the pedals of the instrument was completely destroyed; and when I tried the piano, I found, between many of the keys, sharp pins standing up. I saw them, thank God, before touching the piano. That was my good luck, because I might have hurt my fingers fatally. After that experience, my piano tuner, who accompanied me on that Russian tour, was wise enough to come with the piano into the hall, and remain there for the whole day and night, never leaving it. A constant vigil.

And the reason for all this persecution? Simply that I did not apply to the local piano agency in St. Petersburg, but brought my own piano. I was an intruder! The pedal had been ripped off with great violence. Whoever did it was probably greatly disappointed when I came out and played. It was my début there, and in connection with that début, I shall tell you, later on, several amusing things.

XII

Composer's Interlude

I

But to go on. After my successful *second* tour in America, I returned as usual to Europe. In the summer of that year, 1893, I was living with my boy and some friends in a quiet little place in Normandy called Yport. For the first time in my arduous career in foreign countries, I could invite some people dear to my heart to spend a few weeks with me. My sister came to stay with me, and I was glad to have also my dear old friend Edward Kerntopf. I felt very happy then. It was a holiday time.

This little reunion with my son and friends was a garden spot in a life of constant travel and work. My boy was a child of twelve then, and although he was very delicate, I still had a firm belief that he would outgrow his illness, and everything was being done to bring this about. After ten years of constant labor, this little breathing space was an oasis in a desert of work. I had time for many things then—the harness had dropped from my shoulders. I was free. I began to compose again. I started a composition, a "Polish Fantasia," for piano and orchestra, which I finished within five weeks. That fantasia was performed by myself for the first time at the Festival of Norwich, England, under the conductorship of Mr. Randegger, a fine teacher of singing and an excellent conductor, and it met with considerable success. It was also performed in the same season (by myself) in London with Georg Henschel, who was then conducting many orchestral concerts. Afterwards it was played by several noted artists.

This tour in England was the largest tour I had had so far. I played in all the provincial cities, and in Dublin, Belfast, and

Cork, besides recitals in London. All these concerts were extremely successful.

At the end of the season I made a decision that was of tremendous importance to me, one that made a great change in my career. I decided not to play at all during the following season, but to begin the writing of my opera, "Manru." It happened in this way: a Polish writer and poet, Alfred Nossig by name, had approached me repeatedly with a proposition for writing a book for an opera. So, out of the several outlines suggested, I selected one which was afterward written for me. That book, though not then in its definite form, was sent me toward the end of 1893, and became the libretto for my opera "Manru."

And so I turned all my forces toward the great object, a tremendous undertaking that obliterated everything else. I shut myself completely away from the world. I went to Italy for the first time and took the book with me and began to write the music. My stay in Italy was rather short, for I was suddenly called to Paris on account of my son's illness. I remained then in Paris, living not in my apartment but in a little house which I rented in one of the most secluded quarters of Paris, where I lived quite alone. There was nobody there. Only my servant came every day towards one o'clock and prepared the luncheon.

This little house was in Passy and was a hiding place. No one knew I was there. I shut the world out completely. This was necessary as I was so well known to the public then that my Paris apartment was a rendezvous for friends as well as musicians and was besieged most of the time.

My dinner I usually took in a little restaurant for coachmen. The food was excellent. The company was not aristocratic of course, but it was certainly not unpleasant to see all these good people enjoying themselves after their work. I found a special relaxation and interest in it. At that time there were no automobiles, no taxi-drivers. There were only horse fiacres. It was a peaceful interlude. In no other way would I have been able to work in Paris.

Well, the opera proceeded satisfactorily, because within six months I finished two acts and began the third. Although I was not playing, I still suffered very much from my arm and fourth finger, and upon the advice of a physician I then went to Aix-les-Bains for treatment and, as I hoped, a complete cure. I rented a little château, the Château de Bon Port, on the Lake of Bourget, and made quite a long stay. I took the "cure" faithfully and repeated that for several seasons, but without any permanent results. Nobody, not even the best physicians, seemed to know exactly what the trouble was with my fourth finger. Some tendon had been strained, something had happened that they could not account for. It was all very discouraging.

In spite of my laborious "cure," I enjoyed Aix-les-Bains. It was a charming place with ample amusements to interest one, and one of the many causes of my amusement, I must admit, was my friendship with a little dog that attached himself unexpectedly to me. Now I have had two animals during my life that have shown a certain interest in music. One superficially, because music was perhaps only an attribute to my own personality, but the other one was really fond of music.

It is of the first that we shall speak now, a little dog, that we named Brise-fer. During my cure at Aix-les-Bains, I took my daily bath and treatment at the thermal establishment there. I always went in a little carriage especially ordered, and always had the same coachman, who was somewhat of a philosopher in his way and quite an interesting character. One morning as I was entering the Bath House, a little dog suddenly appeared upon the scene and followed me for a few steps. Two hours later, when I returned from the establishment, I noticed the same little dog and he seemed to be waiting for me, for he wagged his tail delightedly when he saw me. He was a dog of no particular breed, and certainly no particular beauty, but he seemed intelligent and very affectionate, and deeply interested in me.

When I left the establishment, I was very exhausted after the dreadful hot bath, and I hurried into the carriage with only one thought—to get home. To my surprise, however, the dog followed the carriage; he came to the Château with me. He refused to leave, and there he remained for three months, my constant and devoted companion. He never left me. He used to sleep in my room; he ate his meals at my feet and was close beside me day after day as I wrote. In fact, during the whole summer that dog was always at my side. Brise-fer won my heart completely. He was so attached to me and so faithful and sentimental. I have never known a dog like him. My sister, my poor boy, in fact every one who stayed with us, was devoted to him. And then suddenly everything changed. A fortnight before our departure the dog became quite a different animal, so sad, melancholy, and desperate. He sensed our departure, we all felt. Whenever he came to the little tower where I had my studio, he would sit and look up at me just like a human being. He would moan and cry. It was heart-breaking to listen to him. I said to myself, "This is dreadful. I simply cannot leave this dog. I must take him to Paris. It would be cruel to leave him behind. He will die if he is separated from me. There is no other way; he must go with me."

So it was decided and everything arranged with considerable trouble. The day of departure arrived and the dog went with us to the station. I had already bought a ticket for him and I said to Marcel, my faithful and devoted valet, of whom I have many wonderful things to tell you at a later time, "Now Marcel, be sure and put him in the carriage with us. He must not be separated from me on the journey. He must sit beside me as usual." Marcel hurried off with the dog to put him in our carriage, when suddenly he became very ugly. He not only growled furiously, but actually attacked Marcel and tried to bite him. We were dumb-founded. I called him by all his pet names, but he only glared at me, showed his teeth and turned away, vicious and snarling. I called again, "Come here, Brise-fer." I went toward him, but he became more and more ferocious, his tail dropped between his legs and he snarled and shook his head and turned and ran away from us. I stood in amazement at the sight. I could not believe my eyes. It was "all off," as you say in America. What an ending to our friendship! It was a mystery that I could in no way fathom, and so I returned to Paris wondering, and I must say somewhat dejected, without my faithful little companion.

Composer's Interlude

The next year I returned to the Château de Bon Port and began the baths once more. "Perhaps," I said, "I shall see my friend Brise-fer again." I admit I wanted to see him. He was still a mystery to me, a source of irritation. I resented his behavior; I was not used to such treatment. Well, I did see him, the very day after my arrival. There he was at the Baths just as the year before. I called to him delightedly, but he took absolutely no notice of me. I continued my efforts, but without success. Brise-fer would have none of me. Again my old coachman, who was still driving me, watched the proceedings and seemed very much amused at my efforts with the dog.

"Oh, don't bother with him, sir," he said finally. "Let him alone."

"But what is the matter with him? What has happened to him?"

"Oh," the coachman answered, "he is just a fraud, that dog, a fraud! He does not care for *you* any more. He does that to everybody. That's his way, he changes masters. Every year a new master—that is his habit. He's no good. He's a bad dog. Why he's known to every one here, sir." The coachman laughed contemptuously and said, "You can't get him back, sir. Don't try. Leave him alone. He's a fraud, I tell you. He has no gratitude or affection in him."

But I was not at all convinced. I was determined to win him back. Such was my vanity! So, I called him again very affectionately. Still he refused to even look at me. Then I offered him some attraction—I even stopped at the butcher's, much to the disgust of the coachman, and bought a large piece of meat for him, but he never approached me. It was no use. Brise-fer only growled and snarled at me and ran away. Yes, it was "all off!" He knew perfectly well that he was not acting correctly, so he let it appear that we were strangers—he had never known me. A very human trait! I had not expected to find it in a dog, I must say. But after our last encounter, I realized the truth of what my philosophical coachman said—that the dog was a fraud with neither gratitude nor affection in his soul.

In spite of this disappointment, that season at Aix-les-Bains was one of accomplishment, for I finished the sketch for the third act of the opera. It was in this year that my poor father died. I had not seen him for several years. The reason was that I was extremely busy all the time building my career, and though I had the strongest desire to go to him, I could not get a passport, because at that time I was a Russian subject, and being a Pole, I had tremendous difficulty in obtaining a *foreign* passport, and this was the real obstacle. The last passport I was able to obtain, before going to Leschetizky in Vienna, took me more than four months to secure. I had to go to every authority, to the county, to the district, to the province, and even to the Governor. It was purposely made difficult for Polish people to get passports, practically impossible. Having so many engagements, I could not risk going to Poland and perhaps being detained and prevented from fulfilling those engagements.

My father had lived long enough to know of my success. He was an old man then, and he was ill (he had had a stroke), so perhaps he did not realize fully all that had been accomplished in my musical career. But he did know, thank God, that I had made a certain reputation, for he read the newspaper notices I had sent him and had, of course, heard about my success in Paris and London and later in America. When he became so ill and could no longer manage his affairs, I bought a house for him in a little city by the name of Zhitomir. He loved that place and was happy there, in spite of our separation, which I know he felt to the very last. My father ended his days in that little house which I am so thankful I had the money to buy for him. As I began to prosper in life, I gave him also an income, an annuity which enabled him to live in peace and comfort to the end of his days.

His death closed forever a chapter, as the death of a parent always does. He had been everything to me since I can first remember. He was both father and mother. He was a noble man—a fine, upstanding, honest man from the beginning of his life, and even physically he was always a strong, beautiful man. And that is my abiding memory of him.

Composer's Interlude

There was nothing of any importance that happened afterwards until January and February, 1895. I began to play again. I was obliged to. I played then several times in Germany. I had concerts in Dresden. I was invited by the Queen of Saxony, the old Queen Carola, to play for some charity, and since then I have played in Dresden frequently, and strangely enough, always for charities and never for myself. I mention this only in order to point to a certain little fact which took place some years later.

There were short tours in England and France, too, at this time. My pianistic reputation was growing—with the audiences, in the newspapers—everywhere, in fact, I was then established brilliantly throughout Europe, with the exception of Spain, which came a few years later.

These tours, of course, put an end to my work on the opera. The opera, alas, was now enjoying a long rest! It could not be otherwise. You see I was obliged to begin playing again. I needed money. My ten fingers were my fortune.

The year before I had been obliged to accept a new business manager, but the new manager proved not to be as brilliant as all my friends and advisers had assured me! There were more and constant demands for money for the enterprises which he launched and which were not prosperous, quite the reverse in fact.

Now, a lifelong desire of mine was to have a little rural estate of my own, a place with a beautiful forest and a stream of water. That was a dream always close to my heart, but it proved to be an inaccessible dream, and all my attempts for its realization a very costly experience. Instead of one estate, I practically got *three,* and there was never a forest on any of them! I never wanted to make money with these purchases, I just wanted to own a little property that I could enjoy; and so, with this in view, my new manager quickly, one after another, bought for me three properties *without* forests, that I could not enjoy! C'est la vie.

He bought the three properties in succession, and none of them was agreeable to me. The property which I saw first and *did* want, and which proved to be an excellent affair and splendid investment, alas, slipped out of my hands. It was a lovely place with the large forest that I longed for, and the little river running through it, a beautiful river; but ah, I cannot tell you why, my manager did not buy it, but so it was. He delayed; he let it go, and then bought me the others!

The first estate was a forced purchase, a mortgaged purchase. I was induced by him to lend a sum of money to the owners of the estate, and it was a hopeless case. It was in Russian Poland. It was worthless to me because, first of all, there were no trees. It was a good piece of land near a railway station and with a nice little stream, but the forest had been absolutely cut down a few years before. Finally, in order to recover my money, I had to buy it.

The second estate was also in Russian Poland, but near the Austrian frontier. It was, I think, some eighty miles from the railway. With my occupation, I could not go there to reside—so it, too, was impossible. Another mistake!

The *third* one was in Austrian Poland. There were certain nice features about that property, too, because it was beautifully situated, and, although it had no forest, I learned afterward that I could buy a little forest adjoining it, and this I did. For me a forest is the greatest pleasure—to walk among the trees, because I love trees, to hear birds singing in them, and to see not only flowers, but berries, growing. That is an incomparable joy.

Well, I got that little forest, and I loved it, but after a few years I found that even my long lucrative American tours would not be enough to keep it up and preserve it—and me! And so I parted with that third property, at another big loss.

Added to all this, I had great trouble with this manager because when he received all the money that I entrusted to him, he invested that money, not alone for me, but for me and *himself* as partner, and the investments proved to be rather disastrous, to say the least. I lost a great deal and had no satisfaction in any way from them.

So I realized then from these costly and painful experiences that I could not earn one single penny except by my playing. My ten fingers were my only fortune. I repeat, no investment brought me anything. Whatever investment I made, or some one made for me, was always a loss. It was evidently my destiny. Whenever there was a possibility for me to make a brilliant investment, even a fortune, I had not the time to do it because I was an artist and not a business man. When I asked others to do it for me, they always delayed—they neglected it. My orders were not carried out, and everything that was done proved to be ruinous. It is always the same. This fate has pursued me through life.

II

I took up my work again and that summer, 1895, I prepared for the third American tour. It was the most successful of all. That third tour was a tremendous tour, covering the whole of the United States from "Maine to the Pacific" as you say. It was also a very great financial success, which I needed after so many excursions into real estate.

It was then I visited California for the first time, and my experience in San Francisco during that tour was complete and perfect enjoyment. The beauty of the country, the transparency of the air, the kindness and hospitality of the people, made me happy and content.

I met there many people for whom I still personally, or in memory, preserve a warm affection. Incidentally, I had the opportunity of meeting Mr. Herbert Hoover, then a student at Stanford University.

I spent in San Francisco, after these concerts, one week more in order to be able to play in a concert given by the Belgian violinist, Marsick. The weather was gorgeous all the time. It was perfectly enchanting. I was invited to several private houses in Burlingame, and I enjoyed myself for the first time on the tour, because I had that free week. It was a real vacation.

For the American public, it is not without interest to say that when I played in Los Angeles at that time, it was a very small town. Now it has almost two million population. That growth is something astounding to realize. During that same season I played in San Diego. It was a tiny place then, hardly a village, and from the railway station to the theatre (or opera house, as it was called), a distance of half a mile, there was only one house—a little gambling house—and the audience for my concert was drawn mostly from the Coronado Beach Hotel, which was in full swing and crowded. Today San Diego is a very beautiful city of nearly three hundred thousand inhabitants—a miracle in that country of miracles.

In many respects America seemed a fairy tale to me from the first moment. The audiences, for instance, which at the beginning of my career were rather small, were very exclusive. People interested in and caring for music. They came from the small surrounding places, from the little provincial towns, and the majority of them came with their music, with the notes to follow me. They were either students or teachers of music, the first, to have a kind of lesson, and the second, to renew their memories. They listened with a beautiful silence and followed me very reverently with their music. They made a kind of musical congregation, I felt.

It interested me enormously, because music was not then, as it is now, a part of general education. But I am sorry to say that a great change is now taking place. The radio and the records, and especially something that has nothing to do with music and everything to do with speed, the automobile, are injuring music frightfully, in my opinion.

I remember particularly two concerts in Kansas City during my second tour, that impressed me very much. It was rather a remarkable occasion. Several hundred people arrived from Texas, all armed with their volumes of music. It was a wonderful and touching sight. They crowded the hotels; they gathered in clusters at the street corners, and they stood in line in front of the box office—all with their music in hand. The largest contribution to that concert was brought by a great friend of mine from Dallas, Texas, a Mr. White, a music teacher and a splendid fellow. He himself brought fifty pupils to the concert.

During that season, I had in my audience in Los Angeles

people who came even from Phœnix, Arizona, and at Salt Lake City a train full of music lovers, young students from far-away Montana, came to the concert. There was a tremendous blizzard that day and I had to wait for the arrival of their train. It was delayed many hours. At the last moment they telegraphed my manager that they could only get there at nine o'clock in the evening—and would Mr. Paderewski please hold the concert and wait for them? Of course, I waited for them, gladly.

Ah, there are so many beautiful things to remember, revealing that eager youth and the enthusiasm of youth, and it prevailed for many years. I met that spirit again and again, particularly in the West. I often think about it now, and their eagerness and devotion.

They have always showed me affection, my audiences. And I think that an audience is just like a colossal collective individual, and primitive to excess. It is never guided by reasoning, but always by intuition, by feeling and instinct. Audiences, no matter how large (the larger the more so), *feel* just like a collective personality; they always feel whether the one to whom they show their sentiment loves them or not. I have always loved them, and I love them still—the thousands I have played for through the long years!

The spirit of an audience depends in no way upon its nationality, and this is as true of Europe as of America. In Italy I always met the same warmth and touching response from my audiences, and although I was touring practically all Europe and America at this time, it was not until 1897 that I made my first appearance in Italy. My début in Rome took place then. I spent only a few days there, but had a splendid reception, the Queen Margherita being present, and I was very hospitably received at Court and met many important Italian statesmen and artists—and, as always, the statesmen were my special interest. It was a very happy time socially as well, and there were several banquets given me, which added to a brilliant season.

It was at this time that I met the composer Boito. He was the author of several of the librettos of Verdi's great operas, including "Othello" and "Falstaff." Boito himself also wrote a very fine work indeed—the opera "Mefistofele," which had a wide popularity. He was a remarkable musician and an all-round, extremely well-informed man, very sympathetic in appearance, really quite beautiful to look at. Although he was already in advanced years, he was still very handsome. Boito was present at the banquet which was given me by Roman artists under the auspices of the Academy of St. Cecelia and Count di San Martino. San Martino was a very important man. He was practically head of the entire artistic movement in Italy, which gave him an exceptional position.

This banquet that San Martino gave me was an especially agreeable one and I had another glimpse of Italian life on that occasion. There were certain people there that I was interested to meet, such as Sgambati, the composer, at that time the most eminent musician after Verdi; the famous Italian sculptor, Monteverde, came, and the archæologist, Boni, was also among the guests. He had made very important excavations in the Forum. His discoveries, it seems, threw quite a new light on Roman history.

There were two Americans living in Rome then who were very popular, both distinguished men in their line. Julian Story, the sculptor, originally from Boston, and Marion Crawford, also a Bostonian, the very popular author whose books had an enormous sale. He was a delightful host and the most exclusive Roman society was entertained at his house. Story's son afterward married your beautiful Emma Eames.

This Italian tour was delightful. I had contact with so very many stimulating and interesting people, and I found that Roman audiences were very sympathetic—really very wonderful, and such a reception was a great joy to the heart, and balm to the nerves of an artist.

On that first visit I played only in Rome. I played for the Academy of St. Cecelia three times, I remember. It might interest you to know that the Academy is first a school, but most of all an institution that organizes concerts of importance, and gives its

Composer's Interlude

sanction to various musical publications, especially on the historical development of musical art.

At the time I played there, they had only a small hall holding about 1700 people. They now have a colossal hall called the "Augusteo." That hall is circular in form and perfectly tremendous in dimensions, and has something strange about it—because it is the tomb of Augustus. I think he still lies there in a neighboring crypt. It is not often, we might add, that a concert auditorium is built over the tomb of an emperor.

On the whole, the Italian audiences are very enthusiastic and very noisy, often shouting their pleasure. Personally I cannot complain about them, because I am always forced to play many encores, but in general the impression I had was that the audiences were very loud, very spontaneous and cordial, but short in the duration of their enthusiasm.

But for the most part, my audiences have been everywhere the same, Paris, London, Vienna, Brussels, St. Petersburg, New York, Chicago, Boston, always extremely kind and demonstrative and enthusiastic. In America, there is a custom with the people high up in the galleries to show their enthusiasm in a way that is rather discouraging to the European artist, because if they are pleased and satisfied, they whistle, and it very often sounds like hissing to the poor artist. This, of course, applies to the conditions many years ago. Now I think there is not so much exuberant enthusiasm. People everywhere have less passion about things.

There is still one amusing incident that occurs to me now in connection with Italy, something that happened at my house when Boito came to visit me. We had become good friends and I always found him delightful, but, like many Italians, extremely excitable and exclamatory. His visit to me was at his own suggestion—he was passing through Morges and said he would like to stop off and stay awhile in my house. I was, of course, delighted to have him. This was a long time ago, when telephones were just beginning to oppress mankind.

I went to the station to meet him and, before I could greet

him even, he burst forth very violently, "Oh, Paderewski, do you know Count X? What a dreadful bore he is—what a bore!" I tried to divert him, but it was no use. Boito was still in a great state of excitement about him. He could think of nothing else.

"Why," he said, "wherever I go I must see that man. I have just seen him on the train—he is everywhere, everywhere I go. I detest him."

"But," I said, "what difference does it make?"

"Oh," he answered, "he annoys me so—he upsets me. My nerves are all tingling when I see him, and he is always at hand, in trains, in hotels, concerts, even when I leave Italy he must be leaving at the same time, on the very same train!"

Of course it was so foolish I did not know what to say, but, fortunately, we arrived at the house and his attention was mercifully diverted by luncheon. However, he started up again later on and then I determined in self-defense to play a little joke on him—a joke that perhaps could carry a small criticism and put a stop to his obsession. The next day I arranged very carefully with the telephone exchange at Morges, and also with my butler, that at a certain time he was to come in with a telephone message from Count X. And so it came about. We were seated together, happily talking, on the terrace when my servant appeared at the door and said, "Pardon, Monsieur Paderewski, but a telephone message has just arrived for Monsieur Boito. It is extremely urgent. It is from Count X."

"Who?" I said, pretending not to understand the man. He repeated very solemnly, "From Count X for Monsieur Boito. C'est très pressé."

Poor Boito! He had turned absolutely pale. He was glaring at the servant, his eyes fixed in his head. Then the explosion came!

"Did I not say so? Did I not tell you?" he shouted, jumping from his chair. "Here he is again. He has pursued me even here, to your house, even over the telephone."

Poor Boito was actually trembling with rage. He rushed from the terrace, still shouting and talking to himself, and did not appear again for several hours. When he returned he was very quiet, pathetically so. Later on we had mercy on him and told him it was all a joke—a carefully planned joke. Although he was very upset and I think a little angry, my little joke had a very salutary effect. He accepted the criticism and we did not hear anything more of Count X during his visit, which was otherwise delightful.

Nothing particular happened in that year, 1897. I went on to revise my sketch of the opera, and introduced some changes in the libretto to make the action a bit more lively and dramatic, and consequently had to write many new songs and change a great deal of the musical text.

I played very little that year, but I had time to complete the sketch of my opera and begin the orchestration of it. I had been in Dresden, and there, after having played for some charitable institutions, again under the auspices of the good old Queen of Saxony, I had a talk with the director of the Opera, the famous conductor, Ernst von Schuch. He was a conductor of genius, especially of the opera. He insisted upon hearing some parts of my opera and invited me to give the first performance of "Manru" in the Royal Opera House in Dresden. This I was anxious to do, and determined to finish it quickly. On the whole, about two and a half years were spent working on it. I could not write continuously and there were intervals in which I was entirely out of the mood of the composition, but I finally did succeed in scoring the first act. Everything stopped then because I had already arranged for a tour in Russia in 1899. That was my first tour there since the youthful disaster twenty years before.

XIII

Russian Tour

I

I gave three concerts in Warsaw before going to Russia. That was practically my first appearance in the city where I had studied as a boy, and my first appearance as an artist of reputation. These three concerts were in many ways memorable for me, because I was received with exceptional honors on the part of my compatriots. Banquets were given, many addresses made, and so on, and I found it extremely fatiguing to do both public playing and public speaking. But these were all gestures of affection and, therefore, very appealing.

But it was rather pathetic to see some of my old teachers—those who had predicted that I would never be a pianist! Several of them were still there. The man who said I should be a trombone player was no more, but the two piano teachers who always assured me I had better become a cobbler than a pianist were present and looked extremely proud, as though they had said quite the contrary and contributed to my success.

It was at a banquet that I saw again my former beloved teacher of counterpoint and composition, Roguski, to whom I shall never cease to be profoundly grateful all the years of my life. It was an occasion—for us both.

The dear old Kerntopfs were there rejoicing, too, and I played again on their pianos. That did not help me much in producing a good impression. They were not bad pianos exactly, but, of course, not on the same level as the Steinway or Erard. It really was a great sacrifice, but I did it gladly. And at all my concerts in Poland, I played their pianos, and even in Kieff and

Odessa. It was a simple acknowledgment of thanks for a great friendship. But it was hard musically. On that score it was a tragedy. But I made the sacrifice, as I was greatly attached to the Kerntopf family, and to Edward Kerntopf went all my gratitude. He was the axis of the whole wheel. He felt very happy at my concerts, and he was proud and rejoiced that I had justified his faith in me. It was gratifying to a supreme degree.

After that short tour in Poland, I went to St. Petersburg and I played there several times. This was in 1899, and, as I have said, my first tour in Russia.

My first concert was with the orchestra, and after that I gave three recitals. Those concerts were not only very well attended but, artistically too, were extremely successful, though the Conservatory, which at that time was the most important musical institution of the Empire, founded by the great Anton Rubinstein, was absolutely hostile to me.

I do not know whether it was because I was a Pole, but certainly they wanted me to realize that no other pianist could expect to be appreciated in Rubinstein's land, and by his devoted followers. He was dead, but that cult for his *personality* was still so strong and so faithful that it took the form of a positive hostility to any other artist, even though he was recognized throughout the world.

The expressions in the press, especially that I was the successor of Rubinstein in public favor, and really to be compared with him, hurt the feelings of his devotees. For them I was simply an intruder. It was really unpleasant for me, because, whenever I went where there were musicians, they immediately began talking about Rubinstein as if they desired to tell me that I was not recognized by them, and wanted to show me that they were still of the opinion there was no one in the world to compare with Rubinstein.

The audiences, however, were excellent. I did not have that feeling in the concerts. And the press, too, was excellent during that first tour. One critic, speaking enthusiastically about my performances, said that people who wished to make comparisons should remember that a great personality in art was not to be compared with anybody but *himself,* and he added, "Some writers compare Mr. Paderewski with our glorious never-to-be-forgotten Rubinstein, saying that he is a second Rubinstein. That is wrong, because he is the first Paderewski!"

There was another writer who had good words to say about me, too—César Cui. He was a composer, of Italian origin but of Polish descent. He was greatly gifted in many ways and, as you will see, did many things. He was a general in the army and professor at the Military Academy. He taught the science of fortification and was also a professor in the Conservatory of Music. A versatile creature! They were in that way remarkable, those Russian musicians.

Besides César Cui there were several other musicians of real talent and importance, who were extremely versatile in their knowledge and even in their profession, I may add. Rimsky-Korsakoff was not only one of the most prominent Russian composers, but was also a professor in the Naval Academy. Tschaikowsky was a lawyer by education. He was one of the most gifted Russian composers and should have a chapter of his own—many chapters. I want to speak of him specially but shall find a better moment for that. His turbulent life, like that of so many of his countrymen, came to a tragic and dreadful end at the very height of his powers.

Now to turn again to my Russian tour and mention of the composers I saw then. I recall very pleasantly Davidoff, the famous 'cellist, who had been a mathematician by profession and for some time taught mathematics at the University. Borodin, another remarkable Russian composer, was a professor of chemistry. They practised their professions and wrote music as well. How different now! A vanished culture.

That was a very rich period in Russia. Even Nicholas Rubinstein, the younger brother of Anton, was an excellent lawyer before he started his musical career.

But Tolstoi, the most famous of all Russians, I did not see

at all. And I never wanted to, because he has never been a favorite of mine as a writer, nor interested me deeply.

My favorites among the Russian novelists were Gogol and Turgenieff. But Turgenieff at that time was practically despised by the pure Russian writers; he was considered as the representative of the corrupt West—and corrupted by it.

Life in St. Petersburg at that time, and especially at that season, the Carnival season, was something one could never see anywhere else. To give you a picture of it, it will be sufficient to tell a little story.

On one occasion I was approached by somebody connected with the Imperial Court to know whether I would like to play to his Majesty on a certain date. Of course, I said I would, but on that date I was to travel back from Minsk to St. Petersburg and could not have been in time. I inquired at the railway administration whether I could get a special train for the purpose, in order to be able to fulfill that engagement. The next morning I sent my secretary to make the arrangements. He returned at ten o'clock in the morning and said the office was closed and nobody there. He went again at eleven-thirty and returned at twelve and still told me the same story—the office was closed and nobody there. I told him to go again. The office was opened at one-thirty in the afternoon! Before that every one was asleep. It was night life in the full sense of the word! People coming to luncheon, at two or even three, were still under the influence of Morpheus, yawning, rubbing their eyes, stretching their arms, still sleepy!

The engagement to play before the Emperor was put off. Some other important ceremony had to take place, and instead of that I was invited by a certain General Baron von Stackelberg to play with the Imperial Orchestra in its own house, before a group of Grand Dukes and their families. Of course, I was in St. Petersburg and I was a Russian subject, so I considered that invitation an order, and I had to do it—and it proved to be extremely interesting, that experience.

Now, just imagine, in the center of the city, a particular quarter covering perhaps thirty or forty acres, on which were several large houses. In one of these lived the director of the Imperial Orchestra, Baron von Stackelberg, a most charming man, a perfect aristocrat, but what he knew about music, I really do not know. He was a general, and therefore he was in *command* of that Imperial Orchestra corps. Then there was another smaller house, where the conductor of the orchestra lived, and still more houses where the various musicians lived. It was a little colony, in fact. It was unique.

The orchestra was excellent. They had marvellous wood-wind and brass players. Many of them were foreigners, because wood-wind instruments are a particularity of French and Belgian musicians. There were excellent strings, too, most of them German, though some native musicians were playing also. Altogether the orchestra gave me complete satisfaction.

And now comes the most surprising thing. In spite of that tremendous space and all those buildings, there was actually no hall to play in—no place for the orchestra. It was ridiculous. We had to play in a long corridor. It was perhaps eighty feet long, but narrow, and the acoustics were extremely bad, awful.

This corridor was in the principal building, which was a musical museum with a collection of old instruments. There was something also particularly interesting to me in that museum. In one of the rooms there was a collection of portraits of famous Russian musicians, and while looking at these pictures I suddenly found, to my amazement, my own likeness among them, made by an artist in Paris. I found several reproductions of myself, the name underneath, but nothing added to it. Baron von Stackelberg said, "These bas-reliefs are the last addition in this museum. His Majesty was in Paris and accidentally saw them, and liked them so much he ordered several to be bought and put in this museum."

Baron von Stackelberg was pleased to tell me this. But he bitterly deplored the fact that with all their spending and the tremendous sums of money used for the upkeep of the orchestra, there was never a penny to build a proper hall for them to play in. And there was nothing he could do about it. The orchestra, which contained some eighty players, was a very costly affair. It was the orchestra for the private use of the Emperor. What luxury!

The philharmonic concerts, on the contrary, where I played with the regular symphonic orchestra, were given in a large, comfortable hall, and it was in that hall that I afterward gave my recitals. But the orchestra of the Czar had no place of its own. It was fantastic.

I may add that on the occasion of my playing with the Imperial Orchestra, I met several of the Grand Dukes, Vladimir, Boris, and Serge. They were all kind, most courteous, but one of them made a very real impression because he was so entirely different from the others. It was the Grand Duke Constantin Constantinovitch. Quite modest in his bearing, but extremely intelligent and exceptionally well informed about music and art in general. I had quite a long conversation with him, which I thoroughly enjoyed. He was the most intellectual of the whole family, perhaps the only one who did not care about being a Grand Duke at all, because all his life was devoted to studies of art and of literature. He translated Shakespeare into Russian, and was always interested in the works of the Russian Academy of Letters. He was an intellectual in every respect.

No, I never had an audience with the Czar. But once as a boy at the Conservatory at Warsaw, when I was a member of their famous orchestra, we were ordered to play before the Czar. After we had played several pieces, I saw, to my horror, the Crown Prince, later Alexander III, walking directly towards me. I was playing the *trumpet* in the orchestra. He, it seems, was greatly interested in trumpets, because he played the trumpet himself. I was a boy then of fourteen or fifteen and rather shy. He came straight to me and said very eagerly, "Tell me, what kind of a trumpet do you play, my boy?"

For answer, I showed him my trumpet.

"Oh," he said, looking at it closely. "This is not like mine.

Mine is quite different." He then tapped me on the shoulder and went away without another word. My first and last meeting with a Czar of Russia.

The first concert I played in St. Petersburg was for the benefit of poor students of the Conservatory, but this fact had absolutely no influence on them, and they made very hostile manifestations against me. They wanted none of me. The last concert was chamber music and I played two numbers with Auer, the renowned violinist, still a very fine player, and Wierzbilowitch, who was a wonderful 'cellist. That concert was for the widows and orphans of former professors of the Conservatory.

From St. Petersburg I went on to Moscow. My program in Moscow was similar to that in St. Petersburg. The director of those concerts was the director of the Moscow Conservatory, Wassili Safonoff, whom you may remember, as he conducted for several seasons in New York. He was a remarkable musician, a very good conductor, a fine teacher and a very delightful man. But he was afflicted with an exceptional thirst, which, apparently, was unquenchable—a true Russian. Immediately after the rehearsal, he invited me to luncheon, and there I had the first opportunity of seeing to what extent he was thirsty and how difficult it was to try to equal him in his effort to quench that thirst. It was impossible, in fact.

Before luncheon was finished, I was plainly aware of his contempt for my inability in that respect. He was really angry with me. A true son of Russia, I repeat, and therefore, any one who could not equal him in drinking was a contemptible person, a weakling.

He conducted very well at the concert, but evidently had dined just beforehand, and I surmised that the horn-blower of the orchestra must have been his guest, because during the performance that horn-blower did incredible things! He lifted his instrument high in the air, held it as though he were drinking from it and behaved altogether like a drunken or crazy man. This amazing performance of his continued throughout the entire number and completely spoiled my own "Fantasia," which I was playing.

Russian Tour

Safonoff was a terrible fellow in that, like all his countrymen, he could drink without respite. I saw him several times in Russia and Poland, in Paris and later in New York and London.

In London I once invited him to dinner. He accepted, but insisted upon being quite alone with us—my wife was with me then. He said he would be delighted to come. "But there must be no other guests. We must be absolutely alone. I want to talk with you to my heart's content," he said. "There is a great deal to speak about." So naturally I agreed and invited him quite by himself.

Well, he arrived in the best of spirits, but to my surprise did not seem at all eager to begin the long and intimate conversation with me that he was so anxious for. In fact, his whole attention was immediately centered on the drinks. First of all he started with cognac, and drank three or four glasses before dinner; he just tossed them off. Then came two bottles of white wine and one full bottle of claret, two bottles of champagne—yes, I assure you, followed by four more cognacs after his coffee. Then, to my amazement, he asked for beer and, by actual count, drank six large glasses with the greatest gusto. He was built like an athlete, a wonderfully strong man. At that time nothing affected him—he was just like a rock. What a fellow he was! And so lovable, too.

But to return to the concert. It was well received by the audience in spite of the antics of the drunken horn-blower. After my "Polish Fantasia," however, in which he made such a disturbance, there was some slight hostile movement in the audience, and that movement was toward me. I do not know whether it was caused by the behavior of the horn-blower, or by the fact that the composition I was playing was a Polish fantasia. There was already in Russia a decided movement of particular hatred against the Poles, and I was a Pole. But so it was, and it was very disturbing.

The poor horn-blower is dead, and I have forgiven him long ago. Safonoff, too, is dead. I have nothing to forgive him for. On the contrary, appreciation of his conducting and the most happy and jovial recollections of him. Only once did he fail me during the Russian tour, and what happened then showed me that, in spite of his friendliness, he did not really want me to make a success in Moscow. I have always felt this to be true. It may have been for political reasons, I am a Pole, you know, or perhaps we may say it was one of those strange contradictions that occur so often in human nature. At any rate, this was the case with Safonoff.

My first recital there was well attended, but not quite as full as the St. Petersburg recitals, which were absolutely crowded. I looked for Safonoff especially that night and, to my surprise, I did not see him. Not until after the recital did he appear, a strange figure, indeed, as he was still in his morning suit while every one else was in full dress. He had on a shabby little waist-coat and was very untidy, I remember.

"Well," he said casually as he greeted me, "I could not attend your recital tonight because my class was so late. I could not get there."

Now that was not true, I felt sure, but simply an excuse. I very much doubted if there were classes at nine o'clock in the evening at the Conservatory, and besides my concert was in the hall next to the Conservatory and it would have been an easy matter for him to come in and hear me play. But I accepted his excuse at the time. I thought he was simply out of sorts and not in the mood to hear me. But he repeated the same thing at my second recital, and at the third again failed to attend. He only presented himself at the end of the concerts, full of apologies and always in that careless, disreputable attire, which was a lack of courtesy to every one. I must say I felt the whole incident very deeply. It hurt me. I had thought he had a different feeling toward me.

Later on, however, there happened a little incident that explained to me very clearly the attitude of both Safonoff and the hissing audience I have just told you of. One evening a lady came to see me in the artists' room. As she approached, I recognized her and she said in Polish before I could speak, "Ah, Mr. Paderewski, I never, never expected to see you again. What a joy for me! What a happiness!" and she cried and cried, talking excitedly all the time in Polish. All this is easily explained. She was one of my companions and fellow students at the Conservatory in Warsaw years before, studying the violin when I was a boy there, and I played once in a concert with her. I had not seen her for more than twenty years, and she was then married to a judge and lived very far away from Moscow. She had actually made a three-days' hard journey just to hear me play again. That was so kind of her, I thought. Such rare tributes affect one deeply. I was glad to see her, and our meeting was a happy one.

We had a few moments' conversation together which came to a very sudden and disagreeable end. Safonoff and another gentleman, a trustee of the Conservatory, who were standing close to us, were the cause of this interruption. The trustee suddenly turned to Safonoff and said in a loud voice, "Oh, listen to those Poles. Hear them chattering together! It is always like that," he went on contemptuously, "always. Wherever they are, they insist upon jabbering their awful Polish language."

He said all this with an expression of great hatred and contempt. Instantly I turned and faced him, and after a long look, I said in perfect Russian, "You would, perhaps, sir, prefer to listen to us speaking in *Yiddish?*"

There was a dreadful moment of silence. They were both greatly displeased and somewhat surprised, as they had no idea that I spoke Russian. A very unpleasant but significant moment.

II

The Russian tour was full of such disagreeable moments and some of them involved Safonoff. But the most characteristic thing happened at my last appearance, when I had to play again for the benefit of the families of deceased professors of the Conservatory. It was in the small hall of the Conservatory, holding perhaps a thousand people. It was full, and we took our places on the platform—the violinist, the 'cellist and myself. The moment I appeared, hissing began, loud hissing. I looked at my companions and said, "What does it mean?" The violinist answered, "I don't know. I have never seen or heard anything like it in my life, and I cannot understand it. It is an outrage."

Well, the hissing increased and then I said, "What shall I do? This is unbearable."

At that very moment Safonoff appeared, as usual in his shabby little coat, for which I began to think he had a special fondness. But his entrance in the hall seemed to make no difference—the disturbance continued, and it was apparently directed toward me. Then I decided something must be done immediately to put a stop to it. I rose and turned to Safonoff, who was Director of the Conservatory and responsible for the concert, and addressed him personally. I spoke in very good Russian and said in a loud voice so that every one in the hall could hear, "Mr. Safonoff, I cannot play in this hall while this disturbance is going on."

"But why? What disturbance?"

"Do you not hear that—that hissing?"

"Oh, yes," he said, "I hear it, but do not pay any attention to that. It doesn't matter."

"But I have to pay attention to what the public does when I am playing. Therefore, unless the hissing is stopped I shall not play. You must send for the police and put your house in order."

"What," he cried, "send for the police! Surely you do not mean that."

"Yes, I do mean it, and if you do not do it I shall be obliged to do it, and stay here and wait for the police. If they do not appear I shall then put on my coat and return to my hotel."

Safonoff glared at me. "And," I continued, "if any of the newspaper correspondents ask me why I was unable to give this concert, I shall tell the truth: 'Because at the Conservatory of Moscow I have been hissed for the first time in my life! While attempting to play for the benefit of the widows and orphans of former Conservatory professors, I have been literally hissed off the stage!'"

"What! You won't do that!" he shouted; "it would disgrace me, kill me—kill me."

Russian Tour

"No, it would not kill you," I answered, "but it would certainly be very *unpleasant* for you."

He then tried to make some little jokes and induce me to change my position. But I held my ground.

"No," I said, "no, I shall not move until I see a policeman."

This argument lasted for a good fifteen minutes and in front of the audience, interspersed with their continued hisses. It finally ended by his sending for the police. The audience was not hissing then. They had quieted down, as I had already left the stage.

Well, the policemen came. There were several of them. On their arrival I went back again, quite alone, to the platform. The policemen saluted when I appeared and said, "We are here, sir." They stood for a few minutes at attention and the house became perfectly quiet. Then I played. The audience was wonderful, I must say. Their attitude was most sympathetic. You see, it was not the whole audience that had made the demonstration, it was the usual minority—the several cowardly men who did not dare show their hostility against me, a Pole, except in a crowd. It is always so.

The concert was a great success, and afterward Safonoff, just as though nothing had happened, invited me most affectionately to supper, and of course I went. There was no way out of it. Safonoff was in high good humor, most convivial, shall we say, and our other companion, the 'cellist, was quite happily drunk and in a pitiable condition. He imbibed frequently and constantly. We were in the finest restaurant in Moscow, the Hermitage. I do not remember how many bottles the 'cellist drank—so many I completely lost count. I only remember that his last bottle was half champagne and half cognac, and he wanted me, in fact implored me, to drink that poison. Considering his condition, I of course accepted the glass he offered me, but threw the contents over my shoulder and he was never the wiser.

In all this revel, Safonoff led. In fact, it was he who had the great idea of mixing champagne with cognac. What a fellow he was! It was all very merry and he never even mentioned the tragic incidents of the evening. Never. Everything was completely forgotten.

We remained there in that restaurant until six o'clock in the morning, doing nothing but talking nonsense and drinking. I, of course, was as sober as I am now. I only took what was convenient to me. The rest I threw away, but no one noticed it. They were too—happy! Some glasses were emptied by my secretary, who could drink almost as much as Safonoff, he being a good German.

This is a long story about Safonoff and, amusing as it is in spots, it has a deeply tragic side. There is still one thing I must add, a little tribute, a few words more about Safonoff as a conductor and a man. After long nights of revel and constant abuse of alcohol—in spite of all that, he was at the first hour of the morning always at his desk as Director of the Conservatory. He never failed. He was always there at his post, the first of all. Extraordinary fidelity, energy, and a great sense of duty and responsibility were his. He performed all his duties in a most exemplary way. These are outstanding qualities and they were among the noble qualities of Safonoff. Qualities I shall always cherish in my memory of him.

During my stay in Moscow, I stopped at a hotel called the Slavinski Bazaar. It was an absolutely Russian institution and it was an unbearable place. It was Carnival time when I arrived and I did not at first notice anything particularly. I took my luncheon at a restaurant, and saw, immediately upon entering, a very curious object—a perfectly enormous basin in the center of the room, which was as big as a hall, and this basin was full of large fish swimming about. I was somewhat surprised at the sight and asked the waiter why the fish were there and why they were so enormous.

"Oh," he answered, "that is very easily explained. Some of our wealthiest clients like to order fish soup. It is a great delicacy here, and it is a custom of the people in Moscow and Central Russia to order the soup from the live fish. Here," he said, "in our hotel," pointing with great pride to the basin, "our wealthy clients are able to select their own fish. They go and look into the basin, point out the fish (usually the largest they can find) and order the soup. These fish are called sterlet. And," he continued, "sometimes one particularly large, handsome fish costs twenty to thirty rubles!"

Well, his long and detailed explanation was very satisfactory and I had the opportunity during my luncheon of seeing a number of people hurry up to the basin and select their victim.

Apart from that, the evening passed uneventfully enough until midnight, and then, just as I was about to sleep, I suddenly heard,

Hoch soll er leben!
Dreimal hoch!

I was startled and said, "What on earth does this mean? I am in Russia, and yet I am awakened by the singing of a German toast." There was an enormous crowd of people there and they kept on singing that toast, and various others, until seven o'clock in the morning. It was awful. And then, to add to my troubles, the next day promptly at twelve o'clock the shouting began again.

It was impossible to sleep and I sent my secretary downstairs to inquire what could be done. "Go at once," I said, "and inquire into this. If it is just some special festivity they are celebrating, we will stay on in these rooms, but if it is their way of celebrating the Carnival every night, we must move at once."

He returned in a few minutes and said, "Well, we must take other rooms, for it seems there are many old Germans living in Moscow and they are all celebrating the Carnival and will continue to for many days. It will be the same wherever we go." Under these circumstances it seemed useless to move.

So I was practically a prisoner in my apartment; but one night just before my last recital, I said, "I cannot stand this eating in the same room any longer. Let us go somewhere else outside." So my secretary and I went to the Hotel Metropole. It was very full, of course, and they were all in the full swing of the Carnival celebration, day and night. After a little reconnoitering, I inquired if I might have a private room. The proprietor came to speak to me. He knew who I was, and said,

"Why, certainly, Mr. Paderewski, we will let you have a room with pleasure, and," he added very graciously, "a room with a piano in it, too."

"Oh," I cried in horror, "my dear sir, I have just run away from the piano! I do not want a room with a piano in it, certainly not."

"Well," he laughed jovially, "you need not mind this piano. My piano will not disturb you." He then led me to the private room. It was a beautiful room with a fine upright piano. "Here, Mr. Paderewski," he said, "is the room I can offer you, and there is the piano."

I was rather amused at all this and said, "What kind of a piano is it? I must see." So I opened it and tried a note. No response. Then another note. No response. Then still another two or three notes. Not a sound! The piano was absolutely dumb, useless. I began to laugh and to see the joke of the proprietor. A few minutes later he returned to take my order and then I said, "Please tell me your reason for having this piano here."

"Piano!" he exclaimed. "Piano! Ah, Mr. Paderewski, that is not a piano. That is a gold mine!"

"Why, what do you mean?" I said, pretending to be very much surprised.

"I will tell you," he answered, lowering his voice and speaking in the greatest confidence. "Perhaps you do not know our Moscow merchants, and their young sons in particular. They are very wild and they are tremendously rich, too, these people, and they do not know what to do with their money. When they get drunk, they become very violent; they will do anything. First of all, they try to break everything that is breakable, plates, glasses, bottles, chairs, tables, mirrors—everything in the room is broken. When they cannot break anything more, they order champagne in great quantities and pour that champagne into the piano. Yes, Mr. Paderewski, they pour practically all the champagne into the piano. Then, of course, they ask for the bill, and naturally, I charge the regular price for champagne and then make an extra charge, a very large charge, sir, for the destruction of my beautiful piano. So you see I am quite right in saying my piano is a gold mine!"

Life was very extravagant in Russia at that time. Extravagant and sumptuous in the way they did things, beyond anything I have ever experienced. I am speaking now of the aristocracy, of course, and the rich tradespeople and professionals of certain classes. The serfs (or peasants) were poor and downtrodden then as now. But in spite of all this extravagance and riotous living, the Russians always seemed to me like deaf and dumb people. They spoke with caution and in whispers in the streets—they were afraid of the police even then. In fact, the aspect of the whole country was the same as now, they dared not express an opinion, they could have no political opinions—they must remain silent. And there was absolutely no gaiety among them, no real gaiety, no laughter, no smiles. It was only when they were drunk that they became perfectly irresponsible. The country was so gloomy, so sad, so desperate, so vast. Every one was afraid of his own shadow, even in Carnival time.

The Russians are a very strange people. They are gifted, very gifted—still one never quite gets to the depths of the Russian character. First of all, they are fatalistic. They are a little bit Oriental, you know, and they are very curious about their relations with people. They are too polite, too kind, too exuberant, especially when they drink a little. When they realize that they have gone too far, that something may be expected of them, they begin to withdraw; they become suddenly cautious, which of course gives the impression that they are false, which is not quite correct. No, they are not exactly false in my opinion. They simply try to retract a little when they realize they have been too confidential, too intimate, and that is quite natural. You know that is absolutely characteristic of all Oriental people. It is an Oriental trait. They are sometimes too amiable; they always like to appear as a friend, to make a constant impression of charm and courtesy and fine gesture.

As a people, Russians are remarkably musical. One is constantly aware of it. They are a gifted and complex race in spite of a certain primitiveness. Yes, I found everything in Russia complex, but interesting. I was always deeply interested in Russian literature, that is, certain Russian writers. At that time my favorites were Gogol, and, as I've mentioned, Turgenieff. Tolstoi did not interest me so much. But his works were not without influence on the coming Revolution. Besides being a great novelist, he pretended to be a social reformer, and his writings contributed much to the formation of that spirit of more equitable distribution of wealth among the people. He struck the first note. When he was about sixty, we are told, he suddenly renounced all claim to his great estates, though at that time he continued to live on in the same manner. Although he was in a great state of agitation over social conditions, it was not until many years later, when he was over eighty, that he actually left his home and lived among the peasants. He had, however, taken the precaution, if I may say so, to will all his property to his wife.

There are many conflicting stories about Tolstoi, and I am not prepared to say more than is generally known to the public. He was a provocative figure in Russia. In my opinion there was a certain hypocrisy in his living and in his acting; he was posing very much it seemed to me.

I saw again on that Russian concert tour the brilliant Madame Essipoff. She was already divorced from Leschetizky and was professor of music at the Conservatory at St. Petersburg. Madame Essipoff was no longer young, but she was still fine-looking and always brilliant, and enjoyed a great success there as a professor. She had already stopped her career as a pianist.

Directly after the Russian tour I went to England, where I was to give a few concerts, and then on to Leipzig, not to play, but to fulfill my duty as a godfather to one of Nikisch's children. That was after he had been in the United States as conductor of the famous Boston Symphony Orchestra. After leaving America, he became director of the Opera at Budapest.

XIV

Home in Switzerland

I

The Russian tour had been very strenuous, and the concert engagements that followed, equally so. But I had now a place to go after these great concert seasons, a place of repose, my own home. Two years before, I had bought this place, Riond-Bosson, at Morges, and it filled and satisfied a deep and long-felt want in my life. At last there was a piece of land of my own that I could keep. The other properties, as you will remember, were sold almost as quickly as they were bought. But this was different—this house became a home at once, and so it has remained ever since.

I was advised by my physicians to find a quiet place with a fine park or garden for my son, who was still ill, very ill. The Chalet Riond-Bosson, Morges, was advertised for rental. I heard of it first through that dear friend, the Princess Brancovan, who thought it would suit my requirements. It was indeed a lovely spot, with a magnificent view of the Mont Blanc across Lake Geneva. From the terrace window it rises in all its majesty and splendor. Riond-Bosson is about a mile from the picturesque old town of Morges, near Lausanne.

Well, I liked the place and rented it at once. My poor boy was very happy here. It appealed to him from the first. As he was a confirmed invalid then, unable to walk, his life here was easily managed, and this great room, opening onto the terrace, as it does, flooded with sunshine and beauty, was a favorite spot with him.

I spent a year here and the following summer was notified

that the place was about to be sold to some one who had applied for it, but that they would give me preference if I wished to have it. As my son was so happy here, I decided quickly and bought it at once.

It was two years later, in the spring of 1899, that I married for the second time.

And now we come to a moment, a very difficult moment in my life, for it is something I dislike extremely to speak about, not only because it is a very delicate and intimate thing, but also and mostly because it was the consequence of a divorce, and in principle I am and always have been very much against divorce. I consider that people at this particular time are already making a kind of sport, I should say a habit, of divorce. It has become almost an institution, particularly in America. For many people there is no denying the fact that divorce is only another opportunity for going into a new relationship perhaps, a new amusement, a new marriage. My feeling about divorce is and always has been very strong, I am unutterably opposed to it, and yet in the face of all that belief and sentiment it was a divorce that made possible my second marriage.

This new relationship played a strong part in my life and therefore it has a place in this story. When my poor boy was so ill, almost helpless in fact, after much experimenting and being taken from one grandparent to another, he was finally put under the care of the Gorski family, friends of mine from student days, particularly Gorski himself, an excellent violinist with whom I once went on tour. But it was Madame Gorska who took care of my son; she cared for him during all those years like a mother. He became attached to her naturally and was thankful for her attention and her care altogether.

At that time the Gorskis lived in Paris and I was a frequent guest at their house. I saw my son every day during my Paris sojourns and I cannot deny that I was very much touched and also attracted by Madame Gorska. And that attachment developed into love. I can only say it like that, very simply. Gorski himself saw and realized this and was the first to ask for the divorce. It was a difficult time for every one, a time of tension and emotion, but I can say now that Gorski was a noble man and a very loyal one.

Divorce, as you know, is not admitted by the Roman Catholic Church, so there was only a possibility of an annulment of the marriage and it was done the more easily because Madame Gorska had contracted her first marriage when she was very young and without the permission of her father. It was merely a technical formality which had not been observed and which was the basis for the annulment of her marriage to Gorski, and in less than a year after the decision by Gorski it was all an accomplished fact and we were married in May, 1899, in Warsaw.

That same year I went again to America, this time with my wife. I played in more than a hundred concerts, not only covering the whole of the United States, but even going as far as Mexico, and that was a rather eventful journey. At first I was stopped at the frontier by the customs officials, to explain why I was carrying two pianos for my concerts, one the grand piano and the other my usual upright piano, in the private car. As I could not speak Spanish at that time, I should probably have been detained for some days, had not an American officer, travelling in the same train, come to my rescue and explained to the authorities that the second piano was not for sale, but for my daily practice, and that knowing President Diaz, he would complain to him on my behalf if I suffered any discourteous treatment. That evidently impressed the officials, because they let me go at once, with apologies.

But the regular train, through the delay, had already gone and there was no other way of reaching Mexico City in time for my concert except to take a special train, which I had to do.

I took the special train and it had to go at an unusual speed, for *Mexico!* We arrived at one of those very highly situated stations (the railway is climbing higher and higher all the time) when, suddenly, a great shock came. One of the wheels of our private car took fire, it seems, and fell off at the station. It was, indeed, a very fortunate circumstance that there happened to be another Pullman car there, for they took a wheel off that one, and put it on ours at once. We arrived safely in Mexico City, but, instead of being there a day beforehand, I arrived only two hours before the concert. It was a perilous trip.

Upon our arrival, we found all the representative people of the city waiting to greet us. It was a huge crowd and very gay, with a charming way of showing hospitality, just like the Spaniards, who are always very demonstrative.

I gave two recitals and they were very pleasant. Shortly before my second recital, on the same day, I was notified that the President wished to see me, and, though at that time I had no knowledge of Spanish and we had to have an interpreter, I had a great impression of Porfirio Diaz. He was indeed a remarkable man. As long as he was there the country was orderly and prosperous. He was just the man for those people, an iron-handed man. At that time there were no bandits—there was perfect peace and order in the whole country. It is an interesting, beautiful country and very rich. But it remains still what old Humboldt once called it, a beggar. "Mexico," he said, "is a beggar sitting on a bag of gold." Unforgettable words.

There was nothing of particular interest during that American tour. It was just a regular and successful tour like so many others that I have to be thankful for. The only unusual thing that happened was in San Francisco. My concerts there were booked by a theatrical manager, Mr. Friedlander, who was a very nice man, but rather peculiar in his methods. When I arrived in San Francisco from Mexico, I found my concerts advertised very strangely, so modestly, so humbly even, as to give the impression that either the tickets were all sold, or that he had no faith in my success. On reading the advertisements more closely, I noticed that indeed his faith in the possibility of my achieving a success was absolutely *nil*, because he had suddenly reduced all the tickets to *half* my usual price!

I immediately asked Mr. Friedlander to come and see me. He preceded his visit with a splendid basket of flowers for my wife. When he finally appeared, upon my question as to why he had done such a thing, he said, "Well, I did it in order to protect you and to safeguard my own interests as well." I was astounded.

"How do you mean, to protect my interests and to safeguard your own, you reduce all the prices one half? Why?"

"Because," he explained, "because this is your *second* visit to San Francisco, remember, and in my entire theatrical experience I have never yet seen any one able to *repeat* a success!"

Well, I was speechless in the face of such an absurdity. It was ludicrous. You know what an impression it makes on the public when they see that an artist, whom a few years before they paid four or five dollars to hear, can now be heard for two dollars. It was not so much the question of my material interests, but it was the question of my dignity. I protested decidedly, but it was too late to actually do anything, because half the tickets were sold and we could not then raise the price. The house was only half full, naturally. It was a very painful, but fortunately only a local, downfall.

After the concert, Friedlander hurried back to the dressing room. "You see," he cried triumphantly, "you did not fill the hall. It was just as I said. If we had asked your former prices, you would probably have had only a quarter of the hall filled."

Strangely enough, he seemed quite happy about it, even though it was his loss as well as mine. I saw that it was hopeless, no use arguing, and so I let it pass. I will only add that upon my return to San Francisco several years afterwards, under a different manager, I played to sold-out houses.

In connection with the lowering of prices, I must tell you another amusing experience in my career, the only time I cancelled a concert, two in fact, when not being forced to do so by illness or accident. But I deliberately and wilfully cancelled these particular concerts. I refused to play them.

It was in England, in Torquay and Plymouth, which are near each other. I had played there before, and several times after, but on that particular occasion the management of both concerts was given to a local agent who had applied for it. My representative in London was then Mr. Adlington, who was a good friend of mine. He was a musician himself and a good piano teacher. After retiring from teaching, he wanted something to do and bought the rights of representing me from Daniel Mayer.

He was not then experienced in the managerial business and he trusted the man who applied for the privilege of handling these two recitals. He did not know that in those small places there are competitions, rivalries, and all kinds of little conflicts between the local people; so he completely trusted that agent, whose name was Mr. Moon.

When I arrived at the hotel in Torquay, I looked at the announcement as to the hour, and well, I could hardly believe my eyes, I was so astounded at what I saw. The announcement read, "Paderewski, the famous and distinguished artist," etc., etc., and then went on in still larger letters, "Mr. Moon's prices for this celebrated pianist are but *half* his former prices."

I was simply aghast! I sent my secretary at once to Mr. Moon and said that I could not at all understand the advertisement of my concert, that it was absolutely without reason and that I would not, under any circumstances, appear. I was cancelling the concert. My decision was irrevocable and I refused to change it.

Then began a terrible campaign against me in the London newspapers. Mr. Moon survived the event with great difficulty because they made of him a laughing-stock. I think he intended to make a lawsuit, but there was a little correspondence between his lawyer and my manager, Mr. Adlington, and evidently there was no difficulty in convincing his lawyer that it was Mr. Moon's fault because he should not have advertised me in such an undignified manner.

But the campaign against me was especially interesting as it was started by two piano-makers on whose pianos I had never played and would never play. *They* began the attack in the press, but it soon died out. The public understood. Since then I have played several times in Torquay and in Plymouth and had very pleasant recitals.

Home in Switzerland

But there were also really dangerous moments in my life as an artist. Once in California I played in a little town called Santa Cruz. It was in a small theatre. The house was full and many people were unable to get admission. Some boys, interested in the crowd but not in the concert, climbed up to the roof of the theatre. On the roof were various objects, it seems, among them some heavy iron bars. I do not know how it happened. It was not done wilfully, I'm sure children would not be as cruel as that, but an iron bar fell through the roof, perhaps sixty feet. It crashed through the ceiling (there was probably an open skylight there) and hit the edge of the piano with great force, striking close to my hands. If it had been just a few inches nearer, it would have killed me at once. The audience jumped to their feet, but, seeing that I was quiet and unhurt, that I did not move at all and went on playing, they thought all was well; they did not realize that I had had such a narrow escape from death.

Another accident, which proved not to be an accident at all but simply a fear on my part, is such a characteristic story of the West, that it is worth telling, even now.

It happened in Dallas, Texas, where there was a great gathering of the Confederate soldiers from the South, many thousands of them. The city of Dallas, which was very progressive and enterprising, built a special hall for the occasion. It was an enormous wooden hall and held about seven thousand people. I was invited by the Reunion Committee to give a concert there. I had to take a special train from Chicago to reach the place in time, and when I arrived in the morning I saw, to my amazement, that the hall was not yet finished. Everything was in a state of wild confusion. It reminded me of the World's Fair years before. Wood, shavings, and sawdust covered everything. The workmen and many people were walking about smoking and carelessly dropping their cigar and pipe ashes into the shavings. I was terrified at the sight. Fire seemed inevitable. "How can I play here," I thought, "under the circumstances?" I became very nervous about it, I confess, and was really convinced that there would be a terrific fire.

The Paderewski Memoirs

It was an agonizing experience altogether and I was so fearful of disaster that I gave my faithful Marcel, who was with me, directions of just what to do. My wife, who was also there, was to be his first thought. I told him to look out for her if fire started. I would manage for myself. I felt so sure, you see, of some catastrophe because the danger seemed to increase as time went on.

There was a kind of enclosed veranda on both sides of the building where the old soldiers were walking about constantly, and where beds were prepared for them to sleep in at night. It was all a great turmoil and confusion. The old veterans, smoking constantly, roamed about and sat wherever they wanted to, and many of them fell asleep in the aisles.

The day dragged through somehow and I was assured that all would be ready for the concert that night. I had to accept this, of course, but I had grave doubts. When I arrived at the hall at eight o'clock, I saw that a great many of the seats were still unoccupied, at least a couple of thousand, and I had to wait for trains from other parts of Texas with people coming especially to attend the recital. These trains were late, it seems, and the concert must be delayed. There was no help for it, and so we were very late, indeed, in starting.

I was just beginning to play the great Polonaise of Chopin, when suddenly I heard wild shouting, which seemed to my nervous and excited ears to be cries of "Fire!" I thought the shouts were those of panic, that the fire had really started and that we were lost. But, fortunately, such was not the case. The shouts were merely war cries coming from the old soldiers, those happy old veterans of other days, who had fallen asleep in the aisles. My crashing Chopin chords had awakened them, apparently, and they mistook me for a military band! Still half asleep, memories of the old days came back to them, and they sprang to their feet and began shouting their battle cries. It lasted only a minute or two, but it was an eternity to me, although I kept right on playing.

When I saw that the audience was quiet, I understood that

there was really nothing to be alarmed about. The people evidently, who were near the sleeping veterans, could distinguish what their shouting meant. Their cries were "Hooray! Hooray! Hooray!"—instead of "Fire! Fire! Fire!"

So I finished the recital without any accident and with great satisfaction, because the audience was extremely enthusiastic and remained for a long time asking for more. It was a great event. It could happen only in the America of many years ago.

And now to my own affairs a moment. My opera was still unfinished and calling me. I was in a great hurry to go on with the work and I started the orchestration. I must say that rarely did I do any work with greater interest and pleasure. Whatever may be the shortcomings of that opera, those of which I know and those of which I am completely ignorant, I am thankful to say that the orchestration, even when I look back at it after so many years, gives me complete satisfaction.

I finished it in January, 1901, and immediately proceeded on a short concert tour to Nice and Monte Carlo, and then to Rome, where I had to play again for the Academy of St. Cecelia, and in a private concert for Queen Margherita.

After that came a short tour in Spain, which, however, I could not finish, having been recalled from Bilbao by the news of my son's death. He was away from home undergoing a certain treatment of which we both had high hopes at that time. The sudden ending of his brief, mutilated span of life came with shocking force to me. I had still hoped there was help for him somewhere. Death put an end to that hope. I took his body to the Cemetery of Montmorency, near Paris, a cemetery sacred to my countrymen, where eminent Poles were buried in the days of the emigration. Chopin lies there and Mickiewicz, our national poet. There I buried my son Alfred—not yet twenty-one.

II

It was a blessing for me that I had work to do then, that I was forced to work and could plunge into the final details of my opera, which was soon to be produced. So life went on again. The score and the parts of "Manru" had already been sent to Dresden and I went there immediately. The date of the first performance was approaching and we were deep in rehearsals, with the usual difficulties of rewriting and rearrangements. I worked with all the singers, and many of them wanted the usual "complete change" in their parts, demanding not only musical but dramatic change as well. The old story.

As the text of the opera was originally written in German, there was the necessity of a translation and adaptation of music to a Polish text, as the opera was to be performed in Lwów and Cracow immediately after the Dresden performance. So I was forced to work on that too, and I was busy day and night, but that work was a godsend.

For the first performance (May 29, 1901) there was a very large gathering of people from many countries. There came the old master, Leschetizky, from Vienna—that was charming. And Joseph Joachim from Berlin. There came, too, several of my old friends from Warsaw, friends from Paris and from London. There were even some American friends present, who were at that time in Europe.

The première proved to be a decisive success, if one has to judge by the number of following performances.

Later on during that summer, Madame Sembrich attended one of the performances with Maurice Grau, director of the Metropolitan Opera in New York, and they decided to produce "Manru" the next season. Bandrowski, at that time a very popular tenor in Germany, had studied the principal part and offered his services to Mr. Grau. I was glad to recommend him, because he fully deserved it.

In July, "Manru" was produced with Bandrowski and some other excellent artists under the direction of the conductor Spettrino in Lwów, and then in Cracow. There were in the first season thirty performances of the work in Lwów and about ten in Cracow. All of which was very gratifying.

The summer of that year we spent on my estate in Austrian Poland. It was very close to Cracow, and I had the opportunity of going to each performance of my opera from that little estate.

I was satisfied with the Dresden première. It was a very fine one. Not, of course, that every singer was of the highest order. But the chief characteristic of the Dresden Opera was that, although the principal singers were not to be compared with those wonderful artists at the Metropolitan and Covent Garden, the ensemble and the harmony between the solo singers, the orchestra, and the chorus, were absolutely perfect. Nothing could have been better.

During my stay in Dresden—we are still in 1901—I had to play in one orchestral concert given for the benefit of the Opera orchestra. I played no better and no worse than usual, but as my opera was in rehearsal, some of the local critics found many faults with my playing, and were evidently very glad to air their opinions. They were full of complaints and criticism.

"What a pity," one paper commented, "that Paderewski is now composing, for he is no more a great pianist." Another critic wrote even more strongly. He said, "It is to be deeply regretted that Paderewski's time is now being devoted to composition, because his piano playing is being neglected and evidence of this neglect was very manifest at his concert yesterday," and so on.

Ah, well, it was human nature.

Evidently Joachim was not of that opinion, because he asked me to play with him that summer in Bonn, the birthplace of Beethoven, where some chamber music concerts were given in honor of his memory. There were five of them, and I was so glad to take part in that solemnity.

I played several chamber music works, Beethoven, Brahms, Schumann, and so on, and besides in every concert I played one solo number. Musicians from all parts of Germany came to these concerts.

In the first concert, I played Schumann's F Sharp Minor Sonata. The performance must have produced quite an impression, because, after the concert, a gentleman came to me who introduced himself as a Mr. Krebs, and his expression of enthusiasm over my performance of the Schumann Sonata was really unbounded. It is hardly possible to repeat all the superlatives he used. He could not say enough in praise of my playing. I did not know who he was until Joachim said to me later, "You know, Paderewski, you have achieved a tremendous triumph today, as Krebs is one of the ablest and most severe critics in Berlin. He will give you a splendid notice, I am sure."

And he did applaud and approve me after the first concert. I appeared to him then to be superior to anything he had ever heard, and master of my art. And so he wrote next day in his criticism in the *Tag*, the newspaper for which he was writing.

At the next concert I played Beethoven's Sonata Opus III, and I had the great pleasure of hearing from Joachim's lips the most flattering appreciation, the more flattering as Joachim was universally recognized as the greatest exponent of Beethoven's music. "You know," he said, "your playing of Beethoven's Sonata was simply a revelation. I have never heard any performance of that work approaching yours. Never."

But on that occasion Mr. Krebs did not appear, and I lost sight of him until the very end of the Festival. But it was not difficult to guess the reason. You must realize that I was still in the bad graces of the Berlin press since my refusal to play there again, of which I have already told you. I constantly had evidence of their animosity, and even enmity, which pursued me for so many years. Krebs was a Berlin critic, and he approved and applauded me. Then the usual thing happened. An order was given, evidently from headquarters, *not* to write favorable criticisms about me and immediately thereafter in all other concerts I became suddenly just a mediocre piano player. It was a pity, and I am sure poor Mr. Krebs deep down in his heart felt it very much.

It was very characteristic of the Berlin press, which, since my first appearance there in 1890, had disapproved of me. It still rankled that, in spite of their severe verdict, I was enjoying success and recognition everywhere.

There was a very interesting incident at that last concert at which I played Schumann's Sonata for Violin with Joachim. The

unfortunate thing about that Sonata is that it is printed in such
a way that in the playing of it, the turning of the pages presents
the greatest difficulty. The violin part has to be turned without
any interruption, so we first had a rehearsal which went all right.
After we had finished, Joachim said to me, "Now the only thing
we must be afraid of at the performance is the turning of the
page. Let us hope it will be all right because I have arranged for
a very good musician to do this." But it was not all right. The
person who was attending to this momentous duty got so interested in the music, that he entirely forgot to turn the page for
Joachim. "For God's sake," I whispered to him, "quick, quick,
go and turn the page for Joachim." But he went too late. Then
nervousness overwhelmed us both. Joachim could not get his text
and I could not follow him. I was afraid I could never catch him,
and then we began to try to catch each other, and for an eternity
(perhaps it was ten seconds really) it was dreadful! An agony.
We played anything but the Sonata. The audience did not
notice very much, but the musicians did notice, of course. After
we had finished we simply looked at each other, but we could not
say a word. It was a catastrophe.

We had that day a very distinguished gentleman in our audience, sitting just in the front row. It was the then very young
Crown Prince of Germany, the present candidate (if one may
say such a thing under present conditions). The young prince
came to every concert. He was very musical. I think he must
have enjoyed that incident with the Sonata, because he laughed
very heartily, I noticed.

It is amazing to realize what absurd things will interest and
move an audience to laughter. Almost anything—and nothing!—
will often cause them to be as pleased as children and sometimes
they laugh as easily at tragedy as at comedy. Every artist has lived
through trying and agonizing experiences. I have had my full
share of them and there was one audience in my early career,
when I was still quite young, that I furnished unwittingly with a
rare bit of comedy. I remember this concert very distinctly, and
that I was late in arriving and in a great hurry, which did not

often happen. At any rate I came very late to dress and had to hurry. I jumped into a cab and drove to the concert hall, quite unconscious of the appearance I presented. But as I stepped on to the platform I realized that something was quite wrong, for even before I reached the piano, the people sitting near the stage entrance burst into laughter, hearty laughter I may say. I took a few more steps towards the piano, but as the laughter increased, I turned to look at the offenders and found to my horror on turning, that my braces, or as you call them, suspenders, were hanging and dangling far down below my coat! It was an awful moment. There was only one thing to be done.

I ran away, of course, literally made a dash for the exit, which I accomplished successfully but with more laughter. In a minute or two I got myself in order and returned to the stage. I must say that my second entrance was a difficult one to make, but the audience was splendid—there was no more laughter, only very encouraging applause, and the recital went on without further disaster.

Now, in all my talks about the piano, I have neglected one of the most important things of all—*my* piano stool, which is a very special affair. It is both an invention and an innovation. It took me years to discover why I did not feel at ease when playing in public. There was always something wrong. A certain nervousness in my back which imposed a great strain upon me. I began to realize that my piano stool was the difficulty. I was always searching for the right piano stool. I experimented with one after another and tried, I suppose, hundreds of stools in what was beginning to seem an unending search. Finally, quite unexpectedly, I found one at Erard's in Paris which was agreeable to me. It was the lowest one they had; in fact the lowest one I had ever seen up to that moment, and it proved to be the perfect piano stool for me. So I asked them to prepare a couple of such low chairs immediately. This was done and I was delighted. Complete ease and comfort at last! They gave me such ease and repose when I was playing that since then I have never used any other. Of

The Paderewski piano stool

The Chalet Riond-Bosson, Morges, Switzerland

Paderewski's study at Riond-Bosson

course, they get rather worn and very shabby, and I have to have new ones made frequently.

At Steinway's they always have several such stools ready for me. I have two now in my house at Morges, two waiting for me in London and one in Paris. They always accompany my pianos. In fact they always accompany me on my tours and extra ones are always on hand in case of emergency. The piano stool is a vital part of my musical life. It belongs to my pianistic equipment —my life at the piano. I invariably recommend to all my pupils (and any one who plays for me) a low chair. I cannot overestimate the necessity of this and never fail to urge its importance. I myself have my full strength only when I use a low chair. I cannot play on a high one.

Conditions, I mean conditions that affect one, have so much to do with the success of one's public appearance. The atmosphere of the hall, the lighting, the piano stool, the condition of the piano—these mechanical things, how they add to the nervousness and strain of each appearance! For instance, a dimly lighted hall is an absolute necessity for me. And here let me say I have often been criticized and misunderstood on that score, and it has been considered an affectation. But it is really nothing of the sort. I simply cannot stand a brilliant light shining into my eyes when playing. It deprives me of all comfort and repose; it is a nervous irritation that is unbearable, and that is the reason I avoid playing with orchestra. There is so much light on the stage (there must be, naturally, to enable the musicians to see their music) that it becomes a positive torture to me. That torture I had to endure in the early days of my career; as long as I was a beginner, I had to accept everything that came to me. I could not command; I had to obey. But as soon as I could command, I had a comfortable, dim light in the hall and for many years I never gave a concert with a brightly lighted stage. When I had authority to demand certain things with energy, I started that innovation.

Occasionally, a mistake is made and the electricians do just the opposite of what I want. They put down the lights in the hall and put up the lights, very brilliantly, on the platform. That affects me so much that I actually run away from the audience and do not reappear until things have been put into proper order. Naturally, many people fail to understand this and think it pretentious, a pose on my part. But I repeat, it is a necessity for me. I am affected by it as by an infirmity. I cannot look straight into the light.

XV

A Career at Top Speed

I

We were speaking of 1901 and the première of my opera in Dresden. Well, the rest of that year was again devoted to preparation, as "Manru" was to be performed at the Metropolitan Opera House in New York, and I had to attend the rehearsals.

The first performance was extremely well received. Madame Sembrich was quite marvellous, and Bandrowski excellent. Walter Damrosch conducted, and very well indeed. The performance on the whole was beautiful. I had no real trouble, except a slight difficulty with David Bispham, who was then singing at the Metropolitan. He was to play the part of a Polish village sorcerer, and he did not know how to dress that rôle, evidently, for at the dress rehearsal he suddenly appeared in just an ordinary peasant's rags—crowned by (of all things) a Turkish fez! I was amazed at the sight. It seemed impossible that Bispham could have done such a thing. A Polish sorcerer with a fez on his head! I hurried back to his dressing room to expostulate. I told him it was not suitable to represent a Polish peasant with a fez on his head! "Why, it is ridiculous," I said. "How is it possible you could do such a stupid thing?"

But Bispham was not at all disturbed by my excitement, for he answered quite simply. "Oh, my friend, I'm so sorry! But I thought this sorcerer was a Turk!" There was nothing more to be said to that. I was completely defeated by his answer. However, he played his part well and he was an excellent singer, although he didn't know what it was all about, I fear.

My manager, Charles Ellis of Boston, had arranged a tour of

fifty recitals during the season in which the opera was produced, and it so happened that my first recital in Carnegie Hall took place the same day as a performance of the opera at the Metropolitan. As both recital and opera were "sold out," as we say in the usual theatrical language, and there was only standing room, it gave the opportunity to a certain critic to speak about that double performance in a very kind and courteous article, which he rather facetiously called "Paderewski fighting Paderewski."

For reasons I fail to understand, "Manru" was not maintained in the Metropolitan repertoire, though five or six performances were crowded. It was given in New York, Chicago, Baltimore, Philadelphia, Boston, and Pittsburgh. It was performed in Europe in Cologne, Bonn, Prague, Zürich, Warsaw, etc., where it had a very great success, and in Kieff.

But in France we had a great disappointment. Naturally, I had to have it translated into French. The translation was made by Catulle Mendès, a very remarkable writer and a real poet, but he was a dreadful spendthrift and had never enough money. So he accepted any literary work he could turn out quickly in order to earn money, which was so necessary for his habit of luxurious living. Consequently, as he was always pressed for time, he did the translation of "Manru" so carelessly and hurriedly that I could not use it. It was appallingly bad and quite useless. I had many offers to produce the opera, but one and all said the same thing, "The translation is impossible." I could not find any one else at the moment as I was too occupied and had not the time.

According to the rights of authors in France, Mendès would have, through his translation, a right to certain royalties if it were used, but unfortunately, that was out of the question. So it turned out to be a very unpleasant experience altogether—a real loss and a special personal disappointment to me, as I was particularly anxious to have it produced in France, the country of my first début, the land I hold in very special affection.

My tour in America that year was a long and successful one. Like so many others, it was just one concert after another and gave me the deepest satisfaction. I returned then, in 1902, to

A Career at Top Speed

Europe and played some recitals in London, and again I played for Mr. Astor, whose musicales I have told you had become a part of my regular London season.

And then came another very extensive tour in Germany. This was under the management of Mr. Adlington, my new representative in London. At this time, Daniel Mayer, my first manager, had retired and Adlington had bought him out. And all this brings us back for the moment to Mr. Wolff, the head of the great concert agency in Berlin. The same Mr. Wolff who years before, when I was a poor student, had refused me even standing room to hear Rubinstein play. The same Mr. Wolff who in 1890 made such flattering offers for me to come under his management, and who threatened and menaced me when I refused these offers. I have already told this story in our talks, but this time it is the closing chapter.

The tour in question covered almost the whole of Germany except, of course, Berlin, and my new manager, Adlington, and Wolff had come to some kind of an understanding before I went there. I had to pass several times through Berlin, and poor Wolff, who had just been operated on for a fatal disease, expressed a wish to see me. I went to him gladly, of course. At such a time I could harbor no harsh thoughts of our past relations, bitter as they were at the time. He was very ill and weak, but he managed to tell me that he appreciated my visit more than he could express and wanted me to know that he regretted deeply whatever wrong he had done me in the past. Poor man! He hoped that I would forgive him. I never saw him again. He died a few weeks later.

During that German tour I played in every one of the important German cities (always excepting Berlin) and I cannot deny the fact that I enjoyed my playing there to the utmost. Everywhere there were remarkably enthusiastic and appreciative audiences. One of the places where I had particular pleasure, and an especially unique experience in playing, was Bremen, where my audience was made up mostly of old people; I do not know why, but I hardly saw one young person there. They were all old people, and as the concert went on they got so enthusiastic and excited that they began throwing hats and even umbrellas onto the platform, as a mark of appreciation. One did not know what they might throw next. It was perfectly crazy! They completely lost their heads. Anything they had, they threw on the platform, and it really became very dangerous. I can assure you it was a shower of missiles. It was a very odd audience, indeed, which is putting it mildly. Although I was terrified inwardly I remained outwardly calm and went on with my playing. Of course I played many encores in response to their enthusiasm, and then they became quite wild and out of hand.

It was all so extraordinary that when I returned to my hotel after the concert, I asked a friend whether the audience were really as wild and hysterical as they appeared to me. "Oh, yes," he assured me, "they were. Those old people were really crazy with excitement and delight. And," he added, "they simply threw everything they could lay hands on onto the platform. I have never seen anything like it at a concert before." Well, he confirmed my own impression; otherwise I should have thought it all a dream.

My friend also told me that after the concert the audience returned to the hall to look for their belongings and evidently they found everything—most of the articles on the stage!

The other demonstration of enthusiasm which surprised me very much was at Magdeburg. Magdeburg is a typically Prussian town. There was a large colony of military men, and they were as enthusiastic as the young piano students at my recitals in America. They rushed toward the platform at the end of the recital (as you have often seen them do in New York), running down to the platform, and standing there watching my hands.

When did that really begin, that great rush of the audience to the stage? No, it was not in the beginning always so. It did not really start until I had practically crowded houses, because at the beginning of my career there was no necessity for it; there was plenty of room. But since my houses began to be "sold out" as we say (I do not like that expression but there seems to be none better at the moment), the same thing always happens, the audience rushes in a body down to the stage the moment the last piece on the program is finished. The spell of the music is still upon them; they are still held in its invisible grip. It is a very strong and subtle bond that holds the audience and the artist together during a performance.

I always have many people in my audiences, especially in New York, to whom I become accustomed. I know exactly where they are to be found. A certain family will be in one special place in the hall, another family, generally with children, very near the front where they can watch my hands. Certain others will be on the extreme right, others the extreme left, and so it goes.

For instance, there was a certain very refined and extremely handsome gentleman with a rather plain-looking daughter, who came to every recital of mine for more than twenty-five years. They always sat in exactly the same seats. I never missed seeing him there. He particularly became a kind of friendly bulwark on which I found it pleasant to depend. There are always in every audience, you know, no matter how enthusiastic, certain friendly and unfriendly spots, shall we call them? To conquer and win the unfriendly souls is a part of every artist's task, subconsciously of course.

But to go on with our story, my unknown and distinguished friend, for so I shall always think of him, suddenly disappeared. I missed them, the handsome gentleman and his very plain daughter, and it was not only a disappointment but a very real shock to find them gone. I became very anxious to know whether something unpleasant had happened to them. Upon inquiry, I learned that they had gone back to Germany. They were Germans living in New York. He had retired from business and returned to his birthplace, somewhere on the Rhine. I found myself missing them, those faithful, eager friends, and their constant devotion to my music, for a very long time.

One always has an extraordinary sense of welcome when one returns to New York, because it is an audience of *friends*. In that respect there is no place in the world like New York. It is the most inspiring atmosphere, and the people are so kind and so appreciative, though perhaps not so demonstrative as the people, let us say, at Bremen, whom I have just told you about.

I am going to forestall you before you ask about the legend of the priceless gifts showered upon the favored artists of the public. Yes, there are certain artists as you well know, who have been literally showered with gifts during their careers—jewels, pianos, pictures, even houses sometimes are bestowed upon adored heroes, and it is quite understandable that the enthusiasm in an audience can reach a very frenzied height—and with amazing results. Sarasate, that magnificent violinist, used to be constantly bombarded with gifts on his tours. When he returned from Russia, he had trunkfuls of presents, jewelry, cigarette boxes, watches and even furs—all kinds of things.

There is a charming little story of Madame Janauschek, the famous actress, who, after a certain great performance of Macbeth, drove her audience into such a wild frenzy of excitement that several great ladies stripped the jewels from their hands and arms and actually tore the thread lace flounces from their gowns to hurl at her feet!

There is no length to which an audience may not go when moved to great excitement and appreciation. Why, in your own country in the gold rush of California in 1849, even with a mediocre opera company, the miners expressed their delight by showering the singers with gold nuggets which they threw onto the stage from all parts of the audience.

It all sounds very fabulous, but it's true, and most favored darlings of the public receive touching expressions of the affection they call forth. Caruso and the de Reszkes, I remember, and Madame Sembrich inspired a steady stream of gifts of all kinds in the long years of their career. There are, naturally, certain personalities that inspire such out-giving just as there are certain people who are always hosts, and others who are always guests! I think I have already said this; if not I shall probably say it again later on, for such am I—always the host and rarely the guest. I cannot confess to trunkfuls of jewels and pianos studded with gems, for I was always treated as one who should give rather than to receive, but as a mark of great personal friendship I am happy to say I have received many beautiful gifts in my lifetime. This watch which I always carry with such affection was given me by my dear friend, Montgomery Sears, of Boston, during my first tour of America, and he once gave me an exceptionally beautiful gift, some emerald buttons, as a mark of appreciation for my playing in his house.

And there have been touching marks of affection too, especially in America from my compatriots there, the poor Polish emigrants. These humble gifts have always moved me profoundly and such gifts still come even now after all these years, to Morges.

Though rather late in the day, it seems ungracious not to mention certain gifts which came during your days of prohibition and which were most thankfully and gratefully received by me at that difficult time. Certain priceless bottles of fine old whiskey cleverly concealed in beautiful baskets of flowers! These little attentions came regularly from friends and followed me through the country on my long tours. They were a blessing at that time and I make very grateful public thanks for them now in appreciation of the delicacy with which they were concealed and the difficulties which had to be surmounted in sending them to me.

In the past years, I have had certain unusual gifts made me on several occasions, but not as a mark of admiration, quite the contrary. Twice it has happened but it was accompanied each time with remarks that hurt me. The first time was before the war. I received a letter with a document in it, which read as follows: "I hereby give to Mr. Paderewski the property situated in such and such a county, containing some sixty or seventy acres, in order to establish there a school of agriculture for young Polish peasants, and the school shall be founded in, and forever bear, his name, Paderewski." Ah! That was touching. But with the document there came a letter of explanation which was not so touching. It said, "You should not imagine that this is done in order to show you my appreciation for your *musical* ability and accomplishments. Not at all! They bore me. I do not care for music. But I have heard you play several times and I have also heard your addresses, and I know that you are an honorable man worthy of this mark of esteem and trust."

Well, it was certainly a strange communication, and the letter of explanation, admitting me as an honest man though repudiating me as an artist, somewhat took the edge off this gift.

I have had two or three almost identical things. Not long ago another quite large property was offered me for that same purpose (for Polish peasants) but I lost all the documents. I became ill, and lost all trace of that affair. It was a property of some twelve hundred or more acres in Poland. Perhaps it is just as well!

But there was one gift that came to me absolutely without restrictions—a gift outright, and the only legacy that has ever been left to me. It was from a poor Polish workman, who, in 1930, left me everything he had in the world. He left me $50. When I got that little check, I wept. And the message with it touched me as few things in life have ever touched me. On a cheap and worn bit of paper addressed to me, he wrote, "All I have I give to you." The handwriting was so faint as to be almost unreadable. Poor fellow! What it must have cost him to get those few words on paper! It was a princely gift. I tried in every possible way to find out something about him and where he was buried, but I never could trace him. He went to his poor grave unknown to me. An undying memory of his gift is the only monument I can raise to him.

Let me turn back for a moment to my German tour and answer a question that you have asked. It is an interesting question and one that I must answer in the affirmative, for it concerns Germany. Did I feel, even as far back as that German tour, the possibility of war? Yes, decidedly yes. I heard war-talk even then and I felt its menace. I always try to think logically and there were many unmistakable signs to be noticed at that time. I spent many months touring in Germany. I lived in Berlin, where I studied for two seasons. Then I lived in Strasbourg, which was at that time under Prussian rule. I was connected socially with the

A Career at Top Speed

French sympathizers, those patricians of Strasbourg, but officially and professionally I always had to do with the German element. They were the Trustees of the Conservatory where I taught and I had to attend certain functions there. I was often at the house of the Governor of the Province, Prince Hohenlohe, who afterward became the Chancellor of the German Empire. I knew him personally very well and I knew his wife, who had some Polish blood in her veins—her mother was born the Princess Radziwill. I knew Prince Alexander Hohenlohe, the eldest son of the at-that-time Governor and later on Chancellor of the Empire. Alexander Hohenlohe was liberal-progressive and not at all Prussian in his character and sentiments. He was a noble kind of man, and just; he was really a man much above his surroundings and his class. He published certain things in which he condemned his government, especially the attitude of Prussia. I had even not long ago a visit from Prince Hohenlohe here in my house, and was very glad to see him.

So, I knew Germany well, and I knew Prussia well and the Prussian character. Besides, there was something which I may perhaps mention, in this connection—that, being a teacher at the Conservatory, which was under the influence of the Prussian functionaries, I was sometimes at their clubs, I could not avoid it. I recall on one occasion a supper at the Military Casino, when something rather startling happened. Xavier Scharwenka had given a concert at the Conservatory. He was a Silesian, and Silesia, you know, has been Polish for two hundred years, under the Prussian rule, and consequently Germanized very efficiently. So Scharwenka was educated in Prussian schools and considered himself German, though in fact he was Polish by blood, spoke Polish, and wrote Polish music. Well, he came to Strasbourg while I was there, and gave a concert, and all the German officials and military Prussians turned out en masse to show him a special mark of appreciation, so a great supper was arranged in his honor and I was obliged to go.

There were many speeches, and all of them against foreigners. Each in his turn would begin, "We are so proud and so

[323]

glad to welcome here a German artist, etc., etc." I knew well what it all meant; it was unmistakable. The speeches were made, the wine drunk, and the good feeling was at its very height, when suddenly, without any preliminaries, an officer of very high rank jumped from his chair and with his glass raised high in his hand said, *"Und jetzt, meine Herren, an den Tag!"* "To the Day!" And that was in 1886, mind you. Yes, they were preparing all the time—all those years working toward "der Tag"—it had to come.

But let us return again to our music and the year 1902. Early in December I went to Poland just long enough to enable me to dispose of an estate I still owned. An estate so expensive that I could no longer go on with it. I stayed there for several weeks until a purchaser came, and I was glad indeed to sell the place, though at a tremendous loss.

II

My musical career was now really at top speed—practically all over the world—except that I had not yet been to South America nor Australia. I had already been in Spain, but my first tour there was very short. The second tour was in 1902. I gave several concerts in Madrid at that time.

During one of my visits in Madrid I had the pleasure of being invited by the Queen Mother, Maria Christina, to the Court.

I played several times at the Palace, and on one occasion was invited to the home of the Infanta Isabella. She was extremely gracious and brilliant. She was already well on in life, but in spite of her age still most attractive. She received me in a very warm and friendly manner and it was all very informal. It was a tea party at which many members of the royal family were present. After I had played several pieces, the young King, Alfonso, who was then a boy of about sixteen, hurriedly entered the room with a long sword hanging at his left side.

"Oh!" the young King cried, when he saw me. "Have you played so soon?"

"Yes," I replied, "I have already played."

A Career at Top Speed

"Oh, that's too bad, too bad! I wanted to hear you. I came back especially to hear you, Monsieur Paderewski, and you have already played."

"Well, that is very easily managed," I answered. "I shall be delighted to play something for your Majesty now."

"Yes, yes, please," he cried delightedly. "But do me a favor, and play something very, very gay. I love only gay music."

So, I at once began to play some waltzes, which were not real dance music, but pieces from my repertoire, Chopin, Liszt, and Rubinstein. But in spite of his politeness I soon saw that the boy was not very enthusiastic about them, and he finally said, "Have you nothing still gayer in your fingers? Something very gay— lively— something very wild? That's the kind of music I like."

"Yes," I said, "I have"; and I began at once a Hungarian Rhapsody by Liszt. That evidently made an immediate impression on him, because he quickly jumped from his chair with a shout of delight and began dancing swiftly around the table. He was delighted. At one moment he almost fell on the floor because his sword interfered so with his dancing. But he didn't stop, he simply flung his sword on the table and then danced on, wildly, and more and more wildly, just as long as I played. And when I had finished he cried, "Please, once more, just once more. Don't stop now! Give me just one more dance!"

So on I played to his royal satisfaction, and he only stopped when he was quite breathless and dripping with perspiration. It was, I think, the year of his coronation, because there was a tremendous gathering of royalties at the castle, not only the British and Italian but also Scandinavian and Russian members of the reigning houses were present.

After that impromptu dance, I had a short conversation with the Queen, and I said what a wonderful boy he was, with his gay fiery temperament and his marvellous energy, and the Queen replied, "Yes, yes, but really I do not know what to do with that boy. His energy is colossal! There is no stopping him. Do you know what he did the other morning? It is impossible to believe. He came on horseback, riding right up to my bedroom door. Yes,

I assure you, Monsieur Paderewski, he dashed up that stairway on his horse at full speed and landed at my door just to say good morning."

The steps of the great Palace staircase were very shallow but enormously broad, and up this stairway he rode his horse straight to the Queen's door without a thought! What a picture that calls up!

During that tour I played also in Barcelona, where the concert was an enormous success and caused the greatest demonstration I had ever known. On my way back to the hotel, the horses were unharnessed from the carriage, and amid wild shouting and cheers the students themselves conveyed me to the hotel. I might say dragged me there, for they seized the shafts and rushed me at a great rate down the street. Then the whole crowd of several thousand people stood for half an hour before the hotel and refused to leave until I responded to their calls and appeared on the balcony and addressed them in French—at that time I could not speak Spanish.

It was all very exciting and spontaneous. Those gay young students were boiling over with enthusiasm and I was swept along with the great tide.

We are now approaching the year 1903, the most important year in my activity as a composer. When I sold my estate in Poland, I felt much freer; a great burden had dropped away. I decided then to stop playing for a year and write something. So in 1903 I remained almost the entire year at Morges, and began to compose. First of all I wrote my Piano Sonata, which is one of my most important and best works. But it is extremely difficult and for that reason will never be very popular.

The second work was the completion of my third set of Variations, which I had begun years before while still in Strasbourg. I had retained only a few of the variations from that period, so I wrote a series of new ones ending with the fugue. This work is my best piano composition, I think. It is extremely difficult and perhaps too long, but it contains quite a few things which were then almost a revelation in their character and novelty.

A Career at Top Speed

Within a fortnight I also wrote twelve French songs to the words of Catulle Mendès. Madame Modjeska and her husband were staying here at Morges then, and every evening I played a new song to her. It was a happy time.

After that I wrote a sketch of my Symphony. That took several months. The orchestration, however, was done several years later. That composition was written in commemoration of the last Polish revolution of 1863. It was the fortieth anniversary.

When these compositions were finished, I had of course to return to my piano again. I needed money and I must begin to play once more. It was a very prolific year for me artistically and I was happy in it. I never enjoyed myself more in my art than during that year, because there is only one thing that is truly and continuously satisfying in life and that is—*creative work*. Creative work, take it as you will, is the only thing in life that gives supreme satisfaction. Ideas are eternal. In presenting them one reaches the loftiest heights. The form of presentation makes no difference. By creative work one gives one's self new life. Creative work kills death. This theme is a tempting one to elaborate. While you are composing, you live in a certain atmosphere which excludes everything else, practically. For instance, it excludes practising because practising is practically *spade* work, the drudgery. It is an absolute necessity and it is the tragic side of a musical artist, that necessity of continuous practising. If you are a painter, a sculptor or an architect, if you are an engineer, a builder of canals or bridges or towers and so on, you learn your art, or I should say technique, forever. It remains always with you—your technique, your facility. You can remain for years without using the brush or the pencil, and yet when you start again you have the same facility at your command. With the musician, especially an executive musician like the pianist, or the violinist, it is absolutely impossible. You are obliged to practise with your fingers so many hours a day in order to maintain their flexibility. And I repeat this is equally true of both a violinist and pianist. Even the singer's art needs constant practice although it is not as exacting and tiresome in its demands.

The Paderewski Memoirs

Yes, for the pianist it is constant torture and privation. It deprives you of so many, not only pleasures, but necessary things in life. It prevents you from reading, from thinking, from developing your intellect—this practising every day the indispensable hours.

Even now, with my normal work, after I have come to the knowledge that playing is not working, I still need four or five hours a day of practising with the concentration of mind that does not admit any intrusion. It is a slavery from which there is no escape. It has, to be sure, its pleasant moments, but I could say as Gounod once said about Wagner, "Yes, there are divine moments, but oh the unbearable hours!"

Sometimes when I think about the amount of actual physical work I have already accomplished, I do not really know how I could have withstood it, because it was constant labor and effort, and sometimes ungrateful effort, when I had very often to learn something which I knew was only for the moment.

I am often asked by students if it is necessary now and then *to rest* the hands completely. Yes, absolutely. It is not only necessary but it is also very beneficial. I experienced that to the highest degree some years ago when, through my political activities, I stopped playing altogether. I did not touch the piano then for over four years and that was the time when my arm (always so troublesome) got so much better and my fingers became strong again. But I have never had time to rest my hands *regularly* as I should have done, because, when one tour was over, I had to prepare at once for another. So it was unending, not only the strain, but the *pressure* of work. Ah! that is terrible, that feeling of haste. That is the worst of all. It takes away all your courage. It is like a poor swimmer far out at sea who says to himself continually, "Shall I ever be able to reach the shore? Shall I have the strength for that?" Such moments are extremely dangerous. There is only one thing that can be compared in anguish to it, and that is a dream I have so often had when I am obliged to play something that I have not yet prepared, or not prepared sufficiently; the audience is there waiting, the conductor is waiting, the orchestra is waiting, and they come for me to take me to the platform, and I go out and face that great audience and sit down at the piano—ah! that is an agony!

And now I am going to come to a full stop to answer certain questions of yours. You have asked me several times an important and significant question—I should, in fact, say two important questions. The first about the use (or abuse) of Tempo Rubato and the second the use of the pedal. Well, these are questions that must be answered—they are of colossal importance to every pianist. To speak adequately of the great art of pedalling would require a treatise on my part. It cannot be explained in a few words or even a few sentences. It requires a great concentration to make it clear. If I were to prepare a treatise on the use of the pedal, it would take me months.

The pedal is the strongest factor in musical expression at the piano, because first of all it is the only means of prolonging the sound. The piano is a percussion instrument, you know, and the only way of making it appear prolonged is the pedal. Therefore, I repeat, it is the principal factor in expression because it adds to the volume and the duration of the sound. It requires a great study, a special study when trying to produce a real effect with it. In a way it is a science, the use of the pedal. Perhaps it may seem exaggerated to use such an extreme word as science in connection with a little device like the pedal, but it is so. You must know it perfectly to be the master of the keyboard. Its importance cannot be overestimated.

Whenever learning a new piece, one must learn also the proper effect of the pedalling. Each new piece requires a new pedalling, adaptable to the character of the music. Although I had a natural instinct for pedalling when I was a boy, it was only after years of study that it developed into a conscious knowledge.

But we are only skimming the surface of this great subject, for it is all beyond my biography at this particular point. There is far too much to say; it is too big a subject, too vital to the student, to dismiss with these few words. It is of the deepest interest to me and I intend to treat it fully and adequately in the later period of these memoirs.

With your second question, the Tempo Rubato, we fall into still deeper waters. I once wrote a short article on this subject for Henry T. Finck which was published some years ago in a book of his. I remember that I said in that article that Tempo Rubato is the unreconcilable foe of the metronome, and one of music's oldest friends. It is older than the romantic school, it is older than Mozart, it is older than Bach. Why it is called Rubato we do not really know. All lexicons give the literal translation of it as: *robbed, or stolen time*. Although we protest against the use of the words, "robbed, or stolen time," we recognize that the very essence of Tempo Rubato is a certain disregard of the established properties of rhythm and rate of movement.

Chopin made very ample use of Tempo Rubato, and Liszt also, and there is a great deal of interest and value to be said about their use of Tempo Rubato. Tempo Rubato, I may say, to go a little further, is necessary but should not be abused—it should not become *license*.

But again I must refer you to my treatise on this subject, and again I must repeat myself and say that I should like also to use it in the second volume to come.

Yes, it is a fascinating subject. I have always been a defender of Tempo Rubato and sometimes have been violently criticised for using it to excess. To quote your good friend, Mr. Bernard Shaw, who was the music critic on *The London World* back in 1890—he said then of my playing that the license of my Tempo Rubato was beyond all reasonable limit. But, as you know, I do not always agree with Mr. Bernard Shaw.

And now while we are on the subject of the pitfalls and dangers in the pianistic art, I should like with your permission to add a very special word regarding the *development* of the pianistic art and its connection with Bach. A word that I would gladly proclaim to all the world. Every pianist should play Bach. Without studying Bach he would really be no pianist at all, particularly on account of Bach's supreme polyphonic style, which contributes enormously to the technical development of the pianistic art. The pianistic art is a great art because it combines the beauty of ideas with that polyphonic mastership of which Bach was the supreme exponent. He is for me a kind of divinity in music. Musically speaking, Bach is a universal genius. Bach is a giant.

Our full stop has been an interesting interruption I think. But now we must return to my own story. Work again and another tour. I had to start playing again after my year of composing. I had many obligations which had increased very much—I was in need of money and these ten fingers of mine must be put to work once more.

I had given a number of charitable concerts, and then I decided to go to Australia, for the first time. This was in 1904. I had received a very attractive offer and it was arranged for me to go in May. But before that I was obliged to go to Russia again, to St. Petersburg. That was the last time I went there, and it was very dramatic—the last memory of the old Russia that is now no more.

But first I went to Poland. I gave three concerts in Cracow for charitable institutions, because Cracow, our ancient capital, was the only one in which I had not done that. There were some very dear friends then living in Cracow. From there I went to Warsaw and played again.

The visit to St. Petersburg at that time was not pleasant at all. That was a time of most severe treatment of all the nationalities conquered by Russia. The structure of that despotic absolute monarchy was then evidently shaking. The government, at the head of which were the most ferocious reactionaries, started that particular persecution of all aliens within the Empire, to divert the attention of their own people from the activity of the government itself, which was nothing else but license, frivolity, and corruption.

I think at that moment the abuse of the bureaucracy and of certain most influential figures among the imperial families had reached its climax. It was the beginning of the dreadful end.

I had to give three recitals and to play for the Imperial

Musical Society at a symphonic concert, as I had done some five years before.

The sentiment of the people in Russia was very much against the aliens, as I have already mentioned, and very particularly against the Poles. There was a rage against all Poles.

I found, of course, the same old acquaintances, César Cui, Rimsky-Korsakoff, Glazounoff, and so on, but there was something changed. They were not as cordial as they were when they greeted me for the first time; the atmosphere was one of excitement, unrest, and of a deep hostility. Some of them were too timid to show me their former friendship. There was something very wrong altogether. One could feel it in the air, and I felt it immediately in my first recital. For instance, people came very late. It was very cold and they began taking off their furs and their coats in an unusual way, disturbing me so much that I had actually to stop playing several times (without the intention of offending them) because there was so much noise.

Although the house was well filled, it was not the usual St. Petersburg audience. But either through these interruptions or through the influence of the general audience, there was not as much warmth of reception as I experienced before, until the end, when the people got quite wild and enthusiastic.

The next day the newspapers reproached me very severely for interrupting the performance of some pieces. They said there was no provocation for such behavior.

The morning after the recital that good and charming gentleman, General von Stackelberg (the unmusical director of that Imperial Orchestra), came to see me. He was in a very nice mood, smiling and evidently pleased. I could not understand what it was all about.

After warmest congratulations, he came at once to the object of his visit and said, "I am on a very pleasant errand, indeed, today. I have the honor to invite you to play before his Majesty, the Czar. His Majesty has expressed to me his great desire to see you and to hear you at last."

I replied, "Of course, I am at his Majesty's command. The

Emperor of Russia is also the King of Poland, and I am therefore one of his subjects."

The General, I think, was rather surprised that I answered him in this way. I was *not* at the command of the Emperor of Russia, but I was at the command of the King of Poland!

Then I asked the General: "Will you kindly tell me which are the compositions that would meet with the special approval of his Majesty?"

"Oh, yes," he said. "I think anything would suit him but quite particularly Chopin, and some of your own compositions."

I was very glad indeed to hear this because it was at least a mark of interest. The Czar knew that I was a Pole. It was a very gracious act on his part. So I began preparing my two programs, one for the Emperor and the other for my own recital. The days passed quickly, when suddenly on the very eve of the concert for the Czar at the Palace, the General appeared again, but how differently he looked this time! He was really quite pale and drawn and looked so worried and miserable that I knew at once something was wrong. After a moment, in a trembling voice, he said (he was obviously greatly upset): "I am sorry to tell you, Monsieur Paderewski, that the concert at the Palace tonight will not take place. Look at the letter I have received." He handed it to me.

I looked at the letter and, of course, understood. It was very plain, the evidence of rage against the aliens, and especially the Poles. It was very bitter. The Government had stepped in and evidently persuaded the Emperor at the last moment that it would be very impolitic to let me appear at the Palace. They were afraid of my getting in touch personally with the Emperor, it seems. The letter said in very plain language: "I have to inform you that his Majesty, the Emperor, has no time to listen to Monsieur Paderewski's music." It was signed, "The Marshal of the Court."

Well, I did not feel at all offended or humiliated; in fact, I was rather relieved because I knew that I would have to meet some of the worst enemies of my country there, and nobody knows what might have happened then. So I simply said to the General: "That is quite all right, and I tell you frankly that I am glad. Glad that I am not to play for the Czar."

"But why? Why?"

"You do not understand why? Because, for one thing, I would, naturally, have to meet there the man who wrote that letter to you, and do you think it would have been a pleasure to me to meet an *animal* of that kind?"

He simply stared at me, and then he saw it.

"But," he answered, "that is strange that you have that point of view. Don't you see it is a very serious blow? Can't you realize that?"

"No, it is not a blow, but it is an advice."

"How do you mean, it is an advice?"

"I mean that I have nothing more to do here. I shall leave today."

"But you have a concert which has been advertised."

"I shall cancel the concert and the money can be refunded."

When I said that I was going to leave, the Committee of the Imperial Musical Society, that good old César Cui, hurriedly came to see me and said, "But you know you have signed a contract to play in our concert, and by virtue of that contract we have sold many seats for our subscription. You cannot leave now. You cannot. We are bound to make a lawsuit for the nonfulfillment of your contract if you go, much as we would regret it."

Then I explained to him what had happened. "But you know," he said, "that is just politics. You are surely wise enough to understand that it has nothing to do with your *art*. We deeply regret it. It is an uncalled-for insult to you as a Pole, but even so, it is a *political* affair and we are not concerned with politics. We are here on artistic grounds and you promised an artistic institution your co-operation and we are entitled to ask you to fulfill your engagement." There was no disputing that argument and so I had to remain and play.

After I had played that concert—I remember I played a Beethoven Concerto and an endless series of encores—I had the greatest possible success. All my former appearances there turned pale as compared with the tremendous enthusiasm of that memorable night, which proved to be my very last appearance in St. Petersburg, for I had a premonition then that I should never see that beautiful city again. So there was a certain sadness mixed with that triumph.

The next day I went to pay some visits to a few old friends of whom I was very fond and whom I felt I should never see again —for they too were a part of my premonition.

Just before leaving St. Petersburg I went to pay my respects to another acquaintance, an important functionary, an undersecretary of State with the title of Excellency, who for the moment must be nameless for the very good reason that I have forgotten it. When I arrived at his house I saw that he was very grave and serious. But he greeted me kindly and said, "So you are leaving us at this very crucial moment." I looked at him in astonishment.

"Crucial moment," I said, "I don't understand your Excellency."

"But, surely, you must have already heard the news that the Japanese Ambassador is leaving St. Petersburg immediately and at this very moment we are actually at war with Japan. Yes, at this very moment Russian blood, and I am sorry to say Polish blood too, is already flowing in the Far East. We are at a grave crisis. It is extremely serious," he went on, shaking his head gloomily. "We are at war, Monsieur Paderewski. Russia is at war."

He was obviously agitated and deeply moved. He walked up and down the room as he talked. "Yes," he repeated, "Russian blood and Polish blood, your blood and mine, is already being spilt. And let me tell you," he shouted suddenly, "we are going to be licked and it will serve us right too, I tell you. We are going to get licked. Loyal Russian that I am, I declare it!"

He glared at me fiercely, although he seemed oblivious of my presence. In spite of his great rage, he was very melancholy and presented a tragic, if somewhat absurd, appearance.

His prophecy, however, proved to be true, and in short order, as we all know.

I left immediately for Kieff by way of Moscow. At that very hour, just as His Excellency had said, the Japanese Ambassador was also leaving St. Petersburg. My wife accompanied me on this trip and we stayed for a few hours in Moscow to await the arrival of her father, who came from a distant city to see us. We saw him for the last time. He died shortly afterward.

A very interesting and amusing incident, also in connection with the Japanese war, happened while we were travelling to Kieff. At a small station en route, a Russian officer came hurriedly into the train. He could not find accommodations; he searched through every compartment, but there was absolutely no place for him anywhere. He was loaded down with all kinds of paraphernalia. He had with him four or five baskets, a tremendous package with his sword sticking out of it, his great overcoat and, oddly enough, at least half a dozen small pots—of jam!

He stood wretchedly in the corner surrounded by his luggage, and looked so longingly at the one vacant seat we had (for fortunately we had a compartment to ourselves) that it was heartbreaking. He looked at us with such a sad expression that I could not but open the door and ask him in.

It seems he was a captain in the Russian army—a tall, thin man. He accepted our offer of a seat with great joy and began at once to arrange his belongings. He put down his baskets wherever he saw a little space; then he put his pots very carefully and methodically on top of each other. But when he saw there was no room for the last pot, he turned politely to me and said, "Would you perhaps like to have some of these delicious preserves with your tea?" For the precious pots were filled with preserves, it seems. You may know, perhaps, that Russians always take preserves, or jam as you call it, with their tea. It is a custom of the country. I thanked him for his offer and ordered tea, and with the tea we ate the preserves, which proved to be, as he had said, delicious.

After tea he began to talk of the war, and turning suddenly

A Career at Top Speed

to the Polish gentleman who organized our tour, he said, "Tell me, what is the latest war news?"

At that, my Polish manager, realizing that he was speaking to a Russian army officer, made a very sad and melancholy face and said, "I am sorry to say, sir, that things are going badly, very badly I fear."

"How do you mean—badly?"

"Well, do you not know that Port Arthur has already been taken?"

"Port Arthur has been taken!" cried the Russian. "Good. That's splendid news. Wonderful fellows those Japanese. You know that I consider it a great honor for us military men to have to fight such brave adversaries." He was really overjoyed because Port Arthur had been taken. "Are they not marvellous?" he said. "You know, I am sorry, but I think we are bound to lose. We have not been well taken care of. Our army is no good as compared to those Japanese. We deserve to be beaten, and we shall be," he repeated. "There's no doubt of it."

For the hundred or more miles we travelled with him, we heard nothing but his expression of genuine admiration for his adversaries, and the expression of sorrow that the Russians could not compare with the Japanese! It was very amusing. His conversation proved to be simply a repetition of His Excellency's in St. Petersburg.

A strange people, these Russians. One may know them for many years and still not know them. They are always an interesting subject to me, a Pole, and I shall at some time go into it more particularly. This is not the place to elaborate this theme. There will be a better moment later on that you will remind me of. It is of course of the old Russia that I am speaking and the Russians of that time—the splendid Russia of the Czarist rule with its glories and beauties, its cruelties and inadequacies, that has now so vanished in these days of dictatorship and communism. How completely that old régime has passed from the world, from our vision, and almost from our comprehension! Italy, Austria and Germany—the Austria and Germany of my youth and the

beautiful past of my student days. It fills me with a great heart-
ache for what is no more, and a very great sadness. Old Europe
gone forever. I can only pause for a moment and make this
oblation at its bier.

XVI

Australia and New Zealand

I

And now we step into our harness again and go on with our story.

After this last Russian tour, I had still a few concerts in England, and then proceeded to Cologne, where I played in a Rhenish Festival. Then a few weeks later we sailed for Australia. We sailed from Marseilles in May. As my health was not good, and that of my wife left also much to be desired, we took our Paris physician with us on that trip, Doctor Ratynski. We had a great deal of trouble with that young gentleman, because, instead of his caring for us, we had to nurse him all the time. He became ill at once and only appeared on deck for the first time at Suez, just strong enough to take a little walk, and his second appearance occurred in Colombo, where we stopped for some fifteen or sixteen hours. Altogether he was a total loss to us as a doctor.

Of course, Colombo made a tremendous impression on all of us. The rich colors and the wealth of the costumes of those Oriental merchants, who appeared on board the moment we stopped, are still very fresh in my memory. I am longing to see it all once more, but do not know whether it will ever be accomplished.

We had one frightening experience there just as we were sailing. Our friend and companion and manager, Mr. Adlington, got lost. I do not know what happened to him, but we were already on the steamer, which was about to sail, and Adlington was not to be found, but at the last moment, when we were all in despair, I saw, suddenly, a rickshaw running at full speed toward the harbor, and in it sat the lost Adlington! What a relief! He, however, did not seem greatly upset. He had met, it seems, an old friend on shore and forgot all about the steamer—and us!

So we left for Australia, and for almost seventeen days we did not see our doctor again. He was sick all the time. That was dreadful. My wife and I were good sailors and with Adlington, in the roughest weather, we were able to enjoy our meals.

After thirty-five days of journey, we at last reached Melbourne, but what a contrast! At the beginning of our trip we found the heat on the steamer in the Mediterranean very unpleasant, and going through the Suez Canal and Red Sea, it was simply unbearable. There was practically no air to breathe. We spent several nights on the deck, because the air in our cabins was so horrible that we were almost suffocated, even the air on deck, at night, was not much better. I felt as though I were swallowing cotton.

To add to all the unpleasantness, I was not well. I was suffering with my nerves and my stomach. In fact, I was a perfect wreck during that whole journey. I had so overworked for so many years that my labors and my irregular life were now taking their toll. But the worst part of that journey was in the Indian Ocean. During the journey through the Suez Canal and Red Sea, the steamer became red hot, but as long as we could walk on deck it was still tolerable; but when we were obliged to remain in our cabins on account of the very strong winds in the Indian Ocean, we were practically boiling! It was dreadful. It was really something horrible. It was not the proper time of year for that journey. We should have gone in February or January, and it was June! We arrived in Melbourne in July, and in Melbourne we found the climate colder than in any other place in the world. It was full wintertime in Australia then.

We had quite a comfortable apartment at the Hotel Menzies, but we could not eat anything. The food was simply indescribable, so we lived almost entirely at first on pineapples, which were ideal as to taste, but not very nourishing. So my wife then decided to do the cooking herself, and every morning she went with Mr. Adlington, or Mr. Lemmone, who was the local manager of these concerts, to the market and bought food and cooked it herself in our rooms. Fortunately, we had a very nice waiter, who was very much upset, seeing that we could not eat, and said to me repeatedly, "I am sorry, sir, that you cannot eat this food. It's too bad."

Finally I said, "But who is your chef? Tell me, is he a chef, or a tailor or a carpenter?"

"Oh, no, sir," he said very seriously, "he is an *engineer!*"

It was so funny I was speechless. I never expected that answer. Oh, how we laughed!

It was altogether very difficult with the cooks in Australia, because everywhere they had cooks of different nationality. For instance, afterward in Sydney, we had a good French cook. The cooking was good also in the Hotel Australia, and we had a Spanish cook in Brisbane, for a change.

Our doctor recovered as soon as we landed. He felt perfectly well again, and although he had rendered no medical or other service to us on the voyage, he still remained with us.

If it had not been for the bad food, I would have had nothing to complain about. The concerts were quite pleasant, the audiences large everywhere, and the reception extremely enthusiastic. It was in every respect enjoyable artistically. The people were very hospitable. There was a Conservatory of Music attached to the University, and the level of musical education was quite respectable, not only in Melbourne, but in Adelaide, where we went afterwards. It has since become a desert artistically because the Labor Government came into power shortly after our stay there and ruled for some twenty-three years. During that time the whole of the country fell into an almost barbarian state. They considered that people working with their brains, but not with their muscles, were not working at all, and it was a complete decline of intelligence and of good form. I understand that since I was there last in 1927, the Labor Government has been replaced by a Conservative Government and things are going much better. But during that last stay in Australia it was something terrible.

That *first* Australian tour was enjoyable. Our chief recreation was, of course, the parrots. They were a joy and an amusement. I have much more to say later on this subject and the rôle that one parrot played in my life for several years.

Having to play many recitals, in both Melbourne and Sydney, it meant constant work to prepare those big programs.

The authorities everywhere were extremely kind to us. We had frequent invitations to the home of the Lieutenant-Governor, Lord Northcote, and to the Governors of New South Wales, Queensland, and South Australia.

I had in Sydney a concert with orchestra, which brings to mind the triangle story. That orchestral concert was rather amusing for me on account of the first rehearsal I had there. It was not a regular orchestra that was about to accompany me. The conductor, a very talented musician, Signor Hazon, called my attention to the fact that I could not expect a long rehearsal with the orchestra on account of their being already formed into a union. Not a minute overtime could be used for rehearsing, as they would all leave at the appointed hour, leaving me alone with my piano!

I had to play three concertos there, the last one being the F Minor Concerto by Chopin. In the orchestral arrangement of that concerto, in the last movement, there are some eight or nine strokes of the triangle which are very important and effective. Well, the fatal time was approaching, but the rehearsal had to be stopped when there were still about five or six minutes necessary to finish the last movement. I addressed a few words to the orchestra, asking them to please be gracious enough to continue in order to let me play just once the remaining part of the finale. They all consented except one (because there were some real artists among them). Then, imagine my surprise at the very last moment when the triangle player, who had not once struck his important instrument, stopped the whole orchestra and said, "Now, we have played enough. We must stop. It is time to go to lunch." At that, without another word, they got up and left, with only a few more bars to be rehearsed. It must be added, though, that, according to the sacred rules of the union, the triangle player was receiving the same amount of money as the first violin player, and all the other orchestra members who were supposed to be soloists. He, the triangle player, had not even once moved his precious hand, and it was he who said they had played enough, and that it was time to go!

Well, there was nothing to be done. The orchestra left. I asked Signor Hazon who was that important artist, that great triangle player who had stopped the rehearsal. "Oh, he is not an artist at all," he laughed. "He is important in the union, yes, but he is just a cigar-shop keeper!"

And now the obvious question— Did the triangle come in on time at the concert that night? No! Certainly not—he came in, most decidedly—but he came in in the wrong place.

II

I think we went from Australia to New Zealand. The first three concerts took place at Auckland, a large and wealthy city, after which, on account of my not being well, there was quite a long interval between concerts. I wanted very much to enjoy the baths in the district of Rotorua. It is not very far from Auckland, and the principal city of the Maori people.

We enjoyed our stay in Auckland. The hotel was comfortable and the cook, strange to say, was tolerable. He was a Swede. In Wellington we had a Frenchman, in Napier a Scotsman, in Christchurch we had a German, in Dunedin, a Scotch place, we had another Frenchman, and in Invercargill, a Chinaman. In every place there was a different nationality in the kitchen. And the cooking was in accordance.

You can easily realize that, on tour, the cooks make a great deal of difference in my life and comfort, especially as I take only one meal a day—and that after the concert. This was very unfortunate because, as we soon discovered, no hotel kitchen was allowed to stay open after the dinner was served, and, as my first meal of the day was always toward midnight, even later, I could get nothing to eat. So everywhere we were obliged to negotiate with the union authorities. Otherwise, I could only have a bit of cold meat or fish, and it was not possible for me to work under such circumstances. So poor Mr. Adlington or Mr. Lemmone was always negotiating with the union authorities about my food. And it was extremely expensive, too. We were obliged to pay for the extra service, the cook, his assistant and several others. We actually had to pay four fees; then in addition all these people expected very large tips. This is because the money we paid did not go into their pockets, but went of course to the union. So the poor fellows had all that extra work absolutely without pay, except for our tips. I must say I gave them very generous ones, and gladly. In some cases it amounted to even ten or twelve pounds just for their services.

I was still very anxious to try the baths at Rotorua, which had quite a reputation as a watering place in New Zealand, but as a neighboring village was more interesting and comfortable, we decided to stop there. The entire population was Maori. The only white man was a gentleman by the name of Nelson, a Britisher, of course, who came some forty years before to the place as a surveyor and was so impressed, so enraptured by the country and by the people especially, that he decided to live there, and he did live there to the end of his days, which occurred some ten years after our first visit.

We lived in the Hotel Nelson, and it must be said that nowhere in the world have we enjoyed such quiet, pleasant and absolutely undisturbed peace as there. All the Maori people were most interesting to me. They were educated, some of them having been at high school and so on, but they lived just as their ancestors had lived for a thousand years. Some of them even knew who I was, and they showed me so much respect and affection, and such courtesy as I've really never found elsewhere.

From time to time we made some little excursions. Everywhere in that wonderful land there are geysers and hot lakes. The bath I enjoyed there (and which quieted my nerves very

much) was called an oil bath, because the water was so fat
and came from natural sources. It must have been something
very particular. It was very heavy and naturally very hot. I
think it was some 85, or even more, degrees.

Our guide was a Maori girl bearing the poetic name of
Maggie Papakura. She was quite a lady—well educated. She
married, afterwards, some English lord. She was recognized chief
of that little tribe, and she always offered, most graciously, her
services as a guide. to that delightful land. She published an interesting book later about the district of Whakarewarewa. She
guided us most carefully. She would take my wife by the hand,
and then to me, who was following, she would say, "Now be
careful, very careful. Don't go to the right. Just follow me
exactly." I asked why. "Because there is an abyss here which you
cannot see. It is boiling mud—it is on your right, only a yard
away. So be very careful." And then she threw in, by way of
warning, "A few years ago my aunt made a misstep and sank
into that abyss, and disappeared forever." Well, I can assure you
I followed her advice! I was very careful.

On one occasion she showed me a Maori fishing with a line
in fresh and very cold water for trout. He caught one, and without moving from the place where he stood, he threw that trout
right into a little pond only two yards away from him. Then
drew in the line, took off the fish, put a little salt on it, and ate
it! It was thoroughly cooked.

At that time, some of the geysers were playing, but not at
their greatest height and splendor, not high enough for their
guests of honor, as we were considered by the Maoris. They
were extremely proud to have us staying with them. So one
day they decided to give us a "soap of honor" as they call it.
In other words, a treat. What was it? You can never guess. Well,
they brought twenty pounds of soap, put it into the hole of one
of the geysers, and the geyser immediately jumped about 150
feet into the air because the soap increased the gas. It was a
thrilling sight and we watched it in amazement.

We saw the interesting Lake of Rotorua. The lake is of icy

cold water, but right in the center of it there are a few small islands containing geysers of boiling water jumping very high into the air. Another lake, still farther away, had a temperature of 140 degrees. Amazing.

The country was not strictly beautiful, but so uncanny and so interesting, and full of constant surprises.

One day we expressed a desire to go to a waterfall in the neighborhood, which was one of the wonders of the country. Mr. Lemmone applied to the Government for permission to visit it, and the Minister of the Interior, Sir Joseph Ward, notified us that the Government would be very pleased to have me visit the place, and the chief guide of New Zealand, Mr. Warbrick, would call on me in order to make all necessary arrangements.

Mr. Warbrick came to the hotel and to our surprise told us that it was an excursion of at least three days. There was no hotel there, just a cabin, so we had to carry our own food and bedding, which was something of an undertaking. Well, everything was arranged, and we were to start at five in the morning. Suddenly, at midnght, somebody knocked at the door. It was Mr. Warbrick to tell us that the excursion was off. He deeply regretted it, but he had just been notified that there had been an earthquake in that vicinity and the waterfall we were to visit had disappeared!

The Maori people were a source of great interest to me. They were brown in color and very good-looking. They were supposed to have come from Tahiti. They travelled at least a thousand miles before they established themselves in New Zealand, and they are said to have come in boats made from one log of wood. These Maoris are a fine, handsome people, but the women become perfectly abominable when they are married, for they immediately tattoo their chins horribly—an awful sight. As long as they are girls, they are very pretty to look at, but as married women they are perfectly hideous.

They have curious habits, too, and the principal sport of the men is to show their tongues to frighten the enemy. They have very big tongues which hang down very far. Quite dreadful to look at.

Mr. Nelson claimed that they were very intelligent. He said, "Ask any Maori here about his ancestry, and he will tell you, thirty-two generations back, the names, not only of those who founded the colony, but of every one belonging to that tribe. More than that, they will tell you the particulars of every one, at what age he died, and so forth."

I have known several Maoris of exceptionally high education. One was a member of the Cabinet of New Zealand, who received the Duke and Duchess of York during their visit there. He gave an admirable address at their reception, and then took them afterward to the Rotorua district, of which he was a native. Then, to add to his prowess, he actually took part in a war dance before the royalties, and finally, as the grand finale, tried to frighten them by putting his tongue out almost to his navel! Of course, in the dance he had to wear another and special attire which completely disguised him. After the dance he made a little address in Maori, and created a tremendous impression. Later on at the reception he sat with the royalties at table, and the Duke of York said, "Tell me, who was that wonderful dancer who made such a fine address afterwards and who danced with his tongue hanging out so long?" "Oh," replied the Cabinet member, "it was myself. I am a Maori, you know, and a fine dancer."

It is to be added that as well as their own Maori language, they all speak English, which they learn at school.

After that stay we had to begin the concert tour at Napier. Instead of going by sea, we preferred to go in a coach. The first stop was at Waimangu, the most powerful geyser in New Zealand, perhaps in the world. It usually played every day at some irregular hour. The guide said, "The Waimangu is getting more and more irregular every day, and I am afraid it may stop playing altogether. That would mean a disaster somewhere else in the world." He was very serious about it.

I asked if we could see the spot and he said yes, we could

even walk on it. So we went there and walked on it. It was a field, about three acres of stone and sand, and not even damp because sand dries within a few hours in the sun. The guide told us that, when playing, the geyser went up sometimes incredibly high; from the whole place, sand and stones (some bigger than this room) were thrown up just like pebbles into the air. But he added that there was now a grave danger, because the geyser was becoming very irregular. He was not able to speak scientific language; he could not define it, but he made these observations just from experience.

So we left in our coach and arrived at a place called Wairakei. Wairakei was in the desert, but it was surrounded by a tremendous plantation of fir trees, so strong in appearance and so fresh in color, and tall. They were perhaps fifty feet high. Their height amazed me. My first question was "How old are these trees?" The guide replied, "Oh, sir, they are not so old. There used be a house here and these trees were planted a year after the house was built, about fifteen years ago."

Fifteen years old—fir trees as tall as trees of a hundred years here.

On our trip we met a nice, interesting fellow, I remember. A man with some geological knowledge by the name of "Bill"— every one called him Bill. He was a good-looking, fat, strong fellow. He always carried a special watch on which were many marks and signs showing the exact moment the geysers would play. I do not remember how many there were, but at least thirty, each one playing at certain intervals. It was a park of geysers.

We spent the night there, and the next morning Bill led my wife and me to that part of the park where the geysers were playing, again really a most dangerous spot, because if you slipped on one of the little stones you would fall into boiling water. It was very terrifying.

After that visit we had a conversation with the geologist and he told me that he was gravely concerned, as the Waimangu geyser was now so irregular. He assured me that if it ever stopped there would inevitably be a great disaster somewhere in the world. A year later, the Waimangu stopped completely, and there followed destructive quakes in many parts of the world, including the earthquake in San Francisco.

We next arrived at a very small station, the mail coach headquarters. An old man came and introduced himself to me. He said: "I have heard a great deal about you, Mr. Paderewski, and your wonderful piano playing. You are a distinguished man, sir, and we must do everything we can to protect you. The journey from here to Napier is very dangerous. First of all, we have had a great deal of rain. The ground is very slippery and the road is very narrow, and you will need a large coach. Not everybody knows the road and the horses as well as I do, because I belong here and am an old man. I have been here for fifty years. So I will conduct you there myself." This touched me very deeply. I took it as a great compliment and thanked him and gratefully accepted his kind offer. And so we started. It was one of the most dangerous trips I can remember. We travelled for hours and hours along an abyss. There were two rows of horses. In the first row three, and in the second, two—five altogether. It was a rough, primitive road. On one side the mountains—on the other just the abyss. There was not more than a foot between the carriage and the abyss. It was a precipice some 2000 feet deep. If one of the horses slipped, we would go down—and forever.

We were a large party. There were my wife, myself, Mr. Adlington, Mr. Lemmone, the doctor, Mr. Cutler, the piano tuner, Marcel, my faithful valet, and my wife's maid—eight people, and all our luggage on top of the coach.

Finally we came to a place where the precipice ended and we breathed freely at last. We thought it would be that way to the end. But no! It was only a lull in our anguish. During that lull we travelled perhaps three or four miles, when suddenly we saw at a distance a little house and in front of it fifty or sixty people—a little flock awaiting our arrival. Who were they? Well, it was the school of the district, and the teacher had organized a little reception for me. Was it not wonderful? An absolute wilderness. They had been awaiting, for several hours, the approach of our carriage. Unfortunately, we could not foresee the event and so had no candies for the children. We stayed there only a short time and then on we started again on our drive along the precipice. We travelled for four hours, and then I said to the driver, "How much longer?"

"Only about an hour, sir," he replied.

There was still some sun, some little light left in the sky. I looked at my watch. "What time will the sun set?" I asked.

"Six o'clock." It was then about five. I said to myself, "Only another hour. It is not so bad. We should finish with daylight."

Six o'clock came. We were still at the top of the precipice. Again I inquired, "How much longer?"

"Oh, just about an hour, as I told you."

Seven o'clock. We could not see anything. It was completely black. The horses alone were guiding us.

"How much longer?" again I asked the same question and again the same answer, "Just another hour!"

At about eleven o'clock, all shivering with cold, and hungry and frightened, we saw a light at last—a feeble little ray. It was not yet Napier, but, thank God, it was an inn!

Now, I said, anything warm, anything will console us at this moment. The precipice was behind us and there were food and shelter in sight. We approached the inn quickly. Our wonderful old driver jumped down. He was as lively as a cricket and said to me, "Oh, thank God, sir, thank God, it is over. But I must tell you, Mr. Paderewski, that I have never been so frightened in all my life as I have been today. We stayed too long at that school, you know. It was very nice, very pretty seeing all those children, but it was very dangerous—that delay."

We hurried into the inn, but alas, we could get nothing hot— no soup, not even tea, nothing, because there had just been an earthquake and everything was destroyed. But we did get some brandy, which I think saved our lives. Just imagine if there had been prohibition on top of the earthquake!

The next day we had to get up very early, not because we were in a hurry, but it was so frightfully cold and there were not enough blankets in the hotel, so we wanted to be dressed and to proceed. We arrived in the afternoon at Napier without any further discomfort, and there we found a very good hotel and a charming audience awaiting us that night. It was just like playing in London. The contrast of that audience (every one in full dress and the ladies décolleté), after that wilderness, the geysers, the precipice and the discomfort caused by nature and by man, was really something extraordinary. It was like a dream. I could not at first believe in its reality.

From Napier we went to Wellington, and in Wellington the first thing we found were cracks in every room. There had just been another earthquake in Wellington, but they were perfectly calm. They said they occurred often there, and consequently they could not build brick houses, but found wooden ones safer.

Shortly after our arrival, we received two visitors, Mr. Seddon and his wife. Mr. Seddon was then Prime Minister of New Zealand and I had made his acquaintance at Lord Northcliffe's house during Queen Victoria's Diamond Jubilee.

That visit made a profound impression upon all the servants in the hotel, because he had been a miner and worked himself up to the Premiership and, of course, was considered as the supreme authority on all labor questions in New Zealand. So his visit proved an unexpected benefit to me and I will tell you why. I have already spoken about the impossibility of getting any warm food, in fact anything to eat, after my concerts, owing to the labor-union conditions. I was just in the midst of negotiations with the hotel management about the possibility of getting some warm food, but in spite of both bribery and diplomacy on my part, we were at a complete deadlock, when at the crucial moment Mr. Seddon arrived to call on me! It worked like magic—after the visit of Mr. Seddon everything moved on oiled wheels!

The manager of the hotel was overcome with delight. He assured me that if I were so highly connected as to know Mr. Seddon, I should be attended as I wished. "Why, Mr. Paderewski," he said, "there is nothing here in this house that you cannot command. As Mr. Seddon's friend, this hotel is practically yours!"

My stay in New Zealand was in every respect most enjoyable. First, I had all these experiences among the Maori people, then my experiences were so pleasant everywhere, and the social relations most charming. The Governor-General of New Zealand, Sir William Plunket, invited us several times to his house, and I enjoyed very much that hospitality.

In 1927 I was there again, and again had the most charming experiences, but Australia itself was greatly changed—it was really detestable. And of that change which shocked me so much I shall speak at length at another place in my memoirs. Now we must continue on with the present tour.

The concerts in Christchurch and Dunedin were perfectly delightful, but without any particularly interesting episode. The people everywhere were really touching. They were so thankful to me for having come so far to bring them that little message of music.

Our trip continued on to Invercargill, which I remember mostly for my visit to a dreadful place near there called The Bluff. An awful spot—so desolate, so desperately sad and so hopeless. Nothing to look at but water and always a rough sea. There is never a calm day, nothing but bad weather, tornadoes, cold and shipwrecks.

Added to the roaring sea and the horrible weather were the flies! Yes, flies that came in tremendous waves of blackness and literally jumped at you collectively! They left misery in their wake, for at their slightest touch such a terrible itching and burning set up that you had to scratch yourself until the blood came. It was a perfect torment.

Hobart, Tasmania, was our next stop and our journey there was another nightmare. We were travelling in a nut-shell steamer, not much over 500 tons—half the size of the lake steamers, and on a very rough sea. We had to spend almost five days on that miserable steamer and a dreadful tempest was raging and our poor little shell of a boat was at its mercy.

Australia and New Zealand

We were more than a day late arriving in Hobart, so instead of having a day's rest there, as I had anticipated, I was obliged to dress on the steamer and go directly to the hall on landing. That was very hard.

Our doctor, who had so failed us on the journey out, was again terribly sick and became useless. I, too, was very ill and was in anything but good condition to give my concert. However, I survived it as I have survived many other concerts, and there is nothing of any interest about this particular concert, nor was there anything special to enjoy in Hobart excepting one thing, the forest leading to Mount Wellington. A real forest of beautiful fern trees. That was a sensation for me which I shall never experience again, for it was unique in its wonder and beauty. These marvellous fern trees in the remote past, thousands of centuries ago, covered the whole earth, and it is from these trees that we derive our fuel—now in the form of coal.

From Hobart we went to another little place called Launceston, which holds in my memory a very special place, because for that day the whole city was decorated with flowers and banners in my honor and a charming sight it was. The people turned out en masse to welcome me. I was deeply moved.

Upon my return to Melbourne, I gave there my farewell concert at the Exhibition Hall before some six or seven thousand people, which was enormous for Australia.

III

Now, after all this talk, I have left, until the last, one of my most interesting adventures in Australia, for I always think of it as an adventure—the advent of a very important member into my family, the arrival of the wonderful parrot, Cockey Roberts, a parrot who filled me with affection, amusement, interest and considerable agony as long as he lived, Cockey Roberts—and this is his story.

I think I have said before that there were two creatures in my life which had shown great interest in my art, and Cockey Roberts was the second. I shall always believe that Cockey

Roberts was really interested in my playing. He was a very beautiful parrot, and was bought by the gentleman who was locally arranging my tour in Australia, New Zealand, and Tasmania.

We had arrived in Melbourne in July and it was frightfully cold. We hardly knew any one and the first days there were extremely tedious and unpleasant, especially as I had hurt my finger and could not give my first concert, which I was obliged to postpone, and I was lonely and depressed. It was a dark picture altogether.

I was staying at the hotel, and whenever I attempted to go out for a little sightseeing, I was prevented by the most terrific rain. Everything conspired against us and we were not enjoying ourselves very much, as you can readily see. My Australian manager then conceived the practical and sympathetic idea of giving us a little recreation—recreation in the form of a parrot, and he bought a parrot that talked, and talked as I am sure no parrot ever talked before!

That was an unfortunate idea of his, because that parrot made such an impression upon my wife that she bought in addition some thirty or forty other parrots, and we then travelled with a whole flock of birds of all kinds, all ages, all sizes and all colors. With a multitude of cages, we travelled through Australia and New Zealand to San Francisco. How did I endure it? Ah! I do not know except that I am an animal of exceptional patience—if I were not so patient, I should have been dead long ago!

Well, to go on with the story of Cockey Roberts. He used to talk in not exactly the most refined language. It was really very indecent and blasphemous. Cockey Roberts was more than a parrot—he was a real artist in his way. He talked almost without interruption and his vocabulary was extremely rich and very large, but not of the best choice. He was at times very engaging, very hospitable. In fact, he often offered drinks! He asked whether one would have a drink. Sometimes, too, he swore in a terrible way when you displeased him, using the worst possible expressions. But it was a great pleasure to have him in the room

Cockey Roberts—Parrot No. 1

Paderewski and Madame Paderewska in Maori dress on the New Zealand tour

nevertheless. It was constant amusement. "Look here," he would suddenly cry, "have a drink—have a drink." And he spoke very clearly. So distinctly, in fact, that once when we were driving in Auckland, New Zealand, we put the cage with the parrot on the seat with the coachman, and suddenly, in a perfectly kind, human voice, we heard, "Look here, have a drink, have a drink!" And the coachman turned round and said very politely, "Oh, no, thank you, sir, I have had one."

Cockey Roberts stayed with us during the Australian and New Zealand tours, and throughout the whole American tour, and afterwards he lived with us for some six or seven years. He was here, at Morges, an important member of the family. He was an excellent traveller, though he did not like rough weather on board ship; quite especially when we were travelling from New Zealand to Tasmania on that famous Tasmanian Sea, which is the roughest in the world. The ship, a very small one, was rolling all the time and sometimes pitching in a dreadful way. Cockey Roberts's cage was moving constantly from one corner of the cabin to the other, and the poor parrot did not understand what was the matter with it. He was in a state of fury. "Oh, you wretches, you wretches," he would scream. "Go to hell!"

Cockey Roberts always holds first place in my affection, although he was not the only parrot we had. As I have just mentioned my wife bought a whole flock of parrots and we arrived in New Zealand with thirty-six. We had them distributed in various cages, some ten or twelve in one and four in another, etc. But there was one parrot among them that was perfectly tremendous in size and with a voice that was to be heard round the world. He travelled in an enormous cage by himself. We finally landed him in our house in Morges, but I was not sorry to part with him; he was impossible. I was only too delighted when a surgeon from Geneva came one day to see him and I suggested that he take the parrot home with him. He, too, was delighted and glad to accept the bird. He had a very large house and big garden near Geneva. Just the place for him, I thought. But he did not live long in his new home, for he got into a fight with a cow, impossible as it seems, and was killed. A most ignominious but absurd ending.

Ah, but Cockey Roberts was Parrot No. 1. He was a beautiful, lovable bird. But such a voice, especially when he was angry! A voice so shrieking, so penetrating that I could not stand it. But in spite of his voice, I loved that parrot and he loved me. I could do anything with him. He always came to have his neck scratched and he was delighted when I touched him. He used to come regularly to my room when I was practising. I tried to avoid him and would close the doors. When that happened he would knock sharply with his beak. At first I would keep very quiet. Then he would knock again, a little harder, and I would call out through the door, "Who is there? Who is it?" Then an angry voice would answer, "Cockey Roberts." "Who?" I would say, pretending not to understand, and then that angry shrill little voice would come again, "Cockey Roberts! Cockey Roberts!"

Of course I had to let him in after that and he would walk straight to the piano and perch there on my foot for hours while I practised, and the pedalling (and my pedalling is very strenuous as you know) did not seem to disturb him in the least. He would sit perfectly still on top of my foot. And then from time to time, he would say in a very loving and scratchy voice, "Oh, Lord, how beautiful! How beautiful!" Ah, it was touching.

When I stopped and got up, as I generally did once during my practice, he understood perfectly that there would be no more playing for some little time, and then he would walk about the room and amuse himself. But he would not leave me; he stayed close beside me until I began to play again. When I had really finished, then he could be persuaded to go to his own little room, and there he would sit on his perch and was very quiet. But whenever I played, he felt it was his duty to watch me and that his place was by my side, and there he would stay as long as I practised.

His name, and how he got it? That I really do not know. He was called Cockey Roberts when we bought him. He belonged to some one who had been obliged to leave Australia and he had to be sold. Evidently, the owner was not such a friend of parrots as to take him along, so he left him in Australia. We travelled with him, and had a great deal of pleasure and constant amusement while he was with us.

I remember one day in San Francisco, he did something very unpleasant. We arrived there with all our parrots and then decided to reduce the personnel of that troupe of birds. Mr. Adlington took a couple, the doctor took a few, and we left some with a friend in San Francisco. Still, there was quite a number, some fifteen in all, that we brought back to Morges. Quite enough. But Cockey Roberts had always the place of honor. In that big, old Palace Hotel in San Francisco, we kept him always in the large drawing room. The cage stood in the corner and sometimes for hours you could not hear a sound from the bird, and then—oh! what language burst upon our ears!

Shortly after my arrival in San Francisco, a lady reporter asked for an interview. I was just preparing for my concert and did not want to see her, and I asked Mr. Adlington to explain this and say it was impossible. But my wife intervened, saying she was probably a poor girl earning her living by that work and that I must see her for just a few minutes. So I received her, but I said at once that I was very busy and that she should please restrict her curiosity and make her questions brief. But she was very persistent and would have her own way. She stayed over half an hour and evidently intended to continue on and on. Finally I could endure it no longer and said, "Madam, you must excuse me, I really cannot talk further now because I have to play, I have to work. My duty is here, not with the newspaper."

"But," she insisted, "only a few questions more, please."

Suddenly, a tremendous angry voice came from the corner, "Go away; I don't like your voice. Go away." It was extraordinary. That parrot really became a human being in that instant, and it was impossible to believe that it was a parrot and not a person speaking. The poor reporter was completely deceived and terribly upset. She thought it was the voice of my wife. She suddenly jumped from her chair and started towards the door. "Oh, thank you, madam," she said, turning towards my wife. "You have already been very kind to me, I must apologize humbly for being so indiscreet in keeping Mr. Paderewski so long." She would listen to nothing we said and hurried, almost ran, out of the room. And it was Cockey Roberts who did this. Cockey Roberts who saved me from my tormentor. It was unbelievable. That little bird had a soul.

A few months afterwards—it was, I think, in February—we were touring the States. It was a very severe winter. We arrived at Canton, Ohio (the birthplace of Mr. McKinley). My wife was taken ill. Something had happened to the steam pipes in our car, and we had absolutely no heat. It was frightfully cold, so I put on my fur coat. Cockey Roberts was covered in his cage with another fur; still he was shivering with cold.

While I was waiting there in the dining room of the car for the physician, I was feeling very sad and very anxious, and suddenly a muffled, hoarse voice said, "I am so cold. I would like to have breakfast in Australia." Poor Cockey Roberts! His vocabulary was something amazing, uncanny. It had thousands of words.

There is another parrot story, with another parrot, during that tour in Brisbane that might be included here with no disrespect to Cockey Roberts. Brisbane was a terrible place then. The hotel was very bad, but the people were kind and willing to do the best they could to give us all the comforts possible. I had quite a large room, a drawing room with a little space for my piano and I used to practise before meals. One day I noticed for the first time that there was a parrot in a cage in a corner, who behaved very quietly. For some forty-eight hours I had not even noticed he was in the room. He was a big bird and handsome. Suddenly, he started talking, and at that moment an old waiter, very decrepit, with an absolutely blue nose, came into the room bringing the trays, and started to arrange the luncheon. Then the following conversation took place. The parrot in a very loud voice began to shout at the waiter: "John, you are drunk again. John, stop, you idiot! Yes, John, you are drunk again."

John was probably accustomed to those words, for he paid no attention. He went out and came back again. As he entered the room, he appeared to slip. Then the parrot shouted wildly with a shrill laugh, "John, you are drunk again! Don't slip, John, don't slip. If you slip again, John, you will break your bloody neck!"

Well, I was completely enchanted with him. He was the most amusing thing you could imagine. I asked at once if I could buy him. I really wanted to add him to my family; but he was not for sale. John was quite shocked even at the idea.

"Oh, no, sir, you cannot buy him. You cannot buy that parrot. He is a member of the family."

So Cockey Roberts continued to reign supreme as Parrot No. 1. He lived on here with us for several years and his voice finally became unbearable. In fact, when he was displeased with anything (and he was frequently displeased) his shrieking was frightful. It seemed to act directly on my spine. The nerves of my spine became trembly and I was so disturbed in my entire being for days and days after one shriek of his, that I felt I could not have him near me any more. I had to prepare then for a very important concert tour, and so we decided to put him for the summer in with the poultry in the garden, where he had a very nice house all to himself. He was perfectly satisfied, apparently. He talked to the poultry, swore at them too, and sometimes he talked to the gardener.

He would cry for me and I saw him often, but my visits were brief ones.

I returned to America very early that year, in September. It was still very warm weather and somehow—I don't know how it happened, but he was neglected. My sister had not arrived and there were only the servants to look after him. Suddenly, a very severe, unexpectedly cold night came. The gardener had forgotten and left him out in the poultry house, and he caught a cold—a cold that killed him. Poor Cockey Roberts!

I was then in New York, and I remember well that the whole of one night I dreamed of Cocky Roberts. I dreamed about him and saw him, and I heard his funny, shrill, angry little voice calling me and it did not seem so unpleasant to me in my dreams. And somehow, I knew then that Cocky Roberts was dead and there was a very empty little place in my heart. Ten days afterwards we received the news from Morges that poor Cockey Roberts was no more.

XVII

Revolt Against the Piano

I

I returned from Australia by way of San Francisco and began my season there immediately after Christmas, 1904. Shortly after my San Francisco concerts I went to Arden, a little place near Santa Ana in California, which was the home of Madame Modjeska and her husband. We stayed there several days and it was a very painful impression to see these dear people (already aged) and Modjeska herself looking rather sick, living in that forlorn place, for the surroundings of their charming little house were certainly conducive to deep melancholy. It was all so dark—the house so hidden away between the rocks, that there was no light at all. There was only a tiny spot from which one could see the sun. It was very depressing.

I think it was not Modjeska's idea to go there, but her husband's. He had such queer ideas sometimes. For instance, when he chose and bought that place for her, he thought it would be a brilliant business venture to start there a farm for the breeding of goats. So, without knowing anything about them, he got an enormous quantity of goats and then let them all loose—he let them go free to forage for food. Unfortunately, as there was really no grass, only rocks, on the place, the goats died almost immediately.

But the place, in its way, was rather pretty. It looked uncanny, but interesting—those fantastic walls of rock, and that little cottage tucked away in the depths of that canyon. The cottage was beautifully planned by Stanford White, the famous architect, who was their friend. But it was absolutely dark. We spent there two depressing days, and during that time we did not see the sun at all. There was only one place, a small opening in which there stood a little ladder which you could climb painfully up, if you were courageous enough, and from that point, see a tiny bit of sunshine. Yes, the house was actually built in a little canyon. A strange place to live!.

At the time of our visit the goats had already disappeared from the scene. They were either dead on account of the lack of food, or stolen by the neighbors! It was all very absurd, had it not been so sad. I was greatly concerned at this state of affairs and at the effect it was bound to have upon Modjeska's health. I used all my persuasion and logic to induce Modjeska to leave the place and go somewhere into the open world again. I actually pleaded with her. But just at the moment of victory, instead of agreeing with me as I expected, out of a clear sky came that idea of hers to arrange a farewell performance for herself in New York, a benefit performance. Her heart it seems was set on that, and she needed the money. She could think of nothing else. So I promised to arrange all the formalities upon my return to New York. Of course, I addressed myself first to Charles Frohman, whom I knew very well, and later to some other dear friends of hers, and it was decided that her benefit performance should take place somewhere about the beginning of April, 1905, and I was to play. I was to play for her benefit—as she played for mine when I was a struggling young musician, so many years ago.

Unfortunately, toward the end of my tour I met with a serious accident near Syracuse. My private train, en route to Albany, was derailed in order to save not only our lives, but to avoid a catastrophe which would have been exceptionally grave. The details of this accident it is not necessary to go into now, except to tell you that the car was completely overthrown—it was hurled over on its side with great violence. The china and glass were broken and the furniture badly smashed. No one was seriously injured, fortunately, but several members of my party were badly knocked about—and I most of all, because I was thrown forward very violently against the table. I was terribly bruised and lame, and my nerves were very much shaken, which proved more serious than I realized at the time. I found that I could not do anything at all after this accident and I was obliged to stop playing for several months. The shock of this disaster I did not recover from for several years.

I was then under the management of Charles Ellis of Boston, whom I always considered a prince among the impresarios of the world, a remarkable man, and such a generous fellow. Although he is no longer in that profession and we seldom meet, I am glad to say that my friendship with him endures and is just as fresh as if I had continued relations with him and saw him often.*

The saddest and most painful thing about that accident was my inability to appear at Madam Modjeska's benefit performance, which proved to be her last. It was perhaps the only instance where I was deprived of the satisfaction of being able to show my gratitude for a service rendered years before. She was gracious and generous enough to help me as a struggling youth by her appearance in my first concert, and I had felt happy, indeed, to know that I could assist in her last performance in New York. But Fate decided differently.

Anyhow, the result of the benefit was a great rallying of her friends and admirers for the last time and was a real financial success. It enabled her to buy an annuity, which, unfortunately, she could enjoy only a few years. She died in November, 1908. After all these years Modjeska still stands apart in my memory and gratitude. What I have said about her before, and what I say now, is far too little. In the days of my youth our friendship began and I worshipped her goodness and character then—as I worship her memory now.

Yes, it is very hard when an artist must stop working before he dies. He should die in harness—on the battlefield. When an artist is deprived of his work, life is generally over for him. This is so pathetically true that it needs no argument, I think, and I see that you agree to this. There have been, of course, some no-

*Mr. Charles Ellis has since died.

table exceptions, when the artist turned to another branch of his art. Franz Liszt, for instance, was such a one. Liszt stopped playing when very young, only about forty-five, and then devoted all his energy and great genius to creative work. And he had much more satisfaction then, than even in the glorious days of his playing. This is easily understood, in Liszt's case, but for an actor, we must admit, it is quite different. The average opera singer or actor at the end of his career is a very tragic figure. More than any other of the arts, I think, the theatre is the most difficult to abandon.

A man usually maintains himself on the stage much longer than a woman. A man who has been successful say as Romeo— may, thirty years later, still be very great as Falstaff. But it is really a tragedy for a woman who has played the great romantic figures of the theatre to be forced in her old age into small and uninteresting character parts. I repeat, the man has the better of the bargain.

In every way I think it is better for men, not only professionally but even æsthetically. If a man does not look well on the stage, if his features are tired, if his skin is drawn and wrinkled, it does not mean anything to the public, but with the woman— everything! Particularly in your country, America. In England they are far more faithful and not so critical of old age, I think. There is always a distinguished place for their idols and favorites to the very end. Think of the long list of English actresses particularly who have gone on and on until they were past seventy, and still adored by the public. I do not think that happens in America; your standards are quite different.

After April, 1905, I did not play any more that year. I was not well. A complication of things, too subtle to disentangle now and of no interest really to our story, brought this about.

For several years I was not able to use the Steinway pianos as I had had a serious disagreement with the head of the firm, the late Charles Steinway, which had led to his positively withdrawing the Steinway pianos from me. I had asked for certain changes, for different instruments altogether, saying the ones I had were not satisfactory to me, and he had answered saying, "Your telegram is so offensive that I have instructed our representatives everywhere to withdraw all our pianos from you from now on." It was very serious. It ended in a complete break. I had expected him to make some excuses and objections on the part of the firm, naturally enough. On the other hand, he evidently expected me to come humbly forward and ask to be pardoned, to take back what I had said and the demands I had made, etc., and continue to use the instruments they chose to give me, not the instrument I wanted and needed. But that I would not do, I could not do. It was impossible. It was not a personal matter, but an artistic one. It came to an open rupture between us and was most deplorable in every way. It ended my relations with the House of Steinway. It is impossible in this brief mention to give a satisfactory explanation of this disagreement. The demands I had made for changes in the piano were quite justified and I had every reason for demanding them. True, it involved trouble and expenditure on their part but I, at that time, was playing the Steinway pianos all over the world and asked nothing that was not within reason and my artistic rights. And so our relations were completely broken off. It was a deadlock. I felt they were acting most unfairly to me. I then accepted and used the Weber piano, which belonged at that time to the Aeolian Company. In fact, owing to the Steinway disagreement, I played the Weber piano successfully for two consecutive tours.

It took a very long time to get accustomed to another instrument, to make it my friend and respond to my demands. But I succeeded and my tour went on as usual in spite of this added strain. Fortunately, the Steinway disagreement ended a few years later in perfect harmony and with rejoicing on both sides.

It was while I was playing the Weber pianos that I acquired a new tuner, Eldon Joubert, who was with the Weber Piano Company at that time. I mention this now because the tuning and care of the piano is of such tremendous importance to the artist. It is part of the equipment that I have already spoken about, so necessary to every pianist. The tuner of the piano is always a very vital factor in the concert season, and Joubert was remarkable in many ways, so faithful and reliable and one of the best of tuners. When I left the Weber Company and returned to the Steinways, Joubert went with me and has been with me ever since, more than thirty years, I am happy to say.

Now, I must again repeat that I was not at all well in 1905. I still felt the shock of the accident, but nevertheless, in 1906, I made a tour in Spain. I played also in the South of France and Portugal, too. But that playing was not pleasant to me because something was happening to my nerves that made me completely *hate* the piano. I loathed it. I do not know if there was any one particular cause to which I could attribute that feeling. It does not matter now, except to say that it lasted for several years, my feeling of aversion to the keyboard, and still I was obliged to play, and, naturally, it showed in my playing. Yes, I felt it deeply. It was so very inferior to my past performances and it was chiefly due to my resistance to the instrument I was then playing. I could not do justice to myself.

A change of piano is a very serious thing for an artist to face. In Europe, I was then playing the Erard piano which at that time was on the verge of changing its character. Instead of being built, as formerly, completely of wood, they applied their new invention of an iron plate, and from the start it was not a great success. It became extraordinarily heavy to play. I was obliged to use the Erard piano in Europe for two reasons, first because I was accustomed to it, but mostly because of my intimate friendship with Monsieur Blondel, who helped me at the beginning of my career and financed my first concerts in Paris and London. To him goes my everlasting gratitude.

It was the tradition of the House of Erard to do this, to offer to every pianist of importance the hospitality of the house with the instrument; they assumed the entire expense of the recital, leaving to the artist all the receipts without deduction. They were very generous and it helped me greatly in the beginning. But as soon as I began earning large sums of money, of course I refused to accept that kind of subvention and gave all my concerts on my own account.

However, the dreadful fact remains that whatever the cause, and there were many subtle contributing ones then, my feeling about the piano, my dislike for it, grew more and more intense. I no longer wanted to play. No matter what I played I did not feel in touch with the instrument. It was a kind of torture. I consulted several doctors. They said I was overwrought and that I abused the instrument and my strength and that I must not only stop playing but do something else. But first of all they told me to take a complete rest. There was still a certain energy in me which was driving me furiously on to action, but what could I do? Of course, I was always interested in many different things. But what should I turn to at that uncertain moment? Finally, one of my friends here in Lausanne, a great physician and a very wise man, said, "Now tell me what is there—that interests you personally and sympathetically outside of intellectual things?" That was easily answered—I was from an agricultural family and I said that agriculture had always interested me very much. "Good," he exclaimed. "Good! Go and farm. Nature will heal you." I told him that my hands might still be necessary for me later on. He laughed and said he did not mean me to do actual field work myself, but to take a little farm and attend to it—enjoy it—get interested in it, put my heart and mind in it completely, and live close to the healing earth.

That appealed to me at once. I took a little farm not far from here. It interested me from the beginning, and it helped me because I had to live a great deal in the open and spend my days in the peaceful countryside. I went there in the autumn and continued throughout the winter. There was plenty of snow and I enjoyed it thoroughly. That simple life brought a kind of healing with it.

But things happened as they always do, and it soon became a white elephant on my hands, because I began buying and adding land to it all the time. It got bigger and bigger. I bought cows and pigs and other livestock and became a real farmer. That farming experiment lasted for several years. Even when I was playing again, my farm was still in operation and cost me a great deal of money—a very great deal.

But during that time I did not practise at all. No, not at all! No, I did not touch the piano, but after a few months more with my new acquisition, which was growing so rapidly and so expensively, that little farm of mine made me begin to think about *money* very seriously, and I was obliged to face the fact that I must begin to play again. A concert tour was now a necessity. There was nothing else to be done. The rest had already done me some good and I became a little more friendly toward the piano. So I started by giving a few concerts here in Switzerland for charity (to break the ice so to speak) and then in spite of my continued aversion to the piano, I started a tour in America in 1907.

II

During that tour I was invited to play at the White House, on which occasion I met President Theodore Roosevelt, who made a deep impression upon me. A strong, brilliant, and exceptionally well-informed man, knowing a great deal about European conditions, and particularly acquainted with my own country, which was chiefly due to his love of our remarkable writer, Sienkiewicz, who wrote those world-famous novels, *By Fire and Sword, Children of the Soil,* and *Quo Vadis.* He told me then that he travelled for years with Sienkiewicz's trilogy. Certain opinions about my country expressed by President Roosevelt were extremely encouraging to me, and I still gladly and gratefully remember every word he said on that subject. He was a knight. I had a great admiration for him. He was certainly the 100 per cent American he claimed to be, but do not make the mistake of thinking that he was alone in that attribute. Other Presidents and statesmen were just as patriotic as he—though not as violent in their expression of it.

Grover Cleveland, for example, was just as 100 per cent American as was Theodore Roosevelt. President Wilson was just as much of an American as those two, but their tempera-

ments were absolutely different. Cleveland was a great lawyer
and administrator. Roosevelt was a hero and a fighter, and President Wilson was a student and an apostle. President Wilson's
knowledge of history was really exceptionally great and lofty,
and he is still very much misunderstood in America and in
France. But in France they had particular reasons for that, because in the beginning, right after the War, they believed in
his omnipotence. They thought his presence in Paris meant complete fulfillment of his plan during those crucial weeks of struggle and the birth of the League of Nations. The French people
did not know that without the approval of your Congress, his
hands were tied—he could do nothing. They felt he could do anything he wanted, and the feelings throughout Europe even now
concerning Wilson are very mixed. For instance, nations which
have been reconstructed, or resurrected, if you like, through Wilson's appeals (Czechoslovakia, Yugoslavia, and my own country,
Poland), still worship him. France, England, and Italy felt that
they were deceived, and Germany, of course, is inflamed when
speaking of Wilson. They hate him.

But you know, I am of the opinion that if President Wilson
had taken with him instead of General Bliss, who was a lovely
fellow, and Mr. Henry White—if he had taken to France on that
eventful trip of his, Mr. Lodge, who was a bitter opponent of the
League of Nations, and Mr. Elihu Root—everything could have
been accomplished—everything. But he was too partisan in that
respect. Like every important personality, he stood alone. He
could not endure any kind of opposition and difference of opinion—that was characteristic of him and was his principal difficulty as a great leader and as a national figure. It was his un-
doing, his tragedy.

But perhaps I should not indulge in these political appreci-
ations now. One cannot in a few sentences speak adequately of
such momentous happenings and the attributes of the people that
swayed them and brought them about. It is a vast subject that
history must settle and that historians will fight about for many
years to come.

The Paderewski Memoirs

Of President Wilson himself, my great and honored friend, I have at a later time many things that I wish to say, particularly of his unfailing friendship to me and most of all to my country at that crucial time—the ending of the War. My memories of him will always be among my cherished possessions (I sometimes think that memories are the only possessions we have), but this is not the moment to speak of them. They belong with the War in the next volume. They have their right place, their chronological order in my story.

We were speaking I think of the White House musicals which had become a yearly institution of each Administration. They were always very much the same and afforded rather intimate and interesting glimpses of the occupants. I do not think, for instance, that President Wilson had any particular interest in music. There were many sides to his character and he was an all-round highly educated man who recognized intellectually that music was a part of human progress, of human instruction and that it was a necessity even in general education. Whatever he said in that respect was just to the point, but he was so absolutely immersed and pre-occupied with political problems that he had no time or interest for anything that was practically in the sphere of dreams —how else can I put it?—but you agree, I see.

President Taft, whom I knew personally very well indeed, was interested in music perhaps even more than Theodore Roosevelt.

Theodore Roosevelt always listened with charming interest and applauded vociferously and always shouted out, "Bravo! Bravo! Fine! Splendid," even during the performance.

President Coolidge, strangely enough, really looked as if he were delighted with music. This struck me particularly when I played at the White House for him. And, moreover, I think he liked music for itself, and perhaps he liked it even more because while music was going on, he himself did not have to speak, and certainly Coolidge was not fond of talking. Though in contradiction to that I have a little story for you that quite refutes it. I once had luncheon with him at the White House and contrary to all reports, and to my great surprise, President Coolidge talked all the time. Of course, there were only the two of us, but even so, he gave me almost no opportunity to say anything. After luncheon he had his cigar and I my cigarette, and then he began to talk and he talked continuously. And he had something to say. He had, I assure you. He was very firm in all his convictions. There was no changing him, I should think, once his mind was made up. Without particularly looking it, he was a very strong man—and staunch, like your New England granite.

However, to go on, my tour finished in 1908, and then Mr. Ellis, who heard that I had written a symphony, asked that its first performance in America be given with the Boston Symphony Orchestra. That proposition appealed to me greatly, but it also meant extra hard work to orchestrate the symphony, which was yet to be done. Together with that proposal came another invitation to play as soloist in all the concerts where my symphony was to be performed by the Boston Orchestra, to make another little tour in America, the tour to begin in December, 1908. I accepted with pleasure, of course. It was most gratifying.

Then I returned to Europe. Again I played concerts in Paris and in London, and again at those distinguished yearly Musicals of Mr. Astor. And then I started the orchestration of my symphony, which was finished toward the end of November. I worked tremendously.

In December I returned to America and first played in several recitals. Then my symphony was performed in Boston, and afterward in New York, Washington, Philadelphia, and Baltimore, and it was well received by the public as well as the critics. It was altogether a success, *but I had to stop my tour* because my nerves were not entirely cured by that expensive farm I had bought in Switzerland and which we have already talked about, and I was still more shaken by the orchestrating of my symphony. All this, to my despair, brought back again the old *aversion* to the piano.

I could not finish my tour. It was impossible. I had to return immediately to Europe and there tried all kinds of treatments, not only doctors and their medicines but every suggestion even. There was a famous physician at Lausanne by the name of Vitor, who treated me (or tried to treat me) without any result. Another physician here hypnotized me in hopes of a cure, but that was no good. Useless. And so it went, from bad to worse.

Again I tried in 1909 to play. I went to Monte Carlo and Nice, and then, just to find out whether I could play or not, I went on to Bordighera. But it was impossible. The easiest pieces I had in my repertoire I could not manage. My fingers were just like cotton. I could not produce the tone. The touch was so strange to me. The slightest action was an agony of my whole body. It was torture.

So I decided not to play at all! I had a new idea (really an old idea) and it began to absorb me completely. I was then working out the idea of the monument I had planned years before to commemorate the anniversary of the Battle of Grünwald. It was the year 1909. I had ordered the monument in 1908. The artist whom I had selected for that work was a young Polish sculptor, Antoni Wiwulski by name. He was a man of rare genius.

I should like to tell you about him, and a little about the Battle of Grünwald, for it is an interesting story and takes me back to those strenuous moments of my youth, and my burning desire then to commemorate this great historical event.

I was only a boy of ten when I read for the first time about the Battle of Grünwald, which was fought in 1410, a crashing victory for my country, over the Teutonic knights who were then robbing Poland of her most cherished possession, access to the sea. My response to that historical account was so tremendous that I said to myself then, "How happy I would be if I could make a tribute to that splendid victory—if I could live long enough and become rich and powerful enough to celebrate the five hundredth anniversary of that glorious battle by a monument erected to the memory of those great patriots." From that childish moment it became the dream of my life. It never left my heart and consciousness. And in 1910 I accomplished it. The dream came true. All my life I was saving money for that; of all the money I made, I put aside something for it always. And in 1908 I ordered the monument. I ordered it, and then decided to have the ceremony two years later on the five hundredth anniversary, July 15, 1910. Well, it absorbed me completely. It filled me with a great happiness.

I went to Paris and inquired about some young Polish artists who would be able to do such a work. One of them was suggested to me as especially talented, but he was still absolutely unknown. He was a poor student and living very miserably. He had great difficulties to fight against, poor fellow, as he was consumptive. We talked together and his ability impressed me at once. I had faith in him. I asked him if he were strong enough to do the work I had in mind and he assured me that he was, and he became, even as we talked, a new being. My offer and interest gave him hope—something to do—and his health improved rapidly in consequence. He immediately started to work and made a few models. I liked them, and invited him to my house at Morges, and then sent him to a doctor in Lausanne, a dear friend of mine, who treated his throat, which was very much affected. The doctor helped him immediately and he became quite well again. It was a kind of miracle—to all of us.

So he began his model and worked so successfully that in January, 1910, the monument was finished and cast. And everything happened as I had wanted to have it, as I had dreamed it continuously since I was ten years old. The monument was erected in Cracow and is really splendid—a beautiful creation. And for that gifted youth, Wiwulski, it was a great thing too. His health was restored. New life had come to him, but it was not for long, poor fellow! He had been marvellously cured by that Lausanne doctor, who was a great surgeon and famous for his operations on the larynx. He had cured thousands of people as he cured and saved Wiwulski.

We often talked together, and I once asked him how it was possible to perform that very delicate operation of the larynx. And he answered very simply, "Ah, that is God's blessing—that I have such patient hands. They do not shiver (I suppose he meant tremble) at all when I perform the operation." He then went on to explain further and said, "Every one of these operations is delicate beyond the imagination to conceive of and may end with the death of the patient. But, thank God, I have had during my whole long career only one such case, and it was not my hand that trembled. It was, alas, the poor patient himself who became nervous and made a sudden little movement. I do not like to think of it even now," he said—and I saw that it affected him deeply even to talk of it.

But thank God, Wiwulski was cured and went back to his native town, Wilno, and started there on a very great work, the new Cathedral. He was an architect as well as a sculptor of real genius. The war broke out shortly after and he was one of the first to go. There was a certain streak of heroism in that boy and he went to fight, frail as he was. He fought, and nothing happened to him. He was not even wounded. I was already in Warsaw as head of the Government, when I received a letter from him saying that he felt so well and strong and expected, after that attack of the Bolsheviks had passed, to come to Warsaw especially to greet me. He was looking forward to that and so was I. But a few weeks later he was dead.

It seems he was on guard one night before the improvised fortifications and a soldier with him complained of the cold. It was a bitter night, and, without a thought of himself, Wiwulski immediately took off his own coat and gave it to his companion, and remained on guard himself throughout those long, freezing hours. The next day he became very ill, and immediately developed double pneumonia and there was no hope—no help for him. In a fortnight he passed away. His death was a dreadful grief to me. I had hoped great things for him. But he died as he had lived, without thought of himself, just as I had known him, as he had always been throughout his brave young life—always unselfish and ready for any sacrifice. And now, he was dead—the most gifted sculptor of the time. It was a dreadful thing to happen— all that genius and ambition gone forever.

The fulfillment of this dream of youth came as a great and happy diversion for me at that critical moment of ill health. It occupied me wholly. My mind was filled with things that were not only serious in themselves, but politically important, and it was all very close to my heart. Poland was then very much oppressed, and the spirit of the people was very low, so I knew that that anniversary of the Battle of Grünwald would affect the feelings of the people very much. I knew that if there had not been anything of such importance as the unveiling of a monument commemorating that glorious event, the whole anniversary would have passed without notice. I realized that very keenly and, at the unveiling of the monument, I made a short but very forcible address before an enormous crowd of people, who without the amplifiers or microphones of this perfected time, heard every word. It was all absorbing and brought me happiness and content. Something had been accomplished, I felt.

The unveiling of the monument produced a great effect on the mind of the public, not only in the city of Cracow, but throughout the whole country. People came from all parts of Poland. There were some difficulties in crossing the frontier, but many people found it possible to come on foot, not to be noticed by the officials, and so to attend that ceremony. It was, without any exaggeration, an event of great importance, because there was to a certain extent a prophecy in the air—that war was approaching and that we Poles should all stand *together*. Naturally I made no reference to it in my speech, but I did make a reference in the text which is on the monument: "For the glory of our forefathers. For the encouragement of our brothers."

After that, the same year, on the anniversary of Chopin's birth, the city of Lwów organized a series of concerts (combined with lectures) in honor of our greatest composer. Of course, they asked me to play, but I could not, to my deep regret. It was absolutely impossible for me to play then, as you realize. "I am not playing any more," I said. "I do not know when I shall begin to play again." And so they asked me instead to deliver an address at the opening ceremony. I agreed to that gladly and prepared an address. In my opinion, that address was just as satisfactory as if I had given a concert. And perhaps all unknowingly this proved to be my first real entrance into politics, the very be-

ginning of a career that in the farthest stretches of my imagina-
ion I could not have foreseen. As I look back now I feel very
strongly that that moment was a tiny opening of the door into
another world. At this moment I can trace it almost step by step.
Yes, when I had the patriotic idea of that monument, I appeared
for the first time to certain people as a leader. I did not intend
that, or realize it then, but it happened so. There were several
persons who had won the esteem and confidence of the people in
Poland and I was regarded as one of them. It turned out to be
my first, perhaps not decisive, but significant, step in the direction
of politics, and my address about Chopin increased that impression.

During that week in Lwów, I was elected President of the
first Convention of Polish Musicians in the history of our art. Unfortunately I could not attend their conference because there was
so much to do, receiving various delegations, making the addresses, etc., for which I was in constant demand.

As I was not playing then, and had to refuse their urgent request for a concert, I asked my friend and pupil, Ernest Schelling,
to give one Chopin recital, which he did brilliantly.

During the convention there was another concert at which my
symphony was given, and finally my opera "Manru" was performed. So all in all there were many festivities, and I remember
most happily several banquets given for the students. I addressed
these students and it was one of the greatest pleasures of that convention, I think, to greet and talk with that eager youth. I felt at
one with them. I made the opening address and the final one to
bid them good-bye.

All this brought a new turn in my life, a new door opened.
The gates of politics swung wide for me, but still I was not sure,
I did not like to enter. But it was Destiny.

I must not forget to tell you that in that crowded year, too,
came the presentation of the diploma of Doctor of Philosophy
of the University of Lwów. It was a time of great activity.

And now we must again pick up the thread of our story which
has been side-tracked for a moment.

Revolt Against the Piano

My deep aversion to the piano, in spite of my detour into politics, still continued during 1910 and even during 1911. I was considering a tour in South America because I needed money. I had, of course, a certain amount of money, but not enough to live on. I still had to work. My fortune was invested in Polish securities as I considered it my duty, being a Pole, to put my savings into them. Of course, these savings were greatly reduced by the monument. There was still something left to rely upon, and it was quite a nice sum of money, but not enough, and I had to work again—no matter how I felt, and perhaps it is just as well.

So I went to South America and had very successful tours there. I had five successful and pleasant recitals in Rio de Janeiro, three at São Paulo, and seven or eight in Buenos Aires. I intended at first going to Chile over the Andes, but had to abandon that journey, which, considering the altitude, was extremely dangerous for me then.

During that whole tour, the playing was an untold torture, an agony beyond words to describe. I still did not feel at all in sympathy with my work. It was still a fight, not as hard as at the beginning because I felt a little more in sympathy with the piano then. But it was a period of great nervousness and weakness. The climate also contributed to that to a certain extent, and especially in Brazil the discomfort was very great. Though we lived in a hotel about 1500 feet higher than the city of Rio, the air was most oppressive. We could not sleep, and especially as the beds were terribly hard and the pillows, I'm sure, were filled with sand! And the food was very bad. Altogether a time of misery and pain.

The tour lasted from July until November. In Buenos Aires, it was quite different. It was comfortable there.

Early in 1912, I went to South Africa. And a very unpleasant journey it was, and another very unpleasant experience altogether. I was feeling a little better then. Those long voyages had some slight and good effect on me, but the conditions in South Africa were not pleasant at all, for in South Africa there are only incredible things!

But I must add to this that I also had several funny experiences in South Africa, but more amusing to tell about now, than at the time. I recall one very vividly—I had to play in Pietermaritzburg. About half an hour before the recital (I was still in the hotel) my valet, the faithful Marcel, hurried in greatly upset and said that a lady, beautifully dressed, had just stepped out of her carriage, entered the hotel, and *insisted* upon seeing me at once, because she had something very important to tell me. She was very insistent. He could do nothing with her, so I went immediately to the drawing-room and saw there a very nice-looking lady, beautifully dressed as Marcel had said. She seemed greatly agitated and excited, and I asked why she had come. Whereupon she said, "Oh, Monsieur Paderewski, I am here for your autograph. I must have your autograph. I must have it now."

I simply stared at her. I was astonished at the absurdity and audacity of the request, and I said, "Madame, I have my concert in a few minutes, not quite half an hour, and I cannot write beforehand, because it is too dangerous for my fingers. I never write or use my hands just before playing. It is out of the question. I'm sorry, but I cannot do it now."

"Oh, you must do it," she declared. "You must do it for me."

"Impossible," I answered, rising and moving toward the door. "I will do it after the concert, I promise you. But not now. You must excuse me until after my concert."

"Oh, no, no," she protested, "that won't do, for I am not going to your concert. I cannot see you afterward. I am too busy. I must be present at a reception then, and later on I have a dinner party—so I must have your autograph *now*. I am too busy to come to you again. I shall not leave here until you give it to me." And she rose and took her stand in front of the door.

Well, I confess I was terrified. Just imagine the situation. There was no hope for me; no help at hand. I could not escape. I bowed to the inevitable. I wrote the autograph; otherwise I should never have been able to even start for my concert!

It was masterly strategy on her part, and only once before in my career and battles with autograph hunters have I faced such a determined attack, which I really think must be told now while we are on the painful subject of autographs. Some years before, in Leipsig, I was confronted not only with one lady, but with two rather charming young girls, Americans. I had just given a concert for the benefit of Liszt's monument in Weimar. I do not know why, but it was considered something of a sensation, that particular concert, and many people ran after me for my autograph and insisted upon shaking hands, and so on.

The next morning after the concert, without any notice whatever, there suddenly appeared two young ladies in my drawing room. They just walked in without being announced, probably having bribed one of the attendants at the hotel. They were smiling but very determined. They lost no time in proceeding to business. They had brought autograph books with them, and demanded that I sign them then and there. Of course I took the books at once (there was really nothing else to do) and signed them. But whilst I was writing my autograph, one of the young ladies opened her little bag and drew out, with a flourish, a pair of sharp and shining little scissors. At that time, I must regretfully admit, I had much more hair than I have now. It was often an object of comment and curiosity and sometimes even admiration. When I saw the scissors and the look in that young woman's eye, I confess I became very frightened. I realized at once her fell purpose and I realized too at that moment that I might become (without any help for it) completely disfigured for life at her hands.

I wasted no time; I did not stand on ceremony. I jumped from my chair and said, "What are you going to do? What do you want with those scissors, Mademoiselle?"

"Oh, we want some locks of your beautiful hair," the young lady answered smilingly, moving swiftly toward me, scissors in hand.

"Oh, no, no," I cried, "no! You cannot have locks of my hair. I refuse absolutely." And I moved quickly a little further away from her; but it was useless. The young ladies drew closer. There was not a moment to lose. It was then a question of actual seconds and I began to move. Quicker and quicker I moved backward as they advanced toward me, and finally I simply turned and ran for my life, through the drawing room, which was very big, into the next room. I ran with all the speed in my body on to my bedroom, and then, as they were still pursuing, through my room and on to the room of my servant.

They were close upon me then, and as a last resort, I saw there was still another room with the door half open. It was a room belonging to some one else, whom, I did not know or care! I only thanked God for it. I rushed in and closed the door. I pushed it shut with all the force of my body and held myself against it. All the time those girls were racing after me with their scissors ready for the attack. Finally, I locked the door and then I was safe! though I still trembled with fear as they knocked and knocked and tried to force their way in. Thank God, the door held! If it had given way, who can say what might have happened? One Samson and two Delilahs! If it had been one Delilah —ah, who can tell?

But let us return to Africa.

The second experience in Africa was more serious. It was in Durban. I was giving my concert and it happened that it was during Holy Week. I had just started my program, when suddenly I heard choral singing outside, very powerful singing indeed. The hall is very beautiful in Durban, but it was rather empty—not a full house because there is no white population there. It is a black man's country. I could not understand the cause of that choral singing during my concert. I played on for a while, thinking it would stop, but it did not stop! It became louder and louder. It was impossible for me to continue, so I left the platform and went to the artists' room, where I found my so-called impresario and asked him the cause of the disturbance, and said I could not continue. The gentleman in question was a South African. He simply laughed, shrugged his shoulders, and told me to pay no attention to it. It meant nothing, he said.

"But why do they sing now?" I asked. "Why sing in front of this hall during my concert?"

Revolt Against the Piano

"Oh, that is just a religious matter," he replied cheerfully. "There is a congregation here which is very orthodox and they do not at all approve of any entertainment during Holy Week, and so they have come in a crowd to protest against the concert. We cannot do anything. Even the police cannot disperse them. You must simply go on playing. They will not stop. There is no help for it. They will sing and you must play."

Well, they sang for at least three-quarters of an hour, and I played on through all the disturbance; it was an agony and, of course, I cancelled the next concert.

I had still another disagreeable experience, with the critics this time, in South Africa. My prices, as usual in Great Britain or the Dominions, ranged from one guinea for the best seats on down. This happened in Pretoria. It was not an unpleasant place and it was a very musical audience. There were many cultured people there. The house was quite full, but after the concert, some one whom I had known before and who happened to be there, gave me a newspaper, and in it was an article about myself. It was amazing! It said, "Think of a foreigner, a mere pianist who comes here to our country just to play the piano, and has the effrontery to charge one guinea for the seats. What robbery! Why, we had here not long ago, in a beautiful theatre, a man who could play the clarinet, the violin, a triangle, drum, and accordion, and play *all* those instruments at the *same time*, and his price was only a shilling!"

Well, I was glad enough to leave South Africa and to see England again and renew my acquaintance with many old friends. It was upon my return that I saw my dear friend Lord Northcliffe, and he asked me why I had not consulted him before undertaking that long journey to South Africa—whether it would be worth while. He said that was the last country on earth where an artist of great name should go, as there were not enough cultivated people to appreciate him.

XVIII

Tragic Experience

I

After that unsuccessful tour in South Africa, 1912, my nerves began to improve and it was fortunate because I had another shock in store for me. Then began one of the most serious personal and political troubles of my life. It was with the Jews. That was a very dramatic and tragic event with bitter consequences.

While I was living in London at Park Crescent, a gentleman from my own country came to see me. He was a Pole and a political man of very high standing. He had been the representative of Warsaw in the first and second Parliaments of Russia. They called that Parliament the Douma. He was staying at the Langham Hotel, not very far away, and as we had a very large house and plenty of guest rooms, I asked him to move to my house and live there with us during the time we were going to be in England.

My intention was to let him meet and have certain conversations with the most important political men of England, and to promote thereby the Polish question in England. He came, and brought with him a tremendous box. It immediately attracted my attention, it was so big! I naturally commented on its size and asked him what was in the box, and he said to me, "Oh, that box is for you! I have brought it all the way from Poland for you and it contains all the copies of the newspaper which you founded in Warsaw." I was amazed. I could not believe that I had heard correctly.

"What?" I said, "what did you say? I founded a newspaper in Poland? What do you mean? Explain yourself. What newspaper?"

Tragic Experience

"Oh, yes," he easily replied. "I mean your newspaper. That's what I mean. Of course, you did not found it by yourself alone, but the money you sent us helped *us* to establish it. So it's your newspaper, you see."

"But what kind of a paper is it?" I enquired.

"Why, it is an anti-Jewish paper," he answered, "of course."

"An *anti-Jewish* paper! But I do not see any necessity for that."

"Ah!" he exclaimed. "You say *you* do not see that necessity. But we see that necessity. It is very necessary. It is the most important political problem of Poland at this moment."

"No, no, you are mistaken," I said. "It is not! The most important problem is our independence, our *liberty,* not our strife with any part of the population living within the national borders. I do not agree with you at all."

"Well, it is too late now, you cannot help it," he said. "It is done. You cannot change it."

"But what are you saying in it?" I cried. "This is shocking. Horrible. What is the policy of that paper?"

"Oh, we are just boycotting all the Jews. We are trying to establish all over Poland the principle of boycotting every Jewish merchant. That's what we are doing."

"But it is ridiculous," I exclaimed, "and impossible too. There are places where there is not one single merchant except the Jews. It is impossible to do it."

"All right, all right, but it is our principle and we are doing it. And shall continue to do it."

"And with my money," I thought. I was frightfully disturbed. It was a great shock to me and I again looked into the newspapers he had brought me, and it was really ridiculous.

At that time all the Jews who came from Russia were victims of persecution by the Russian nation—victims of pogroms, wholesale massacres. They came to Poland to escape persecution, but strangely enough, once in Poland, they started to show their excessive Russian patriotism, which was not very much to the taste of the Poles, and naturally these newcomers brought a great deal of disturbance and ferment into the whole community.

They were persecuted in Russia, but in Poland they were very welcome to the Russian Government, because, you know, that principle which is expressed in Latin, "Divide et impera"—"Divide and rule"—that was very convenient to the Russian Government. They *wanted* to have that disturbance, that ferment and discontent of the Poles. It suited their purpose.

Now it so happened that in that very year there came new elections to the third Russian Parliament under the old régime, and though the Jews were not in the majority in Warsaw, they managed so well with the consent, and even with the assistance, of the officials, that they got the majority of votes—and could elect the representative from Warsaw to the Parliament, not the Poles, but the Jews.

The Polish gentleman who was then in my house was again a candidate as a representative from Warsaw to Parliament; he had been twice elected. The third time he was beaten by the Jews, and *that* newspaper in my opinion was a kind of retaliation.

As to the money I sent them, it was when the first elections were announced. Of course every one had to give some money, every one who felt the necessity of having proper representation in the Parliament, and every one who could afford to give money did so. I gave each time for the election a certain sum. It happened that at that particular election, as I had a little more money and the necessity of fighting was more acute, I gave a little more than usual. I gave about $1000. I sent that money for the election *fund*.

Now, you cannot establish a newspaper with $1000. Any one knows that. It was ridiculous. I most distinctly said I was sending that money for the Election Fund, as everybody else did.

Evidently the Committee which was in charge of the election, seeing that the prospects for the election were very weak, decided to revenge themselves on the Jews, which was stupid.

Yes, that was stupid, but the Jews were still more stupid, because instead of electing some one from among themselves who was an intelligent and respectable man, and who would have been a worthy representative of a community, they elected an almost illiterate Polish workman without any education, a man who was not capable of saying ten words. It was an insult to the city.

That was the reason for their establishing that newspaper. But I could not agree with that, and I said it was ridiculous and dishonest to say that I founded the paper. I protested strongly.

"Well," my friend said, "we had to say something. You have a big name in Warsaw, and somebody has to be behind that newspaper. We had to have a figurehead, an ardent patriot. When we were asked who gave money for it, well, we said that you did. You can't do anything about it now."

"But," I said, "first of all that is not true, and secondly, it is dishonorable."

"Yes, but you cannot deny it," he retorted, "you cannot. If you deny it, you know what it means. You will have not only the whole of our party against us (you may pay no attention to that) but there will be even worse consequences—there will be riots, because there will be people who will join you, who will oppose us. We are going to fight them, and the result will be riots and disorders everywhere. It will start something—a fight which may end very seriously."

What a situation! But I realized the truth of what he said. "Well," I thought to myself, "I must bear the consequences because I am not going to start anything which would direct the attention of the whole world on Warsaw." You can easily realize that the Press of the whole world could make out of that something very scandalous. So it was better to keep quiet and do nothing. I could privately say it was not true, but I could not then make a public statement. I was in a very bad situation, but powerless to act. What he said was all true. "If you make a public statement, however short, denying your connection with our newspaper, it will result in riots." It was a bad business.

So when I came to Warsaw in 1913, after having played in several German places and in Cracow and Lwów, I gave a concert for the Fund of the Literary Men in Warsaw, and then

I could see with my own eyes in what a state the place was on account of that conflict with the Jews. The paper was still going on, and went on for some years after that. There was nothing to be done about it.

It was, I think, the second month of its existence when I got those first copies and learned there was such a paper. I had been in London five or six weeks when that gentleman arrived and brought me the great news and the copies in his tremendous box!

The aspect of that poor city of Warsaw was really quite revolutionary. Everywhere there were bands of suspicious-looking Jews or Poles. Of course, the Poles were in a large majority, but that majority was not organized. It was a small group of people who had started the newspaper. The whole of the nation was by no means in harmony with that object, and all the Jews were against it naturally, because they were the attacked.

So they decided to oppose it and to fight. Then there came to me several Jewish people, very decent men who asked me to make a denial of these charges. I told them frankly that it was impossible. Although I had had nothing to do with it, I could not make any public statement which would tend to increase this already serious disturbance, a disturbance which might lead to further riots and even fighting. I could not lend my hand to such a thing. They agreed and accepted that verdict as it should have been accepted. So I had to bear the consequences, which were hard—bitter.

When I arrived in America in the fall of 1913, I found to my surprise the Jews there already strongly united against me. They had even sent out circulars all over the country. There were several newspapers which reproached me with having done such an abominable thing as founding a newspaper to boycott the Jews, and to excite the whole of the Polish population against the Hebrew part of the country.

The propaganda in that direction achieved such proportions that even some of my friends (and I had among my friends several prominent Jews in New York) became deeply concerned. They said that something drastic must be done, that it was in-

...........y ...d with the money he earned in the United States.

Paderewsky gave $20,000.00 to establish the newspaper *"Dva Grosha"* published for no other purpose than the agitation of killing the Jews of Russia.

Paderewsky's generous contribution made that agitation successful; and to-day, everywhere in Russia, desolate women are weeping for their slaughtered babies, husbands and fathers.

Will you help Paderewsky again to contribute Twenty Thousand Dollars for murder?

.... of humanity, will not help the slaughter of innocents.

Stay away from the Paderewsky concerts.

Respectfully,

THE JEWISH PROGRESSIVE CLUB

THE JACOB GORDIN DRAMATIC CLUB

WORKMEN'S CIRCLE, No. 114

WORKMEN'S CIRCLE, No. 511

A fragment of one of the handbills

tolerable to have such libelous propaganda and persecution in a civilized country. They were greatly disturbed.

Those circulars or handbills were worded in a very drastic way. For instance, to quote one, "Are you going to patronize Paderewski's concerts? Do you know that Paderewski uses all the big sums of money he earns in America to organize pogroms of women, children, and old Jewish people in Poland?" It was all very serious. There are many of those handbills still in existence and I shall be able to show you one, I trust.

I myself received many, many letters, anonymous and signed, saying that it was my duty to call a mass meeting and justify myself as to all these crimes of which I had been, and still was, accused. There were hundreds of letters of menace, too, with threats to my life, and they came in such quantities that my manager, Mr. Charles Ellis, actually found it necessary to appeal to the authorities, and the authorities decided the situation was so grave that I should not travel unprotected. So a number of detectives were assigned to accompany me during the whole tour of 1913.

The season started in October and lasted till the end of April. For the entire tour I had that company of detectives, who on several occasions informed me of very dangerous conditions and happenings. Everywhere the same kind of persecution; everywhere those circulars and handbills. The situation was extremely serious and my life was often in danger. In several places the Rabbis in the synagogues actually preached against me. They appealed to their congregations not to attend my concerts, because I was such a bitter enemy of their race.

To a certain extent it affected my audiences, but not very much. Not as much as you would have thought.

At the same time, not a few Jews came to me personally as they usually came, to ask me for assistance. I never refused them in spite of these attacks.

There were two cases in particular when, in spite of that ferocious propaganda, a number of Jews came to ask me to help them go back to Poland. And I did it gladly. I gave money for those two families to return to Poland, and that represented quite a nice little sum, I assure you. But in one case I was specially pleased to do that because the petitioner happened to be the son of my old friend Schmul, whom I shall mention later, in my political activities. During the war he had no luck in America. His family was large also, and he wanted to go back to Poland and appealed to me to help him. And I was happy to send him back.

During that tour, as an addition to my troubles, I had a severe attack of neuritis in my right arm. It was so painful that I played with extreme difficulty, and I felt that the moment soon would come when I should have to interrupt my tour. Well, that moment came at Seattle. I could not play any longer. I could not even lift my arm, the pain was intolerable, and as I was to proceed from Seattle through Portland, Oregon, to San Francisco, I cancelled the concert in Seattle and went directly to San Francisco. This condition was not only aggravated but actually brought about by the terrific nervous strain and anxiety of the past months. The situation in which I found myself upon arrival in America, through these attacks of the Jews and their violent propaganda against me, was one of great difficulty, and in spite of my innocence, was deeply disturbing.

A good friend of mine, Mr. Urchs, of the Steinway firm, met me upon my arrival in San Francisco. He was gravely concerned at my condition and said, "I shall go at once and inquire about the best doctor for you."

I was very anxiously awaiting the arrival of that doctor when Mr. Urchs returned, not with the doctor but with another friend of mine, a musician from San Francisco, Sir Henry Heymann, and he said, "Now, there is no use calling a doctor, because a doctor cannot cure you immediately and that's what you want. But there is something else for you to do. You must go at once to Paso Robles and take some of the mud baths there for your arm. They are magical," Heymann said, "so many of my friends have been cured, and I am also enjoying the treatment myself because I too have neuritis badly. It is almost infallible, that treatment at Paso Robles."

It was only six hours away from San Francisco and worth

Tragic Experience

trying. So we started immediately for Paso Robles, and there I had my treatment for three weeks, after which I could continue my tour and finish it in comfort. My neuritis had left me. That place is absolutely unknown, and, as I know by my own experience, the result of that treatment is really miraculous. There is a bathing establishment and a large hotel, very comfortable too, but there are very few guests—only people from surrounding places. Why it has not been developed, I do not know. All these mud baths contain a large amount of radium and are of the greatest benefit. It can only be a question of time, I think, before this place becomes a well-known "cure."

Yes, I was cured and filled every one of my engagements. But the dreadful situation in connection with the Jewish persecution was still upon me, still going on, for while I was in Paso Robles, to my great surprise, an official of the Administration in Washington came to me and said that I must now make an affidavit stating that these accusations of the Jews were unfounded.

But I asked, "Why do you come to me *now* about it? I have made no complaint."

"No," he replied, "you have not, but the Administration at Washington is now aware of all these regrettable things that have happened, all these threatening letters, all the circulars, which were current and are still current all through the country, and besides you must now be informed that there has been a strong petition sent to the President by some of your influential friends from New York (and among them some of the notable Jews) asking the President to put an end to that propaganda which is unworthy of a civilized country." That was President Wilson.

So I had to make an affidavit at once that I had not established a newspaper, that I had nothing to do with organizing pogroms and that all these accusations were absolutely false.

I think it will be interesting to include that affidavit in these memoirs of mine. Painful as all this is to recall, it has its place, and an important one, in the story of my career. This is the time to tell it, to put it in its chronological order, the year it occurred and such details as make it now, after so many years, an integral part of my memories.

The affidavit was made at El Paso de Robles, California, on February 5, and is now in the possession of a friend. It follows:

February 5, 1914.

State of California
County of San Luis Obispo:

SS

Ignace Jan Paderewski, being first duly sworn, deposes and says:

My home is at Morges, in Switzerland; I am temporarily so-journing at the Hot Springs at El Paso de Robles, California. During the last year I have been publicly subjected to many un-just charges which have caused many of my friends indignation and concern. For the satisfaction of those good friends, and for such use as they may make of this affidavit, and to all whom it may concern, I hereby swear and declare:

That I never gave money to any anti-Jewish newspaper what-soever.

That the establishment of the newspaper of which I am ac-cused of being the founder, was absolutely unknown to me and, in fact, I only heard of its existence for the first time some two months after the date upon which (as I am informed) it was founded,

That I never initiated or supported the boycotting of the Jewish trade in Poland, being entirely out of, and not taking any part in active politics in Poland.

[Signed] I. J. PADEREWSKI

That affidavit was sent, I understand, to all the New York newspapers. I, of course, was not in New York at the time, but I was informed that *The Evening Post* was the only New York newspaper that published the affidavit. This was due in some measure perhaps to my lifelong friendship with Henry T. Finck, the music critic of that famous journal. Although I never saw it, I wish to add that the affidavit was also published in *Musical America* a short time afterwards.

But the persecution continued as before. It was not stopped for the rest of the tour, and for all the consecutive tours the Jews continued to attack me violently. They never believed my statements. Never.

Some of my friends in New York even went to a Jewish newspaper protesting against such treatment, saying it was not true. The only reply was, "Oh, yes. We know it is not true, but it is good publicity! It sells the newspaper."

The only result of the affidavit was that the promoters in Poland who were responsible for starting the paper got furious and turned on me and attacked me in that very paper! My own paper, as they called it. What a fantastic situation!

All this took place in 1914, the year of the Great War, and this war, little as we realized at that moment, was almost upon us. War was already in the air, and it was in the interests of certain Jews to have that propaganda continue, not personally against me, but against Poland. Even after the war, during my last few tours in America, I found these circulars still being distributed in some places. Still going about—still making mischief.

But, for the moment, I shall leave it at that. At another time there is more to say but it does not belong to this year of 1914. At a much later period the attack was renewed.

I now want to tell you of an important new interest in my life. It was in February, 1914, that I bought my ranch in Paso Robles. There were two reasons for buying that large property, which has since been a cause of much trouble and expense. First of all, I was under a feeling of great gratitude to the place itself for my recovery, and secondly, I was persuaded constantly, and I may say, almost violently, by the physician of the establishment who had a decided passion for the real-estate business, and I was completely at his mercy! He used to come to me and preach about acquiring land there because it was so profitable, such an opportunity for investment for the future. He was as deeply interested in that as he was in his patients, apparently. It had its amusing side, of course, because I was helpless—at his mercy. His attacks upon me took place when I was in the baths—in mud up to my neck! I could not protest, I could not resist, and he never let up. I was in a trap. I must add in justice, however, that I was probably quite a willing victim, for I really loved the place and was very grateful besides.

There are plenty of those healing mud baths on my estate and I know there are several sources of mineral water of the same kind used in the Thermal Establishment in Paso Robles, so there was reason in the arguments of my physician.

Paso Robles, by the way, is a Spanish name meaning the passage of the oaks.

I developed the place greatly. I planted many hundreds of acres of almond trees, prune trees, walnut trees and even a vineyard, which for a time had great success because of the Swiss-Italian colonists who live not far away, and who bought the grapes to make their own wine. But it is expensive to keep up. I have there a very good man, who was practically educated at my expense because he made his apprenticeship in Switzerland. For a time my garden here at Riond-Bosson in Morges has been considered as a model orchard in the whole of the Swiss Confederation.

Yes, I loved Paso Robles before and after I bought it. It proved to be another gold mine, as I have already said, a mine that you pour gold into but never take any out! There have been many such gold mines in my life.

XIX

Fête Day

I

But we must now go back to our tour. After that tour in 1914, I played once in London and then came directly to Switzerland, to my house at Morges, longing for a much-needed rest, but the air was full of menace. Even then peace was slowly receding from the world. The shocking murder of the Austrian Archduke Francis Ferdinand a few days before had horrified the whole world. The consequences of that assassination could not then be foretold, but a dreadful fear gripped all Europe at that time. At any moment the tension might break and then—? We all waited from hour to hour, I may say, in the gravest suspense. Already in the beginning of July I had several unexpected but important visitors, whose object it was not difficult to guess. They talked about certain important changes in the map of Europe. War was in the air. I knew it was coming. In spite of my joy at being again in my own house, in all the peace and beauty of that lovely spot, the days were full of a great unrest and sadness that nothing could alleviate. The hour of doom was approaching slowly, but oh so surely, and still life went on in the old accustomed way. Friends came and went; we laughed and talked and made music, and a particularly beautiful summer lay lovingly upon all the land.

On the 31st of July, the day of my patron saint, St. Ignace, which has always been a day of festivity in my house, there was a very large gathering of people from various countries, and of many nationalities. It has been a delightful and happy custom for many years to make that a kind of fête day, and all the countryside, people from Geneva, Lausanne and elsewhere, come with their greetings. It is one of the most touching things that have come into my life, this lovely gesture toward me by my neighbors. The children come, too, lots of them. They come in their pretty white dresses with bouquets and little gifts, sometimes to sing to me and sometimes to dance or say a poem. It is all very touching.

The festivities go on all day. A big luncheon is served to all my visiting friends, and the good will and gaiety, and I may add food, goes on throughout the afternoon. It is a happy time for everybody.

The luncheon at this special festivity was a large one and friends came from all over the world, I can say. Now there is something that I must mention just here, something in connection with the gentleman to whom we have already devoted some attention, head of a large and strong political party in Poland, the same gentleman, you will remember, who organized that newspaper in my name against the Jews. He, too, had arrived that morning to celebrate my fête day.

During the luncheon, at which there were some forty people present, I had to acknowledge with thanks all those who came to give me the evidence of their affection. In a little address I said that in spite of our happiness at being together, we must all realize that it was a moment of extreme gravity and that even while we sat there the fate of Europe was perhaps swaying in the balance, that the ominous mutterings of war were already vibrating through the land, and that if war came, my own country, Poland, would be among the first to suffer, I felt sure. She would be torn with battle for a very long time and would become a sea of blood and tears, but she would emerge free at the end—please God.

It was a tense moment for every one at the table, broken by the quick retort of our political friend, who jumped to his feet and answered me rather gaily and confidently that I was too pessimistic, and in spite of my protest that Austria-Hungary had already declared war on Serbia, he went on still in the same vein, declaring that there was no real cause for alarm, that there would be no war, there could be no war, that conditions were not yet ready for war, and so on.

Every one drew a long breath as he sat down, and all leaned back in their chairs as coffee was brought in by the butler. But just as the last cup was served, a telegram was handed to him. He opened it quickly and sat staring at it, absolutely pale. Then he rose quietly from his chair, and came to my side. "I am sorry," he whispered, "but I must leave at once. I do not understand why, but they are calling me to return immediately." In a second he was gone from the room. After a few minutes, I excused myself and joined him in the hall and said good-by. He was still stunned and overcome at his orders, but still protesting as he went out of the door, still denying as he shook hands, saying "there will be no war. It is impossible. No one is ready. We cannot have war now."

This was an ominous interlude to me and the few people who noticed his departure. But the day went on with gaiety and happiness, and the dinner that night was a beautiful one. My wife had given it her special attention. All my dear and close personal friends and artists had come especially at this time. They had come from Paris, London, and New York.

On this particular 31st of July, 1914, my friends decided to make that day an unusually memorable and gay one. It was to be a gala occasion, more brilliant than any that had preceded it. A great number of artists, Polish, Swiss, French, and American, were there. Everything was propitious and great preparations were on foot. They decided to have some kind of a fantastic play, I know of no better word for it, and they organized a pageant of exclusive Chinese character. I have a little collection of Chinese curiosities, for which I had quite a particular fondness, and that probably gave the impulse to my friends to arrange that pageant.

During the evening, splendid fireworks were displayed, and then from the farthest end of the park which surrounds the house, a tremendous Chinese dragon, spitting real fire and flames (it seemed to the onlookers), advanced majestically toward the house. It was something terrific, uncanny, and prophetic, too, at the same time, I felt—and was really frightening.

During the evening, a rather large number of my visitors, who were young and middle-aged Swiss gentlemen, arrived for supper and I noticed that each one was carrying a little valise. It struck me at the time as rather strange, but that was all. Nothing happened, however, until we were seated at table, when the supper was interrupted by the telephone, which rang continuously, and the messages were evidently of such importance that every few minutes one of these Swiss gentlemen was called to the telephone and obliged to leave the table. It was noticeable and very strange.

There was also a peculiar atmosphere among all the guests. Every one, without knowing exactly why, was under the impression that something was about to happen—that something must happen. It affected the whole gathering and threw a strange kind of gloom over the gaiety at supper. Of course, I must tell you, there were already rumors in the newspapers, justifying, to a certain degree, our unrest and nervousness, but the matter did not become quite clear until late that night, at one o'clock. Suddenly, from another room, all my Swiss guests appeared at the door in military uniform! That explained the valises they had carried. They were all very tense and very solemn; and without a word, each man came up to me, shook hands, and said very simply, "Au revoir, and perhaps good-by."

It was a dreadful moment. I found myself unable to say anything. But as the last one left the room I ventured to ask, "Where are you going, my friend?"

"To the Frontier," he answered, and then they went quickly out of the house without another word.

It would be interesting to recapture now if one could the awful sense of the moment when that staggering news reached us. We were overcome by it. It fell upon the whole household—with dreadful import. Our happy fête was turned to mourning.

Among the guests present at my house on the 31st of July,

Fête Day

1914, there were a great many artists of various nationalities. Mme. Sembrich was there with her husband, Ernest Schelling and Mrs. Schelling, Felix Weingartner, the famous conductor, with his wife. The brothers Morax, René the poet and playwright, and Jean, the painter. There was Gustave Doret, the famous Swiss composer. Also Wiwulski, the sculptor of the monument in Cracow, Tim Adamowski with his wife, my good friend and trusted English manager, Mr. L. G. Sharpe of London, and Miss Alma-Tadema, and many other dear friends.

Oh! I knew that something was in the air because during that month of July, I had so many visitors who pointed out to me the possibility of a tremendous change in the map of Europe. I was quite aware of the forthcoming events, and the declaration of War did not surprise me at all. I knew it must come.

Early the next morning I went out alone and walked to the station, and there I saw the two brothers Morax, my Swiss friends living at Morges, both in uniform guarding the station. I went on to the Post Office, and there I found another friend, also in uniform, Gustave Doret, guarding the post and telegraph. We saluted—but had no word to speak on that fateful day, August 1, 1914.

War had been declared. The fate of Europe, perhaps the whole world, was in abeyance and all mankind with it. A new world, a new era was at hand, I felt sure, and I, too, must enter this new era, the era of an unexpected and fated career. "This is the end of my artistic life for a time," I said to myself. "Perhaps forever. It is finished." I realized it absolutely. My heart was heavy.

War had come! War had come to every one.

A silent pall lay over that whole beautiful, peaceful countryside. A pall, alas, that was not to lift its black curtain for many years.

THE END

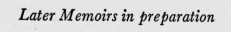

Later Memoirs in preparation

Index

Index

Index

Index

Index

Index

Steinway, house of, 189, 190, 192, 196
Steinway, William, 198, 222
Steinway pianos, 219, 220, 248, 249, 265, 266, 364, 365
Stengel, 203, 204
Stepmother, Paderewski's, 20, 21, 31
Stockhausen, 103
Stokowski, Leopold, 124; father, 132
Stolypin, 245, 246
Stool, piano, 312, 313
Story, Julian, 278
Strasbourg, 88, 322, 323, 326; Conservatory, 101–103, 107
Strauss, Richard, 35, 60
Stuart, Lord Charles, 242, 244, 245
Students, from Montana, 277
Studzinski, Mr., 36
Sudylkow, 9
Suez Canal, 340
Sully, Monet, 149
Suspenders, 312
Swietochowski, Alexander, 109
Switzerland, 368, 393
Sydney (Australia), 341, 342
Sylva, Carmen, 163
Symphonie Espagnole, 69
Symphony, Paderewski's, 138, 327, 371, 376
Symphony Orchestra, New York, 124

Tadema, *see* Alma-Tadema
Tadema piano, 177, 178
Taft, President, 370
Tag, the, 310
"Tannhäuser," 145, 146
Tasmanian Sea, 355
Tatra Mountains, 81
Tavern Club of Boston, 210, 212
Tedesco, 27
Tempo Rubato, 329, 330
Terry, Ellen, 149
Texans, at Kansas City concert, 276
"Thaïs," 139
Thalberg, 161
Theatre, 93, 94; court, 124, 125
Thomas, Theodore, 124, 216–218, 265; orchestra, 262
Times, London, 158, 159
Tolstoi, 284, 298
Torquay, 303, 304
Toscanini, 124
Toulouse, 125
Tours, 128–130
Transcript, the (Boston), 201
Tree, Beerbohm, 180, 181
Trélat, Madame, 115, 116
Tretbar, Charles F., 189–191, 193, 197–202, 215, 216, 218, 223
Tribune, The (Chicago), 201
Trombone, 37, 38
Trumpet, 37, 38
Trusteeship for orphans, 57
Tschaikowsky, 115, 284
Tunbridge Wells, 226
Turgenieff, 285, 298
Twain, Mark, 205

Union Square Hotel (New York), 191
University of Berlin, 61
Urban, Professor, 77

Urchs, Mr., 388
Utrecht, 151

Vacaresco, Helene, 163, 164
Valse Caprice, Rubinstein's, 100
Vanderbilt, George, 209
Variations, Paderewski's, 70, 71, 85, 326; Beethoven's in C Minor, 117
Verdi, 277
Victoria, Queen, 181–184, 237–239
Vienna, 63, 83, 85, 89, 91, 93, 94, 108, 111–113, 119
Viennese, the, 94
Violin, lessons, 57, 58
Vitor, 371
Vladimir, Grand Duke, 287
von Bülow, Hans, 123, 124, 165–172, 191
von Schuch, Ernst, 281
von Stackelberg, Baron, 285, 286, 332

Wagner, 63, 92, 122, 123, 145, 146, 328
Waimangu, 347–349
Wairakei, 348
Wales, Prince and Princess of, 185
Walter, Bruno, 124
Warbrick, Mr., 346
Ward, Sir Joseph, 346
Warehouse, Paderewski practises in, 196
Warrender, Lady Maude, 176
Warsaw, 31 ff., 54, 67, 68, 72, 97, 107–109, 282, 331, 384 ff.
Washington (D. C.), 223, 224, 371
Washington Arch, 210
Weber piano, 365
Weimar, 379
Weingartner, Felix, 397
Wellington, 343, 351
Whakarewarewa, 345
White, Henry, 369
White, Mr., 276
White, Stanford, 361
White House, 368, 370
Widor, Charles-Marie, 139, 140
Wierzbilowitch, 288
Wilde, Oscar, 186
Wilno, 374
Wilson, Woodrow, 368–370, 389
Windsor, 181, 183, 184, 238
Windsor Hotel (New York), 192, 196, 255, 256
Wiwulski, Antoni, 372–374, 397
Wolff, Rubinstein's manager, 104–106, 164, 317
Wolves, 29, 30
Wood-wind instruments, 286
World, The (weekly), 162
World War, 244, 393 ff.
World's Fair, Chicago, 262 ff.

Yates, Edmund, 162
York, Duke and Duchess, 347
Yorke, Mrs., 173
Yport, 267
Ysaye, 65, 66
Yugoslavia, 369

Zakopane, 81
Zaslaw, 27
Zhitomir, 272